The Year of Liberty

The Year of Liberty

The History of the Great Irish Rebellion of 1798

THOMAS PAKENHAM

Random House New York

For Val

Library of Congress Cataloging-in-Publication Data
Pakenham, Thomas, 1933–
The year of liberty: the history of the great Irish rebellion of 1798/
Thomas Pakenham.—1st U.S. ed.
    p.   cm.
Originally published: London: Hodder & Stoughton, 1969.
Includes bibliographical references (p.) and index.
ISBN 0-679-74802-4 (pbk.)
1. Ireland—History—Rebellion of 1798.   I. Title.
        DA949.P3   1993
941.507—dc20   93-24770

Manufactured in the United States of America
9 8 7 6 5 4 3 2
First U.S. Edition

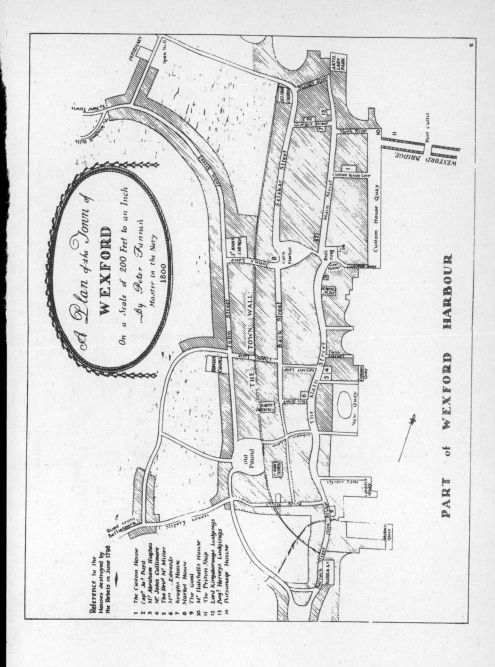

PART of WEXFORD HARBOUR

QUESTION: What have you got in your hand?
ANSWER: A green bough.
QUESTION: Where did it first grow?
ANSWER: In America.
QUESTION: Where did it bud?
ANSWER: In France.
QUESTION: Where are you going to plant it?
ANSWER: In the crown of Great Britain.

(From the United Irish catechism)

CONTENTS

MAPS

Preface

Who fears to speak of Ninety-Eight?
Who blushes at the name?
When cowards mock the patriot's fate,
Who hangs his head for shame?

The Memory of the Dead

THE REBELLION of 1798 is the most violent and tragic event in Irish history between the Jacobite wars and the Great Famine.

In the space of a few weeks, 30,000 people—peasants armed with pikes and pitch forks, defenceless women and children—were cut down or shot or blown like chaff as they charged up to the mouth of the cannon.

The result of the rebellion was no less disastrous: Britain imposed a Union on terms that proved unacceptable to the majority of the Irish people, and there was a legacy of violence and hatred that has persisted to the present day.

How did this catastrophe occur?

The story must be seen in the context of the war between Britain and France and the wave of Jacobin revolutions, impelled by France, that swept through Europe at that time. It is in this context—of ideological war to the death—that Britain and her Irish Allies were fighting in Ireland. A successful revolution in Ireland, and then Britain would be the next to go.

But there are other themes that need to be stressed, as they have tended to become obscured by later Irish history.

The rebellion was not provoked by Pitt and the British government, as most Irishmen came to believe, in order to pass the Union. On the contrary, it was the result of Pitt's failure to have *any* policy for Ireland. Pitt recognised that all was not well. The Irish Catholic peasantry were some of the most wretched in Europe. The country was governed by a grotesque colonial partnership: a weak British viceroy with British staff, bullied by a narrow oligarchy of Irish Protestants of British settler stock. Pitt could have corrected the abuses of power that had brought the country to the brink of revolution. Distracted by the war with France, he hoped for the best. Ireland was left to its fate.

Equally misplaced was the optimism of Wolfe Tone and the Irish revolutionaries—the "United Irishmen". Tone recognised that there could be a terrible irony in that name. Himself of Protestant stock, he knew that the Irish ruling class would be no friends to the revolution. He pinned his hopes on the have-nots: the Presbyterian businessmen and artisans, and the Catholics. With French help, he planned a war of independence—a "fair and open war" as he called it. In fact the rebellion turned out to be a ferocious *civil* war—Irish loyalists against Irish rebels—with many of Tone's closest friends committed to the loyalist side.

Most tragic of all were the illusions of the Irish peasantry, intoxicated by the fumes of the French revolution and the heady doctrines of Tom Paine's *Rights of Man*. They were all for Liberty if it meant the end of tithes and taxes and an oppressive government. They were quite unprepared for war.

I have tried to weave these strands together into a coherent narrative using contemporary sources. It is nearly a hundred years since the appearance of the last full-scale history of the rebellion—itself part of Lecky's monumental *History of Ireland in the Eighteenth Century*. Today sources are embarrassingly rich on the loyalist side—ten thousand odd documents in the Rebellion Papers from Dublin Castle; a complete run of Irish newspapers; and the confidential letters of almost all the chief protagonists. Sources that have come to light recently include the private letters of Pitt in London, Lord Camden in Kent, George III at Windsor and Dundas in Scotland; a new cache of Auckland papers at Keele; and an important series of letters from Lord Wycombe in the British Museum.

On the rebel side, lack of sources makes it impossible to do justice to the movement. I have found fewer than a hundred revolutionary documents of 1798. For the most part I have had to make do with second-hand (and sometimes second-rate) material; contemporary spy reports, mid-nineteenth century biographies, folk-songs and hearsay. My picture of the revolutionary underground in '98 is, of its nature, a reconstruction.

With the volume of written sources weighted so heavily to one side, it is impossible to avoid giving offence. I have tried to be fair.

In a book of this sort so much depends on the goodwill of the staff of the libraries and record offices where papers are deposited. I have been especially fortunate in the help I have received from the following:—Mr. B. MacGiola Coille of the Irish State Paper Office, Dublin; Dr. P. Henchy, Mr. John Ainsworth, Mr. T. P. O'Neill, and countless others on the staff of the National Library, Dublin; Captain K. Danaher and Dr. T. Wall of the Irish Folklore Commission; and Mrs. Olive Goodbody of the Society of Friends; Mr. K. Darwin and Mr. B. Trainor of the Public Record Office, Belfast; Mr. Kenneth Timings of the Public Record Office, London; Mr. I. Fraser of Keele University Library; and the staff of Kent County Record Office, the Scottish Record Office, the London Library, the British Museum, Greenwich Maritime Museum, and the National Registrary of Archives.

A number of historians have generously given me advice and encouragement during the writing of this book. I owe an especial debt to three members of the staff of University College, Dublin: Professor Desmond Williams, Professor Kevin Nowlan and Dr. Maureen Wall; and to Dr. R. B. McDowell of Trinity College, Dublin. I have inflicted my problems on them, and shamelessly picked their brains.

Mr. F. MacDermot generously let me see his draft of an unpublished article on Arthur O'Connor. For this, and other help, I am most grateful.

I am equally in the debt of my tutor at Oxford, C. R. Stevens, who somehow introduced Irish history into a course devoted to Ancient Rome.

I must also gratefully record permission to quote manuscript material from the following sources: for the Percy, Wyndham, Wellesley, Pelham, Holland and Auckland MSS in the British Museum acknowledgement is due to the Trustees; for the Irish State Papers to The Taoiseach; for the Camden MSS in Kent County Record Office to the Marquis Camden; for the Wellington MSS in Apsley House to the Duke of Wellington; for the Bunbury MSS to Mr. B. McPeake; and for the Sneyd MSS at Keele University to the university authorities. In quoting contemporary material, I have used contemporary forms as far as is practicable without confusion.

I must add a tribute to the friends who encouraged me during the enterprise: John Vaizey, who gave me the idea; Adrian Lyttelton, Patrick Chorley, Angus MacIntyre and Karl Leyser who gave invaluable advice; Laurence and Linda Kelly, and Patricia and Timothy Daunt who helped me at a critical hour; Paul Thompson and Daria Chorley who read drafts of the book in manuscript; Bruce and Mavis Arnold who helped provide the illustrations; Anthony Sampson, Richard Simon and Robin Denniston who spurred me on.

To Mairin Garrett, who helped with the research, I owe an immense debt.

Finally, a word of thanks to my long-suffering relations who had the Irish rebellion around the house for so long. To the many other authors in the family I owe an especial debt. They were unsparing in advice, regardless of the risk of reprisal.

Prologue

A Protestant Wind

Bantry Bay, December 21st-27th 1796

Ara ! but why does he stay behind?
Lillibulero, bullen-a-la.
Ho ! by my soul 'tis a Protestant wind.
Lillibulero, bullen-a-la.

ON THE night of December 16th 1796, the last great French invasionary force ever to set sail for the British Isles slipped past the British squadron blockading the port of Brest. Five days later the French fleet—thirty-five ships with 12,000 troops on board—arrived unopposed at its destination.[1]

It was to land at Bantry Bay in south west Ireland. The French planned to invade Ireland, expel the British with the help of the Irish revolutionary party, and set up an independent Irish republic.[2] It was to be the first step in the conquest of England, the English revolution and the creation of an English republic modelled on France.

The prospects for the Irish part of this scheme could never have seemed brighter than on that day in late December. Ahead of the French fleet were a number of beaches suitable for a landing place. There was a light wind and little sea. There were no signs of any hostile preparations on shore. There was no reason to believe that the British fleet were on their way to intercept. Less than ninety miles from Bantry, the large military and naval base of Cork lay almost undefended. In a few days the whole south of Ireland could be theirs.[3]

On board the 80-gun flagship, the *Indomptable*, was the Irishman whose irresistible enthusiasm had been the mainspring of the expedition. Strange to say, his name would have meant nothing at this time to most of his compatriots. He was a pale, slightly-built thirty-three year old Dublin barrister called Wolfe Tone.

The son of a Protestant coachmaker, Tone had won a scholarship to Trinity College and in due course had been called to the Irish bar. In 1791, frustrated by the lack of professional and political prospects for someone without family connections, and dazzled by the ideas of the French Revolution, he had helped found an Irish radical movement called the United Irishmen.[4] The aim of this "brotherhood of affection", as the United movement was called, was to throw open the Irish Parliament—at that time the preserve of a Protestant oligarchy—to all Irishmen irrespective of their rank or religion. At first the methods of the movement were to be non-violent.[5] But soon after war broke out between Britain and France in 1793, the reformers became revolutionaries. The Irish Government regarded the movement as a nest of sedition and drove it underground.[6] On their part, Tone and the United Irishmen recognised that without French assistance they would achieve nothing, and believed that the French would not intervene for less an object than a complete revolution in Ireland.[7]

And so it had turned out. Expelled to America for his political activities in 1795, Tone was soon informed by his friends that the United Irish organisation was nearly complete. Would he go at once to France to collaborate with the French army of liberation?[8] With little money and virtually no contacts, Tone had brilliantly succeeded. He had somehow persuaded the new rulers of France—the French Directory—to embark on the perilous scheme. General Lazare Hoche, most experienced of all French generals in the field at that time, not excepting Bonaparte, had been appointed Commander-in-Chief.[9]

Such was the situation on December 21st 1796, as Tone, a slight figure in the heavy blue surcoat of a French adjutant-general, paced up and down in the great gallery of the *Indomptable*. Only one thing marred the prospects of success. To avoid the British naval blockade, the invasionary force had followed a difficult channel out of Brest harbour five days before. In the darkness and confusion, the frigate carrying the Commander-in-Chief, General Hoche, had become separated from the fleet and had not been seen since. It was now agreed to delay the landing to give him a chance to catch up.[10]

All that day, the great ships, their decks crowded with soldiers, hovered close to the shore. Ahead of them the mountains were covered with snow. They would have a cold bivouac when they landed. Soon they were so close to the land that it seemed to Tone's fancy that he could touch the sides of the bay with either hand. After so long an absence from Ireland, he was surprised to find he felt so little emotion. One loves ones country, he wrote in his diary, no less for not having romantic feelings about her.[11]

But now the extravagant good fortune that had brought them so close to triumph, suddenly deserted them. For five weeks, the wind had hung in the east, first frustrating the British naval blockade, and then spiriting the invasion fleet to Ireland.[12] For one day—the 21st—the wind was light and the sea calm. In Hoche's absence, no landing was made on that day. On the 22nd, the east wind resumed, and now they had turned the headland it blew straight in their faces. Inexorably, the wind freshened, and in the squalls of rain and snow, more than half the fleet parted company with the flagship.[13]

Hour by hour, the hopes of a landing faded. On the 24th, the easterly gale became a storm. At about six that night, the admiral signalled to the *Indomptable* to cut her cables and run. Still Tone and the French staff officers with him clung to the precarious hope of landing. At last the wind came round to the south, but the storm continued. One by one, the fourteen remaining ships cut their cables and turned for France. On the night of the 27th the storm turned to a hurricane. A huge sea caught the *Indomptable* on the quarter, stove in the gallery and one of the windows of the great cabin, and filled the cabin with water. Tone, who was woken by the crash, thought the ship was lost and lay quietly in his hammock, determined to die like a man.

When the storm blew itself out, the *Indomptable* found herself alone. As Tone put it, England had not had such an escape since the Armada.[14]

All over Europe, people felt the harsh breath of that east wind. In Paris and London people were found frozen to death in the streets.[15] In Ireland, the Irish army, bracing themselves for the invasion, were caught in a blizzard.[16] At Bandon the militia, led by their colonel, twenty-seven year old Lord Castlereagh, huddled for shelter in a deserted church;[17] at Birr the peasantry were set to dig the artillery out of the snowdrifts;[18] and in Dublin, the garrison was issued with flannel waistcoats specially sewn by ladies of the viceregal court.[19]

But the hurricane blew, scattering the French fleet, and one of the great Cork magnates, Lord Shannon, hummed the lines from "Lillibulero".[20] It was a Protestant wind.

I

Conspiracy

1

Britain's Difficulty, Ireland's Opportunity

Britain and Europe, January 1798 and before

What would these gentlemen have? France is revolutionised!
Holland is revolutionised! Italy is revolutionised! Switzerland
is revolutionised! Europe will soon be revolutionised. But this,
it seems, is not enough to content them.

Bonaparte to the ambassador of the United Irishmen,
February 1798

A FEW DAYS after the start of the year 1798, the King's First Minister,
William Pitt, sat down in his study at Bromley to draft a letter to the King.
The subject was of such delicacy that even Pitt, after years of exceptionally
cordial relations with the King, felt the impertinence of broaching the
matter. It concerned a proposal for a multi-million pound voluntary fund
to support the war with France. Pitt now respectfully informed His
Majesty that it was absolutely essential for the safety of the kingdom that
he should make a sizeable contribution from the privy purse.[1] Back came
the reply in the King's meticulous Italic hand. The King of England, he
lamented, was "not so rich a man".[2] He gave £20,000—less, it turned out,
than some of his subjects[3]—and complained that it ruined him.

If the war had embarrassed the King's finances, it had brought the
country itself to the verge of bankruptcy. Despite a swingeing new tax on
personal wealth, despite taxes on the rich man's coach and the poor man's
beer,[4] the Treasury's deficit had soared to close on ten million pounds.
Consols, the measure of the nation's self-confidence, had fallen at one time
to 47—the lowest ever recorded.[5] And still the cost of the war mounted:
for new regiments and new ships, and loans to shore up Britain's new
allies abroad, and to defend Britain and Ireland from French invasion.[6]

It was Ireland that remained the weakest link in Britain's chain of
defence. The escape from the Bantry Bay expedition the previous year
had been providential. It reflected only discredit on the British navy. For
nearly a month that armada of ships had crossed and recrossed the sea

between Ireland and France. Three British fleets had been in a position to intercept—and only stragglers had been taken.[7] The defence preparations made by the Irish army had proved equally inept.

And now there were reports of dangerous unrest in Ireland. No doubt Lord Camden, the Irish Viceroy, was exaggerating; he had forecast a revolution at the time of the Bantry Bay invasion, and yet Ireland had stayed quiet and loyal. Still, on one score the Irish crisis was real enough. The country was still closer to bankruptcy than Britain. The Irish army was costing three million pound a year, nearly half the revenue; unless Britain bailed out the Irish Treasury, neither business nor Government could continue.[8]

Pitt was not insensitive to the dangers. Yet he did not interfere much with the running of that kingdom. He left it to the minister responsible— the Duke of Portland, ex-Irish Viceroy, now Home Secretary and leader of the Whig wing of the Government. He remained unruffled by the threat of a new attempt at invading Ireland. Still, to his close friends—to the men with whom he shared the port at White's, and the pies at Bellamy's—Pitt seemed aged prematurely by the strains of the war, and the war-time coalition.[9]

In a sense, Pitt the Younger had never been young. At twenty-one, he had sprung fully-armed into the Commons, a master of rhetoric and a master of patronage, cool and brilliant like the Greek hexameters he so much admired and could recite with so little effort.[10] At twenty-four he had been invited by the King to form a Government. He had stepped serenely into his father's shoes, the youngest Prime Minister in British history. After fifteen years of continuous office, he was still unchallenged in his craft, despite the setbacks of his war policy.[11]

The previous year, 1797, in fact had been a catalogue of disasters. Despite the four and a half million pound loan from Britain, the Emperor of Austria had made peace with France; the Czar of Russia and the King of Prussia had followed suit; and so ended the Triple Alliance.[12] At home there had been riots, and mutinies and an incipient revolutionary move- ment.[13] And at their backs, a constant irritant, was the problem of Ireland —still unresolved, as it had remained for so many hundreds of years.

In 1782, weakened and humiliated by the loss of the American colonies, Britain had agreed to a new deal for Ireland.

Britain had had no choice. A self-styled Irish Volunteer army had been formed by the Irish ruling class to protect the country against the French.

Then, encouraged by the success of the Americans, they demanded some
form of self-government or threatened an Irish War of Independence.[14]

Ireland, like America in the previous decade, posed the delicate problem
for England of reconciling the national aspirations of a colony with the
strategic needs of the mother country. Yet Ireland, half-independent as she
had become, was geographically part of the British Isles. It was to this
unique geographical predicament—too far from Britain to be assimilated,
too near to be allowed to be separate—that so many of Ireland's anomalies
and miseries could be traced.

For six hundred years she had been consigned to a political limbo—poor,
weak and divided. The proud and talented Celtic people who had once
imposed their own Christian culture on decadent Britain and Europe had
sunk under the weight of Norman invasion and annexation. In the Middle
Ages, when small countries like Scotland, far from centres of power, had
their own kings and parliament and a history of nationhood, Ireland remained divided and misgoverned. To some extent, this was Norman
policy, based on strategic interests. The Normans had no wish to see a
strong, united and potentially hostile neighbour on their western doorstep.
But the only real alternative—a powerful colony in the island—had proved
elusive except within the Pale surrounding Dublin. The Normans had
swallowed the Anglo-Saxons in England in one bite. For four hundred
years they nibbled at Ireland. And still by the reign of Elizabeth she was
only half digested—part colony, part dependency, part nation, a source of
more weakness than wealth for Church and Crown, and a prey to each
successive enemy of Britain.[15]

The Reformation added a new barrier to a country already so cruelly
divided by race and culture; it also made Britain still more hag-ridden by
fears of her security. The political map of Europe was now crudely defined
along religious boundaries. If Ireland stayed Catholic, she stayed an ally
of the Catholic states with whom Britain was at war. Yet the Elizabethan
Reformation in Ireland was as ineffectual as the Norman conquest. In the
name of God and their Queen, the Elizabethan adventurers harried the
native chiefs, persecuted their religion, and hunted down their people like
wild beasts; in fact behaved with the cheerful savagery of the Conquist-
adors. But Irish Catholicism could not be rooted out like the pagan
religions of the New World. Do what they could, the Elizabethans left
Ireland still predominantly Catholic, still poor and burning with hatred for
her English oppressors.[16]

The next century saw an attempt at an even more drastic solution: large-
scale colonisation of the more fertile areas, and eviction of the original

inhabitants. But successive plantations—of Scottish Presbyterians in Ulster, and English emigrants in the Midlands and South—did not secure Ireland. The Catholics' watchword remained: "England's difficulty is Ireland's opportunity." The Irish Catholic uprising of 1641, the hideous reprisals of Cromwell, and the Jacobite wars confirmed the dangers to Britain. After his victory at the Boyne, King William decided on a final settlement. A formal bargain was struck with the Irish Protestant planters. They would keep a complete monopoly of political power, and control most of the land. In return they would act as a British garrison to preserve the peace and stability of the island. To protect their settlement the Catholics must be kept weak. The Protestant garrison was therefore authorised by Britain to pass a series of penal laws against them. A century of peace and some prosperity—for the Protestants—succeeded.[17]

It was this Williamite settlement that the Irish Volunteer army of the 1770s had found inadequate. In trade and politics they were treated like a colony—their goods kept out of the British market, their Parliament kept subordinate to Westminster. Now they took their cue from the people of Boston. "Free trade—or else," said the Volunteer army. "O Lord open thou our Lips," said the placards slung round the mouths of the Volunteers' cannons, "and our mouths shall sound forth thy praise."[18]

The British Government, embattled with both America and France, had no wish to see if the Irish were bluffing. In 1778 almost all trade restrictions were lifted. By the Irish new deal of 1782 the Irish Parliament was made —theoretically—equal with Westminster. Only one fragile link held the two kingdoms together now: the British Crown, and the golden chain of Crown patronage—jobs, sinecures, and titles—that secured the loyalty of the Irish Parliament. At a price, the catastrophe of an American-style revolution had been avoided.[19]

Yet it soon became clear that, from the British point of view, Ireland might be out of the frying pan only to fall into the fire.

For the Irish Volunteer army, the "revolutionaries" of 1782, were not victims of the settlement, descendants of the men who had been evicted from their lands and hunted down like wild beasts. They were of the garrison, the "Protestant nation" of settler stock. Their national aims had little more to do with the mass of the Irish people than George Washington's with the Red Indians. And Britain's concessions to this small, selfish and corrupt oligarchy had only exacerbated the grievances of the rest.

The survivors of the Catholic upper class, aroused by the Volunteer movement, wanted equality with their Protestant neighbours: the right to serve in the army, to hold a commission of the peace, and above all to exercise political power. The emergent Catholic middle class wanted equal rights in the professions—the law was closed to them—and they, too, wanted political rights.[20] By giving increased power to the Irish Parliament, Britain had only increased the frustrations of those excluded from it.

Still more explosive than these grievances were those of the submerged peasantry, the hidden, Gaelic-speaking Ireland of the countryside. Their grievances were economic and social—high taxes and low prices, and an impossibly harsh land system—and were exacerbated by the differences of culture and religion. For them, the Irish Parliament was the Parliament of the alien landlord and the heretic. New power for this Parliament meant new power to persecute them with tithes and taxes and Acts against sedition and insurrection.[21]

Such was the situation, ominous enough, in 1789 when France exploded into revolution. Millions believed in most countries of Europe that, here was the solution to their grievances and frustrations—a democratic revolution. In turn, half the countries of western Europe were revolutionised—Holland, Switzerland and northern Italy. In each a French-style republic was established by French arms.[22] And what material could be more combustible for revolution than the oppressed people of Ireland?

These next few years had seen an attempt by Pitt and his Government to redress some of the worst Irish grievances. A reluctant Irish Parliament agreed to relax most of the penal laws—but refused to grant complete emancipation by giving Catholics the right to sit in Parliament.[23] Nothing was done about the land system, which pinched hardest on the mass of the people; and the partial relaxation of the penal laws only raised expectations to see them dashed once more.[24] The war with France, that began in 1793, caused a slump that crippled the Irish economy in town and country, exacerbated the resentment against the war—and made the French revolutionary cause still more attractive.[25]

By 1797 it was reported to Pitt that a secret Jacobin-style army was being prepared by Wolfe Tone's associates in Ireland, the newly founded societies of United Irishmen. The movement was also stirring up trouble among English Jacobins. And that spring, connected in some way with the Irish movement, the revolutionary crisis exploded in England.

The naval mutinies at Spithead and the Nore brought the country to the edge of the abyss. For three weeks the entire Spithead fleet—the thin blue line protecting London from a French invasion—was in the hands of the mutineers. The Admiralty had no choice but to meet in full the demands of the men for better pay and conditions and better officers.[26] But meanwhile a still more serious mutiny had broken out at the Nore and the ships of Admiral Duncan's fleet, blockading the Dutch fleet at the Texel, struck their colours and joined them. The Dutch fleet were known to be preparing an invasionary force. Now there was nothing to stop them. To cap it all, the British army seemed to be catching the infection. One night Pitt was woken to be told the marines were marching on London (the report, as it happened, was false). But England, no one could doubt, was nearer civil war than at any time since 1688. The Nore fleet flew the red flag, declared a kind of republic—the "Floating Republic" as it was called —and prepared to blockade London until their demands were met. All along the banks of the Thames people watched and waited for the fleet to begin the bombardment. Others fled inland, dragging their belongings as though from a foreign invasion.[27]

And then, quite suddenly, the naval mutinies and the British revolutionary crisis evaporated. In the last resort, it emerged, the British sailors and soldiers, like other working people, were loyal to King and country. However badly paid or badly treated, however republican their sympathies, they were still not prepared to join Britain's enemies to make a revolution. The habit of loyalty was too strong. On the day of the King's birthday the mutineers found themselves singing "God Save the King"; and one by one the red flags were hauled down and replaced by the royal standard.[28]

In October Duncan's sailors—the same men who had mutinied—won a crushing victory over the Dutch invasion fleet at the Battle of Camperdown. And despite the financial crisis, there were improved reports from Ireland.[29] Pitt's unshakable optimism seemed once again to be redeemed.

★　　★　　★

The same week of January, 1798 that found Pitt writing his delicate letter to the King, found the rulers of France pressing on with new plans to invade England and Ireland.[30]

The French Republic at this date—the Fifth Year of Liberty according to the new calendar—had just passed the second climacteric of the Revolution. For several years, the glory of French arms abroad had only been matched by the chaos and corruption of French politics at home. The *coup d'état* of the 18th Fructidor (September 4th 1797) was supposed to have cleared the air. The new Directory's purges were almost on the scale of the Terror: hundreds of political prisoners, including priests, were condemned to the "dry guillotine", the fever-ridden penal settlements of French Guiana.[31] Yet still the political power struggle continued.[32] Meanwhile a vast new

invasionary force was being assembled at the Channel ports.[33] Its commander-in-chief was to be the man who had smashed the Triple Alliance
in Europe, brought the Pope tumbling from his pedestal and made even
the French Directory quail—General Bonaparte.

The previous October, after his military triumphs had imposed peace
on all France's enemies except Britain, Bonaparte had written to the
French Foreign Minister: "Our Government must destroy the English
monarchy, or expect itself to be destroyed by those intriguing and enter-
prising islanders. The present moment offers a capital opportunity."[34] The
fifty thousand veterans of the Italian campaign were now released for
service elsewhere. And where better to send them, as Wolfe Tone pointed
out to the French Directory, than to invade the weakest part of the British
Isles, the Kingdom of Ireland?[35]

For Tone and the Irish revolutionaries in France, Bonaparte's new
command was a godsend. They had suffered a crushing series of disappointments since the fiasco of the Bantry Bay expedition.

In June 1797 they had heard the electrifying news of the British mutinies
at Spithead and the Nore. A Dutch and French invasion fleet—both
possibly destined for Ireland—were in preparation at Brest and the Texel.
But owing to the hopeless state of the allied navies, and the Ministry of
Marine, neither could stir. Finally, when the mutinies had collapsed, and
the sails of the British fleet appeared again off the Texel, the Dutch fleet
was ready. In early July, 13,500 Dutch troops were embarked, and Tone
was among them. For six weeks the wind hung in the west, as unremit-
tingly hostile as the east wind six months before in Bantry Bay. In mid-
August the troops were disembarked, and Tone was posted to the staff of
General Hoche in Belgium. A few weeks later the flagship on which he
had embarked and the rest of the Dutch fleet were blown to matchwood
by Admiral Duncan.[36]

And then in September the two Frenchmen, to whom the Irish most
looked for support, had both been lost to the cause. Hoche, the lost leader
of the Bantry expedition and Tone's friend and patron, had died suddenly
of consumption; Carnot, their chief ally in the Directory, had fled to
Switzerland after the *coup* of the 18th Fructidor.[37]

Everything now depended on Bonaparte. Already the French Directory
had given Tone encouragement; Talleyrand the Foreign Minister, even
mentioned a date for the expedition—April. And then, a fortnight after
Bonaparte's triumphant return from Italy, Tone found himself being
shown into the small, neat house with the classical furniture in the Rue
Chantereine where the great man had made his headquarters.

"Nature has exhausted her energies in the production of a Bonaparte," Barras the Director had thundered the week before, in his sycophantic speech of welcome. But the man whom Tone now found facing him across the room seemed to have been exhausted by his achievements. At this period he was only twenty-nine, but looked ten years older. Tone was also surprised to find that his appearance gave no hint of those extraordinary mental qualities for which he was famous—the marvellous enthusiasm and the explosive energy. His face looked more like a mathematician's. "He has a fine eye," Tone noted in his diary, "and a great firmness about his mouth; he speaks low and hollow."[38]

The interview itself was something of an anti-climax. Bonaparte showed remarkable ignorance of Irish affairs; he had got it into his head that the Irish population was only two and a quarter million (in fact it was about four and a half million—a third of the population of the British Isles). He let the Irish do the talking. Edward Lewins, a Dublin solicitor who had come to France as unofficial ambassador for the Irish revolutionary movement, had accompanied Tone. Bonaparte invited them to return shortly with a report on Ireland and the possibilities for invasion.[39]

In January 1798, Tone and Lewins returned to the house in the Rue Chantereine, bringing a sheaf of documents. In these it was stated bluntly that Ireland was still a British colony, and the colonists—450,000 Irish Protestants of the Established Church—were devoted to the British connection. It was accepted that until recently the Irish Dissenters were also part of this garrison. But now, inspired by the ideals of the French Revolution, the Dissenters were prepared to unite with the Catholic peasantry.[40] It was Presbyterian rationalism and Catholic nationalism that would combine to effect a revolution.

Bonaparte thanked Tone and Lewins for the documents. As before, he said little himself. They were taking their leave when he asked Tone where he had learnt his soldiering. Tone explained that he could not really claim to be a military man at all. "*Mais vous êtes brave*," said Bonaparte brusquely.[41]

Bonaparte's manner was hardly encouraging. And indeed, two things were becoming clear about him, both in different ways, ominous for Ireland.

First, Bonaparte's war machine was vastly expensive to run. France, like England, was trying to raise money by loans and contributions. But even these, and the coffers of the Pope and the treasury of Italy, were not enough to feed and clothe and arm the army destined for the British Isles. To pay his army, Bonaparte needed a war of conquest, not a war of liberation.[42]

Second, Bonaparte, whatever his ultimate political ambitions, showed no sign at present of wanting to force a show-down with the French Directory. He could not, therefore hang around Paris, resting on his laurels, while the veterans from Italy sat on their bayonets. For this reason, too, he had no alternative but to find a new country to conquer—and find it quickly.[43] If Ireland, then, was to be the object of the expedition—as part of the invasion of England—the obstacles were daunting. Somehow the demoralised French navy must produce the immense number of troop-ships, and the vast quantity of stores. Somehow the Irish patriots must organise their underground army to rise at the right time and place. Every-thing must be ready in a matter of weeks. Otherwise, impatient for glory and riches, Bonaparte would pursue his dreams elsewhere.

If the Irish exiles felt misgivings about Bonaparte, he gave them no ground for complaint in the next few weeks. On February 8th, he set off on a whirlwind tour of the channel ports. At Dunkirk, the dockyard was in the usual demoralised state. Bonaparte ordered the engineer-in-charge to prepare fifty large pinnaces and to move heaven and earth to get ships to embark 4,000–5,000 horses, 50,000 men with artillery and the necessary provisions. All must be ready in three weeks. Other Channel ports were alerted. In addition, Bonaparte sent a message to the Dutch authorities that he would require 20–30 gunboats and 200–300 fishing boats, to be ready at Ostend.[44]

Up and down the coast, tremendous efforts were made to keep the target dates. On the road to Lille, it was reported, "every useful tree cut down, and sawyers at work cutting planks and other scantling, and carts trans-porting it to the coast in great numbers." Flat-bottomed boats "without number" were being built at Le Havre; there were 25,000 troops at Rouen ready to march at an hour's notice. At Douai ninety-one pieces of artillery were observed at the churchyard *en route* for the coast.[45]

A few days later, these spine-chilling reports found their way to England, by way of a spy based on Jersey, and in due course were passed to the Irish Government.[46] Whatever country was to be invaded, no one could now doubt that Bonaparte was in earnest.

2

"Are They Above Or Are They Come?"

Dublin and the South, January 22nd–March 12th 1798

A wet winter, a dry spring,
A bloody summer, and no King.

Irish prophecy for 1798

THE NEWS of the impending French invasion found Lord Camden in Dublin Castle, the medieval fortress that dominated the teeming capital.

Dublin, second largest city in the British Empire, seventh largest in the world, was visibly collapsing under the weight of its 200,000 inhabitants. In the Liberties—the weavers' and mechanics' quarter a few hundred yards to the west of the Castle—the squalor and disease were frightful even by the standards of that age. It was common to find sixty (or even seventy) sharing a house. Recently one of the outside walls of a house had collapsed exposing the occupants to view; for want of alternative, they had continued living there till the rest of the house fell.[1] Meanwhile, on the other side of the Castle, houses were being torn down in an orgy of street-widening, speculative building and jobbery. Domed and pedimented, the palaces sprang up along the muddy river banks of the Liffey: the new Courts of Law, the new Customs house, the new Parliament itself, none smaller, less tasteful or less convenient than those of London itself.[2]

The Castle itself had remained aloof from both the horror of the Liberties and the glamour of the new Dublin. To the Irish people, looking at the Castle from outside, the place still had an air of absolute authority and of military force to support it. In fact, as Camden had been depressed to find when he took over as Viceroy three years before, the Castle was only a fortress in name, its towers and battlements little more than scenery. Inside, the place had a ramshackle colonial look.

There was a battered statue of Justice (whose scales tilted when it rained); there were two muddy courtyards; and there was a handsome classical building decorated by an artist fashionable in England long before.

Behind the façade were the real symbols of the King's Government in Ireland: a string of seedy offices, botched together at various dates, their locks continually being changed because thieves lurked on every staircase, and the great apartments of State, "dirtier and worse furnished", according to one Chief Secretary, "than any private gentlemen's house in England".[3] It was in one of these great apartments that Camden was now conferring with his colleagues on the current crisis in Ireland.

Camden himself looked the very type of the British aristocrat. He was young and tall and fair-haired; he was high-minded and humane; but three years of trying to govern Ireland with a cabinet and Parliament drawn from the corrupt and selfish Irish oligarchy had utterly demoralised him.

In theory Camden's Irish cabinet were simply the Government's advisers. Executive power was supposed to rest in the hands of the Viceroy, responsible to Pitt and the King. But the Irish cabinet—or "Junto" as their detractors called it—were fast becoming the real rulers of Ireland. The cabinet itself was dominated by three men: John Beresford, the elderly Commissioner for Revenue, John Foster, the Speaker in the Irish Parliament, and the formidable old Lord Chancellor, Lord Clare. They had all had years of experience at managing British viceroys. Once, it was true, a viceroy had shown real independence: Lord Fitzwilliam, Camden's immediate predecessor. He had sided with Henry Grattan's party—the Irish Foxites who were lobbying for Catholic emancipation—and given Beresford the sack. But fortunately for the Junto (and unfortunately for the Catholics) Fitzwilliam had greatly exceeded his instructions, and was recalled after a few weeks by Pitt.

Of Camden's personal staff at the Castle, the Chief Secretary, Thomas Pelham, shared his despondency. Pelham was already showing signs of the illness that would shortly remove him from his post. One of the under-secretaries, William Elliot, was also ill; he was nicknamed the "Castle Spectre" because of his ghastly complexion, supposed to be the result of the Irish climate. More robust was Edward Cooke, the under-secretary for the civil department.[4] But Cooke tended to side with the Junto. Finally, there was the Viceroy's nephew, the protegé of Pitt himself, Irish-born, Cambridge-educated, brilliant, icy, twenty-nine year old Lord Castlereagh.[5]

These were the men—young, and (except for Cooke) totally inexperienced—who were to be Camden's support in the impending crisis.

Towards the end of January disturbing reports about the state of Ireland were once more being despatched to London. On the 22nd Camden informed the British Government that he had "very unpleasant" accounts of the Midlands. Gentlemen's houses had been raided for arms, and gentlemen's ash trees cut up for pike handles. In Queen's County, the magistrates were about to ask the Viceroy to proclaim the district, according to the recent Insurrection Act, impose a curfew and call in the army to deal with the outrages.

"My opinion," Camden reported, "is that the gentlemen are much more alarmed than is necessary." The regular army were at hand in the garrison towns. The gentlemen, in their dual capacity of magistrates and yeomanry officers, should be able to keep the country quiet without declaring what amounted to martial law in their district. "But the privy council," Camden added despondently, "will not be able to withstand unanimous requisition, and I shall be under the necessity of agreeing with it."

The Irish country gentlemen, he explained in a sudden outburst to the Duke of Portland in London, were making government impossible. Their absurd jealousy of England, "their nonsensical and short sighted pride of independence", and the careless, not to say cruel, way they behaved to their inferiors had done much to bring Ireland to its present state. Now they were shirking their responsibilities. Some had even threatened to give up their commissions unless the regular army were let loose on the people. It was blackmail, but for the time being the Irish Government would be forced to submit.

A fortnight after proclaiming Queen's County Camden heard still more unpleasant news from the South. The only active magistrate in a vast mountainous tract between Cork and Tipperary, Colonel St. George, had been assassinated in circumstances of peculiar savagery. Only a fortnight before, Colonel St. George had written a confidential letter to the Castle describing how the neighbouring gentry, terrified by threat of assassination, had let their trees be cut down for pike handles by the local peasants. "A gentleman about a quarter of a mile from this passively observed the people cutting down fifty of his trees in Daylight in view of his house." The mob had taken over control of the country: "one may say the Revolution had commenced."[6]

Colonel St. George, a veteran of the American campaign, was not easily intimidated. Escorted by a bodyguard, armed with blunderbuss, sword and pistols, he declared he would "quiet" Captain Doe, as the local peasant leader was styled, if he had to burn every house in the district, starting with his own tenants'. That night, after he had dismissed his bodyguard from the house where he was staying it was surrounded by men armed with swords and pitchforks. His host and hostess, Mr. and Mrs. Uniacke, were just lighting him to his bedroom, when fourteen men appeared on the landing place from the backstairs, while others showed themselves below. Mrs. Uniacke threw herself in front of her husband. They flung her over the staircase on to the pavement of the hall. They stabbed her husband through and through, and flung him down beside her. Colonel St. George, defending himself at the head of the stairs, was hacked to death by a man with a rusty scythe.[7]

As the grisly details of the treble murder were multiplied in successive editions of the national press, further assassinations of the few remaining active magistrates were reported. Near Parsonstown, in King's County, Mr. Dooling, a respectable gentleman of more than a thousand a year, was shot dead in front of his wife by a gang of forty assailants.[8] At Richmond, Cork, Sir Henry Manix was killed in his garden.[9] While, only an hour's ride from the capital Mr. Johnson Darragh of Eagle Hill, Kildare was "amusing himself in his field with a spade and a shovel", when a gentleman rode up and shot him in the stomach.[10]

For Camden there was little comfort in the thought that for many years back there had been an open season, in certain parts of Ireland, for shooting magistrates. In Tipperary and the South the land-hungry peasantry had formed secret societies to protect their interests. If landlords accepted the unwritten code of the society, giving security to the tenant and a reasonable rent to the landlord, then the landlords had nothing to fear. But if they tried to fight the code, and the magistrates supported them, then the local Whiteboys—the boys with white shirts over their heads—would pay them a visit, and it might be the start of a long, bitter, agrarian war.

In the last decade these agrarian troubles had spread northward, and developed into many distinct forms of violence and anarchy. In Wexford there were riots by peasants protesting against conscription for the new militia. In Ulster there was not only a war between landlord and tenant, but between two rival groups—Catholic tenants, called Defenders, and Protestant tenants, called Peep-O'-Day Boys. In the Midlands the Catholic peasantry then adopted the name of Defenders for their own agrarian outrages against the tithe proctors and clergymen. It was a confused and perplexing picture, but two striking features emerged—the grievances were local grievances, in one way or another connected with the land, and, what followed, the disaffected had no serious political aims.[11]

How far was the new wave of outrages in Ireland in this tradition? Up to this time Camden had continued to apply the time-honoured remedies: letting the magistrates make an example of the district with as savage penalties as they chose.[12] But in the spring of 1798, the Irish gentry had become impatient with the conventional methods of pacification. Inflamed by press reports of assassinations, often accurately described, they were now pressing the Government for new measures of repression. Something dangerously like panic was spreading through the splended demesnes and trim glebe houses of the gentry.

In County Tipperary, a general attack on the town of Templemore was believed imminent—a false alarm, as it turned out. But "in a moment the garrison was on the alert, fired a signal gun, rung a large bell to alarm the county—had grenades ready, matches lighted."[13] The Protestant ascendancy was fast becoming a beleaguered garrison. Refugees began to flock to the towns of the South and Midlands. Country houses, when still inhabited, were turned into strong points; windows and doors barricaded; alarm bells installed on the roof. John Beresford, in Waterford, wrote to a British cabinet minister that they were daily threatened with massacre, and the Governor of County Cork, Lord Longueville, wrote grimly to his solicitor in Dublin, "Send me a form of prayer for the Last Day. I fancy it will not come in time here."[14]

In the face of mounting pressure for the declaration of martial law throughout the kingdom, Camden still hesitated. In late February he was still reassuring Portland that, once the country gentlemen put their mind to it, and found an opportunity to "feel their own strength", they could keep the disturbed counties quiet.[15] A week or two later he contrasted bitterly the cowardly way they behaved in the country with their violent language in Parliament. If they would not co-operate, how could the Government tackle the delicate and intractable problem on whose solution the safety of the Kingdom seemed to depend[16]—crushing the great United Irish conspiracy before the French landed?

A few days after those spine-chilling reports of Bonaparte's invasion fleet at Dunkirk had reached Dublin, via London, the Castle heard a rather different report of the French plans from their own intelligence network. They had one group of servants who were to prove loyal in the coming crisis—their secret agents and informers. But their information was obscure or conflicting, and to some extent this explained the hesitant way Camden had so far tackled the conspiracy. It was also to prove a crucial handicap in the weeks ahead. The current reports were characteristically confusing. According to one Irish intelligence report the French, not to be disheartened after the Bantry Bay fiasco, were indeed planning to invade Ireland, but would not be ready till April. More recent news from France made no mention of any expedition in preparation. It began to look as though Bonaparte had other plans.[17]

The same fog hung over the informers' reports about the strength of the United organisation in the country. According to one account, the United Irish leaders were using the present breathing space to perfect their military organisation. Meanwhile, they had issued the strictest instructions to their members to avoid all incidents which might provoke the Government into more severe counter-measures.[18]

This report raised a particularly difficult problem. If the report meant anything, it must mean that the United Irish movement was strongest where there was *least* disturbance. Those outrages which had sent the country gentlemen scurrying for cover in the towns and cities, abandoning the country to the rebels, could not be, directly at any rate, a prelude to revolution. It was merely the old agrarian war under a new name. The real threat must lie in the peaceful state of Dublin and the politically conscious counties around it. It was here that the Government should seek out the root of the conspiracy.

It was to Leonard McNally, radical barrister and popular playwright, that the Government owed their best blow-by-blow reports on the conspiracy. We shall probably never know exactly why McNally, a self-made man with a wide circle of friends in the United Irish movement, had agreed to betray them. No doubt his personal fears played their part— fear of the violent course the Irish revolution would take if it ever broke out, and fear of his own arrest and imprisonment if he did not co-operate with the Government.

On March 4th, McNally reported to the Government that the latest instructions had just arrived from Wolfe Tone and his colleagues in France. Nothing was to be done that might even hint at a plan for rising; on no account must houses be robbed for arms or trees cut down for pike handles. The movement must at all costs remain underground. At present, McNally reported: "the organisation goes on astonishingly—what is more, astonishing numbers in respectable and independent situations."[19] In another letter he described the rapid spread of the revolutionary movement among Dublin's middle classes. The law officers were organising. The yeomanry were coming round. The bank clerks, the merchants and the traders could be "reckoned upon almost to a man". Even the men servants were uniting in revolutionary committees. The new tax on men servants had "completely settled them".[20]

The Castle tended to take McNally's reports with a pinch of salt, but by early March it was clear from its agents in half a dozen places that a critical new phase in the revolutionary movement had been reached.

The headquarters of the conspiracy, the Government had known for some time, had shifted from the dissenters' city of Belfast to the capital itself. The precise identity of the Irish Directory was still a mystery, indeed it was not certain if one had yet been formed, but the Government knew who the main trouble-makers were. The Directory (or the "Directors of Politics", or the "Supreme Executive", as different informers called them), included some of Dublin's most affluent and respected citizens.

There was the successful radical barrister, Thomas Addis Emmet, son of the official state physician; William McNevin and John Lawless, respected doctors; John Chambers, secretary of the Irish Whig club, and a personal assistant to the great Grattan himself; John Sweetman, a brewer in Dublin; Richard McCormick, secretary of the Catholic Committee; Arthur O'Connor, friend of the English Whigs and nephew of Lord Longueville, and, by far the most influential as regards his family connections, Lord Edward Fitzgerald, brother of Ireland's first nobleman and largest land-owner, the Duke of Leinster. Catholic and Protestant, lawyer, doctor and landowner, they were a cross-section of Dublin's upper crust; only one component—the new rich—was missing. But two wealthy businessmen, according to McNally, were waiting in the shadows: Oliver Bond, the woollen merchant, and Henry Jackson, the ironmaster, whose astonishing new factory was powered by steam.[21]

Intellectually, the dominant men in this brotherhood were Thomas Addis Emmet and Arthur O'Connor. Emmet could wax eloquent on the technicalities of universal suffrage; O'Connor's special study was econo-mics. O'Connor "talks a fine page out of Adam Smith in lieu of conver-sation," remarked one of his friends that winter. Neither man had the kind of qualities that capture the hearts of the people. But in this respect one of the Directors was pre-eminent—Lord Edward Fitzgerald. Wild, handsome, hot-headed, idealistic and (if provoked) violent, Lord Edward had been an early convert to the philosophical ideas of Rousseau and Thomas Paine. In 1793 he had resigned his seat in the Irish parliament after an extraordinary outburst against the Government. He had married a beautiful French girl, Pamela, reputed to be the daughter of the Duke of Orleans. And how could they fail to set people's hearts on fire, that pair, as they drove through the streets of Dublin—Lady Edward dressed in Irish-made muslin, Lord Edward a dashing figure with the plain brown suit and the cropped revo-lutionary hair style of a French Jacobin.

On their broad political aims it was clear that the Irish Directory, like

Wolfe Tone and their colleagues in France, were now more or less agreed. Originally they had been, as ostensibly they still were, for reform by constitutional means, like the Whigs and the radicals. But by now they saw that only a complete break from England would give Ireland the economic rights, and the Irish professional classes the political power, that justice demanded. This, in turn, could only be accomplished by revolution.

But how could these conspirators hope to achieve the revolution in a country divided against itself by class and religion, with the balance of wealth and military strength so clearly on the side of the pro-British party? On this all important question the would-be revolutionaries were, as the Government now began to learn, fatally divided.

First news of the split had reached the Castle from neutral Hamburg, the centre of British intelligence in Europe. The report came from a Belfast businessman, code-named "Richardson", who was a member of the United Irish mission there. Turner, as his real name was, warned the Government that there was a move for immediate rising without waiting for the French. The Catholic members of the United Directory in Ireland violently opposed the idea, and McCormick had denounced its sponsors as "dangerous men and traitors to the cause".[22]

McNally's information was fuller. Despite repeated assurances that help was on the way, the French gave no proof of being ready to invade Ireland. At length an influential section of the executive, led by the aristocrat enthusiasts, Arthur O'Connor and Lord Edward, had announced that in their view the country was sufficiently well organised and equipped to go it alone. This was violently opposed by the lawyers and professional men—Emmet, McCormick and McNevin. The dispute ran high and O'Connor accused Emmet of cowardice. They disagreed, McNally went on, not only about when to act, but the manner of acting. Emmet, cautious and humane by nature, believed in securing life and property; O'Connor, the real revolutionary, in "severity that would strike terror". Emmet's moderate line carried the day, after a message reached them from France promising immediate invasion. At which O'Connor had left for London "much displeased and irritated even with his confidential friends".[23]

O'Connor's party, however, was still a force to be reckoned with. They controlled The Press—the semi-official paper of the movement. This had been set up by O'Connor the previous summer soon after his release from prison, taking over from the movement's Belfast paper, the Northern Star, which had been sacked by some Irish militiamen with the connivance of the authorities, and the presses thrown into the street.

The Press was less provocative to Government, or at any rate the Dublin authorities were more thick-skinned. To Emmet and his friends, it now seemed, if McNally was correct, extremely mischievous. Its tone was not, they believed, in the least calculated to calm the peasantry during the critical phase of forming a huge underground army.

"Ireland is singular in suffering, and cowardice; she could crush her tormentors, and yet they embowel her; she *could* be *free*, yet she is a slave."[24]

"Let the tree be cut down, and cast into the fire, it has too long cumbered the ground."[25]

"The time is not far distant when our *passive virtues, impregnated with the active ones*, shall procure for Ireland her rights; shall hurl confusion and destruction on her enemies; shall avenge the murders of her slaughtered patriots."[26]

If *The Press* alarmed Emmet, the *Union Star* drove him wild. This was a clandestine broadsheet run as a freelance venture by a Catholic gunsmith called Watty Cox. The *Union Star* disarmingly claimed that its policy was "to establish the empire of universal benevolence and fraternity from [the] Wicklow hills to Belfast, from the Channel to the Atlantic".[27] But it frankly exploited the racial and religious hatreds of the submerged Catholic peasantry. The clergymen to whom they paid their tithes were "idle and voluptuous drones", their doctrines "impious".[28]

"The lands which royal villainy wrested from murdered Irishmen shall be the rewards of the deliverers of their country. No more will the lazy lord enjoy the fruits of your labour . . . no more shall you be as you have been for centuries, rearing and watching the ox or the sheep whose flesh you never tasted, or whose fleece never warms you."[29]

"Revenge! glorious revenge! Your name is as sweet as Liberty."

In subsequent numbers it developed the theme of Brutus, the brave tyrannicide.[30]

"Yes! Prince of patriotic assassins, thy noble and virtuous spirit should pervade our land: the infant whom a British, or a British Irish butcher has left fatherless should be taught . . . thy example . . . as an honest duty."[31]

To the relief of the moderate United Irish, the Government had managed to track down Cox the editor, in mid-December, and the career of the *Union Star* ended abruptly. Emmet would have been less pleased had he known that Cox, as a condition of being left at liberty, had agreed to tell the Government all he knew about his fellow members.[32]

Despite all this new information about the United Irish leadership, and the new danger that O'Connor's violent party, now led by Lord Edward, might attempt a rising without waiting for French help, the Castle still hesitated. Then at the end of February Camden learnt some cheering news from London.

Arthur O'Connor had been arrested on a charge of sedition, and was safe behind bars in the Tower.[33] At last Camden screwed up courage enough to close down *The Press*[34]—and then almost regretted it. For among the United Irish leaders the arrest of O'Connor and the seizure of his paper did not have quite the effect anticipated. According to McNally, the party as a whole had now swung back behind the moderate leadership of Emmet and McNevin. O'Connor's arrest would hardly be noticed. McNevin and McCormick were rather relieved at the way things had turned out, because of their fear that O'Connor would stir up trouble if he got to France. As for *The Press*, the Government would be surprised to hear that its suppression had been well received because of the danger of its sparking off a premature explosion.[35]

Such was McNally's story, and there was much independent evidence to confirm it. Since O'Connor's departure, the party had issued a series of bulletins to its members, and half a dozen had fallen into the hands of the Government. Stern, even puritanical in tone, these were clearly aimed as a counter-blast to the heady doctrines of *The Press*. Once more, they reminded the brotherhood, they must warn them against choosing unsuitable members for their societies. Mistakes in this respect were responsible for the recent hardships they had suffered. They must beware of rival organisations. People had disgraced the name of United Irishmen by their violence. If one of their own members stole arms and was imprisoned, he would forfeit the support of the society.[36]

This denunciation of the recent Defenders-type outrages in the South and Midlands was followed by more general hints on deportment. The brethren must be more discreet about the way they dressed and the language they used. "Party articles of dress", French-style clothes and cropped hair were forbidden, and so were secret party signs. Sobriety must be their watch-word in every sense. They must boycott the heavily taxed foreign goods, like wine, sugar and tea. "A Government which draws its resources from vice (such as GAMBLING and DRUNKENESS)" must soon be brought down by the new brotherhood based on "Union and Love" and teetotalism.[37]

Through the reports of their secret agents the Government had now been following the conspiracy, stage by stage, as it approached its climax. They had watched it grow from a perfectly legal society of reformers, before war broke out with France, to a huge underground army, incorporating it was claimed, 300,000 Irish sworn to join in armed revolution. They might be ill equipped, and the numbers greatly exaggerated. But if the leaders chose their moment well, they had some chance of success, and if the French joined them, then Ireland might for a time be lost to the Empire.

Why not, then, arrest the leaders? The Government, of course, had often considered the idea. The problem, as Camden saw it in the beginning of the year, was not only to detect the plot but to expose it to the world. The information they had already collected through Turner and McNally went far to establish the connection between the disturbed state of the country and the United leaders in Dublin, and the links in turn between them and their allies in France. But Turner and McNally refused to let their evidence be used in a court of law or a parliamentary enquiry. Even if they had been prepared to come forward, they were not sure themselves who were at the heart of the conspiracy. So it was agreed in London and Dublin to make no arrests for the moment.[38]

This had been the position at the end of January. A fortnight later, Camden had written to Portland to say he was under strong pressure from the Irish gentry. "It seems their opinion that the system of Union is spreading, that the Counties into which it has been introduced are organised, that the Publication of *The Press* is spreading still more widely that System, whilst no Measure seems to be taken to counteract it."[39]

At a cabinet meeting, the Speaker, John Foster, put the case vehemently for arresting the known conspirators, although they could not be brought to trial. Foster was the most powerful man in the cabinet after the Chancellor. He was emerging as the leader of the right wing, the party of the squires and the Orange lodges, the *ultras* who were still unreconciled to the relaxation of the penal laws against Catholics. With some justice, Foster argued that the comparative calm of Dublin and the country around was not, as Camden then believed, the result of the Government's strong measures. On the contrary, it meant the region was successfully organised and patiently waiting the instructions of the Dublin executive. By arresting their leaders, the Government would "disconcert their proceedings". He added, "It might possibly produce an insurrection in some part of the kingdom, but under all circumstances the event might not be unpropitious, as it would be more in our power to quell it, than if such event happened when the enemy were off the coast."[40]

The London cabinet was shocked to read Foster's proposal. Portland wrote hurriedly back to Camden that these measures would be both "dangerous and inconvenient".[41]

A few days later, however, entirely new information came into the hands of the Irish Government, which was to tip the balance sharply in favour of Foster's plan. And in a few days more Portland reluctantly conceded to Camden that he could arrest the conspirators at his discretion.

The latest acquisition to the Castle's intelligence network was a twenty-seven year old Catholic silk merchant, called Thomas Reynolds. He had useful connections. Wolfe Tone had married his sister-in-law. Lord Edward was, he claimed, a distant relation. He had joined the movement more than a year before, believing that its aims were limited to its published programme—Catholic emancipation and Parliamentary reform. At first his membership seems to have been more or less nominal. Reynolds was preoccupied with the task of getting out of trade and setting up in style as a country gentleman. Lord Edward obliged by helping him buy the lease of Kilkea—one of the smaller Fitzgerald castles. In December, as Reynolds was choosing the wallpapers and family portraits for the baronial hall, Lord Edward asked him a favour. His own activities for the movement had drawn the suspicion of the Government. Would Reynolds mind taking over his place as United colonel for County Kildare? Reynolds could hardly refuse such a compliment from the brother of the Duke of Leinster—his landlord. The Kildare Committee received him enthusiastically, and soon he rose from county treasurer to a place on the Leinster Provincial Directory itself.[42]

At the beginning of the new year, when O'Connor's violent party, as we have seen, challenged the moderate leadership of Emmet, Reynolds at last saw the movement in its true colours, according to his own account. Two members of the county executive took him aside and showed him their "diabolical plans". The rising was imminent—the first step, the assassination of eighty leading members of the Government. Prelates, noblemen, gentlemen, some of them my own relations, noted Reynolds in horror. In each case a man servant sworn to the cause was ready to do the deed.[43]

On February 25th, Reynolds rode down from Dublin to do some business with a friend called Mr. Cope, merchant of Cope & Co. They dined with some local gentry. Conversation turned to the distracted state of the country—magistrates murdered in broad daylight, houses raided, threats of a French invasion, and the prospect of revolution. Reynolds had been in Paris when the mob took over. His mind was now made up. Riding back to Dublin he confided to Cope that he knew "someone" who could give the Government all the information they needed.[44]

Without disclosing Reynolds' identity, Cope went immediately to the

Castle. The Chief Secretary, Thomas Pelham, authorised Cope. to offer him virtually a blank cheque in exchange for the vital information. Reynolds assured Cope he was not interested in a reward. He only made four stipulations: he should not be prosecuted; nor be asked to prosecute others; his identity should be kept secret; and some ready cash—500 guineas—should be paid him in case he had to leave the country suddenly.[45]

As a first instalment, Reynolds now produced a copy of the actual minutes of that week's meeting of the Supreme Executive. It was, he said, taken from a set in Lord Edward's handwriting. It confirmed the Government's worst fears. The revolutionary army—on paper, at any rate—outnumbered the Government forces by more than five to one, totalling, according to the returns, precisely 279,896 armed men. This huge secret army was distributed fairly evenly over three of the four provinces; no returns were included for Connaught, the poorest and least organised of the four.[46]

On one vital issue Reynolds' report added to the bewilderment of Camden and his advisers. Those outrages in the South and Midlands, were they in fact directed by the movement? Or were, on the contrary, the tranquil counties in the North and East the better organised?

The returns of armed men confirmed the first view. Queen's County, proclaimed in January as in a state of insurrection, boasted the largest army after Wicklow, parts of which had been proclaimed the previous winter. Dublin and Meath, little disturbed, were little organised. Wexford and a couple of other peaceful counties on the fringe of Leinster were so apathetic as to have sent no returns.

Yet according to the minutes of the meeting, the counties that declared themselves ready for immediate rising were Meath and Carlow, in the Midlands, and Down and Antrim, in the North—all of which had recently proved completely quiet.

The Supreme Executive, at any rate, were now putting the finishing touches to their plans for the rising. Each county was to appoint an adjutant-general to report direct to the Executive the tactical strength of the county contingent. Every road and bridge, every scrap of land must be surveyed with an eye to its use as a patriot rallying point, or a place for ambushing a Government convoy. When the French landed, patriots must gather together all the horses they could find, take three days' rations for the men, and march forward immediately to join up with the patriotic militia and yeomanry.

Though Reynolds, like Turner and McNally, refused to give evidence in court, Camden and his advisers devised a scheme which would enable them not only to seize the conspirators, but to bring them to justice.

On March 12th, according to Reynolds, the twenty odd delegates of the Leinster Directory were to meet in Dublin. It was a critical moment. Once again a motion for immediate rising, unassisted by the French, would be put to the meeting, and this time it would probably be carried. Lord Edward, as military expert, John McCann, as the provincial committee's secretary, were both in favour. One of the violent party, according to Reynolds, had told him a few days before, "We were nearly equal to them at the last meeting, and we have all the new Delegates to our side at this time." All over the Kingdom new recruits were joining them. More than half the soldiers in the barracks of Dublin and the camp at Loughlinstown were now sworn to the cause. They desired "but twenty minutes' notice to seize the camp and march to Dublin".[47]

Completely unsuspecting, the Executive continued to keep Reynolds up-to-date with their plans. Reynolds in turn passed the information to Cope, and Cope to the Government. On March 10th, they learnt that the meeting would be in a room on the first floor of the house of Oliver Bond, the woollen merchant in Bridge Street. It would begin punctually at ten. The passwords were: "Are they above or are they come?" "Is Ivers of Carlow come?"[48]

The night before the meeting Camden wrote to Portland to tell him why he was going ahead with the arrests, despite the British cabinet's misgivings. First, the United leaders were doing "inconceivable mischief" organising the country. The Irish cabinet unanimously agreed that they must be stopped, even at the risk of precipitating a rebellion. Second, the spring assizes were approaching. The gentry were completely demoralised and it would be impossible to get juries unless the Government showed they were not afraid to strike. Third, if they delayed any longer, their "best friends" in Parliament would turn against them. Camden concluded: "it is therefore with infinite anxiety I look to the success of the measure."[49]

Next morning shortly after ten, Town Major Sirr, Dublin's notorious chief of police, rushed into the first floor room in Bridge Street and surprised the Leinster Directory in conclave. At one swoop Sirr seized ten provincial delegates, two members of the Supreme Executive and their papers. Meanwhile, the houses of the other leaders had been surrounded. Sweetman was taken in his brewery, Emmet in his chambers, Jackson in his iron foundry, and McNevin in his consulting room.[50]

Several of the country delegates, however, were late in arriving at Bond's, and so escaped. Though arrested, Thomas Traynor, the Dublin City delegate at the meeting, outwitted the Major. "Hold up your hands," bellowed Sirr, as he entered the room. Traynor managed to slip one incriminating document into his mouth. Then, pretending to be faint with terror, he persuaded the Major to give him a glass of water, and so swallowed the paper.[51]

Only two members of the Supreme Executive escaped. Richard McCormick, the Catholic, had despaired of being able to restrain his violent colleagues. Attacked and abused by them for cowardice, and in fear of his own life, he had gone into hiding just before the meeting at Bond's, and soon fled abroad to safety.[52]

When he had gone, the sole survivor of the Executive, on whom the hopes of tens of thousands of peasants were now pinned, was Lord Edward, the leader of the violent party.

3

A General's Prophecy

Dublin, March 12th–30th

"... in a state of licentiousness which must render it
formidable to everyone but the enemy,"

General Abercromby of his Irish army

"Poor creature I pity him ... he is quite in his dotage."

General Lake of General Abercromby

THE ARREST of sixteen leading revolutionaries raised surprisingly little
stir in the capital. The Lord Chancellor, Lord Clare, it is true, was hissed on
his way to the Council Chamber. He rounded on the mob, according to
one account, "cursing and swearing like a madman".[1] He said himself, in a
reassuring note to a friend: "Some forty or fifty blackguards did follow
me down Castle Hill; but, as I never go out unarmed, on my facing them
suddenly with a pistol in my hand, they retreated with precipitation."[2]

Characteristically the Government had made no effort to forestall a
riot, let alone a serious attempt to rescue the prisoners. After the scuffle
with the Chancellor, however, a massive show of strength was given by
two thousand loyal Dublin yeomanry—lawyers, doctors and parsons
who spontaneously left their work to rally in the streets, and patrol there
till morning.[3] There were no further incidents, and Camden was able to
report to London the almost unqualified success of the raid on Bond's.[4]

Next day the gossips were busy. The man who had informed on the
conspirators was supposed to be John Binns, the London Jacobin, who had
slipped in and out of Ireland the previous month, and was reported to
have turned King's evidence after his arrest with O'Connor.[5] The purpose
of the arrests, people said, was to make hostages, as the French and Spanish
fleets had combined, and invasion was imminent.[6] Everyone had a different story to explain Lord Edward's escape. In one version, the sheriff had
actually caught him breakfasting at McNevin's, but the warrant had been
sent to a different address, so he escaped.[7] In another, Lord Edward had

been saved from the trap by a premonition of his faithful Negro servant, Tony.[8] A thousand stories were told of where Lord Edward was now hidden. He had fled to his brother's house in the North. He had sailed for France. He was concealed in Dublin, disguised as a woman. For some days the Dublin papers fanned the gossip with conflicting reports,[9] then the story faded, and the attention of Dublin ladies turned to a still more tasty Dublin scandal—the forthcoming murder trial of Robert, Earl of Kingston, for shooting his daughter's seducer.[10]

In the Fitzgerald family circle, Lord Edward's flight caused, naturally enough, rather more agitation. His aunt, Lady Louisa Connolly, whose husband, Tom Connolly, commanded the Derry militia, was in *"horrors* about his *having* invited the French, or his being punished for it".[11] His conventional older brother, Lord Charles, who had a minor post in the Government, was "so overcome" that he shut himself up in his villa and refused to see anyone.[12] Other respectable relations rallied round. Lady Louisa Connolly happened to be connected by marriage to both Lords Camden and Castlereagh. The latter was vaguely reassuring: "You may rely on the earnest wishes of government to do all they can for Lord Edward, who is so much loved, and as he can't be found, no harm can come to him."[13] Lord Castlereagh gallantly offered to return to Lady Edward her private letters seized during a raid on Leinster House.[14]

Lord Edward's French wife, Pamela, was reported by Louisa Connolly to be bearing up well during this trying period. "Poor little Pamela's *fair, meek* and pitiable account of it all moved her to the greatest degree," her sister Sarah wrote in her diary.[15] Louisa had gone straight to Leinster House after seeing Lord Castlereagh, and Pamela was told very firmly that, if she knew where Lord Edward was, she was to keep her mouth shut. Appearances were unpleasant, it was true, but the family still clung to the hope that Edward was innocent—or at any rate had made good his escape. They had some reason for optimism. Just before Lord Edward had gone underground, the Lord Chancellor told one of the family: "For God's sake get this young man out of the country. The ports shall be thrown open to you, and no hindrance whatever offered."[16]

There was more to this policy of the Government's than respect for Lord Edward's influential relations. As we have seen, Camden's overriding aims were first to prevent revolution in Ireland, and second to expose to the world the international Jacobin conspiracy.[17] Lord Edward's arrest seemed now more or less irrelevant. The cabinet did not, in any case, have a particularly high opinion of his talents. "Lord Edward is zealous but not fit to command a sergeant's guard," a Castle informer had written earlier.[18] One thing that never seems to have crossed anyone's mind in Government circles at this time was that in this wayward and idealistic young aristocrat Ireland might find a more potent symbol for national rebellion than in any of the more serious conspirators.

What worried Camden and his advisers was not Lord Edward's absence. It was the comparative innocuousness of the papers seized at Bond's with the other revolutionaries.

The only papers of any great significance found at Bond's were some provincial committee resolutions and subscription lists written by the provincial secretary John McCann and hastily thrust under the grate.[19] These papers, John Beresford reported to his crony Lord Auckland a day after the arrests, "confirmed to a certainty what we knew before, their treasonable designs and actions".[20] But it was one thing to justify to themselves the policy of seizing the conspirators; it was quite another thing to prove in a court of law that they were guilty of high treason. And as the days passed it became increasingly obvious to Camden and his advisers that they were still no nearer obtaining the evidence necessary for a successful prosecution.[21] A list of 67,295 people ready "to act in concert with the Nation"[22] was hardly going to bring anyone to the scaffold unless the *object* of the meeting could be made plain. To achieve this they needed the testimony of the informer who had betrayed the meeting—Thomas Reynolds. His identity was still unknown to the Government, but the message came back to them by way of Cope. He refused point blank.[23]

At this discouraging period the Castle received the latest bulletin from that Dublin Cassandra, Leonard McNally. "You will be surprised at being assured," he wrote of the arrests at Bonds's, that they have "scarcely affected any man except the very near connections of those imprisoned, and even those connections do not despond but evince pride mingled with their apprehensions." McNally warned the Government that the arrests had not, as they thought, broken the back of the revolutionary organisation. "The societies met yesterday," he wrote on the 13th, "in the midst of the tumults and calmly proceeded in their business." Orders were sent to each society: "When a secretary is taken up, instantly meet and elect another!"[24]

McNally's story was hard to swallow. On the 19th, the Under Secretary at the Castle, Edward Cooke, wrote confidently to London: "Dublin is broken in its organisation by our late captures, and certainly there is much confusion among the rebels."[25] Yet it was hard to dismiss McNally's story completely. Francis Higgins, the editor of the pro-Government *Freeman's Journal*, heard from his private spy ring that some Dublin business men who were in the plot had set up a special committee to help get Jackson, Bond and the others out of prison; they were confident that they could not be prosecuted and delegates had been sent north to assure their friends there of "their Continued and Invariable zeal".[26] An informer called Boyle reported that "there will be a new directory or Convention appointed, in the room of such as are taken up or run away." Neilson, the Belfast printer arrested in 1796 and recently released, was one of the leaders.[27] Later in the month, Boyle announced he had attended one of the five hundred branch meetings called to receive instructions from the new directory. Expresses were to be sent shortly with the new plans. "Pikes are making in Abundance in every part of Dublin . . . some very desperate Attack will be made and that very soon."[28] By the end of the month one informer was claiming that the arrests had been worse than useless. "For they say unless the great Ones suffered in their Cause it would never come to pass."[29]

Whether they believed these reports or not—and they seem to have been sceptical—the Castle authorities recognised their perilous situation, as long as the state prisoners were unpunished. "If these villains escape with a temporary imprisonment only," wrote the Lord Chancellor, Lord Clare, "there will be no possibility of living in Ireland."[30] But how to get evidence? Would attainder be justifiable? "I fear we cannot convict *legally*," wrote Cooke, "but they *must* be punished, or the country is gone."[31]

This delicate question was still unresolved when a political storm burst which was to drain the last reserves of the Castle's strength and solidarity. It was to be the worst political crisis since the fiasco of Lord Fitzwilliam's viceroyalty three years before—and the Government's last chance of avoiding the catastrophe of rebellion and civil war.

Two days after the arrests at Bond's, an exceedingly tiresome letter had arrived from London. There was consternation over there, reported the Duke of Portland, at what purported to be a general order of the Commander-in-Chief, General Sir Ralph Abercromby, accusing the Irish army of atrocities. The Irish gentry in London were convinced that nothing but death and destruction would follow; they must collect up their belongings and leave Ireland for ever.[32] A couple of days later, Camden received a still more ominous sign—a letter from Pitt himself. Had he really authorised this extraordinary order? Such "a public and indiscriminate censure" of the whole Irish army was "almost an invitation to a foreign enemy".[33] Other members of the British cabinet—Lord Auckland[34] and Lord Westmoreland—wrote privately to enquire what on earth was going on in Ireland.[35]

The copy of the general order that had created such a sensation in London was perfectly genuine. On February 26th, after returning from a tour of the South, Abercromby had sent a circular to all generals and commanding officers, which began with the striking statement that the Irish army was "in a state of licentiousness which must render it formidable to everyone but the enemy". This was proved, Abercromby went on, by the "very disgraceful frequency of courts martial and the many complaints of the irregularities in the conduct of the troops in this Kingdom". Commanding Officers were now instructed to enforce the strictest discipline and restore the good name of the army. At the same time they were reminded that standing orders expressly forbade troops to act on their own initiative against the disaffected, without being called on by the magistrates, unless they were themselves attacked.[36]

A few hours after writing this order, Abercromby left Dublin again— this time for a tour of the North. He did not consult the Castle, he did not even inform them about this remarkable document. For him it was simply a matter of discipline. "It was necessary to speak out," he later explained. "The order is strong, but be assured it was necessary." The abuses of all kinds "can scarcely be believed."[37] One of his friends added in his defence: "Nothing I am sure could be more remote from Sir Ralph's mind . . . than any idea of politicks."[38] And that, of course, was his undoing.

Abercromby was a capable commander in the field, as he had shown in the recent campaign in the West Indies. But in his long career he had made still more mark as a humane and efficient administrator. He had helped re-build the morale of the British army, shattered by the fiascos on the Continent.[39] His politics were liberal, and free from party. As a young man he had, like many serving officers, sympathised with the American struggle for independence.[40] He now shared the views of his friend Henry Dundas, and the other more liberal-minded members of the British cabinet, who hoped shortly to establish an honourable peace with France.[41]

From the first he had had misgivings about his new post in Ireland. Although he was assured by the English cabinet that he would have a free hand, he knew that the peculiar nature of Irish Government put the Commander-in-Chief in a most difficult position. As the King's representative the Viceroy was in theory the head of the Irish army. In practice, this merely created endless delays and obstructions, for the Commander-in-Chief had to get the sanction of the Viceroy on the most trivial questions; it also laid the Irish army wide open to intrigue, as officers could appeal to the Viceroy over the head of their Commander-in-Chief.[42] Despite the re-assurances in London it took Abercromby only a fortnight to realise this system had not, after all, been changed. He pressed Camden to honour the promise to give him a free hand—or let him return to England. "A divided command," he pointed out, "is perfectly incompatible with those principles by which military affairs are guided."[43] Camden's reply was characteristically evasive: he could not formally delegate his power to him, but he would have it in substance.[44]

The more Abercromby saw of the way the country was being run, the less he had liked it. He had one clear aim—to reform and remodel the army to be ready to meet the threat of French invasion. The task was daunting: "On my arrival here," he wrote to a friend in England a few days after disembarking, "I found an army of upwards of 40,000 without any arrangement made for their subsistence" in case they had to take the field. A Commissary-General was appointed—the best that could be found, though "not altogether qualified".[45] Other military preparations were equally defective. "No artillery were in a condition to move," he told his staff officer, General John Moore. "Even the guns attached to the regiments were unprovided with horses. No magazines were found for the regiments. Little or no order or discipline."[46] The cavalry, Abercromby found, were "in general unfit for service", and the infantry officers "very little able to command them".[47] But to a professional like Abercromby, the most alarming feature of all was the way the regular army were scattered in small groups all over Ireland. In December, he wrote to General Lake, the commander of the northern district, to impress on him "the absolute necessity" of concentrating the troops in larger bodies. "In their present state they are exposed to be corrupted, to be disarmed and made prisoners."[48] Instead of leaving the regular army to the garrison towns from where they could be rushed to meet any attempt by the French at landing, the Government had allowed more than half of them to be dispersed in small parties for protecting the gentry in disturbed areas. This kind of police work was the job of the local yeomanry. In special cases Abercromby was prepared to let regular troops do duty alongside the yeomanry, but their strategic role should be completely different. Their present dispersed state was "really ruinous to the service. The best regiments in Europe could not long stand such usage."[49]

After a frustrating month in Dublin, Abercromby set out for his first tour of the country. He travelled south, reaching Cork in late January. He was pleased to find that the country people were quiet. There was dissatisfaction, it was true; and a "watchful eye" must be kept on the disaffected.[50] The trouble was, he reported to the Duke of York in London, in a private letter, "The upper orders of men have fallen, in general, into a state of despondency, and seem to have given up the cause." He had tried as far as possible to resist their appeals for regular troops to protect them. The present system could ruin the troops' discipline and lead them "into a thousand irregularities contrary to law, which would bring disgrace upon themselves". By withdrawing the troops, he could not only restore the troops' discipline and concentrate them at strategic points ready to ward off invasion; he might also, as he put it to the Duke of York, "force the gentlemen to exert themselves".[51]

Many years before, Abercromby had been stationed as a junior officer in Ireland. What he now saw of the Irish gentry only served to confirm his earlier impression, that their petty tyranny was the root cause of Ireland's troubles. As men they were ignorant; as landlords oppressive. Still more shocking to Abercromby's Scottish soul, their chief interests were "the pursuit of pleasure or political intrigue". Now, when their country most needed magistrates of integrity and courage, they were deserting their posts, or crying to the army to rescue them from the peasantry they had goaded to rebellion.[52]

On his return to Dublin Abercromby gave Camden a confidential report on the preparations to defend Ireland. If the French landed on the eastern side of the country, they could be sealed off between the two great rivers, the Slaney and the Barrow. If they chose the South-West, which was more likely, they would be blocked by the large garrisons at Kinsale and Cork, which were in a good state of readiness. Right across the South he was forming a chain of depôts for arms and ammunitions, forage and provisions. New batteries on the Shannon were being erected, the old fort at Duncannon was being reversed so that its guns faced out to sea, while far up the Shannon the medieval castle at Athlone was being hastily fortified. All these measures were essential to protect the country from foreign invasion.[53] As for the enemy within, Abercromby repeated once more that the internal security of Ireland must depend on the "firmness and resolution" of the country gentlemen.[54]

Camden was well satisfied by this report. He had found in Abercromby "great military experience," he told Portland, "combined with remarkably good sense and knowledge of the world". Sir Ralph's conviction that the country gentlemen should be given "the opportunity to feel their own strength" coincided exactly, as we have seen, with the view of the Castle. After sounding several gentlemen, Camden had convinced himself, as he reported to Portland on February 24th, that he would adopt the suggestion, and accordingly they would be able to regroup the army as proposed.[55]

Two days later Abercromby issued his remarkable order: that the Irish army was "formidable to everyone but the enemy". The Castle saw it—and gasped. But Camden was politician enough to see the enormous damage that the order could do if exploited by the Opposition in Parliament. Only six days before in the Irish House of Lords, Lord Moira had accused the Irish army of illegal methods of repression, and Abercromby's order seemed to provide complete confirmation. At a cabinet meeting it was unanimously agreed to try to hush up the whole business.[56] If it came up in Parliament they would have to explain it away as best they could.

However, the days passed and no mention was made of it in the Irish papers, and when the Opposition brought a censure motion in the Commons on March 5th, only one oblique reference to the order was made which was quickly smoothed over by the Government.[57] As for Abercromby, he had left Dublin a few hours after its despatch, and the Castle decided to say nothing to him, in the hope that the whole business would soon blow over.[58]

The very day that Camden received news from Portland of the extraordinary sensation the order had created in London Abercromby returned to Dublin. Camden summoned him peremptorily to the Castle. Abercromby would not come till next morning. A painful interview followed. Abercromby, not trusting himself to speak off the cuff, read a long statement of self-justification.[59] He understood that his order had been construed as a political manoeuvre in support of the British and Irish Whigs. The facts were these: he had lamented the "general alienation of the minds of the People from Government", he had regretted the "supineness and despondency of Individuals", he had seen with anxious concern "the loose texture" and "relaxed discipline" of the Irish army; he had issued the order to correct these abuses, and to "stimulate the exertions of the country". If, however, he did not enjoy the confidence of the Irish cabinet he would gladly resign his post.[60]

At this Camden backpeddled hurriedly. Without a man like Abercromby, he simply could not carry on as Viceroy.[61]

In London the cabinet received this news with some relief. The hullabaloo caused by the London-Irish lobby was apparently diminishing, and the Foxites had not, as anticipated, made capital in Parliament out of the Abercromby indiscretion.[62] Accordingly, Pitt's Minister of War and a personal friend of Abercromby's, Henry Dundas, was asked to act as peace-maker. He wrote to Abercromby immediately to convince him that nothing would injure his reputation more than to resign because of "imaginary doubts or suspicions" about the Irish Government's confidence in him.[63]

Before this soothing letter could reach him, however, Abercromby had received news apparently confirming his darkest fears of a plot against him in the Irish "cabinet".

Events had, in fact, moved fast since the interview with Camden. That very evening, the Government's attempt to hush up the business had received a completely unexpected reverse: the unfortunate order was leaked into the Irish papers—reprinted from the London papers of five days before.[64] "Licentious . . . Disgraceful . . . formidable to everyone but the enemy." It was too much for the officers of the Irish army and the rest of the Irish gentry. All their bitterness at what they called the Government's policy of half-measures towards the people rushed to the surface.

The solidarity of the Irish cabinet was no match for this assault. The Lord Chancellor, Lord Clare, inured to unpopularity by twenty years of Castle politics, held his ground. It was provoking, Clare confessed to a friend, not to be able to resent the "peevish indiscretion" of "this Scotch beast" Abercromby as it merited.[65] But the other principal adviser of the Government, John Foster, canvassed the order openly, formed a cabal against Abercromby which held a council of war in his own chamber, and lobbied furiously for his dismissal.[66] It was reported to London that both Houses of Parliament were "in a state of smothered flame".[67] The crisis reached its climax when Foster, as Speaker of the Commons, moved an address to the Lords, expressly contradicting Abercromby's order.[68] In private there was serious talk of impeaching him.

The crisis showed the Government the violence of the gentry's feelings against concessions to the people, and the grave risk of further alienating the gentry. Foster, their spokesman, was able to seize on one part of Abercromby's order which plainly contradicted the Viceroy's proclamation of the previous year,[69] the part which forbade the army to act without authority of the magistrate.[70] General Lake, the northern commander,[71] and most senior general after Abercromby, firmly sided with the gentry against his chief. By withdrawing regular troops from the North, "he appears to me to be doing everything he can to lose it," he had written to a fellow general.[72] As for the conciliation, "Poor creature I pity him . . . he is quite in his dotage."[73]

As the breach between Government and Parliament widened day by day, Camden still dithered. Cooke and the Chancellor were turning against Abercromby. Despite the success of the arrests at Bond's, disturbances seemed to be on the increase again. This was all grist to the mill of Abercromby's detractors. "The state of the country is dreadful beyond description," wrote that stalwart member of the Government party, John Beresford. "The late military orders have done unspeakable mischief."[74] "For God's sake, what is doing . . . with our Commander-in-Chief?" said another Irish Privy Councillor. "He may be an excellent general in the field, but he's a miserable bad Politician. I wish he had stay'd with the Negroes on Martinico."[75]

To Pelham and other well-intentioned Englishmen in Ireland—fellow civil servants like Elliot and Knox, soldiers like Craufurd and Moore—the campaign against Abercromby was deplorable. They recognised that Abercromby's remarks, though unfortunately worded, were perfectly true—and no less wounding for that.[76] From his sick-bed, Pelham drafted a long plaintive letter to Portland: London had given countenance to the Irish cabal and condemned unheard not only Abercromby, but the Viceroy himself.[77] Moore threatened to resign in sympathy, if Abercromby went; Craufurd and other officers expressed their solidarity.[78] Tales of the plot in the Irish cabinet to force Abercromby to resign, began to reach London, spread by Abercromby's supporters. To Portland, still blind to the power of the Irish Parliament and so greatly underestimating Camden's difficulties, the idea of an Irish cabinet undermining the Viceroy's position was worse than unconstitutional. It was "preposterous".[79]

But in Dublin, the Viceroy had at last made up his mind. Instead of further arguments to persuade Abercromby to stay, he decided to instruct him to countermand his order, and at the same time he saw no choice but to lay before His Majesty Abercromby's request to resign his command.[80] In the cabinet and in Parliament the balance of power had now shifted decisively towards Foster and the party who favoured strong measures. They were not slow to exploit their advantage.

For many months, as we have seen, the Government had been pressed to adopt tougher measures to tackle the chronic agrarian troubles in the Midlands and the South. These troubled areas now seemed to be slipping out of Government control into the hands of the Jacquerie of local peasantry.

About one o'clock in the afternoon of March 28th, a body of nearly a thousand country people led by officers dressed in blue and scarlet regimentals, marched into the town of Cahir in Tipperary and, having posted guards at the avenues, proceeded from house to house disarming the inhabitants. They surrounded the house of the local magnate, Lord Cahir, and stripped this too of all its arms. And then, after an address by their commander, warning his men against any deeds of violence, they marched peacefully away again.[81]

From other parts of Tipperary and the South, the reports were of open acts of rebellion. "Every night the enemy are out," wrote the formidable High Sheriff, Thomas Judkin Fitzgerald. "So far as I can learn they have a General and inferior officers—their army are kept in the mountains . . . They are extending themselves every night."[82] Their immediate objects were to collect money and arms. As their leaders became more desperate, they did not scruple to use assassination to remove anyone who stood in their way. From Queen's County, Lord Portarlington sent an S.O.S. for reinforcements. They were "surrounded by a numerous Banditti whose ravages have caused a General Alarm". Unless help came, "those gentlemen who have hitherto stood on their defence must abandon the country".[83] From Templemore, Sir John Carden reported: "This country is now so bad that it should be declared in a state of *absolute rebellion*. Every house for a considerable distance round this place was robbed of its arms last night, and the insolence of the people is astonishing. They look upon their plan as on the eve of being accomplished."[84] It was the same wretched story from all over Munster and many counties nearer Dublin: attacks on villages in broad daylight; gentlemen helpless after being robbed of their arms; more troops an absolute necessity or panic would ensue; martial law the only solution.[85]

As the situation deteriorated day by day, Camden's Irish advisers adopted an increasingly violent tone. The Chancellor pointed out that, because of Abercromby's order that troops needed authority of magistrates, not a soldier could stir when the rebels marched into Cahir. In Kildare an army patrol had surprised a gang of twenty or thirty rebels loaded with looted arms: the rebels did not attack the patrol, so the patrol did not dare molest them. Lord Clare added: "The people do not cultivate the ground so that, if this proceeds much further, the best which we can expect will be famine."[86]

Cooke remained cool, but sided with the Irish cabinet. The South was "troublesome". Had it not been for the recent "relaxation of vigour", it would have been subdued long ago. They must treat "Rebellion as Rebellion" and all would be well.[87]

Camden, weak and desponding at the best of times, and now unsupported by Pelham who had suddenly fallen gravely ill, reluctantly agreed once again. On March 30th the Privy Council signed a proclamation that declared the country in a state of actual "rebellion", threatened the disaffected with the most summary measures unless they surrendered their arms, and although the civil courts were still sitting, imposed something more than martial law over the whole kingdom.[88]

In one respect alone, Camden was able to mitigate the severity of the new measures. The army was still commanded by Abercromby. Camden appealed to him to go south and to quell the disturbances before he gave up the command. It was asking a great deal. He must not only revoke his own order, but actually carry out the new measures of which he so strongly disapproved. Abercromby told Camden that it was a sacrifice which he did not expect would have been demanded of him, but consented.[89] He countermanded his order, and next day he left for the South.

In Dublin feeling still ran high against Abercromby. To protect his own reputation in England he had allowed the news of his resignation to be made public. "I should suppose that Sir Ralph Abercromby must have lost his senses," said Lord Clare when he heard this, adding that if he didn't act with spirit in the South, as he had promised, "then they should disgrace him".[90] The same day, another of Lord Auckland's Irish friends reported: "The Spirit and Resentment in both houses of Parliament are at present very high—I dined to-day in Company with Eighteen of the first men in this Kingdom—from the language heard, it would not surprise me to see Sir Ralph [Abercromby] *impeached.*"[91]

Camden had resolved the worst political crisis since his well-meaning predecessor, Lord Fitzwilliam, had been thrown to the wolves three years before, after trying to sack Beresford and Cooke. But the settlement was a disastrous one. In the last few months Camden's Government had tried to introduce some English discipline into the licentious army of Ireland. At the same time a gesture, feeble perhaps but sincere enough, had been made towards conciliating the disaffected by introducing the rule of law.

Both experiments were now cut short. The law was to be put in the hands of the army, and the army in the hands of Lake, a run-of-the-mill general, of little intellect or military skill, who believed in the reckless exercise of military power. Often in the months ahead the Castle were to ponder that two-edged prophecy of Abercromby: the people goaded to madness by a reckless and ill co-ordinated policy of disarming, the army utterly contemptible in the face of a real enemy. Only the mistakes of their enemies could now save the Government from destruction.

4

The Triangles

Dublin, Cork and Midlands, March 31st–May 9th

But Ninety-Eight's dark season came,
And Irish hearts were sore,
The Pitch-cap, shears and triangle,
The patient folk outbore.
The Blacksmith thought of Erin
And found he'd work to do.
"I'll forge some steel for freedom,"
Said Pat O'Donoghue.

Pat O'Donoghue

THE PROCLAMATION of martial law on March 30th, following so soon after the arrests of the Leinster Directory, proved a crippling blow to the United movement—far more so than the most sanguine of the Castle hawks could have supposed.

In the last fortnight the Dublin arm of the movement had made a brave effort to close its ranks. "*The organisation of the Capital is perfect,*" announced a hand bill distributed five days after the arrests. "No vacancies existing . . ."[1] The same confident message, as we have seen, reached the ears of Government through its network of informers.[2] In fact the new Executive was of very different mettle from the old.

Two ardent young republican barristers, John and Henry Sheares were its leading lights.[3] Hovering in the background was Samuel Neilson, imprisoned after the suppression of his Belfast Newspaper, *The Northern Star*, and since released on parole.[4] But the Sheares were hardly the stuff to lead to a revolutionary army, while Neilson, who did have some of the necessary qualities of mind and character, was now an alcoholic. On Lord Edward and his friend, Surgeon Lawless, were centred the hopes of the cause. But both were marked men—a handicap for leaders of even an underground movement.

In the country, the arrests dealt a double blow to the local branches of the movement. Not only had they lost the ten most active leaders, who had gone as delegates to the fatal meeting in Dublin. But their confidence in the secret Executive, the invisible men in the capital whose commands had held such magic for country minds, was now shaken. People consoled themselves by the thought that the Government could have had no legal evidence against their prisoners—an impression that the new Dublin Executive did its best to confirm in a hand bill. "For us, the keen but momentary Anxiety, occasioned by the Situation of our invaluable friends, subsided, on hearing all the Circumstances of the case . . . that they are as safe as Innocence can make men now." The hand bill added that Irishmen should treat with "dignified contempt" the suggestion that the Leinster Directory had been betrayed to Government by one of their number.[5]

Kildare—the county of great wooded demesnes, liberal landlords[6] and the most highly organised United movement in Leinster—had come off relatively lightly from the arrests at Bond's. Of its three delegates who were due to attend the Dublin meeting that day, only one—George Cummins the apothecary—had been arrested. His place was quickly filled by a respectable farmer called Michael Reynolds.[7] The other Reynolds, Lord Edward's nominee, Thomas Reynolds, had not of course been arrested; though it would have been safer for him if he had been. He soon learnt that the Sheares brothers in the name of the Dublin Executive had officially reported to the Kildare Committee that he was the man who had betrayed the meeting at Bond's. Reynolds retreated to his new castle, understandably disturbed.[8] That spring a number of prominent men had disappeared without trace—a Catholic priest, a respected doctor and so on. "Moiley [a bogeyman] has eaten them," people would say light-heartedly.[9] And all *they* had done was to warn people against the movement. With no illusions about his own prospects, Reynolds barricaded himself in the ancient keep of Kilkea.

Meanwhile the second counter-measure—the Proclamation of martial law—had dealt a crushing blow to Kildare's capability for war.

Apart from Kildare, there was only one other county of Leinster which had not, it appears, been seriously disorganised by the arrests. This was the rich corn county of Wexford. The Wexford delegate, Robert Graham, had been late for the Dublin meeting and so escaped. Undisturbed by magistrates or informers, organisation continued smoothly. "Nothing could exceed the readiness and goodwill," one of the Wexford leaders, Miles Byrne, confessed later, "to comply with the instructions they received to procure arms, ammunition, etc. . . . Every man had fire-arms of some sort, or a pike. The latter weapon was easily had at this time, for almost every blacksmith was a United Irishman." But now the Proclamation of martial law threw Miles Byrne and his friends into confusion. "Everyone considered himself as walking on a mine ready to be blown up."[10]

In Carlow, to the west of Wexford, the Proclamation caused nothing less than panic. No county had suffered worse loss by the arrests, as their chief delegate, Peter Ivers, had kept virtually all the Society's business to himself. "As none of us had any occasion to meddle in such things," one of the Carlow committee later recalled, "we were quite a set of novices without him." The Proclamation caught them still struggling to fill up vacancies. Terrified of informers, they changed the normal meeting place— a public house in Carlow—in favour of a hide-out in the country. So many of the committee refused to be nominated as delegates that balloting had to be abandoned. Eventually a farmer called Mick Heydon agreed to go on the perilous mission to Dublin.[11]

The meeting of the new Provincial Directory in Dublin was a near fiasco. There was the greatest difficulty in organising it at all; few of the members turned up, and those that did were in fear and dread of being arrested. Every man in the room had a case of loaded pistols before him on the table.[12] The Dublin Executive was apparently told that if the order to begin was delayed much longer, the chance for a general rising would be lost for ever. The Executive would not budge. "Again and again, we warn you," they had announced after the arrests, "against doing the work of tyrants by *premature*, by *partial* or divided exertion. If Ireland shall be forced to throw away the scabbard, let it be *at her own time*, not at theirs."[13] This was still the policy of the Executive, who clung to the hope that a French landing was imminent.[14] The trouble was, as the county delegates must have pointed out, that when the piecemeal disarming began in a few days time the country people would have no alternative but a partial and unco-ordinated uprising—or surrender.[15]

The Government had made the most of the lull between the Proclamation of martial law at the end of March, and the date when the first of the series of ultimatums would expire and the generals would begin to let loose their troops on the people.[16] The Lent Assizes was proving successful —almost too successful in some places. In Queen's County, Camden reported to Portland, the juries were "almost too anxious to convict".[17] The country gentlemen, who had seemed utterly incapable of defending themselves before the Proclamation, did not now shrink from condemning to death thirteen men accused of thefts of arms and other outrages. "We were very fortunate in our juries," wrote Wellesley-Pole, one of the future Duke of Wellington's younger brothers, to his eldest brother, Lord Mornington. "There was not a single jury upon any of these trials that I would not most cheerfully have submitted myself to . . . I've hanged eight of the thirteen and respited the remainder."[18] Wellesley-Pole had come over from London especially for the Assizes and was delighted to find that his own tenants were "completely out of the scrape", surrounded as they were by the most disturbed parts of the county, and in consequence "not one farthing was levied off his barony", though the county as a whole had to find £800 as compensation for the arms robberies. Wellesley-Pole had no illusions, however, that his tenants were in league "as well as the rest of their country to assist the French upon their landing." He was much struck, as indeed was Camden himself, by the dying confession of a condemned United Irishman called Fitzpatrick, that the plan was to murder all Protestants when the French landed.[19]

Camden was, as usual, bewildered by the reports from the disturbed counties. He was glad to hear that systematic creation of a rebel army had not got very far in Queen's. Yet he was terrified of the contest becoming a religious one—as would certainly happen if the United organisation passed into the hands of the ignorant Catholic peasantry, who believed themselves, with some justification, to be the victims of centuries of oppression.[20] On this score the latest intelligence gave no comfort.

In his confidential report on the Assizes, Leonard McNally, the prisoners' official defence counsel, and secret Castle's spy, had warned Cooke that in Queen's County the Defenders' agrarian movement had not been absorbed into the United system. Fitzpatrick, the man who had revealed the massacre plot was the only one who had been instructed in the military organisation, and even he had not used the prescribed United Irish oath. The absence of a defence fund at the subsequent trial, McNally added somewhat bitterly, was another sure sign of undeveloped organisation. To that extent, the conspiracy in Queen's was less dangerous than those in Kildare or Carlow. McNally continued: "Yet I never knew a peasantry bear a more inveterate antipathy to their superiors owing, as I understand it, to great oppressions under which they suffer."[21] Exacerbating the tensions between tenant and landlord were distinctions of religion. Although now legally allowed to serve on juries, Catholics were still apparently excluded. Queen's was one of the few southern counties in which the Orange movement had yet shown itself publicly. Extremists of either side were now pitted against each other, and the juries made no secret of which side their sympathies lay. "Some gentlemen of fortune wore orange ribbands and some barristers sported *orange* wigs with emblems."[22]

Less spectacular than the assizes at Queen's, the others were satisfactory enough to the Government. At Kildare, according to the judges' reports, the juries did their duty, though some of the new Catholic jurymen were reluctant to convict.[23] In Wexford, it is true, there were few convictions, and it looked as though the juries were tainted or intimidated.[24] But in the rest of the Midlands and South, till recently so demoralised by outrages, the juries acted remarkably "properly" and in all a hundred men were convicted. In the North, by contrast, the judges all declared they could never remember so little criminal business. The slump suddenly seemed to have ended; the booming linen trade had filled the bleach greens, and although, characteristically, Camden had doubts about their sincerity the people appeared happy and loyal.[25]

So far so good. The leaders of the conspiracy had been arrested, the outrages punished, peace restored. It was now time to defuse the bomb by disarming the rank and file of the movement. The planning of this delicate operation had been left to Abercromby to work out in detail. The method he had chosen was, he believed, the most humane that could be used in the circumstances. Instead of taking up individual suspects, as General Lake had done in the North the previous year, stopping at nothing to extract information about concealed arms, Abercromby had decided that the troops would use collective punishment to force the surrender of arms. If all else failed, troops would be sent to live at "free quarters" in the disturbed districts. Punishment would be systematic, not indiscriminate. The aim was "to excite terror" as one of the generals put it, and so "obtain our end speedily."[26] But the troops were to use as little actual force as possible.

As a military measure this plan of Abercromby's depended for its success on several conditions. That notoriously ill-disciplined army, "formidable to everyone but the enemy", had first to be brought under control. At the same time the co-operation of the country gentlemen was essential, for the army would be almost helpless without the local knowledge and practical help of magistrates and yeomanry. On the latter score little progress had been achieved.

Before he left Ireland Abercromby had gone South to make the final arrangements with his generals. From his headquarters at Kildare he issued a solemn warning to the country that unless the plundered arms were returned within ten days he would be forced to send the army to live at free quarters—to billet themselves among them.[27] The assizes were on at this time but it was noted that Abercromby made no move to keep the gentry informed of what he intended. He passed on to Queen's County where they said he refused to meet a delegation of the Grand Jury to ask for reinforcements. More or less the same story was repeated in King's and Tipperary. At Cashel, it was said he would talk to no-one but General Sir James Duff; they agreed on the plan of free quarters which was to start as soon as the ultimatum there expired.[28] Perhaps Abercromby *was* tactless, or perhaps he was misreported by the gentry. Camden, at any rate, sided with the latter. If Abercromby believed that the country could never be kept quiet without the assistance of the country gentlemen, why for heavens sake did he continue to snub them? And why give the rebels such protracted notice of the severe measures? Camden wrote testily to Pitt to complain that Abercromby had not performed his last service either "with zeal or ability", and he would be sorry if he were re-employed in the King's service when he returned to England.[29]

But the truth was that in many parts of Ireland the Irish country gentlemen, whose reckless treatment of the lower orders was the cause of so much of the disaffection, had no wish to co-operate with Abercromby's humane plan. They now asked for the plan for free quarters to be postponed. "It will unavoidably involve the innocent with the guilty," wrote Sir Charles Coote from Queen's County.[30] "Surely this is a more violent and coercive system than burning the houses of those who are known to be delinquents?" Coote seems to have persuaded General Sir Charles Asgill, the Commanding Officer in Queen's and Kilkenny, to write to Government to the same effect.[31] The guilty were the lower orders with little property to lose; free quarters could only make fresh enemies to Government. Even if it were theoretically possible to discriminate between innocent and guilty, the officers would need the help of the country gentlemen, and almost all of them had now left the country since the assizes. But Camden, despite his anger with Abercromby, believed it was too late to change the plan, and the generals were instructed to disarm their districts accordingly.

Within a few days of each other the first ultimatums expired; Tipperary first, then the three adjoining counties of Leinster—Kildare, King's and Queen's. The choice of these four counties might have appeared an odd one, had the swoop been based on the secret intelligence reaching the Government. But Camden, as we have seen, was far from clear in his own mind where the greater danger lay—in the counties that were apparently lying low according to the instructions of their leaders, or those in which the bare-faced robberies for arms showed they were only partially corrupted. In the event, he found himself, as so often before, doing what the country, which meant the country gentlemen, expected of him. He instructed the army to disarm the most disturbed districts. The organised ones, if any *were* organised, would have to wait.[32]

The ten days' notice expired in Queen's County, one of the few areas where the gentry were prepared to co-operate, on April 22nd, the day before Abercromby left Ireland. A last minute appeal to the inhabitants was made by the commanding officer, Sir Charles Asgill. If they gave up their concealed arms, pikes and ammunition, they could still avoid ruining themselves and their families.[33] They were offered the chance of handing them over to their priests, without any questions being asked. "They were told we knew there were pikes and fire-arms dispersed throughought the country," wrote Wellesley-Pole. "And they must be delivered to us or we would lay the country waste. We reasoned, threatened, tried to bribe, beseeched, but all to no purpose."[34]

The free quarters began—with amazing results. "To my utter astonishment in two days we got in nearly all the fire-arms that had been taken," Wellesley-Pole later reported. "About 250 muskets, blunderbusses and pistols—and above 300 pike heads which had been buried in peasants' gardens." At the end of a week's free quarters, good order was "miraculously" restored. The peasantry confessed they had been deceived by their leaders. The gentry, too, gained such confidence that they "threw down their barricadoes, opened their windows, and went to live in their houses as they had been wont to do."

The disarming of Queen's County showed Abercromby's scheme for free quarters was practical provided it was executed with discipline. Wellesley-Pole, who was later to prove a successful Chief Secretary, described the scrupulous care taken to avoid indiscriminate plundering. Local yeomanry corps were sent to escort the troops into the most notorious areas and the local gentry asked to point out who should suffer. "We generally took poultry, pigs, calves, hay and corn from these people, but with moderation; and we usually left them with a threat that if arms and pikes were not brought from their side of the country next day we should visit them again the day after . . . very few persons were twice plundered." All the soldiers he saw were "perfectly humane and orderly"—except for one military detachment commanded by John Beresford's nephew, Lord Waterford, who "would have been very ready to have destroyed the whole country indiscriminately had we suffered it."[35]

These drastic measures seemed equally successful in parts of the South where General Sir John Moore was sent to organise the disarming. The same ten days notice had been issued in the coastal belt to the west of Cork, called the Carberries. Moore marched five companies of Light Infantry and a detachment of Dragoons into the Carberries, "to show them that I was serious". To his surprise this had no effect. He appealed to the priests—with no more result. At length he despatched the light companies to "forage the whole of the country" from Crookhaven to within seven miles of Skibbereen.[36]

Moore had instructed his men to "treat the people with as much harshness as possible, as far as words and manners went, and to supply themselves with whatever provisions were necessary to enable them to live well". As he was present everywhere himself, there was no fear of any very great abuses. "On the second day, the people who had denied they had any arms began to bring them in. After four days we extracted sixty-five muskets. Major Nugent in Coharagh was obliged to burn some houses before he could get a single arm." Moore moved his men from district to district, "always entreating that the arms might be delivered without forcing me to ruin them". Few parishes had the good sense to do so. "The terror was great. The moment a red coat appeared everybody fled." After three weeks of this unpleasant police work, Moore's haul totalled 800 pikes and 3,400 stand of arms—presumably guns stolen from the loyal inhabitants. The latter were "delighted with the operation except where it touched their own tenants, by whose ruin they saw they themselves must suffer". On the other hand, "they were pleased that the people were humbled and would be civil." In the whole area, he had only met two gentlemen "who acted with liberality or manliness"; the rest seemed to be "actuated by the meanest motives". Unless they changed their ways, or the Government stepped in to protect the people from them, Moore concluded, the pike would appear again soon enough.[37]

By the last week of April, Camden's weekly bulletin to Portland seemed almost optimistic. Arms were coming in; outrages had ceased; of the midlands there were particularly good accounts. In King's County Colonel Dunne had recovered seven hundred arms in the first few days. Sir Charles Asgill had been mopping up in Queen's and Kilkenny. There were flattering accounts of the work of General Dundas in Kildare.[38]

In South Kildare free quarters were indeed in full swing but carried out with the reverse of Moore's and Wellesley-Pole's restraint. From his headquarters at Athy, Colonel Campbell of the 9th Dragoons had sent out bundles of threatening notices, and in due course had let loose the army on disturbed districts. At Ballitore, a pretty village in the much disturbed lowlands on the edge of the mountains of Wicklow, a small community of Quakers had had to give billets to a detachment of the Tyrone militia, composed of professed Orange men, wearing orange ribbands. They plundered the inhabitants. After complaints to Colonel Campbell, some of the property, though not the food, was restored. Meanwhile the local yeomanry had been out foraging and returned to the village loaded with hay, oats and potatoes.[39] Their Commander, Colonel Keating, was a popular magistrate, suspect to some for his liberal sympathies.[40] According to Mrs. Leadbetter, one of the Quakers, he unsuccessfully appealed to his men to "take with a sparing hand—to remember that this was the scarce season, between the old and the new food coming on." He then went to the chapel "and, with tears, besought the misguided people to surrender the stolen arms". For one night the patrol was to be withdrawn to give the people the chance to bring them in secretly. If this failed, the neighbourhood would be burnt. Soon the arms began to come in.[41]

Paradoxically, it was on Thomas Reynolds—the man to whom the country owed the arrests at Bond's—that the full force of the free quarters campaign now fell. About five miles from Ballitore, Reynolds was preparing a farewell banquet for twenty of his friends and relations in the newly restored baronial hall of Kilkea. After two attempts on his life by the Kildare committee he had decided to leave Ireland as soon as it could be arranged with Government. About eleven o'clock on the morning of the banquet three officers, including Captain Erskine of the 9th Dragoons, and three troopers entered the great hall with pistols and drawn swords. Erskine announced that he had instructions to take possession of the castle and place Reynolds under arrest.[42]

As a district commander, Colonel Campbell had no inkling that Reynolds was a Government agent. Nor as yet had he any proof that Reynolds had been a United Irishman. But Reynolds was not only politically suspect, like any other gentleman with Fitzgerald connections. He was supposed to have repaired the battlements of Kilkea to make it an arms depot and headquarters for the Kildare rebels; the bell in the clock tower was believed to be a tocsin to call the county to arms; and deep inside the fortress Lord Edward himself was supposed to have found a secure retreat.[43]

Captain Erskine had already made himself a reputation in these arms searches. He now showed exemplary thoroughness. After spending several hours inspecting the wine cellars down in the ancient vaults, he requisitioned the banquet, seating himself at the head of the table. After dinner Erskine and his men began in earnest the search for Lord Edward and the secret arms depôt. They tore up the expensive new flooring on all three stories, they tore down the valuable old wainscoting, they tore off the wall-paper and canvas in the newly decorated rooms, they broke up the stairs, and pierced the cupboards, ceilings and floors in many places. Inside the ceremonial rooms they carved names and dates on the dining-room tables, broke up the lighter furniture, and smashed every piece of glass in the place. They made short work of three pianos: the strings were cut out, the sounding-boards split and the outside hacked about. A pedal harp was a particular object of their wrath, as the harp was the symbol of Ireland and the harp without the crown the United emblem. Paintings were cut from their frames or used for target practice, including some valuable portraits given to Reynolds' grandfather by his namesake, Sir Joshua.[44]

Meanwhile Erskine's men were living off the land. All the hay in the barn, all the corn in the granary, and all the livestock on the farm, were taken by the troops. Even the milking cows and draught oxen were slaughtered for food. Every morning and evening they brought out wine in buckets on to the lawn of the castle, and a pint was duly measured out to every soldier and camp follower. Pleasure parties came out from Athy to see the castle, consisting of officers' wives and families, and the soldiers' wives and girl-friends. They brought back as trophies anything that was portable—linen, blankets, quilts, books and china. For nine days the party lasted. When it was over, and Captain Erskine was finally convinced that there was neither an arms depôt nor Lord Edward in the castle, the place was an empty shell.[45]

The sack of Kilkea was not an isolated incident. It was part of Colonel Campbell's plan. A few miles away, another Kildare liberal, and distant connection of Lord Edward's, received a visit from the 9th Dragoons. Thomas Fitzgerald of Geraldine, Thomas Reynolds' maternal uncle, occupied a large mansion outside Athy, and was second-in-command of the Duke of Leinster's Athy yeoman cavalry. On April 28th a detachment of 120 cavalry and infantry took possession of the house, placed Fitzgerald under arrest and commandeered all the property and food on the estate. The bill that Fitzgerald sent to the Government, when his complete innocence was proved some three months later, included the household linen and plate, hogsheads of spirits, ten cases of white wine and a flock of sheep, all consumed by the military. The same treatment was given to other gentlemen's houses nearby.[46]

We do not know how much Abercromby's system of collective punishment by free quarters was abused by the commanders in the field. But it is clear from various reports, including the caustic comments of the Whigs and radicals in Dublin, that men like Colonel Campbell greatly outnumbered men like Moore and Wellesley-Pole. "I hope the example that is likely to be made of it." Campbell reported to Lake's office on the day that Captain Erskine sat down to dine at Kilkea, "will induce the people to bring in their arms."[47] Having dealt with the rich man in his castle, Campbell turned to the poor man at his gate. All the liquor shops in Athy were destroyed—to protect the troops from temptation. Many shopkeepers were almost ruined.[48]

Dr. Drennan, the fashionable *accoucheur* who had helped Wolfe Tone found the first United Irish Society in his heady youth, wrote to his sister in Belfast to tell her that Wogan Browne, the Kildare liberal, had thirty soldiers at free quarters in his house, "for as the cabbins afford little or nothing for the entertainment of man and horse, the castles of the country gentlemen must pay for it without much discrimination."[49] Lord Wycombe, unofficial Irish correspondent for the English Whigs, went to see the seat of war for himself. Driving down from Dublin in a chaise and four, he at first noted nothing odd except the long lists of names of inmates posted outside each according to the new regulations. At Monasterevin, on Kildare's western border, where Lord Edward Fitzgerald had an estate, he was stopped by a militia captain organising the search for arms—"a very plausible young gentleman, advantageous as to his person and correct in his manner."[50] The captain turned out to be one of the Wicklow militia whom *The Press* had accused, with justification, of attrocities the previous autumn and winter.[51] After proving his identity as an English peer (and Irish landlord), Lord Wycombe was welcomed into the Wicklow militia headquarters. The captain explained that the country was "in a dreadful state", that they were liable to be attacked at any moment, that his troops were harrassed by fatigue". Their orders, he went on, were "to treat the country as an enemy's country". They took forage or what else the people had, one man having property of one kind or another. However, persons of good character were protected. Many pikes had already been surrendered, and he expected new orders the next day to "burn and destroy certain parts". They must "follow up one vigorous step with another till arms were procured".[52]

Lord Wycombe duly reported to Lord Holland, the leader of the Foxite Whigs in the Lords: "His Majesty's forces have obtained the most decisive advantage over the domestic enemy, which in truth is reduced to its last shift. I wish I could send you some of the fat sheep, the good wine, and the greasy pigs that have rewarded the valour of the troops." The only trophy he did send was "the sample of a barren harvest, an Irish Pike," given to him by General Sir Charles Asgill. Privately, Lord Wycombe regarded the troops at free quarters as "mercenary ruffians" who had done more to disturb the country than any other "species of miscreant". Nothing could be worse than this "bedevilment—unless an absolute Vendée".[53] What Lord Wycombe saw, however, was the first phase of disarmament, executed more unsystematically and brutally than Abercromby had proposed, but still recognisably Abercromby's plan. A new phase was now beginning, when the new Commander-in-Chief would apply methods, much more to the liking of the Irish gentry.

Despite the apparent success of Abercromby's plan for collective punishment, Camden had, after only a week's trial, suddenly countermanded the free quarters. He gave two reasons to Abercromby's successor, General Lake: the practical difficulties of distinguishing between the loyal and the disaffected, and the damage that would be done to military discipline if free quarters were continued for any length of time.[54]

The real reason, of course, was the howl of rage from the Irish gentry when they discovered that their own property might be injured, directly or indirectly. A few of the more sophisticated, it is true, saw the point of Abercromby's plan: they were the ones, like Wellesley-Pole, who were prepared to collaborate with the army to prevent abuses. But to most of them Abercromby was the man whose mistaken lenity and ridiculous general order had egged on the rebels. He and his fellow Scotsman, General Stewart, might be good soldiers, but they had shown themselves "damned Blockheads", as John Lees reported to Auckland.[55] And now this perverse plan for free quarters was "playing the very devil with the country"[56], as another loyalist put it—and no doubt that was Abercromby's malicious intention. All they wanted was "prompt punishment" of the guilty. It was no time to observe the niceties of the law, or even the semblance of the law that still existed.

Lake's first instructions from the Government were to discontinue free quarters and adopt "other vigorous and effectual measures". What these were to consist of was never made quite clear. But Lake, a heavy-handed English general, had apparently succeeded in disarming Ulster the previous year, earning the praise of Parliament, Camden and his advisers, and even Portland in London. Not an articulate man, like Abercromby, he does not seem to have been preoccupied by abstract principles. His general aim was to give the army its head. "You may think me too violent, but I am convinced it would be mercy in the end," he wrote to Pelham when recommending house-burning in the North. Characteristically, his comment on the *Northern Star* affair—the wrecking of the United Irish newspaper offices by a detachment of Irish militia—was that he was sorry the officers had intervened before the business was finished.[57] Whether Lake now issued specific instructions on disarming we do not know. He was not the man, at any rate, to cramp the style of his local commanders. And they, like everyone else, were now impatient for results.

About May 1st, a remarkable apparatus appeared in the main street of Athy—a large triangular piece of wooden scaffolding. The triangles, as the thing was called, were designed for securing a man while he was flogged with a cat o' nine tails. People knew what it was, of course. Flogging was an accepted social instrument in eighteenth century Europe. Ten or twenty strokes of the cat were the normal way to treat a petty thief; for breaches of the military code the punishment could be much more severe.[58] But Colonel Campbell, the local commander, had decided to put the cat and the triangles to a completely new purpose.[59] He would use a little "correction" to discover the concealed arms. Not to put too fine a point on it, he would use the cat as an instrument of torture.

We do not know his exact circumstances at the time. Kildare was certainly the strongest organised county in Ireland, and Athy one of the centres of the movement. Free quarters, so successful in nearby Queen's and King's, had not achieved full success here. Large numbers of arms had been stolen and only a small part of them recovered.[60] Many of these were broken or useless. Outrages had been frequent, and still continued. The parish clerk at Narraghmore had been murdered; so had the Catholic priest nearby who had denounced the United movement from the pulpit;[61] and what touched the military still closer, their own expresses were frequently way-laid, robbed and even murdered on the roadside.[62]

The first men to be arrested were the blacksmiths. Government believed —and with justification as it turned out in many parts of the country— that most blacksmiths were forging pike heads. Along with carpenters, commissioned to make the handles for pikes, and the whiskey-house keepers, privy to the plans for their use, the blacksmiths could lead them to the heart of the conspiracy.[63]

In Kildare the blacksmiths were now told to reveal where the pikes were hidden—or else be flogged till they did. One day, Mrs. Leadbeater, the Quaker, noticed a posse of the notorious Welsh Fencible regiment, the Ancient Britons, ride into Ballitore, "dressed in blue, with much silver lace". They took the local blacksmiths, Tom Murray and Owen Finn back to Athy, the latter walking in tears beside the car carrying his smiths' tools. Meanwhile, Captain Erskine and Cornet Love, having made an example of Kilkea were all ready to make an example of Ballitore. Mrs. Leadbeater's diary records what followed:

"They set fire to some cabins near the village—took P. Murphy the father of a family, who kept a shop of spirits in the house where B. Wills had lived—apparently an inoffensive man—tied him to a car opposite to his own door, and these above-mentioned officers degraded themselves so far as to scourge him with their own hands. James Carney, tied to a tree, underwent a similar punishment—the torture was excessive—they did not recover soon. Guards were placed to prevent anyone coming into, or leaving, the village. The village, so peaceful, exhibited a scene of tumult and dismay—the air rang with the shrieks of the sufferers, and the lamentations of those who beheld them suffer. These violent measurers caused a great many pikes to be brought in— the street was lined with the numbers who came to deliver up these instruments of death."[64]

In Athy the blacksmiths were now tied to the triangle and, with the full authority of martial law, flogged to exort confessions. A local man called Thomas Rawson was one of the Athy interrogators. He acted on "speculation" to make men "whistle" as he termed it. "He would seat himself," we are told by one of the arrested men, "in a chair in the centre of a ring formed around the triangles, *the miserable victims kneeling under the triangle until they would be spotted over with the blood of the others.*" Two of his victims were father and son. Another received 500 lashes, and was then found to be innocent.[65]

The operations at Ballitore and Athy were duly reported to the Government, both officially and unofficially. Colonel Campbell described how "a little military discipline" had brought in pikes and useful information.[66] Another informant begged Edward Cooke, the Under Secretary dealing with security, not to pay attention to the "rebel petitioners" who were lodging complaints against Captain Erskine and Cornet Love's exertions in recovering concealed arms at Ballitore. Those two officers were "very useful men". The "new necessary roughness" had been successful in smoking out rebels and tracking down arms. "Cornet Love's temper and manner is peculiarly adapted to make a successful impression on the hardened feelings of these barbarous rebels."[67]

"Military discipline . . . exertions . . . successful impression." How far Camden and the Castle in general recognised the realities behind these reassuring phrases, it is difficult to say. Edward Cooke, certainly, believed in "severity beyond the law". But we do not know whether the Castle had yet come to accept torture as *official policy*. What is certain is that confronted with the first evidence of its use the Castle made no effort to condemn it. A new phase—Lake's—had now begun, in which the recklessness of the Irish army would be given full rein. Events were now moving rapidly towards a climax. "A scene of horrors" was to open, to quote Lecky's famous phrase, "hardly surpassed in the modern history of Europe."[68]

5

Pacifying Wicklow

Dublin and the South East, May 10th–19th

> Some of the Administration would fain lay at our door [the Catholics'] the distracted state of the country—a state which is partly the consequence of the ferment which reigns over Europe but chiefly, I fear, the result of the weakness and cruelty of their own measures.
>
> *Daniel O'Connell to his wife,*
> *Spring 1798*

BY THE beginning of May the Viceroy could flatter himself that Ireland was at long last on the mend. In the disturbed counties the campaign of collective punishment by free quarters had produced "striking" benefits. These included "the total cessation of those dreadful murders and outrages which had disgraced the country. No mail arrived, some weeks ago, without accounts of savage cruelties or excessive pillage." Camden was satisfied that now, whatever the other effects of the campaign, "at least the lives of the loyal and well disposed have been protected, their confidence in some measure restored, and the general appearance of the country much improved."[1]

If some impression had been made in the minds of the common people, by the Government's show of strength, their confidence in the Government had yet to be restored. Otherwise, as Sir John Moore had remarked, "the pike will appear again very soon." Conciliation had not, however, a high priority in the Castle. There would be time for this in due course. All the Government's energies were now concentrated on one daunting task—breaking the rebels' organisation before the Executive gave the signal for rebellion.[2]

The bumper crop of rebels arrested in Kildare certainly seemed to confirm the need for strong measures. Their previous intelligence reports about the underground movement in Kildare had if anything underestimated the extent of the conspiracy there. In the other disturbed counties of the Midlands—Queen's and King's—the United system seemed only skin-deep among the disaffected peasantry. But behind the noisy Jacquerie of Kildare, Government saw lurking what they most dreaded—an articulate middle class revolutionary movement. It was one of their leaders who, to Camden's intense satisfaction, now offered to play a decisive rôle in crushing the conspiracy.

This political windfall was none other than that would-be country gentleman, Thomas Reynolds of Kilkea. As we have seen, the Government did not know that he was the man to whom they owed the arrests at Bond's. Through the medium of Mr. Cope, they had learnt that his anonymous informant, despite his pleading, had refused to give further information and would not appear in court to prosecute. Nor again, did Colonel Campbell know, when he gave the go-ahead for free quarters at Kilkea, of Reynolds' equivocal position.[3] But Reynolds' ex-colleagues, now convinced of his treachery, unwittingly achieved what Mr. Cope's pleading, and Colonel Campbell's free quarters had failed to do. Five of the men in his regiment reported him to the Government. As their colonel he had told them to fill the vacancies after the arrests at Bond's, reported that he had put Lord Edward safely "into the box and out of harm's way", and instructed them to be ready to rise when the invasion came.[4]

Accordingly Colonel Campbell sent out a detachment of the 9th Dragoons to arrest Reynolds. He was soon lodged in Athy gaol. Appalled at what might happen to him there, Reynolds threw off the mask, and told Campbell of his dealings with Government.

The same night a *cri de coeur* reached his friend Mr. Cope: "I have this day been arrested and thrown into the common jail here. My hope, my dependence, my existence is on you. Get me instant relief." A few hours later he scribbled—"Give me to my wife and little baby again, and do with the rest of my substance as you please. Mr. Cope, I'm a father and a husband."[5] When the message reached Athy to convey Reynolds to Dublin, he was in no mood to refuse anything that the Government asked.

A good bargain was soon struck. In exchange for his personal immunity Reynolds made a sworn statement about the underground army of Kildare and Lord Edward's role as general. Further, in exchange for a lump sum of £5,000 and a life pension of £1,000 he agreed to appear in court as the principal witness in the treason trial of those arrested at Bond's. If Reynolds was relieved at his escape from summary justice, the Government were frankly delighted at their part of the bargain. For months they had been trying to get to grips with the huge underground army in Kildare supposed to be organised by Lord Edward. But their intelligence reports were confused and conflicting, and none of the leaders they had arrested would confess to their part in the business. Here at last was a complete confession from one of Lord Edward's staff officers, who would actually stand up in court and expose the whole conspiracy. Already the news of the confession, as Camden noted in his report to London, had leaked out to the Kildare committees—with excellent results for the Government. The organisation was broken, great numbers of pikes were being surrendered and for Reynolds, now branded as the traitor, there could be no turning back.[6]

But the Reynolds affair, however successful, gave Camden no respite in his losing battle with Foster and the ultra-loyalists. The "friends" of the Government, he reported abjectly to Portland, would be difficult to satisfy without more active measures in disarming the capital itself. Yet he himself did not believe they were either necessary, politic nor feasible.[7]

He did not exaggerate his difficulties. Commissioner Beresford, one of the stalwarts of the Privy Council, wrote that week to his crony Lord Auckland a letter bitterly denouncing the failure to take strong measures in Dublin: "Certain I am that without much outrage hundreds would peach . . . a very few of them being executed would change the face of things." The Government would be forced to authorise more "exertion". Everyone thought so in both Houses of Parliament. It was inconceivable that the Irish ascendancy should sit patiently waiting "to have their throats cut".[8]

Another enthusiastic member of the Foster party, John Lees of the Post Office, reported to London that "people are getting impatient, and I am myself one of the number that wish to see, and that soon, prompt punishment". If only Lord Camden "had a little of the devil in his disposition, and that he would, as occasions arise, forget that law, or the semblance of law, exists among us". Foster's party believed passionately that the right sort of "severity" was not being used against the rebels. The known leaders of the conspiracy were still left at large. If Camden "could steel his heart" to being firm, the "whole thing might be put down in a month".[9]

In response to mounting pressure the Castle made two concessions. First, a great purge was conducted in Trinity College. The Chancellor, Lord Clare, conducted a three-day ceremonial visitation. In fact the United cell in the college had been broken up some weeks before: its leader, Robert Emmet, Thomas Addis Emmet's younger brother, had gone underground. But the Dublin ascendancy were comforted to hear the Lord Chancellor thundering against French principles in the college, and indeed it was a rôle that the Chancellor performed with admirable gusto. General satisfaction was felt at the formal expulsion of 19 seditious undergraduates, even if Wolfe Tone's old friend, the physics tutor, Whitley Stokes, was only temporarily suspended.[10]

The second more serious step by the Government was to offer a £1000 reward for the arrest of Lord Edward Fitzgerald."[11]

It may seem odd that the Castle had observed such restraint in their search for this aristocratic revolutionary. He was related by marriage, it is true, to both the Viceroy and the Chief Secretary, and even the Chancellor had a soft spot for his aunt, Lady Louisa Connolly. But ties of blood or political allegiance would hardly explain the lack-lustre way the Castle had conducted the pursuit. No doubt the Castle had believed the brains of the movement were now behind bars. Now the news from Reynolds had at last alerted them to the danger of leaving Lord Edward at large. The price of £1000 on his head was more than a sop to their supporters; it was calculated—and well calculated as we shall see—to bring him to justice.

Edward Cooke was the man in charge of these matters. In early May he was still very much in the dark about the plans and even the identities of the main conspirators. "We are very bad," he wrote to London the week before Reynolds was brought to Dublin. "Although the head committee is disorganised, some power has started up which directs the Dublin committees of which I am not yet competent—Certainly the spirits of the lower orders are kept up—military orders are issued—Pikes are making in numbers—and the idea of a rising prevails."[12] Reynolds' new information added some details, particularly about Lord Edward, but Reynolds had been out of touch with the movement for the whole of April. Cooke strained every nerve to discover more from his network of informers, professional and amateur. The radical barrister, Leonard McNally, was little help, as the moderates in the United movement, on whom he relied for his sources, were in prison or in hiding.[13] But another Dublin barrister —a Catholic called Francis Magan—was now prepared to act secretly for Government, provided it was made worth his while.

For some months Cooke had been angling for Magan's services through the medium of Francis Higgins, the eccentric editor of the ultra-loyalist *Freeman's Journal*. Higgins already boasted of seven private informers on his pay-roll, planted by him at various levels of the United movement. The recruiting of Magan was by far his biggest *coup*.[14] Magan was drawn from much the same background as Reynolds; his father had run a Dublin woollen shop claiming royal patronage, and he himself was one of the first Catholics to be called to the bar since the Catholic Relief Act of five years before.[15] Ostensibly he belonged to the respectable Catholic party of Lord Fingall and others who were pressing for full emancipation. But like Thomas Reynolds, he had been invited to join the revolutionary movement and, with the disappearance of all but a handful of the original leaders, soon occupied a strategic place in its counsels.

Inured as he was to the wild tales of informers, Cooke could not fail to be startled by Magan's first report. Not only did he claim to know the hiding place of Lord Edward. He warned Government that the new directory were planning a rising at "Old May Day"—in about a fortnight. Even Higgins seemed to be uncertain how to take this latter information, which conflicted with another from an "unquestionable" source that the rising was still timed to coincide with a French invasion, expected forthwith.[16]

Hardly had Cooke received this report when his attention was diverted to a still more remarkable recruit for his intelligence service. On May 10th a young militia officer called Captain Armstrong had been browsing in a fashionable bookshop in Grafton Street when the bookseller, called Patrick Byrne, offered to introduce him to two of the leaders of the new United Directory, the Dublin barrister John Sheares and his brother Henry. From his taste in left-wing pamphlets Byrne had attributed to Armstrong a taste for revolutionary politics. In due course he led Armstrong to the back room, where he introduced him to Henry Sheares with the words: "All I can say to you, Mr. Sheares, is that Captain Armstrong is a true brother, and you may depend on him." In this he was sadly mistaken. Armstrong promptly reported the interview to his colonel, was advised to act the part of the revolutionary, and what purported to be the latest plans of the Directory were, in a matter of hours, on Cooke's desk in the Castle.[17]

Armstrong's information dramatically confirmed Magan's. The conspirators had definitely decided not to wait for French aid. Unable to restrain their troops any longer, they would launch the general rising in the next few days. In the Dublin area it would take the form of a simultaneous night attack on the camp at Loughlinstown, the barracks at Chapelizod and the capital itself.[18]

The real state of United movement was still unknown to the Government. In fact it was in a pitiable condition, its few remaining leaders under overwhelming pressure for a last desperate throw. The makeshift Executive that had emerged after the arrests at Bond's was still agonisingly divided. Their dilemma was no longer whether to fight on now or to wait for the French. It was whether to fight or surrender.[19]

The huge citizen army, built up over the years round country forge and the city tavern, was crumbling away before their eyes. Already, they knew, the arms had been squeezed out of parts of Kildare, Queen's and King's. If those tyrants applied the same, or still more savage methods, to disarm the other areas round Dublin—Wicklow and North Kildare—they must abandon all hope of revolution.

The free quarters campaign had caught them by surprise. True, the army's reckless violence had been self-defeating in many areas, and many who had fled from their homes were now burning for revenge. But, on balance, the Government's campaign had succeeded in disastrously weakening the movement. They had no reply except to urge heroic patience on their followers.[20] About the same time a second and no less disastrous blow had fallen. The coded reply from France to the request for news about the French invasionary force, at length reached Lord Edward: the French had refused to make an advance of £5000 on his estates, "saying they could make no payment short of the entire, and that they would not be able to effect that for four months." The advance of £5000 referred to the limited expedition of 5000 men that had been asked for. The "payment in full" referred to a French expedition of at least 15,000 men. But no help would reach them till August.[21]

Lord Edward, as we have seen, was suspicious of French designs—hence the demand for a limited force. He had also been a leader of the violent party who believed in pushing ahead with the rising without waiting for the French, despite the risk of civil war.[22] We do not know his reaction to the latest twist in the crisis. But when the move to go it alone had been canvassed in March, a rising still had a fair chance of success, and Lord Edward was free to direct it. He was now preoccupied with the struggle to avoid arrest—a rôle for which he showed little natural aptitude.

At his first hiding place—when he stayed under an alias with a widow lady by the banks of the Grand Canal—he had left his boots with his name in them outside his room to be cleaned. The family retainer, who polished them, told his mistress that he knew "who the gentleman upstairs was". Fortunately he proved loyal.[23]

Till mid-April Lord Edward had stayed in this retreat, and at night he used to walk out along the canal bank, "accompanied generally by a child", as Tom Moore his biographer says, "whom it was his amusement sometimes to frighten by jumping into the boats that were half sunk in the canal." The widow, hearing his laughter echoing along the canal, tried unavailingly to impress upon him the need for caution. Another prank shared with his young companion was a plot to dig up the flowers at the bottom of the garden—a bed of orange lilies.[24]

He was next brought to a hiding place in the centre of Dublin—at the house of a feather merchant, called Murphy, in Thomas Street. His friend Lawless brought him there "wrapped up in a countryman's great coat, and, in order more completely to disguise him, wearing a pig-tailed wig." (Lord Edward's own hair, of course, was cropped *à la revolutionnaire*.) Here, his high spirits had an unpleasant result. He insisted on visiting his wife in her lodgings nearby, and disguised himself this time as a woman. The shock was too much for Lady Edward, who was expecting her third child, and brought on a premature confinement.[25]

For safety Lawless moved him to the house of another feather merchant, called Cormick, in the same street. But even here he exposed himself freely to the risk of detection. Cormick's house was one of the chief meeting places of the new Directory. When Hughes, a Government spy, called on Neilson in late April, he was taken to Cormick's where he found Lawless and Lord Edward playing billiards upstairs.[26] Later they had a convivial evening together—we do not know where the other spy, Francis Magan, met Lord Edward, but it may well have been at Cormick's too.

Lawless seems to have been the most active man in the new Directory, after the Sheares. At the time Hughes visited him, he seems, in common with all the rest of the company, still to have doubted the feasibility of a rising without French aid.[27] But by early May he had thrown in his lot with the violent party, and plans were laid for a rising before the end of the month. Emissaries were sent out to parts of the country warning them to prepare. The other provinces were told to co-ordinate their risings so that the news of them reached Dublin at the same day as the rising broke out there. The main rising would, of course, be in the capital. Two strategic strong-points — the army camp at Loughlinstown and the artillery camp at Chapelizod—would be handed over by their respective garrisons.[28] Dublin would fall, perhaps, without a shot, and as a crowning enterprise, Camden and the hated Castle junto would be seized as hostages.[29]

This was the United strategy, as far as we know, at the beginning of that ill-fated May—a plan for a *coup* more than for revolution.

For success it depended, above all, on the attitude of the 4,000 militia and other Irish troops in the Dublin garrison. The militia were mainly Catholic and great efforts had been made to win them to the cause, by appealing to their patriotism and warning them of the sufferings of their families at the hands of the local Orangemen. On the day after the Proclamation of martial law the new Directory had put out a special bulletin entreating them "not to turn their arms" against their fellow men, "whose crimes are hatred to tyranny and oppression and a love of liberty".[30] This particular appeal is stamped with the characteristic idealism of John Sheares. It appealed to the Irish soldier not only as an Irish Catholic conscript, or even as an Irish nationalist, but as a member of the new international brotherhood based on the philosophy of Tom Paine and Rousseau, and given practical expression in France. It even appealed to the Scotch and English regiments to make common cause with their Irish brothers against the men who had betrayed the rights of man. "Our tyrants talk of treason, forgetting there can be none except against the rights and interest of the people. The people *could* flourish and would flourish without them, but what are they without the people?"[31]

How far such philosophy stirred the hearts of the English and Scotch regiments, it is hard to judge. Many of the Irish Catholic troops were certainly believed by the new Directory to be loyal to their cause. But in their efforts to win over the King's County regiment stationed at Lough-linstown Camp, Lawless and the Sheares brothers staked all on the loyalty of one fellow free-thinker—Captain John Warneford Armstrong.

They knew, no doubt, that he read *The Rights of Man* and *The Age of Reason*, perhaps secretly subscribed to *The Press*. There was loose talk, it seems, that he had been a republican at Trinity, and had once offered to "cut off the head of the King of England". More remarkable still, he had been quoted as saying that he doubted the existence of the after-life.[32] But to stake everything on the loyalty of a chance acquaintance: this was a desperate throw, which only the desperate state of their affairs could justify.

The new Directory, led by John Sheares and Lawless, while Neilson and Lord Edward lay in the shadows, had now almost lost touch with the organisation its predecessors had created. In Westmeath the terror of the Government's impending campaign of disarming had so stricken the county that only the southern barony could supply its returns to the Executive. Its colonel begged one of Lord Edward's bodyguard, Patrick Gallagher, to see that his own contingent of 3,400 would not be sacrificed "thro' the neglect or intimidation of other baronies".[33] No returns had been received from two other Midland counties—King's and Queen's— since two months before the disarming began there. It was to be feared that the large contingents there, who had reported their strength as over 15,000 in February had now been broken by "free quarters". The last official return from the best organised counties—11,900 from Kildare,

11,300 from Carlow, 10,100 from Meath and 14,000 from Wicklow—dated from April 19th, three days before the disarming began.[34] Since then southern Kildare had carried the full weight of a savage military campaign to disarm them, and its numbers must have been halved. The other three counties might have kept their organisation intact, but their morale must be shaken by the fate of their fellows and the failure of the Executive to offer any reply. If there was hope, it lay in the disciplined calm of the northern and extreme southern counties. Despite the North's savage beating the previous year, the Northern executive still met, though no returns had been made to the Dublin Executive. While in the rich corn lands of Wexford, a county with sturdy traditions of yeoman farming, the United system might be yet developing, aided not only by the sympathy of a few unusually radical gentry, but by the goadings of their political opponents—an unusually bitter Protestant party.[35]

Meanwhile the Castle was poised to continue with Lake's phase of its campaign to disarm the rebels. Camden was, as we have seen, heartened by the successes in the South and Midlands, and under correspondingly heavy pressure in Parliament for stronger measures to finish the job. Since the discovery that the United Executive planned to act within a few days, he needed no encouragement to disarm the counties reported to be still ripe for revolution.

The first district after South Kildare to feel the troops' new rigour, was the county of Wicklow, strategically sited astride the mountains south of Dublin. For some months Wicklow had featured in the alarming intelligence reports reaching the Castle, and Camden himself reported that it was "extensively and formidably organised". According to the Leinster returns in their possession, its forces mustered 12,000.[36]

The political centre of Wicklow's United organisation seemed to be at Arklow—on the county's southern borders with Wexford. The previous autumn, the local clergyman, Mr. Bayley, had reported to the Castle that the principles of the United Irishmen were making "rapid and alarming progress in Arklow, and its vicinity". Arms were preparing and pikes making—"and in the usual style of that faction the most savage threats openly thrown out against all loyalists". In his own case, the "confidence and regard which I have been accustomed to, and I may say have merited", had suddenly been withdrawn, and in its place substituted a "gloomy reserve". He felt sure, despite the impenetarble secrecy of the party's organisation, that the Catholics were all sworn United men, and the

Protestant loyalists in danger of massacre. Bayley appealed for the Government to make Arklow a garrison town, double the strength of the yeomanry, and embody the Protestant fishermen as a home guard.[37]

But nothing of this sort seems to have been done. The Government had no troops to spare for a county which was apparently quiet. There was a garrison at Wicklow and one at Bray. For the rest they relied on the local yeomanry, scattered in small detachments over the bogs and mountains.

At the beginning of the year the garrison commander, Major Joseph Hardy, made his own report on Arklow, confirming the view that a religious war was impending in South Wicklow. "The Romans," he wrote, "are strengthening themselves by every means possible." The Protestants, threatened with death and destruction, did not dare give information to the magistrates. What was especially ominous was that the wealthy Catholics who had "an unbounded influence over the lower class" were behind the movement, and the Catholic priests added their moral authority. Every Catholic in the yeomanry corps was corrupted. Hardy recommended depriving some of the weaker magistrates of their commissions, and strengthening the hand of an especially active one, by giving him jurisdiction both sides of the Wexford-Wicklow border.[38]

The magistrate in question, who was later to acquire a national notoriety for his part in these events, was a man called Hunter Gowan. He was of humble origins, having started his career as a professional hunter of outlaws—hence his sobriquet. The Catholic gentry of the neighbourhood regarded him as an upstart, and one of them—old Garrett Byrne of Ballymanus—horse-whipped him, for daring to ride to hounds. In due course Byrne's son Billy became one of the delegates of Wicklow's United party, and Gowan the leader of a group of irregulars called the "Black Mob" who roamed the country hunting for rebels including, of course, Billy Byrne.[39]

In late March the Castle had received a third warning about the organisation of South Wicklow. A mysterious horseman was arrested taking a back road across the mountains near Rathdrum. He turned out to be a cousin of the county delegate lately arrested at Bond's He said he had business with Mr. Philip O'Neill in Arklow but would not reveal its nature; he was then going on to see Mr. Bagenal Harvey in Wexford, and would return to Dublin next day.[40] As both Philip O'Neill and Bagenal Harvey were believed to have positions in the United high command, everything pointed to the fact that the Government had arrested one of the couriers taking instructions from Dublin to Wicklow and Wexford.

Despite all these warnings, however, no serious steps were taken in South Wicklow against the rebel organisation—except for a move by Hardy against Billy Byrne by stationing a sergeant's guard ("under his nose", as Hardy described it) at Aughrim.[41] When the Castle acted it was, as usual, only to conciliate local feelings. Twenty-eight magistrates denounced to the Government the Bray infantry—a yeomanry corps commanded by another Bray magistrate called Captain Edwards—as a hotbed of traitors.[42] The loyalty of other corps was similarly impugned. Under strong pressure, the Government agreed to the purging of more than a hundred men from five corps, most of whom were Catholics, and the whole county was proclaimed "likely to be in a state of disturbance".[43] But they sent little or no reinforcements to Major Hardy's handful of regulars in the garrison. If there was trouble it was left to the gentry to settle as best they could, and—from their point of view—there seemed some sense in this policy. The worst incident in the county had been on the day when a detachment of Welsh Fencibles, called the Ancient British, got drunk at the fair in Newtown Mount Kennedy and ran amok, flogging and torturing the supposed rebels in the village.[44]

So matters stood, while the more disturbed counties to the west were disarmed, until troops marched into Wicklow to break the United organisation.

We can well imagine what the leaders felt when they read the fatal ultimatum. For more than a year they had laboured to build up a disciplined organisation from the motley ranks of the disaffected—unemployed fishermen at Arklow, the national-minded shopkeepers of the towns and villages, and the land-hungry peasants of the mountain sheep-folds. When the Executive gave the call to arms, they believed they had created the biggest citizen army in all Leinster, bigger even than Lord Edward's army in Kildare. They had 13,000 fighting men divided into eleven regiments, and 110 companies. They had 700 lb. of gunpowder stored at Arklow, smuggled in on the cattle-boats that returned empty from Wales. They had more than a thousand guns, rifles and pistols, hardly less than ten times that number of pikes. And, the best stroke of all, they believed they had won over many of the militia to their side, including those at Wicklow, the county town, and at Arklow, the southern gateway to the county.[45]

The new phase of disarming appeared brutal but effective. On Sunday May 13th General Craig's ultimatum was posted up in the towns and villages, warning the people to surrender their hidden arms. If they complied, "they would not suffer in person or property the smallest injury". But if they did not, the troops would use "rigid severity".[46] At first, according to the garrison commander's report, the leaders tried to make the people resist, but it was "the last effort of an expiring party". After the first arrests, the discovery of arms gathered speed, as people knew that the game was up. Many people fled from their houses, taking anything that they could move. Others surrendered: sergeants leading their whole companies of twelve men, blacksmiths bringing the list of the men for whom they had forged pikes. In ten days Major Hardy was pleased to say that the "spirit of insurrection is fairly broken". He himself was amazed at the way the "evil had so spread and pervaded the whole county". A few "staunch Protestants" were loyal but there was "hardly a Papist not corrupted". Even some of the garrison were tainted. Hardy was particularly glad to report that "violence" and "rigour"—house-burning, half-hanging, and flogging—had completed a general surrender, with "as little injury happening to the loyal as possible". In his ten-day blitz he had captured 600–700 stand of arms and over 3,000 pikes; he had rounded up the secretaries and treasurers of the committees, so shattering the county's finely-spun organisation, and he had made important discoveries about the organisation of the neighbouring part of Wexford, whose leaders included, he claimed, a well-known Catholic baronet. Only one obstacle remained, he concluded, and that was the presence of two or three "temporising magistrates" who were allowing people to surrender without bringing in arms. He had written to the worst offender to warn him to desist. "If he don't, I trust you will prevent his acting."[47]

The "temporising magistrate" who had fallen foul of Major Hardy was the same man—Captain Edwards of the Bray yeomanry—whose troops had earlier been denounced to the Government by his fellow magistrates. His case illustrates the predicament of that rarity—a liberal-minded Irish gentleman—when the wild Irish army was in command. Edwards had opposed the request to the Government for reinforcements, as this would disaffect the loyal and make the wavering decided enemies. "I deprecate dragooning such people—it is a bad system except in open rebellion ... Where is the man whose blood will not boil with revenge who sees the petticoat of his wife or sister cut off her back by the sabre of the Dragoon—merely for the crime of being green, a colour certainly with them innocent of disaffection." The military outrages at Newtown Mount Kennedy were proof enough of the working of martial law. He had been eighteen years a magistrate among these people. He had now pledged himself to protect them from outrage as long as they observed the law.

And he threw down this challenge to Major Hardy: if the troops came to Bray and committed outrages "under the semblance of law" he would use every means to punish them.[48]

When the order to start disarming the people reached Edwards he found them as submissive as he had foreseen. He was shocked to learn that the ultimatum expired in two days, instead of the usual ten. He then learnt privately that a whole district was willing to surrender on two conditions. First, they must not be forced to give information, and second, they must all be promised free pardon. The offer came from a district that was not even in Edwards' part of the county, but after obtaining permission from the local landlord he set off that night into the mountains, attended only by his son, the corps' first lieutenant. At midnight Edwards found himself among an army of self-confessed United men who crowded in from all sides to throw down their arms and solemnly swear loyalty to the King. More than fifty were accordingly given protections, and many more would have surrendered, had not the approach of daylight forced Edwards to return home. The fugitives were not, however, to be granted a second chance.

For that evening Edwards learnt from Hardy that he and his yeomanry corps were relieved of duty till further notice. Meanwhile the Bray district offered to surrender to Edwards. But Hardy would not grant even a twenty-four hour truce to make this possible, and Government upheld him.[49]

Few things illustrate so clearly the utter recklessness of Lake's campaign of disarming as this strange episode in Wicklow.

In disarming the people there were three great dangers. First, the very minimum of force must be used or the violence itself could drive people to rebellion. Second, there must be a co-ordinated plan for disarming, or the terror excited in one area would trigger off a rising in the adjoining districts. Third, the people who had surrendered their arms must be given confidence in the Government by some form of conciliation.

Abercromby had recognised these dangers. In a few districts, like Wellesley-Pole's and Moore's, his plan for collective punishment by free quarters had been successfully carried out.

But then Abercromby had gone and his plan had been abused by local commanders. Next the system of torture, as begun by Colonel Campbell at Athy, and cheerfully accepted by Lake, had been applied without discrimination in parts of Kildare.

Now, by a culminating act of folly, Lake had allowed the pacification of Wicklow to follow the same reckless pattern. He gave, it seems, no

warning to commanders like Major Hardy about the risks of excessive
force. He made no co-ordinated plan with the other commanders in
adjoining districts, like Carlow, who had somehow still failed to start
their own campaign for disarming. The last thing that came into his head
was any plan for conciliation.

Yet that part of Wicklow, above all, was a district that would have been
easy to disarm. That huge secret army of Wicklow, that was to bestride
Leinster like the Wicklow mountains themselves, existed only in the
fancies of its leaders. The people were mainly country people, poor and
politically unsophisticated compared to their neighbours in Dublin, Kildare or even Wexford. They had cheerfully pledged themselves to a movement whose leaders promised not only to free them from their old material
grievances—high rents and tithes, and low prices—but to give them a new
place in society and a new country to belong to. Now that vision had
turned to nightmare. Abandoned by their leaders, hunted down like
animals by the yeomanry, they were desperate to surrender, provided only
they could trust the good faith of the Government.

But the Government—both the Castle and the thirty-odd families of
peers and squires and parsons who ruled the county of Wicklow—
believed in "prompt punishment" and "salutary shocks". Refused an
amnesty, many hundreds of men took their arms, and what little else they
could carry and fled into the mountains with no choice now but to attempt
an insurrection.

6

"The boys will all be there"

Dublin, May 18th–23rd

The boys will all be there, says the Shan Van Vocht;
The boys will all be there, says the Shan Van Vocht;
The boys will all be there, with their pikes in good repair
And Lord Edward will be there, says the Shan Van Vocht

And what will the yeomen do? says the Shan Van Vocht
And what will the yeomen do? says the Shan Van Vocht
Why, what should the yeomen do, but throw off the red and blue,
And to Liberty prove true: says the Shan Van Vocht

The Shan Van Vocht

EVENTS WERE now moving rapidly towards a crisis. By the third week of May, the Government forces, engaged in Lake's reckless campaign for disarming the rebels, were approaching the capital itself. At Celbridge, only twelve miles to the west, where Swift had once found a safe retreat, the flames of burning houses lit up the night sky. All day the Connollys who owned the town had pleaded with the people to give up hidden pikes. "Celbridge as yet holds out," wrote Lord Edward's aunt, Lady Louisa Connolly, to his step-father, Mr. Ogilvie in London, "though five houses are now burning. Whether obstinacy or that they have them not, I cannot say." But one by one the chain of Kildare towns along the road to Dublin were surrendering. "Some houses burnt at Kilcock yesterday produced the effect. Maynooth held out yesterday, though some houses were burnt and some people punished. This morning the people of Leixlip are bringing in their arms." The Scotch officers engaged in the disarming were "fortunately two most humane officers, that do not do more than is absolutely necessary from their orders".[1] Other parts of Kildare were less fortunate.

In the country round Dublin the ordinary people were trapped between rival terrors—the army and the rebels. In Dublin itself, an eerie gaiety prevailed, accentuated by the extraordinary cheerfulness of the weather. Under cloudless skies, the fashionable world paraded in the Green, drove in the Park and were borne in their litters to and from the routs and ridottos. The news of the day included abductions and elopements, and the arrival of an extraordinary new musical instrument called a grand piano.[2]

In this last hectic week of junketing before the storm broke, people later remembered the peculiarly self-confident atmosphere. For three years, they had lived with the idea of revolution, and had shuddered at the Government's stories of plots to massacre them in their beds, and the rebels' claims that the city was all but theirs. But nothing, in Dublin at any rate, had ever happened remotely like the forecasts of either party. A few broken pikes in an old timber-yard, a revolutionary committee of teen-agers with a seditious paper hidden in a teapot—so far this was the only evidence put forward by the Government to confirm their story of the impending massacre.[3] Equally, nothing had emerged to confirm United Irish claims that the city would be theirs almost without a shot. The streets were unusually peaceful at night, and absolutely no attempt had been made to check any of the counter-measures taken by the Government.

In this carefree mood, Dublin's high society prepared to enjoy what was to prove the last great Parliamentary spectacle ever to take place in the capital. On Friday May 18th was to be held the trial of Robert, Earl of Kingston, for the murder of his illegitimate half-brother, Colonel Fitzgerald, after the latter had seduced his sixteen-year-old daughter. Few people believed Lord Kingston's claim that he had shot the wretched man in self-defence, though certain facts of the case were piquantly obscure: what, for instance, *was* Colonel Fitzgerald doing that night in a public house on the edge of the Kingston estate in Cork, after travelling incognito from London. People said Lord Kingston had shot him in mistake for a United Irishman, but then people saw a United Irishman under every bed. All that was clear was that it would be the trial of a life-time.

Lord Kingston, a commoner on the night of the shooting, had suc-ceeded to the family title before he came up in court and had chosen to go for trial before his peers. It would be the first trial of this sort for forty years. The Dublin newspapers whetted appetites with a full column on the grand and awful legal ritual. All seventy-one peers of the realm would serve on the noble jury—far too many for the House of Lords itself. The House of Commons had been fitted out with due solemnity to accommodate them, that newly rebuilt Commons whose immense cupola and gallery for 700 spectators already gave it a magnificence far exceeding that of the Mother of Parliaments herself. Robed according to rank, each carrying a white wand, the seventy-one peers would move in procession to the scarlet-covered seats, led by the Lord Chancellor. The noble prisoner would then be summoned to the bar, dressed in deepest mourning, his armorial bearings carried by the King-at-Arms at his side. On the other side of him would stand a man dressed as executioner, bearing an immense black-painted axe. According to the forms laid down by precedent, two inches of the blade were to be of polished steel, and the axe itself must be held at precisely the same height above the ground as his Lordship's neck. And then at the climax of this awful ceremony, the names of the prosecutors would be called out three times, and all eyes would turn to the back of the chamber where these unknown men (or women) would emerge.[4]

In actual fact the trial proved an anti-climax for the peers in their scarlet seats and the commons in the galleries as no one at all emerged from the back of the hall to prosecute Lord Kingston, and each peer duly declared him "not guilty upon mine honour". Yet unknown to any of them the trial nearly provided a theatrical climax exceeding the wildest dreams of the columnists. The new National Directory of the United Irishmen, consisting of Lord Edward Fitzgerald, the two Sheares brothers, Surgeon Lawless and Samuel Neilson, met in Dublin the day before the trial and reconsidered their plan for the rising. Instead of the proposed triple attack on Castle, barracks and camp—the plan the Sheares' new friend Captain Armstrong had forewarned the Government of—the Directory considered a scheme of breath-taking simplicity. Attending Lord Kingston's trial next day would be the Viceroy, the Lord Chancellor, the Chief Secretary, the other members of the cabinet, in short the entire Government of Ireland. The United army had only to surround the Houses of Parliament, while the trial was in progress, and seize the members of the Government, and the country would be theirs.[5]

The scheme might seem hare-brained, but the Directory was, as we have seen, in a mood of some desperation. By every post came letters from the organised counties, who were bearing the brunt of the disarming. They reproached the Dublin men for their inaction; they reminded them of their claims that the Irish militia was true to the cause; and they warned them that, if Dublin did not rise now, they themselves would have no choice between premature insurrections or surrender.[6]

In these circumstances, the Directory put to the vote the scheme for the attack on Parliament. Its chief advocates, it appears, were the Sheares brothers. Lawyers by profession, enthusiasts by temperament, they never doubted the army's loyalty to the cause. If they were right, the Government might be seized almost without a shot fired; if they were wrong the attack would cost them at best thousands of lives, at worst end in fiasco. The voting was exactly even, until at length negatived by the vote of one man—Francis Magan, the Government spy, now a member of the National Directory.[7]

If, at this time the Government had any counter-plans against the conspiracy, it was largely the work of Francis Magan. Nothing illustrates the state of the United movement better than that in their last desperate reshuffle they should have pushed forward to the position of supreme responsibility this singular candidate—a young Catholic barrister with little talent and no record of loyalty to the cause. Magan was, however, assiduous in supplying the Government with the reports of all the meetings he attended.[8] He found it hard to keep up with events, so rapidly was the position changing day by day.

The inner strains of the alliance between the United movements in town and country were now cruelly obvious. In Dublin, Belfast and Cork, the middle class movement, founded seven years before by Protestant intellectuals, was fast evaporating. That notion of social revolution, of a new order based on universal suffrage and national independence was hard to reconcile with the current prospect of a peasant revolt, in which all men of property, whatever their political colour, would be swept away.

It was an appalling risk, they had known all along, to mobilise the primitive forces of the countryside in an ideological struggle. This was one of the main reasons, as Emmet was first to admit, for waiting so long for the French expedition.[9] They were desperately conscious of the lack of trained officers able to keep the popular army in control. But the French had failed them at the supreme moment. Even before the Government campaign of disarming had begun, the peasantry had shown scant regard for the orders of their officers: robberies had betrayed their plans, assassinations disgraced the ideals of the movement. Since then the finely spun net of organisation, those tenuous links of sacred oath and local loyalty, had been subjected to the rigours of counter-revolution. The country people had now lost their best leaders, many had been driven from their homes by the hangings and house-burnings, and those who remained were blinded by desire for revenge.

The day of Lord Kingston's trial, the Directory met once more to try to resolve the split in its ranks. Lawless and the Sheares brothers were, apparently, adamant that it was too great a risk to let the country people march on Dublin. They still pinned their hopes on the garrison coming over to them, particularly the militia at the camp under Captain Armstrong. Lord Edward, Neilson, and the others, insisted that the only chance for revolution was to rally the combined armies of the four surrounding counties—Dublin, Kildare, Meath and Wicklow—and march in over-whelming strength on the capital. "Tens of thousands," Lord Edward declared, "will instantly flock to the standard." This plan was adopted, but the cost was high. The Sheares brothers resigned and formed a splinter group. Lawless threw up the whole enterprise and fled from Ireland.[10]

The date of the rising was now more or less agreed. It was to be on the following Wednesday, May 23rd. Hurried arrangements were now made by Lord Edward to co-ordinate the march of the four rebel armies. Kildare he knew he could count on: five weeks before, he had sallied out with Neilson to reconnoitre the route of its march to Dublin. At Palmerstown, a few miles west of Dublin, their jaunt had attracted the attention of a Government patrol and they were placed under arrest. Fortunately Lord Edward persuaded them he was a doctor attending to an intoxicated patient, a rôle that came naturally to Neilson.[11]

Lord Edward now made arrangements for his friends in Kildare to ad-vance on Dublin in three columns—leaving a detachment to seal off the strategic bridge over the Boyne at Clonard. Similar instructions were sent to the armies of Dublin, Wicklow and Meath.[12] The latter had proved exceptionally well disciplined. No incidents had disturbed the quiet pre-parations for war, nothing had provoked the army to disarm them, and according to the returns their army now numbered 12,000. Part of their forces would join with Kildare's left column at Kilcock and march to-gether along the main road from the west. Another Meath column would converge on the capital from the north, joining the men from County Dublin near Dunboyne. He himself would leave Dublin the next evening —Saturday 19th—to prepare a rallying point for the armies at Finglas within sight of the capital. For the assault on the Castle Lord Edward wrote a final note of his requirements: 50 hammers, 50 groove irons, 150 hooks for scaling-ladders, and so on.[13]

That evening Lord Edward had an ominously close brush with the police. For his last night before leaving Dublin he had decided to leave Moore's in Thomas Street, and move down to Ushers Island, where Francis Magan, the new member of the Directory had a house on the quayside. (No doubt a visit to Lady Edward, staying at Moira House nearby, was also in his mind.) Accompanied by an armed body guard, he had just reached the edge of the Liberties—the handloom-weavers' ghetto which served as the United headquarters throughout this period—when the notorious police chief, Major Sirr, appeared in the road ahead. Sirr was knocked down in the scuffle, and received a stab from the stiletto off one of the bodyguard called Gallagher. However, it glanced harmlessly off his stock, and Sirr's party managed to grab another member of the bodyguard called McCabe. Meanwhile Lord Edward had ducked through the net, and dodged back to the safety of the Liberties, where he lodged once more with Murphy the feather merchant.[14]

Next morning Lord Edward had a heavy cold and a sore throat, and lay on his bed in the backroom. There was an anxious moment when a party of soldiers, led by Sirr, were seen outside the house of Moore's that Lord Edward so recently left. Lord Edward took refuge for a time in the attic—then the hunt seemed to be abandoned, and he returned to the backroom.[15] About lunchtime Neilson called. As usual, he took not the slightest precaution to conceal himself but contented himself with a message urging caution on Lord Edward. Later someone called with Lord Edward's revolutionary uniform—a bottle green braided suit with crimson cape, cuffs, silk lace, and a cap of liberty two feet long. The summer day passed peacefully.[16]

Neilson called again at four, and stayed to tea. He went off in a hurry, leaving the door ajar, and Lord Edward went back to bed. Outside the Liberties, Dublin was en fête: Lord Camden and his party left the Castle and took their seats in the Theatre Royal for a gala performance of *Robin Hood* (a comic opera written, oddly enough, by McNally, the Government spy).[17] In the backroom of the feather merchant's, Lord Edward lay on in bed, reading *Gil Blas*.[18]

And then, without any warning, the blow fell that seemed to remove the last lingering chance of success from the great conspiracy. It was just seven, and Murphy went upstairs to tell Lord Edward that he had a drink of whey ready for him.[19] As he stood there, two men peered round the door—the Police Chief, Major Swan, and a Dublin editor and yeomanry officer called Captain Ryan. Swan carried a pistol, Ryan a swordstick. "You know me, my lord," were Swan's first words, "and I know you. It will be vain to resist,"[20] Lord Edward sprang up "like a tiger," as Murphy described it,[21] and stabbed Swan three times—in the side and under the left arm and breast. Swan snapped his pistol, missed, shouted "Ryan, Ryan, I am basely murdered," then ran downstairs to fetch Major Sirr and his party of eight soldiers left below to keep off the mob.[22]

It was now Ryan's turn to face Lord Edward's stiletto—a special "revolutionary" model with a zig-zag design issued to the party leaders. His sword-stick bent like a reed on Lord Edward's ribs. The two rolled over and over, crashed through the door, and fell locked together down the flight of stairs. Here Major Sirr at last came to the rescue of Captain Ryan, still clinging to Lord Edward's legs, though his stomach was ripped open by fourteen stab wounds.[23] "Without hesitation," Sirr later reported to Ryan's son, "I fired at Lord Edward's dagger arm, and the instrument of death fell to the ground. Having secured my titled prisoner, my first concern was your father's safety."[24] But Ryan's wounds were mortal. Lord Edward, only slightly wounded, it seemed, in his right shoulder, was secured by the soldiers and taken off in an open sedan chair to the Castle. The bottle green uniform and the green and crimson cap of liberty followed, carried in triumph by the soldiers.[25]

All this time the bodyguard that were to escort Lord Edward to head the combined armies at Finglas were being entertained in a public house in nearby Queen Street. At last they heard the appalling news. Their leader, Rattigan the timber merchant, desperately tried to organise a rescue, but the Major had removed Lord Edward to the Castle.[26] Had the bodyguard acted more promptly they might well have succeeded, as there were hardly any patrols in the streets, owing to a review of the yeomanry corps that happened to be taking place that evening. As it was, the news of the arrest blocked the streets with a riot of the Dublin mob: traditional rivals—the butchers of Patrick's Street and the weavers from the Liberty—joined forces to attempt a rescue, and had actually collected pikes for it, when they heard a report that a squadron of cavalry were advancing on them from the Castle. They took to their heels.[27]

The news reached Lord Camden, watching *Robin Hood* in his box at the Theatre Royal. It was overheard by some of Lord Edward's relations who were in the next box with Lady Castlereagh, and the Lieutenant General of the Ordnance, Captain Pakenham. The latter insisted on their remaining in the theatre, as he was afraid it would create panic if they suddenly left. Even Camden did not dare leave his box.[28] But the news spread in ever widening circles—to Lady Louisa Connolly at Castletown, appalled to find that he was still in Dublin, to Colonel Napier who exclaimed that Lord Edward had been "*seduced* and *betrayed*", to Lady Sarah Napier who had hysterics, and to Lady Edward herself who still clung to the hope that the Government had no evidence against him.[29] Others took a less favourable view of Lord Edward's prospects. Lord Clare predicted that the reprobate "now bids fair to make his exit on the scaffold".[30]

To the Castle the news of the arrest came as no less of a shock than to anyone else. Camden and Castlereagh probably had no warning that it was imminent.[31] Cooke, who had passed on a tip-off to Sirr, seems to have thought that his information was too good to be true. At any rate, he had failed to make the elementary military precautions to ensure success. But to the Castle the arrest seemed the crowning victory for Cooke's network of informers, some blackmailed into helping them, others attracted by the smell of blood-money.

Ever since the beginning of May Francis Higgins, the editor of *Freeman's Journal*, had been playing Magan as delicately as a trout. Higgins, a strange mixture of coarseness and humanity, whose social pretensions had won him the nickname of the "Sham Squire", finally received a signal from Magan on the Friday afternoon, to say that he expected Lord Edward to visit Ushers Island, where he lived, that evening. Cooke passed the message to Sirr, and as we have seen, the first attempt at capture ended in fiasco. But Lord Edward had been driven back to his old haunts in Thomas Street. Now it only needed a little luck for Government and the complete recklessness of Samuel Neilson to bring Lord Edward's last hiding place to the notice of Major Sirr.[32]

It was high time for the Government to pull in the other members of the Directory—especially the Sheares brothers, whose daily movements had been reported to them by Captain Armstrong for nearly a fortnight. Armstrong was instructed by Castlereagh to have a last interview. He went as before to their elegant Dublin house in Baggot Street. John Sheares gave no hint of the split in the Executive, though he admitted that Lawless had absconded. He claimed the authority of the Executive to offer Armstrong the colonelcy of the King's County regiment and to each of his men a plot of King's County land, once the revolution was over. As far as Armstrong gathered, the plan for the rising in Dublin early next week still stood. There would be a pincer movement on the Castle, from the garden in the rear as well as the main gate. The barrack on the quay would be sealed off. Five or six men would be sent to attack the houses of each Privy Councillor[33] (Sheares had realised at length that a night attack on the Castle would find the seat of Government empty.)

As for the plan for the attack on Loughlinstown camp outside Dublin, where Armstrong was stationed, he still appeared confident that "throughout Ireland the Militia regiments would join". When Armstrong told Henry Sheares that the only militia sergeant whose name they had actually given him had refused to acknowledge that he was in the movement, Henry declared himself "much surprised at that", but attributed it to his caution, adding that he "and his brother escaped by that caution, for Government then thought them inactive". Such was the story that Armstrong reported back to Lord Castlereagh.[34] He did not add certain other details of the meeting that were to haunt "Sheares Armstrong" for the rest of his long life, try to deny them as he did: that he had stayed to dinner with the family, where Henry's wife had played the harp to entertain them, and he had fondled one of the infant children of the man he was soon to send to the scaffold.[35]

The arrest next morning of both the Sheares brothers, Henry in their own house in Baggot Street, John in Lawless' abandoned house in French Street, seemed to complete the decapitation of the conspiracy—except for Sam Nelson, now believed to be a harmless alcoholic. Moreover, in Henry Sheares' writing box the redoubtable Major Sirr found a most powerful weapon to turn against the rebels: a draft proclamation in John Sheares' handwriting, that would finally dispel anyone's misgivings about Government's firm measures against the conspiracy.[36] For once the Castle did not fumble. The text was leaked out to the Government's supporters, who were curiously encouraged to read the rebel Proclamation.[37]

"Irishmen—your country is free," the scrawl began. "That vile Government, which has so long and so cruelly Oppressed you is no more. Some of its Most Atrocious Monsters have already paid the forfeit of their lives and the rest are in our hands. The National Flag the Sacred Green is at this moment flying over the ruins of Despotism, and that Capital, which a few hours past witnessed the debauchery, the plots and crimes of your Tyrants, is now the citadel of triumphant virtue and patriotism. Arise, then, United Sons of Ireland . . . Arm yourselves by every means in your power, and rush like lions on your foes." The call to arms was followed by a statement of the new revolutionary ideals: "We will never sheathe the sword until every being in the country is restored to those equal rights, which the God of Nature has given to all Men . . . no Superiority shall be acknowledged among the Citizens of Erin but that of virtue and talent." After a few hints on regular and irregular warfare—"Where you cannot oppose them in full face, constantly harrass their rear and their flanks, cut off their provisions and magazines"—the proclamation sounded a solemn call for "Vengeance, Irishmen, on your oppressors . . . for the wretch who turns his sword against his Native Country let the national vengeance be visited him. Let him find no quarter."[38]

With the discovery of this stirring manifesto, the last piece of the jigsaw seemed to the Viceroy and the Castle authorities at length to fall into place.

Who could now doubt the plan for the Dublin rising, first revealed to them by Captain Armstrong ten days before, since confirmed in the "most extraordinary and convincing manner" by a member of the Ulster executive, and two other independent informers, including Magan, now actually a member of the National Executive?[39]

There was one essential counter-measure. For weeks, as we have seen, the more violent members of the cabinet had been pressing Camden to use force to disarm the capital. Knowing the uncertain temper of the yeomanry, and the certain hardships of imposing a curfew on a quarter of a million people crowded into a couple of square miles of city, Camden had first temporised, then agreed to a limited search.[40]

Beresford and the hawks were still not satisfied. Only a day before the Sheares' capture John Beresford wrote testily to London: "We have the ball at our feet, and if Government will allow us to disarm the city, which we can easily do now . . . the rebellion will be crushed; but there is backwardness and timidity in certain people, which makes them dreadfully unwilling to enter upon any exertion, even in times like these."[41] Beresford was a moderate—for a man of his party. "Lord Edward—damn him—" wrote John Lees, "continues in great pain—the ball's not extracted—his life was not considered in danger from his wounds—The rope I hope, however, will soon dispose of it."[42]

A motion was got up in the House for the summary execution of all state prisoners without trial, and it needed all Lord Castlereagh's tact to dissuade the House from adopting the proposal.[43]

In these circumstances, Lord Camden agreed at last to let loose the yeomanry in the capital itself. On Monday evening, a few hours after John Sheares' arrest, Castlereagh despatched a public message to the Lord Mayor, informing him of the proposed rising. It requested his co-operation in "preserving tranquility within the bounds of the metropolis," and at the same time for adopting "such measures of general precaution as shall appear best calculated to defeat the designs of the rebellious against the King's Government and our invaluable Constitution."[44]

Next morning, the city magistrates, assisted by 800 of the Dublin yeomanry, none of whom were trained soldiers but mostly lawyers and professional men, set out on their delicate task. The scenes that had become commonplace in the villages of the Midlands, since the disarming began there in April, were now repeated in the suspect areas of the capital.

In Thomas Street, where Lord Edward had found his last hiding place, houses were ransacked, and furniture thrown into the street.[45] Buildings in which pikes or fowling pieces were found were dealt with in the usual way. The timber warehouse belonging to Rattigan, the leader of the bodyguard, was searched, found to contain pikes, and duly reduced to ashes.[46] Suspects, too, were dealt with in the usual way. Some, who it was thought could help with the enquiries, were hung up on the triangles in the Castle yard.[47]

Even Beresford was delighted by the success of the operation. "It is surprising what quantities of arms of all kinds have been detected," he observed next day. "The quantities of the pikes are prodigious, but scarcely any are produced without acts of violence. Numbers have been flogged who have been caught with pikes, and all but one peached and discovered. I have seen none of the flogging, but it is terrible to hear the perseverance of these madmen. Some have received three hundred lashes before they would discover where the pikes were concealed. The extent of the conspiracy is amazing. Many people, on being terrified by the appearance of triangles and cat o'nails have discovered and peached their brother committee men. All the gaols are full."[48]

John Lees, however, complained that the discovery had not been conducted by any means "to the extent expected."[49]

Dublin, so recently the scene of the legal pantomime of Lord Kingston's trial, was battened down for the siege. Seized with sudden energy, Camden and his cabinet had stationed troops at strategic points and in commanding avenues. An extra regiment had been brought in from the Camp. Beyond that, however, little was done.[50] To remedy the grave defects in the city's defences somehow posed insuperable problems. A series of experts had pointed out to the Government that the Castle could not be defended against mob assault. Tear down part of Secretary Cooke's house and build a strong-point there, said Captain Pakenham.[51] Surround it with *Chevaux Defrises*—a sort of barbed wire entanglement—said General Vallancey, the seventy-six-year old bridge-builder, cartographer and antiquarian. Furnish the Castle with small hand-grenades, he later reported, as there was "not a more offensive species of ammunition against a mob in the city".[52] But, as usual, nothing had been done, except for an attempt to fortify the Pigeon House on the quays as a last citadel for the Viceroy to retire to, convenient for the return passage to England.[53]

No one had bothered to fortify the bridges on the two canals that girded the city like a moat. There were no check points at the city limits. There were no mines, nor mining tools, in the whole of Ireland with which to blow the Liffey bridges. Even the Royal Barracks was indefensible.[54] The problem of military defence, like so many others in Ireland, had not been recognised till it was too late to remedy it.

It was now the morning of Wednesday, May 23rd. Cooke wrote to Wickham, "There is great joy and enthusiasm among the loyal: the attendance of the yeomanry has been full and their conduct zealous . . .

the search conducted regularly." If anything, Cooke rather regretted that the insurrection would not now take place. Not that Cooke was a blood-thirsty man: but as he was to admit later, "How could that conspiracy be cleaned without a burst?" There was another silver lining that a realistic English civil servant like Cooke could not blind himself to: an insurrection would "prove many things necessary for the future settlement of the country". Not to put too fine a point on it, Cooke meant that the disaster could be exploited to help the British Government to impose the ultimate solution to the problem of Ireland—Union with Britain.

With these mixed feelings Cooke and his friends viewed their escape from insurrection. For Camden it was a moment of unqualified relief. The last patches of fog were lifting—the fog of conflicting evidence that had for so long hidden the great United Irish conspiracy. Step by step the Castle's agents had penetrated to the heart of the movement. The leaders had been hunted down or put to flight. The rank or file had been disarmed. Lake's rough and ready methods of pacification appeared to be redeemed.

Even that baffling question of the geographical distribution of the move-ment seemed to have resolved itself. There was no special pattern. Some of the strongholds of the movement were in the disturbed counties like Kildare. Other well organised areas had never been disturbed. Both types of district had felt the rigour of Lake's campaign. A few more days would see the last ultimatums expire—in parts of Carlow and Meath—and then the campaign would be complete.

Almost cheerful, for once, Camden reported to London that, owing to General Lake's able disposition of the troops, there could be now "no apprehension of insurrection or even tumult.'59 Then one by one reports began to reach them that threw the Castle into the wildest confusion.

The silk mercer, who had been planted by Sam Sproule as a spy in one of Dublin's local Committies, arrived breathlessly with the news that his troop had just been told to mobilise in half an hour at their mustering point at the Old Bridge. The message reached Cooke by four-thirty. "Seen two deputies set off," ran the almost illegible scrawl, "loaded with pistols—one for Kildare the other for Wicklow—to raise them immediate —it is believed they will *rise tonight.*"60

Earlier Sproule's informer had predicted that a gang of thirty desper-adoes would make an attack on Newgate to try to release Lord Edward Fitzgerald; a horse would be at the gate ready for his escape.61 Later that day Sproule sent a second message to say that he had just heard that the whole ring of counties round Dublin were to rise that night and march on Dublin.62 A third message informed Mr. Cooke: "No official order as to the hour—all expectation Neilson pushing it on by every earthly means— distressed about Arms but determined on the tryall."[63]

The news of Neilson's organising simultaneous risings *outside* Dublin, in a combined assault on the capital, came as a bombshell to the Government. On Sunday, it was true, they had received the report of Magan, who claimed to be a member of the actual Executive, on very much the same lines: he described the plan for the assault on Dublin—by "a circuitous chain from the Naul and Garretstown and round by the mountain to Dunleary foot." Magan added that instructions had already gone out to the captains and colonels of the surrounding counties. But Magan confessed he did not know whether the arrest of Lord Edward on Saturday would scotch the plan, nor did he know the date.[64] This information, like most informers' reports, was too full of detail, much of it conflicting. The Government had relied instead on Captain Armstrong's soldierly account of the Sheares plan for a rising *inside* the city on Monday or Tuesday, confirmed by the actual Proclamation in John Sheares' hand, and the report of a spy on the Ulster executive.[65] They had had every reason to believe that the trials, arrests and the subsequent disarming of the city had frustrated this. What they could not have guessed was that the Sheares' plan, and indeed the brothers themselves, had already been discarded *before* that fiery Proclamation was drafted.

As the evening wore on, messages poured into the Castle, conflicting in many respects, but confirming the main lines of Sproule's and Magan's reports. It began to emerge that the country yeomanry, not the militia in the camp, were the men the rebels relied on. Many had recently been purged on suspicion of United sympathies, but had retained their firelocks. Others were to form a fifth column in each scattered village corps.[66]

The Dublin Unitedmen's new rôle in the proceedings was still, however, obscure. According to one informer they were to burn the outgoing mail coaches, so as to spread the news of the rising to the four provinces.[67] According to Sproule they were not to rise till the night after the four counties had. Magan believed they were still intending to assassinate the "three C's"—Camden, Clare and Cooke. Whatever hopes remained of revolution within, all informers agreed that the main battle for Dublin would be conducted from outside, and tonight was the night.

It was now too late, of course, to warn most of the scattered garrisons in the towns round Dublin of the impending attack, though a message was sent to warn Lord Gosford at Naas.[68] It was task enough to try to rally the garrison for the defence of the capital. As the drum beat to arms, people heard that immense bodies of rebels were actually assembling at Santry to the north and at Rathfarnham to the south. The yeomanry were ordered to occupy Smithfield—the main open space to the north of the river.[69] Sir Jonah Barrington, who paraded with the attornies' corps that night has described the scene: "The regular garrison, and the yeomanry, prepared themselves with the utmost animation, but nobody knew his station, or could ascertain his duty—orders were issued, and immediately revoked —positions were assigned and countermanded—more confused, indecisive and unintelligible arrangements of a military nature never appeared."[70]

Despite the apparent danger to such a huge body of men, confined between narrow streets, they treated their situation with good humour. It was noticed that the bravest spirits were those who had dined best; others made a forced loan of bottled porter from a shop around the corner. As darkness fell, the hilarity increased among the great army defending the capital: "All the barristers, attorneys, merchants, bankers, revenue officers, shopkeepers, students of the University, doctors, apothecarys, and corporators, of an immense metropolis, in red coats, with a sprinkling of parsons, all doubled up together, awaiting in profound darkness (not with impatience) for invisible executioners to despatch them without mercy . . . a running buzz occasionally went round, that the videts were driven in . . . In the meantime, no further orders came from the general, and if there had no orders could have been obeyed."[71]

At midnight Dubliners heard the clatter of the artillery train returning from the camp to reinforce the capital. A pair of cannons were trundled out to guard the medieval gates of the Castle.[72] For some people this show of strength only seemed to confirm the wild rumours of the fifth column in their midst. Horish, the fashionable chimney sweep, was understood to have tried to burn down the Houses of Parliament.[73] All the servants were sworn into the conspiracy. An apothecary had admitted selling enough arsenic to poison the whole city.[74] The lamp-lighters, too, were in the plot. Indeed, the lights were now beginning to go out, "better to favour their deeds of darkness," as Bishop Percy remarked. Later the loyalists were relieved to see the lamp-lighters driven through the streets by the yeomanry, "with a bayonet in the breech to compel them to light the lamps".[75]

For those who lived on the outskirts of Dublin, there were more than rumours. For some nights they had seen signal fires on the Wicklow mountains to the south; someone who watched them through a telescope claimed that they varied in intensity to answer the purpose of a telegraph. In the suburbs people observed significant chalk marks on the doors of the most loyal yeomen destined, no doubt, to be the first victims of the massacre.[76]

Some people, of course, did not take their predicament too seriously. Lord Wycombe, the Irish correspondent of Fox and the British Whigs, was out at Sandymount where he had set himself up with a villa, and a "sporting heifer" of a mistress called Rosy. He was well prepared to face the revolution: "I have arranged a little plan of defence," he had written to Lord Holland a few days before, "and sleep with a loaded Blunderbuss by my bedside determined to defend the Golden Fleece, which is born by Rosy, and my own life to the utmost of my power. I fear I must, in case of attack, abandon the lower part of the house in which the coachman and footman repose, for you know we cannot count upon our servants . . . but I think Charles [his butler] and myself can take a position in the staircase from where we should very successfully annoy an enemy that meditated an invasion of the upper."[77]

Lord Wycombe was a radical who might have been spared. Some of Dublin's loyalists seriously wondered if they should live to see another dawn. Incredibly, the Government had still not imposed a curfew, and crowds of ordinary people were milling about the streets, as though an earthquake was imminent. This only added to the confusion of the military preparations. Military posts were surrounded by people seeking asylum. Beresford's notorious interrogation centre, converted from a riding school, was besieged about ten o'clock by "a number of well-dressed women" according to his friend, Sir Richard Musgrave, "to claim the protection" of the fearless croppy-hunter.[78] In the almost total darkness, people reported shadowy figures assembling in St. Michan's churchyard, where pikes in plenty were known to be buried.[79] Two carts had passed through Rathfarnham with "a dreadful rumbling sound" from the load of pikes inside, and the couriers had cried frequently "Liberty, and no King".[80] There were various accounts of sabotage: two smiths had been bribed to spike the cannon at the Castle. One of the Ordnance forges had been stolen and then inscribed "God damn the King". The watch-house guards had left their carbines loaded ready for the rebels to seize.[81] Only one thing was lacking: no one had actually seen a rebel.

The truth was, of course, that in Dublin there were precious few rebels to see. During the last few days the Dublin arm of the movement, whose strength had been failing before even the arrests at Bond's, had virtually disintegrated. It was not simply a collapse of the leadership. The split with the Sheares, the flight of Lawless, the recklessness of Neilson, Lord Edward's curious state of paralysis: these all reflected a complete demoralisation in the rank and file of the movement, that had by now reduced its paper army of 8,000 to a few scattered groups. The arrest of Lord Edward was the last straw. By the 23rd, the United Irish army of Dublin consisted of a few hundred men wandering round in search of their instructions.[82]

Even now there was still a Directory, but weak and utterly despondent. That night about eight o'clock they met in Abbey Street to try to coordinate Dublin's efforts with the main body of insurgents marching on the capital from the surrounding counties. So intimidated were they, we are told, by the fall of their predecessors in office, that there was no one they could trust to carry the message to the colonels of the few societies still intact. In the event Neilson volunteered on this dangerous mission, and about nine o'clock the old revolutionary, a sick man after his years in Newgate, stumbled off into the night.[83]

Neilson, a huge, shambling man, and latterly a slave to drink, somehow made his way through the milling crowds of yeomen and loyalists and safely reached his destination in the Barley Fields near Newgate. The colonels asked him to return to the directory for further instructions. At that point his old weakness reasserted itself, according to the story of a man who knew him well, and he felt unable to continue without refreshment. When he emerged from the public house, he had lost all sense of direction and had even forgotten the purpose of his mission. Drawn by an irresistible force, he staggered across to Newgate, where his old friend Lord Edward lay wounded, and began to shout incoherently to his old enemy, Gregg the gaoler.

It was still light and Neilson was not a figure to mistake. Gregg slipped out of the prison, called a party of yeomanry, and in a few moments Neilson, fighting heroically to the last, was carried bodily inside. Reports of his arrest spread rapidly to the officers he had left such a short time before. Telling their men to fend for themselves, the officers hastily dispersed.[84]

II

Rebellion

1

The Mail Coach Signal

Dublin and surrounding counties, May 24th–25th 1798

Tell me, tell me, Shawn O'Farrel,
Why it is you hurry so?
Hush *ma bouchal*, hush and listen,
And his cheeks were in a glow.
I bear orders from the captain,
Get you ready quick and soon,
For our pikes must be together
By the rising of the moon.

The Rising of the Moon

IT WAS Neilson, during one of his sober moments, who was said to have devised the ingenious idea that the signal for the rising should be the stopping of the mail coaches.

The main body of insurgents, instructed to converge on the capital from the adjoining country, now waited for this signal to begin. They did not yet know, of course, of the catastrophic events in Dublin during the last few hours: the collapse of the Directory, the arrest of Neilson at the gates of Newgate, and the virtual disintegration of the movement inside the capital. As it was, their own numbers had been drastically reduced in the last few days by defections—and of leaders in particular. Still, thanks to Lake, a sizeable army still remained for the march on Dublin.[1]

Not far from the city boundaries were the men detailed to stop the coaches. Beyond this, all along the outside of the county boundary, in a broad crescent extending five to fifteen miles from the capital, parties of armed men now began to take up their positions. Near the Naul, in an area which Lake's commander had still failed to disarm, 2,000 men surrounded the Westpalstown barracks. At Curragh and Greenoge, another area where the ultimatum had yet to expire, about a thousand marched up and down the village street, waving pikes and firelocks.[2] After dusk, road blocks were formed on the Navan road, and a party from a third district, yet to be disarmed, began to converge on Dunboyne in Meath.[3] On the Kildare side, where the violence of Campbell's soldiers had goaded the people to rebellion, parties took up their positions along the Galway road.[4] To the south, people had been gathering in the foothills of the Wicklow mountains; some, no doubt, the men Major Hardy had driven there. As darkness fell two groups, each perhaps five hundred strong, converged on the fashionable suburbs of Rathfarnham and Dalkey, while other parties began to assemble near Tallaght and Rathcoole, along the strategic road to the South.[6]

This whole force spread out in a crescent around the capital numbered perhaps ten thousand men.

The plan for the signal, on which so much appeared to depend, had a certain macabre beauty, one must recognise. It turned one of the Government's most powerful strategic weapons against them. The mail coach system, surprisingly well run by Lord Auckland's crony, John Lees, was much more than a postal service. It was a finely spun web of communications that held the country together. Apart from the odd military express, all Government messages went by mail coach: an S.O.S. from a beleaguered magistrate, a reassuring reply from the Castle, a peppery general order from military headquarters, a spy report from Wexford, an ultimatum from the Privy Council and so on.

Destroy the mail coaches, and you would not only spread panic in the garrison towns; you would paralyse the Government of Ireland.

In military terms, too, it was eminently practicable—more than could be said for most of the instructions from the United High Command in the last few weeks. Once the mail coaches were held up, no power on earth could stop that invisible message spreading to the regiments beside every hedge and ditch along the roads from Dublin.

Yet vital as it was, the mail coach signal was only a trigger in the United army's mechanism. If the revolution was to explode at the right time and place, some tactical planning was needed: battle orders for the march of different regiments, battle plans for the rising in each area, plans above all to train men to shoot straight and stand a charge without flinching, plans to make an army out of the great mob of peasants who made up the republican forces, and had never yet heard a shot fired in anger.

On all these crucial tactical questions Neilson and the Directory had been unable to offer the county committees much assistance.[6] On the strategic side they had adopted in turn a bewildering variety of ideas: the grand slam on Parliament; the triple attack on the Castle, camp and artillery; the four counties' assault on the city from outside. But the first two were plans for a *coup*, with no more tactical sense than a revolution in *opéra bouffe*. The latter was a last desperate throw. What was now cruelly obvious was that faith in the power of the French army to paralyse the Government forces in Ireland had blinded most of the Directory to the real nature of the war ahead.

Lord Edward, the only military man in the Directory, had believed, it is true, in going it alone without French aid, and had given some thought in consequence to the tactics to be adopted by the revolutionary forces. But he seems to have been far from clear in his mind what would be suitable, and how it could be reconciled with the strategy proposed by his colleagues. He had not, at any rate, made his ideas plain to some of his closest associates, let alone to the actual leaders of the great army he had helped to mobilise.[7]

According to one source,[8] he rightly recognised the danger of pitched battles. From his experience of irregular fighting in the American war, he had seen that Ireland would be ideal for guerrillas, as most of the country was conveniently divided into small fields, and protected by high banks. In this sort of terrain, he is said to have pointed out, every hedge was a fortification, every ditch an entrenchment.

Lord Edward was also said to advocate irregular tactics *inside* the capital, complementary to the risings and ambushes outside it. This, at any rate, was the gist of a curious little pamphlet captured at Leinster House and attributed to him. The main battle would be fought in Dublin, pikemen against riflemen. The usual advantage of regular troops—in fire power and discipline—would count for nothing in the narrow streets. The pikemen would charge at "a smart trot". The townspeople would give supporting fire from the housetops with "bricks, coping stones, etc.". Others would block the streets with "hogs heads, carts, cars etc.". Trapped between these barricades, unable to hear the word of command or the beat of a drum above the roar of popular fury, the regular troops would be nothing more than a "mob in uniform", and as soon disposed of.[9]

Yet other people who claimed to know his mind said that Lord Edward shared Neilson's ideas for the frontal assault on the city using conventional military methods of attack. The armies of Kildare and the other counties around Dublin were to assemble at a number of points of rendezvous in open country, and then march on the city with flying standards.[10]

Again, as regards the crucial question of how to teach the revolutionary forces a disciplined use of arms, Lord Edward believed, according to one account, that drilling should be adopted but arms training was unnecessary. Others said he had much more unusual ideas. He had noticed in

America that the Indians who were excellent shots with the gun, had originally learned with a bow and arrow, and had proposed accordingly to train the army of Ireland for national warfare by the same economical method.[11] As a possible variant, he would teach them to shoot with catapults. But in the event, as far as we know, the Directory did not adopt these methods of training—or indeed any others. People were expected to fend for themselves—pitchforks against fortified positions, faith and enthusiasm against musket ball and grape shot.

The Directory's weakness in this respect only reflected, of course, their fatal isolation in the last few months, from the movement they had created. Most of the local commanders now thrown back on their own resources were men of little education and military understanding. In the strategic county of Kildare, however, there were leaders of exceptional enterprise, as events were now to reveal.

No other county had suffered more from the army in recent weeks. Yet so recklessly had the job been done that the organisation was still partly intact. Its leadership was still in the hands of comparatively educated men. The chief of these was a respectable Catholic land-holder from Johnstown called Michael Reynolds. He had emerged from one of the young farmers' groups sponsored by Lord Edward—the rustics he was supposed to have joined in republican sing-songs around the bonfire.[12] After the arrest at Bond's of Cummins, the Kildare apothecary, Reynolds had been promoted to the Kildare executive. A man of short muscular build, celebrated for his physical strength and his skill at horsemanship, he had shown himself uncompromising in debate. In a powerful speech to the county executive in March he had put the case for executing his namesake and predecessor on the Directory—Thomas Reynolds of Kilkea.[13] The traitor would destroy the Society, if he was not himself destroyed. His advice had not been accepted till the opportunity was lost. But the new Reynolds was now the driving force behind the county's plans for battle.

At his side on the county executive was another Catholic of still greater respectability, though less forceful character, Dr. John Esmonde of Sallins, brother of a Catholic baronet from Wexford. We do not know how deeply Esmonde felt himself committed to the business. Some Protestant gentry of Kildare—ordinary liberals like Colonel Keating, the popular new member for the county—were taken, quite erroneously, for revolutionaries.[14] Probably Esmonde was a moderate in the Party like Emmet and the other doctors in the Dublin Executive—McNevin and Lawless. In addition to Esmonde there were three other recruits from the gentry: William Aylmer, son of the squire of Painstown near Kilcock, George Luby, his brother-in-law from Maynooth, and his neighbour Hugh Ware. All three of them were, like Reynolds and Esmonde, of the same religion as the men they were to lead.

Nothing indeed is more striking than the absence from the movement of Protestant nationalists in even the best controlled and best educated of counties like Kildare.

Yet Kildare did to some extent confirm one optimistic belief of the party. They had always said that in raising a home guard to defend the country—the 40,000 part-time soldiers of the local yeomanry corps—the Government had unwittingly trained and armed the hard core of the United army. Reynolds and most of the other Kildare leaders had received some formal military training in this way. Reynolds had recently had to leave the yeomanry corps, taking his arms and accoutrements with him. Esmonde, a trusted lieutenant in the Sallins loyal yeomanry, was in a still better position to serve the Cause.

The plan now adopted by these men shows how little even those sketchy ideas of Lord Edward had percolated to the country. It was a simple, desperate scheme for seizing the town of Naas and the neighbouring garrisons. As such it had all the strength and all the weakness of the old Defenders' tactics: a midnight raid in overwhelming strength, a half-armed mob rushing forward to seize arms and release prisoners. But the town of Naas was not a loyalist outpost defended by a few old gentlemen with blunderbusses. It was one of the most heavily defended garrisons in Ireland. To succeed against such odds in Naas, courage or luck could hardly suffice. The attackers needed an organised fifth column in the town, ready with barricades to cut off the cavalry and protect their men from the cannon. And little if any arrangement of this sort had been made.

On one score alone had Michael Reynolds and his followers any reason for confidence. They were still complete masters of surprise. They knew the enemy's military dispositions, they knew which of the yeomanry would desert them, they even had the password to the garrison at Prosperous. And best of all, they could see that little or no preparations had been made by the Government to counter any attack of theirs.[15]

The Government, relying on Lake who relied in turn on commanders like Colonel Campbell and Major Hardy, believed that they had broken the conspiracy in Kildare. They had tracked down all the known leaders, except for a few like Michael Reynolds, who had fled. They had made an example of places in the south of the county like Ballitore. And now at last the spirit of rebellion seemed crushed. It was "affecting", as the District Commander, General Sir Ralph Dundas, reported, to see the "poor deluded people" giving up their arms, and flocking to his headquarters at Kilcullen to receive protections, declaring that moment to be "the happiest in their lives".[16]

From all over the county came reports that the trickle of surrendered arms had suddenly swollen to a flood. With a little "persuasion" the people of Monasterevin, on Lord Edward's estate, had brought in 300 pikes; at Naas 150 pikes and 10 firelocks; at Old Kilcullen 30–40 pikeheads; at Athy "inconceivable quantities" of arms. All told, 5,000 pikes and 5,000 other pieces of arms were reckoned to have been surrendered "through the humanity" of the Government.[17] If captured documents were correct, this was virtually the whole rebel armoury in the county. With evident satisfaction General Dundas had reported to the Castle: "Be assured the Head of the Hydra is cut off—and the County of Kildare will, for a long while, enjoy profound peace and quiet."[18]

By May 23rd the end of mopping-up operations was in sight. Near Athy the yeomanry corps reported a blank day. Night after night they had been out hunting for pikes—in the saddle sometimes ten hours at a stretch. Now yeomanry captains like Captain Weldon could feel they had earned the respite. "Slept till two, read till dinner, dined at home . . . very fine day,"[19] he wrote in his diary. Everywhere people commented on the cheerfulness of the weather, which had transformed a cold, late spring into gloriously precocious summer.

And then quite suddenly the extraordinary news, that had reached the Castle a few hours before, burst on Kildare. An express galloped into Dundas's headquarters at Kilcullen: a rising was expected at any moment in Dublin and the adjacent district. Commanding officers were instructed to call in their scattered parties and concentrate them in the towns. Lord Gosford at Naas and General Wilford at Kildare were alerted. But it was now nearly midnight and obviously no warning could be given before morning to the dozens of other detachments of troops scattered in small parties across the county, nor to the loyal civilians they were trying to protect.[20]

One such party was at Prosperous, a small cotton town built twenty years before in the false dawn of Ireland's industrial revolution alongside the Grand Canal to the north of Naas. Its looms were now idle—casualties of the same war-time depression that had thrown out of work the hand-loom weavers of Dublin and the miners of Kilkenny. Billeted in the old cotton factory were a dozen Welsh Dragoons of the Ancient British Fencibles—and as many again were billeted around the town. The main garrison consisted of thirty-five of the City of Cork militia, a largely

Catholic regiment commanded by a zealous Protestant called Captain Swayne. These were stationed in the main barrack in the centre of the village.

Swayne's party was the only one in the county still pursuing active measures against the rebels.[21] On Sunday, people said, he had burst into the Catholic chapel while the priest was saying Mass, called on the people to give up their arms, and told the priest, "If you don't have it done, I'll pour boiling lead down your throat."[22] By Wednesday, at any rate, he had burned fifteen houses, and put twelve men in the guard house. One of these he tortured by hanging him from a beam with his foot resting on a spike, to make him inform against his friends. That night he posted sentinels as usual, and then retired to his room on the upper floor of the barrack.[23]

Three miles to the east of Prosperous along the canal was a small village called Clane, where fifty men of the Armagh militia under two subaltern officers had·been stationed. They had the assistance of the Clane yeomanry —about twenty men, Catholic for the most part, tenants of the local landlord, a liberal Protestant called Richard Griffith, whose estate of Millicent lay a few miles on the Naas side of the village. No hint of danger of any sort had reached him that night. The yeomen were not even on permanent duty. Only about twenty of them, with an officer and sergeant, remained with the militia in the town. The rest had dispersed to their houses as usual. Now they were waiting for orders—including those who had sworn to fight that night for the United army.[24]

It was now a few hours from dawn on May 24th, and in the area around Dublin the great insurrection to liberate Ireland seemed to be degenerating into a few scattered risings by aimless and leaderless men. At the Naul in County Dublin where the crescent-shaped attack was to have had its northernmost camp, the insurgents had proved nothing more than a marauding band, reminiscent of the Defenders. The western camp was formed, it is true, at the appointed place near Dunboyne, and a small success achieved with the attack on the police post there, and the shooting of two Highlanders and the capture of their baggage.[25] But these affrays were not particularly well conducted, as the police post at Dunboyne was only defended by four old men, who were butchered, and the Highlanders were caught by accident on the road.

The attempt to form the southern rendezvous near Clondalkin had ended in fiasco. About five hundred farmers and tradesmen had collected in Rathfarnham and the district under the command of a respectable

Catholic yeoman called Ledwich, ready for the great march on Dublin. When they approached Clondalkin they found that no one had come to meet them; instead they were told that the garrison was waiting for them. "Go home," shouted one of the yeomen they knew, "You are too late".[26]

After a hurried council of war, it was agreed to give up the enterprise till a more suitable opportunity presented itself. Most of the party took to their heels, dumping their pikes in a quarry by the side of the road, or tossing them over the hedges into the fields. Soon only nine were left and by ill fortune they happened to meet a posse of the Fifth Dragoons near a pub called The Fox and Geese. Lord Roden, commander of the Foxhunters, was a freelance member of this group. A volley from the rebels sent a ball through his steel cavalry helmet. The Dragoons fired back with their carbines and saw several of the rebels rolling on the ground. They finished them off with their sabres, and sent a wagon-load of pikes and three mangled bodies to be displayed as trophies in the Castle yard.[27]

To cap it all, the mail coach signal had completely miscarried. The men detailed to stop the mail coaches had somehow failed. In the confusion, four of the five mail coaches had passed unscathed, including the Cork and Limerick mails that passed by the scene of the battle of the Fox and Geese at Clondalkin, and the Enniskillen mail which had run the gauntlet of the Dunboyne rising. Only one coach was stopped in the appointed place. About a thousand men had gathered in the fields by Santry, three miles to the north of Dublin, and a party of them went forward and waved the coach to a halt by the wall of Santry demesne. They were loyalists, they told the mail guard, and must warn them of the rebel army lying in wait for them ahead. The guard and passengers were being escorted to safety, when they noticed some of their rescuers cheerfully setting alight to the coach, their baggage, and the royal mail.[28] But this remarkable bonfire did not achieve the results on which the northern army had set their hopes. North of Santry was an area of counties Dublin and Meath supposed to be particularly loyal to the cause. They had appointed their officers, and drilled their men, and collected arms and ammunition. The nearest Government guard post was at Balbriggan nearly twenty mile to the north. The nearest garrison town at Drogheda, ten miles beyond. Otherwise the country was virtually undefended. The unmistakable message blazed out from the great bonfire by the wall of Santry demesne—and fizzled out. On the strategic road to Belfast no one stirred.

These disasters were of course unknown to the Kildare United army as they prepared to launch their attack on Naas, Clane and Prosperous. The first they knew that something had gone wrong was when the Munster mail was reported to be approaching Naas.[29] We do not know how far Michael Reynolds himself was responsible for what followed. A party of men, at any rate, attacked the coach, set fire to the contents, and hacked the passengers to death. It was a momentous decision did they but know it. Kildare was at last committed—and more than Kildare. As the Munster coach blazed up, the sparks were flying that would set alight the whole south-east of Ireland in the greatest national conflagration since the civil war a hundred years before. It was to take many months, and to cost 30,000 lives before those flames were to be extinguished.

About three in the morning Richard Griffith, the commander of the Sallins yeoman cavalry, was wakened by a violent knocking on the door of his house by the canal. On running to the window, he learned that his guard at Clane had been attacked by a body of more than three hundred men and several of the Armagh militia had been piked to death in their billets. Less than a quarter of an hour later he galloped into Clane to find that the yeomanry had managed to beat off the attack by firing a few rounds from their carbines, while the militia turned out. Griffith took command and together with the militia and yeomanry drove the attackers across the commons beyond the village. Some took refuge in some huts, which were duly burned. Many were killed and six prisoners were taken— four of them Griffith's own tenants. One of them was shot after being condemned at the drumhead, the others hanged with less ceremony.[30]

On their return to Clane after dealing with "the rascals", the party heard the news of a massacre. Three miles away at Prosperous, Captain Swayne and his little garrison had been surprised by a great mob of rebels, believed to be commanded by Griffith's own first lieutenant, Dr. Esmonde. Fifty of the garrison had been butchered. Griffith took a roll call of his corps and found that three of the twenty supposed to be on duty that night had in fact deserted to the enemy, taking with them their own and other yeomen's arms. He had hardly time to regroup his yeomen and the Armagh militia when a second wave of attackers swept down on them along the road from Prosperous.

A volley from the carbines brought down six or seven of the leading men—a company of rebels riding the horses and wearing the accoutrements of the vanquished Ancient Britons. Behind, the infantry continued to advance. "The party made a very formidable appearance," Griffith later told a friend, "not so much from its numbers, though very considerable, but from the brightness of the Arms, the Scarlet Coats, Helmets, etc". Unable to secure their flank, Griffith's yeomanry and the militia made a tactical retreat to a field beside the commons. The rebels opened a smart fire towards their position, but directed it, fortunately for their assailants, at an angle of forty-five degrees upwards. "Our fire had better effect," Griffith later reported, "we killed or wounded a considerable number of the enemy—they very soon fled in great dismay. I then charged them with my sixteen yeomen and cut down several rascals whose heads were ornamented with Ancient Briton's Helmets Cork Militia Hats etc. —the roads and fields over which we rode were instantly covered with pikes, pitchforks and musquets".[31]

Despite these heartening moves, Griffith decided that the rebels at Prosperous were too strong for him. Moreover orders had arrived for his troop to retreat to the safety of the garrison at Naas. While the men were preparing to march, and the wounded were being loaded onto cars, a yeoman called Philip Mite, who had not been on duty that evening, confessed to Griffith that he had actually accompanied Esmonde when he led the rebels for the attack on Prosperous, but had made his escape before the action began. Hardly had Griffith heard this confession when Esmonde himself appeared in his usual place at the right of the troop, "His Hair dressed, his Boots and Breeches quite clean and himself fully accoutred." Griffith, speechless with astonishment and indignation, rode beside him into Naas. The troop was drawn up opposite the gaol, and five minutes later their first lieutenant was lodged "in the body of it".[32]

There was little exaggeration in the grim tale of the attack on Prosperous. We do not know how far Esmonde was actually responsible, but he and Mite appear to have planned the attack. There were five hundred men in the party, mostly farmers, with a sprinkling of cotton workers from the defunct cotton factory including, strange to say, the son of the English proprietor. All day they had been gathering in the woods by the eighteenth lock of the canal. At dusk they began to march towards the barracks. A desperate courage carried them on past the sentinels into the guard-house. The twelve men inside were piked and shot. Four of the party managed to climb the stairs to Captain Swayne's bedroom on the upper floor of the barracks. He was shot with a blunderbuss. Then they set fire to the barracks. Meanwhile others had rushed the cotton factory where the Ancient Britons were stationed, and others again had hunted down the troops billeted in private houses around the town. They set fire to the powder magazine in the barracks, which blew up with a tremendous explosion. The route became a massacre.[33] Out of the fifty-seven soldiers, who had formed the garrison, mainly Catholics from the south, only nineteen were spared or made good their escape. All the rest were piked or burned or shot in their beds.[34] In a ghastly sort of carnival, Captain Swayne's body was ceremoniously burned in a barrel of tar.[35]

Meanwhile, perfectly synchronised with the assaults on Clane and Prosperous, Michael Reynolds had launched a regular military attack on the large, and well armed garrison at Naas. About half past two a dragoon from an outpost galloped into the town and reported to the commander of the company of Ancient Britons there that a "very considerable armed body" was approaching rapidly. The garrison mustered about a hundred and fifty men of Lord Gosford's Armagh militia, fifty-nine cavalry of the Fourth Dragoons and Ancient Britons, and sixteen yeomanry of the local landlord, Captain Neville. Instantly the drum beat to arms and the men together with two all-important pieces of artillery were drawn up in defensive positions, according to the plan formed for just such an emergency.[36]

The main column of the insurgents, nearly a thousand pikemen with a few musketeers, some wearing green cockades, others like Michael Reynolds in their scarlet regimentals, advanced silently towards the gaol, at the centre of the town. Meanwhile a second column was pushing on towards the barracks and the depôt for arms. Others again crept in unnoticed by the side streets, and narrow lanes, to converge on the barracks from the opposite side.

Reynolds' party had nearly reached the gaol when the main street was swept by grape-shot from one of the field pieces. One of the officers of the Ancient Britons received a mortal wound from a pike. At this the troops charged recklessly down the street, losing half a dozen men, and worse still, blocking the cannon's field of fire. Reynolds's men made a second desperate charge, and a third. Eventually they were flung back.

For nearly an hour the battle raged in the narrow streets around the barracks. Here, too, the insurgents fought with a crazy courage against the overwhelming superiority of the militia's cannon. But at last they broke and fled in every direction. And now Lord Gosford was able to deploy the weapon that inevitably turned defeat into massacre. "The cavalry took advantage of their confusion," he reported dryly a few hours later, "charged in amongst them, and pursued them all over the country in almost every direction and killed a great number of them."[37] As they fled, the insurgents threw away their arms. Next day, eight hundred pikes and more than twenty firelocks were picked up, many of them dumped in pits near the town. Three men wearing green cockades were also found there. They were brought in and hanged in the public street. Then they were sent to join the three hundred odd rebels whose mangled bodies littered the streets and fields for several miles around the town.[38]

Lord Gosford's triumph was marred by two misfortunes. He had lost twenty-two of his troops. And though his men captured Michael Reynolds' horse, its rider made good his escape to the safety of the Wicklow mountains.

Lieutenant-General Sir Ralph Dundas heard the news of the risings as he breakfasted at his headquarters at Castlemartin near Kilcullen. As the Commander of the Midland district, it was his job to crush the insurrection before it spread. But how to organise the counter-attack when he was himself beleaguered? Three hundred pikemen had occupied a strong position in the churchyard at Old Kilcullen, only a couple of miles from the gates of his own house. Dundas, an old man, whose eyes were so weak that he sometimes could not see to write his own despatches, had only sixty troops at his disposal. Only a third of these were infantry—a party of the Suffolk Fencibles. The rest were cavalry, Romney Fencibles and the Ninth Dragoons, whose short swords made them almost useless against pikemen. Nonetheless, they galloped away down the hill, eager for the honour of first engaging the enemy. The leader of the Ninth Dragoons was Captain Erskine, the man who had entertained himself so well at Kilkea Castle six weeks before.[39]

The parish church at Old Kilcullen stood about a hundred feet above the fair green, a little beyond the point where the Cork turnpike separated from the road to Athy. The village itself was partly ruined—token of a previous visit of Captain Erskine and the Ninth Dragoons. About three hundred pikemen had now set up their camp in the churchyard on this little hill. Indefensible from artillery, or even ordinary musketeers, it was more or less impregnable to cavalry, as one side of the churchyard was sheltered by a wall, the other by a quickset hedge with a ditch before it, and the only approach was by a narrow lane. Alongside this the first line of pikemen had been posted.[40]

To the amazement of the spectators, the cavalry were ordered to charge. And charge they did—dashing themselves to pieces against the ten foot long pikes. By the third charge they had lost twenty-three men, including the Commander of the Romneys, Captain Cooke. Another ten were wounded, most of them mortally. As for Captain Erskine, his horse had stumbled on a gravestone and thrown its rider, breaking his leg. He was soon put out of his agony. According to Thomas Reynolds, it was an old beggar-woman who found him, recognised him, heaped him with abuse and then stabbed him to death with a rusty clasp-knife.[41]

After cutting his way out of Old Kilcullen when the infantry had come up, Dundas retired with his little force to the village of Kilcullen Bridge, commanding the strategic crossing of the Liffey. Here he was able to collect together the yeomanry corps of the local landlord, Captain La Touche, with about a hundred men all told. Meanwhile the rebels had crossed the Liffey lower down, and re-emerged astride the line of his retreat to the north, their numbers swelled by their success. They were now drawn up in a regular line three deep, with three stands of green colours, completely sealing off the road ahead.[42]

This time Dundas did not under-estimate his opponents, and superior tactics more than made up for the disadvantage of fighting without regular troops or artillery against an enemy ten times as numerous. On the left of the road the United forces had occupied a strong position with a hill at their backs. On the right they were dug in behind the characteristic-ally high-banked fields of the locality. To flush them out from these positions Dundas sent out two small parties, strictly instructing them not to risk an engagement, and the feint succeeded.[43] The rebels chased these parties down towards the road, where they were first caught by the concentrated fire of Dundas's musketeers, and then cut to pieces by the cavalry. As in Naas, the army was in no mood to give quarter. In his official report next day Dundas recorded: "The slaughter was considerable for such an action—about 150 lay dead. No prisoners." He added that it was "a great consolation" to him, after the heavy losses in the morning's engagement, that his party had this time suffered not a single casualty.[44]

It was now nearly twenty-four hours since the first rebel parties had assembled for the assault on the capital. Fourteen engagements had followed and in every single case, except two, the meanest little garrison of soldiers had managed to repulse the rebel army. Certain villages, it was true, had been virtually undefended, and several of them—north and south of the capital were now occupied by the rebels. But no military threat to the capital had ever materialised, and in most cases the rebel attack had ended in fiasco. Even the two rebel victories, which had cost the Government about a hundred men, had won the rebels nothing of any direct strategic value. Prosperous was a backwater in the great Bog of Allen and at Kilcullen on the road to Cork the rebels had now been forced onto the defensive. In short, there was much reason to think that the rebels had shot their bolt and the rebellion would swiftly collapse unless something quite extraordinary occurred.

But occur it did, and in a few hours the blaze that had seemed so easy to extinguish, was spreading almost unchecked towards the far more inflammable areas of the South.

The extraordinary fact was that Dundas, far from driving home his advantage after he had re-opened the strategic road to Kilcullen Bridge, had given a general order for the retreat. The disaster at Old Kilcullen seems to have completely unhinged him. Without any foundation, he believed an attack on Naas was impending. He allowed his men a mere two hours rest, destroyed eight hundred stand of arms picked up after the battle, and then retreated northwards to Naas. Meanwhile he had instructed all Commanding Officers in the county to evacuate their posts and concentrate their troops at Naas. Obediently the Armagh moved out of Clane, the Tyrone militia out of Ballitore, the Suffolk Fencibles out of Monasterevin, even General Wilford's garrison out of the town of Kildare. In Monasterevin the yeomanry were left to guard the loyal inhabitants. In the rest the yeomanry too were evacuated and the loyalists left to follow as best they could. Only one town retained its regular garrison, and this was Athy on the border of County Carlow. The messenger with the order to retreat lay dead on the turnpike—intercepted by the rebels.[45]

It was here on the borders of Carlow and Wicklow that Dundas's fears for the garrison might have seemed to be justified. Along this turnpike came the coaches to Cork. When Michael Reynolds had fired the mail coach in the early hours of that morning the signal had passed along this road, and the news of the attack on Naas had followed, transformed by rumour out of all recognition. The gaol in Naas had been taken. The prisoners had been released. The Castle was theirs. Even the loyalists had to admit that something serious had happened. How else to explain the stopping of the Cork mail? To the United men it was clear that their hour had come.

Village by village, along the mail coach route in the wake of the wild euphoric rumour, men had snatched up their pikes and swords and green cockades, and run to the points of rendezvous. By seven o'clock the news burst upon Old Kilcullen. By eight o'clock the tidal wave had swept to Ballitore. At nine it reached Castledermot. Due south along the line of the turnpike it ran, spreading out and engulfing the villages at either side.[46]

The chaplain of Lord Aldborough's yeomen had happened to be at Castledermot fair that morning. He saw the actual moment of impact. "All was quiet there till about 9 o'clock when on a sudden the whole fair dispersed and ran in all directions with their cattle towards their respective homes." News had arrived that the people "had risen in Dublin, Naas,

Ballymore and had beaten the King's troops, had possession of the Cannon, had let out the prisoners, and were rising everywhere over the kingdom".[47]

The news that Dundas was ordering a general retreat now seemed to provide complete confirmation for the wildest rumour. At Ballitore, ten miles to the north, an express arrived from headquarters to tell the garrison to retreat to Naas. The loyal inhabitants watched grimly as first the Suffolk Fencibles, then the Tyrone militia, marched out of the town. "All was hurry, tumult and confusion," Mrs. Leadbeater wrote in her diary. But one thing was clear: the United party believed the day was theirs. As the troops retreated, a man she knew appeared at the door of the shop dressed in green uniform. There were reports that fighting had already broken out at Narraghmore nearby. For the loyalists the alarm increased with every hour.[48] In the town of Kildare the garrison under General Wilford retreated so precipitately that they left their camp equipage in the town, and took no steps to destroy the large numbers of pikes and firearms surrendered by the rebels in the previous few days. About an hour after the last of the King's troops had left the town the market bell was rung to show the coast was clear, and the rebels who had surrendered the arms returned to collect them. By nightfall about two thousand rebels occupied the town, led by a man called Roger McGarry. They took over the houses of the loyalists who had fled. They seized the mail coach from Limerick, which reached the town just before midnight. And having plundered the coach and killed a young officer who was a passenger in it, as well as some of the Protestant loyalists of the town, they marched out again in three long columns, bent on attacking the neighbouring garrison of Monasterevin.[49]

Hour by hour the news of Dundas's withdrawal spread southwards along the mail coach road, bringing a new fever to the villages already bemused by the reports of victory. Most formidable of all, a mass attack on the garrison of Carlow was planned by the United party of that county, supposed no less than eleven thousand strong, in concert with a large contingent from the adjacent county of Queen's.

The driving force behind this plan was a young brogue-maker called Michael Heydon, who had assumed control of the Carlow party after the news of Ivers' arrest. He had needed all his strength to prevent it disintegrating. In Carlow, the ultimatum for forcible disarming had yet to expire, but the grim lesson of a flogging at Athy, ten miles to the north, had not been lost on the rank and file of the party. The only alternatives were to fight or to surrender. Some of them had surrendered their arms already, which had led to the local commanders extending the amnesty. The great majority had been still wavering, caught between their mystical faith in the invisible National Executive in Dublin, and their very human fear of being flogged. The Government's ultimatum was just expiring when Heydon announced the plan for a midnight attack on the town. Four large parties would converge on the potato market at the centre of the town—three from the surrounding districts of the county, and the fourth from Queen's County across the river to the west.

William Farrell, one of the leaders who had actually surrendered his arms, tried to dissuade the country people from the attempt. "Why, man," he told a friend, "if they do come in, they will be shot like rats in the streets." But an enthusiastic speech by Heydon and a certain amount of intimidation by his followers carried the day. "I have help enough in the town," Heydon told the country people he had enrolled. "I have nearly all the yeomen, nearly all the militia ready armed and a great number of the Ninth Dragoons, besides all the townsmen and you have nothing to do but march in and give a shout and they will all flock to you in an instant and there will be no one to oppose you and the town will be taken without any trouble."[50]

About two o'clock Heydon's column poured into the town down Tullow Street. It seemed completely defenceless. Only once were they stopped—by the parish priest, Father O'Neill of Tynryland, who came out of his house and begged them, dropping on his knees in the dusty road, to go back before it was too late. A thousand strong they pushed past him and reached the point of rendezvous, the potato market. And then the streets reverberated with their shouts, as a signal to their friends to begin.[51]

2

Counter-Attack

Dublin and surrounding counties; London, May 25th–27th

> In Dublin, the traitors were ready to rise
> And murder was seen in their lowering eyes.
> With poison, the cowards, they aimed to succeed,
> And thousands were doomed by Assassins to bleed
> But the Yeomen advanced, of Rebels the dread
> And each Croppy soon hid his dastardly head.
> Down, down, Croppies, lie down
>
> *Loyalist song, July 1798*

MEANWHILE IN the Castle at Dublin the Government had at last roused itself for war. "The Sword is drawn," the Viceroy declared. "I have kept it within the scabbard as long as possible. It must not now be returned until this most alarming Conspiracy is put down."[1] "We shall lose many lives," wrote Beresford, "but we'll conquer."[2]

Already that morning the first battle trophies had appeared outside Lord Castlereagh's office in Lower Castle Yard—the three mutilated bodies of the men cut down by Lord Roden and the Fifth Dragoons. The sight shocked even John Beresford.[3] Barrington called the display the most "frightful spectacle which ever disgraced a royal residence, save the seraglio". It was a hot day and visitors to the Castle had to run the gauntlet of the trophies on the pavement, "cut and gashed in every part covered with clotted blood and dust".[4] A further sensation was caused during the afternoon when one of the bodies came to life, was taken into the guard-house, and duly pardoned by the Viceroy, after making a full confession.[5]

The reanimated corpse proved to be a handsome young man called Thomas Keogh—son to an opulent farmer of Rathfarnham. The tale he told of the rebels' plans was music to the ears of the Government. The Rathfarnham rising had been a miserably ill-conducted affair: a party of men he hardly knew had thrust a rusty sword into his hand, and taken him to the Fox and Geese at Clondalkin "with four or five carts loaded, as he heard, with Blankets, Provisions, Powder and Ball". Suddenly their leaders, two of the local yeomen called Ledwich and Wade, shouted "Make away as fast as you can or you'll all be killed" and the next moment the Dragoons were upon them.[6]

Ledwich and Wade, who had been captured uninjured, told much the same story, protesting that they, too, had been forced into the business, but the court martial that tried them as deserters from the yeomanry did not accept this part of their evidence, and to the bodies in the Castle yard were soon added two more, swinging from a convenient lamp-post, as a cautionary tale for the corps of yeomanry.[7] A few other executions followed. According to Barrington, some of the lamp-lighters paid with their lives for their failure to light the lamps the previous night.[8] An elderly volunteer officer, Major Bacon, was hanged from the scaffolding on Carlisle Bridge as a suspected United officer, after being found skulking in a handsom cab disguised as a woman. Later, huge crowds gathered to see the despatch of Dr. John Esmonde, the Kildare United leader, from the same makeshift gallows, his yeomanry coat turned inside out to brand him as a deserter.[9]

Apart from these popular diversions, and the display of a few other rebel corpses, tastefully decorated with pikes, Dublin remained singularly undisturbed.[10] True, searches for arms and men continued. A blacksmith was carried through the city on horseback, "his bellows borne before him and his person hung over with the pikes which had been found with him".[11] An eminent merchant, Mr. Braughall, suspected, with some reason, of being involved in the United movement, was hauled off to Kilmainham Gaol. Behind the closed doors of the Royal Exchange, now a temporary barracks, the yeomanry continued "improving themselves", as an eyewitness put it, "in the science of flogging".[12] But compared to the wild scenes of the previous day—the house burnings in the Liberties, the panic and confusion of the loyalists—Dublin was restraint itself.

For this Camden and his Government could take some of the credit. That afternoon, May 24th, the Viceroy's proclamation had been read out in the Castle Yard, solemnly requiring His Majesty's subjects to take notice that the whole country was now subject to martial law, and that Lieutenant General Lake and other general officers had been ordered to punish "by death or otherwise" all persons "acting, aiding or in any manner assisting in the rebellion which now exists in this Kingdom".[13] In his turn Lake had imposed a belated curfew on Dublin except for servicemen and state officials. The Lord Mayor had ordered all householders who had not registered their arms to surrender them forthwith, on pain of transportation.[14]

The public response to these war-time restrictions, was heartening. There was a rush of new volunteers to the local yeomanry, bringing the total to about six thousand men.[15] Hardly a professional man was to be found in the streets wearing civilian clothes, though some had joined up, no doubt, either to keep up appearances or to dodge the curfew. Even in the civil courts it was noted that only the prisoners wore civilian clothes. All the rest—bar, juries, attorneys, even one of the judges—appeared in service uniform. Despite the curfew and the closing of the theatre for the duration, people were intent on showing their public spirit. Alarm bells were put on house-tops. Amateurish efforts were made to fortify the bridges over the canals.[16] A riding-school master called Parker offered his services free during the crisis. He could "drill and complete gentlemen in cavalry manoeuvres at his Equestrian Academy" in Foster Place, taking only three days to "complete an attentive pupil for the field".[17]

At the same time the rival Archbishops of Dublin were rallying to defend the Constitution. The Protestant Archbishop issued a circular to his clergy expressly recommending military service.[18] The Catholic Archbishop sent out a Pastoral, to be read from every pulpit, denouncing the rebellion and warning his flock of the moral necessity of submission to the law "at this awful and alarming crisis". The Pastoral was followed by a solemn declaration in the newspapers, signed by virtually the whole Catholic Establishment, including four peers of the realm, two baronets and three archbishops, to testify to the benefits of the Constitution for Catholics and to express horror at the rebels' atrocities against the Protestants.[19] One of the signatories was John Keogh—the man who had sent Tone to seek French assistance.

Finally, even the Irish Whigs, who had never shown much sympathy for the war against France, declared themselves in favour of the war against the Irish rebels. Plunket and Bushe both pledged their support in Parliament for the Government's exceptional measures; while Sir Laurence Parsons, who had resigned from the militia at the time of the Abercromby crisis, now advertised his intention of fighting for King and country in the yeomanry.[20]

Government and Opposition, Church and State, men of rank, and men of property, all seemed united against the enemy—all that is who belonged to one class or another of the "respectable inhabitants", as Camden called them. But how to deal with the great mass of the people who were not respectable, who had little to lose in a revolution, and much perhaps to gain, and had been led to believe that it was now theirs for the taking?

Camden's first report to London of the outbreak was, characteristically, indecisive. "Acts of open rebellion" were only to be expected after the strong counter-measures, but there was a general "spirit of loyalty".[21] From a political point of view there was reason for Camden to feel relieved. But temperamentally he was a pessimist and the state of the country was conducive to it. He saw beneath the loyalty of the respectable class an ominous spirit that could prove no less destructive than the United movement itself. "The indignant feelings of the loyal part of the country," he wrote to Portland, "aroused to such a pitch that I almost tremble lest their zeal should drive them to acts of Retaliation."[22] Camden was not exaggerating the danger, for unless the loyalists could be restrained, the rebellion could develop on religious lines, tearing open the old wounds healed over by a century of more or less peaceful co-existence. And then, as Camden put it, "political enthusiasm" would combine with "religious animosity", to goad the Catholic peasantry to try to regain, by a holy war against Protestants, the estates forfeited by their Catholic ancestors.[23]

Already some of the loyalists were embarrassingly active. In the Commons, on the morning of the outbreak, Colonel Maxwell tried to carry a measure for summary trial and execution of suspected rebels arrested *before* the rebellion—including of course the leaders against whom there was no legal evidence. This amazing proposal was applauded in the Commons with cries of "Move! Move!" At that point Lord Castlereagh had intervened. Honourable Members, he had reminded them, should not wish the warmth of their feelings to run away with their understanding. If the times required the "exemplary punishment" of particular criminals it was up to the Government to select them. Rebels in arms would be treated with the "utmost severity", but they could not close "the door of mercy" against other "deluded inhabitants".[24] Castlereagh's speech quieted the House for the time being, but the trouble would clearly recur. Even Beresford was disturbed by the violence of the loyalists.[25]

The indignation of the extreme Protestant party was fed by the atrocity stories now sweeping the capital. Some were complete fabrications; like the story of the Catholic baker at Rathcoole who had tried to dispose of the garrison by poisoning their bread. Many were wildly exaggerated; like the case of the intoxicated kitchen-maid who had confessed in her cups that 20,000 Catholic maids had sworn to join the rebels.[26] Others, like the tale of Horish, the Castle sweep, having advanced money to the rebels in exchange for an option on Lord Charlemont's villa, were merely absurd.[27] Unfortunately there were still other tales that were true. At Dunshaughlin, it was learnt, the mob had broken into the house of the inoffensive local school-master and killed him and a gardener and then mangled their bodies. They had stripped a third man and put him in a cauldron of boiling pitch. At nearby Dunboyne they murdered several civilians, and then plundered their houses. In every case the victims were Protestant, and Catholics were pointedly left unmolested.[28]

Hour by hour, fresh accounts were received of looting and lynching by the infuriated Catholic peasantry who had born the brunt of the disarming. The destruction of Captain Swayne and his garrison at Prosperous had been followed by the indiscriminate killing of any Protestants identified with Government "The Kingdom is ours . . . down with the Orangemen!" cried the mob weeping with joy. They dragged out of bed Mr. Brewer, the English cotton master whose enterprise had created Prosperous. "Behold the body of a heretic tyrant," someone shouted, as his workers dragged him out into the street, his skull split open by an axe. They hunted down and shot Mr. Stamers, the landlord who owned most of the town, and had rashly come himself to collect the rents. They murdered an old man of seventy who had once been a sergeant in the army. "Where are the heretics now?" cried the women of the town. "Shew us the face of an Orangeman!"[29] Again it was noticed that Catholic loyalists were left unscathed, while no one else was safe from the popular fury. In the town of Kildare, now abandoned by the army, the mob had piked to death an old Protestant lodge-keeper, his fourteen year old granddaughter and the faithful dog that had tried to defend him.[30]

It was now two days since the outbreak of the rebellion and as fresh news of disasters in Meath and Kildare reached Camden he began to feel serious alarm about the military problem presented by the rebellion. Camden himself had never shared the cheerful view of other members of the Castle staff like Edward Cooke who, as we saw, welcomed the rising as "the salvation of the country", because that conspiracy could not be "cleared without a burst".[31] It was true, no doubt, that the army should be able to deal with the rebels fairly swiftly, now they had been forced into the field. But *would* it—an army in fact, officered by the same class of Irishmen who now showed their zeal in Parliament, and commanded by a British general in whom Camden could now put no confidence? In his earlier reports to London, Camden had repeatedly asked for more rein-forcements from Britain, and he now urged on Portland and Pitt the "absolute necessity" of sending them.[32] "The conspiracy is so general," he wrote, "that it will require every exertion to put it down." It might tempt the French to accelerate the invasion plans. The reinforcements could be spared, he hoped, "without any danger to Great Britain".[33]

The day that the rebellion had broken out around Dublin, Pitt and the British cabinet in London were, for once, considering the problem of Ireland. The subject of their deliberations, however, was not tragedy, but farce.

A few months earlier, the Bow Street runners had arrested five men in most peculiar circumstances in a Margate hotel. The men had walked along the sands from Whitstable the previous day carrying a monstrous amount of luggage, including several boxes of papers, a mahogany trunk with a secret drawer, and a quantity of gold. Two of them gave their names as Colonel Morris and Captain Jones, and claimed the others were their men servants. But on examination the military gentlemen turned out to be Father Quigley, an Irish Catholic priest from Dundalk known to be a leader of the United party, and Arthur O'Connor, aristocrat, revolutionary and bosom friend of Lord Edward Fitzgerald.[34] (Lord Edward's comment on the arrest was, "O'Connor had nothing odd with him but twelve hundred guineas.")[35]

The English Government had been playing cat-and-mouse with these two United Irishmen for some weeks. They hoped to find out more about their British counterparts—the shadowy Jacobin conspiracy of the United Britons. The arrest confirmed their belief that the two organisations were linked. One of the arrested "men servants" was John Binns, whom they knew from their Intelligence network was just back from Dublin, where he had delivered a message of solidarity from the United Britons. Quigley had accompanied him there, and on their return attended the United British committee in London. In his riding coat when arrested at Margate was found a highly incriminating letter from a body called the "Secret Committee of England", addressed to the French Directory and inviting an invasion of England by "the hero of Italy and his invincible legions".[36]

Whitehall did not take too seriously the United Britons' plans to revolutionise England on the French model, but were glad to have an opportunity of crushing the plot in its infancy. If the French invaded England, which was undoubtedly their aim, the United Britons, and the corresponding societies in various parts of the country, could make some mischief. A few weeks after the arrests at Margate, Portland had authorised a round-up of Jacobins in London and Manchester. In case of difficulty in finding legal evidence to convict them, the British law was brought into line with the Irish by suspending habeas corpus.[37]

The legal case against Quigley, O'Connor and the others seemed solid enough. It turned on three documents found in their possession. There was the Secret Committee letter inviting invasion and the French passport, both of which incriminated Quigley directly and the other indirectly, if they could be shown to have known of them. Thirdly, there was a coded letter from Arthur O'Connor to Lord Edward Fitzgerald, in which, by a strange chance, the key had been left attached. This revealed that O'Connor was going to France where he would be "very active" in the United cause.[38]

To convict O'Connor, a member of the Irish Directory, was obviously of supreme importance for the Irish Government, and in this Whitehall had acted as agent for the Castle. An interminable correspondence had developed, in which every contingency had been covered: Leonard McNally, the Dublin informer, had wormed out of the United lawyers the line of defence to be adopted; two other informers—Cox the gunsmith and McNally's own illegitimate son, Leonard Howard—had been sent over to Maidstone to help with the trial. While John Pollock, Lord Downshire's political adviser, had briefed the British prosecutor with discreditable details about the Irish witnesses, who included Grattan.

Yet in his trial at Maidstone on May 21st O'Connor had out-manoeuvred everyone, friend and foe. He was helped by the fact that a meddling clergyman, the son of Arthur Young, the economist, had written a letter to some of the jurymen urging them to convict. He also had the good sense to avoid calling any Irish witnesses. The heart of his defence was a dazzling series of testimonials from the great English Whiggery. Mr. O'Connor is a friend of mine and firmly attached to the Constitution, said Charles James Fox. No man was ever more opposed to the idea of a French invasion, said Richard Brinsley Sheridan. These lofty sentiments were echoed by Samuel Whitbread, Thomas Erskine, and five Whig Peers—Lords John Russell, Thanet, Oxford, Suffolk and Moira. O'Connor's only fault, as his counsel put it, was his excessive openness and frankness. The Constitution of the United Irishmen was read in court as evidence that a man like O'Connor could have had no connection with it. The letter to Lord Edward, which had an offensive reference to the Whigs, was similarly turned to his advantage. The British jury, the British judge, and the British Whigs were all equally beguiled by O'Connor. The persecuted patriot was triumphantly acquitted. Father Quigley, whom no one had bothered to defend, was condemned to be hanged as a traitor.[39]

The trial concluded on May 22nd with one of the strangest scenes in a British court of justice. O'Connor could be re-tried under Irish law on exactly the same charge of which he had just been acquitted under British law. Accordingly, two Bow Street runners were waiting by the dock ready to re-arrest him. But no sooner had the death sentence been pronounced on the unfortunate Quigley, than O'Connor rushed from the dock to the bar, and from the bar into the body of the court, with the police in hot pursuit. The court was plunged into confusion. Outraged Whigs, including O'Connor's Counsel and Lord Thanet, tried to snatch him to safety. Swords were drawn—the swords that were lying as evidence on the table. Furniture was smashed, and heads broken. O'Connor might have got clean away, but for the quick-wittedness of the judge's coachman who brought him crashing to the floor.[40]

The news of the bungling of O'Connor's trial, and the unseemly brawl that followed, reached the British cabinet next day, May 23rd. Pitt was in a sensitive mood. Some sort of invasion attempt by the French was imminent. In the Mediterranean a vast fleet was assembling for an unknown destination—perhaps Ireland.[41] On the Normandy coast the French were reported to have flat-bottomed barges ready to launch. In the port of Ostend a large fleet was mustered. The cabinet had decided earlier that month to strike at the Ostend fleet with a commando raid on the Ostend-Flushing canal. The news had just reached London that, though the dykes had been destroyed, the entire British force had been ignominiously captured, unable to re-embark.[42]

Two days later, on May 25th, Pitt finally lost control of himself. It was at a debate about manning the navy, which was being rushed through all its stages in a single day, such was the emergency. As usual, the Whigs were tweaking the Government's tail. Tierney, an Irishman and leading Foxite, opposed the bill as precipitate. Pitt accused him, in a grossly unparliamentary outburst, of opposing the bill "from a desire to obstruct the defence of the country".[43] Tierney appealed to the Speaker for protection, but Pitt icily repeated the phrase, and insisted that he meant every word of it. He had had, it was clear, more from Fox's party than he could take.[44]

The next step, though illegal, was obligatory for two men of honour. The Prime Minister made his will, and on Sunday May 27th drove solemnly from Birdcage Walk along the road to Putney Heath, where he met Mr. Tierney. The seconds, Whig and Tory, paced out the ground and loaded two cases of pistols. Nearby the Speaker, a personal friend of Pitt, stood watching from a small hill where a felon hung from a gibbet. A crowd of sightseers waited, as the fate of the British Empire hung in the balance. Tierney and the Prime Minister both fired—and missed. They fired again—with no more result. The seconds intervened.[45]

As the tale of Pitt's escape sent a shudder through the nation,[46] an express reached Whitehall with the news from Ireland that Pitt and the cabinet had long dreaded: the rebellion had begun.

In Dublin, Camden's gloomy predictions were fast being realised. General Dundas's hasty withdrawal on the first afternoon of the rebellion had opened to the rebels the whole county of Kildare. By May 26th an army of about thirty thousand United men had occupied the towns of Kildare, Prosperous and Kilcullen, and the villages of Rathangan, Newbridge and Ballitore, and a couple of hundred thousand acres of the richest farmland in Ireland within twelve miles of the capital. To those who had family or property in this area it was no consolation that the rebels seemed to be united only in name—a half-disciplined mob with little idea beyond plunder. All that could be said was that so far they had failed to break out of the county. But unless they could be forced onto the defensive, this would be only a matter of time.

On the western side of the county, where it marched with Queen's, the rebels were clearly massing for a thrust. Along the Galway turnpike, the only main road open after Dundas's withdrawal, came desperate appeals for Government help. At Monasterevin, the town on the Queen's border, the withdrawal of the regular troops had left about eighty part-time yeomanry to hold this fort as best they could. The first attack had come about in the morning of the 25th, the morning after the first outbreak. A party of variously armed men tried to rush the town using much the same tactics as their fellows at Naas. Three columns of attackers poured down the narrow streets and captured part of the church. Outnumbered by more than twenty to one, the garrison had succeeded in driving them off by concentrated musket fire, but at the cost of nine yeomen killed and wounded. Despite their own casualties—sixty-three lay dead in the streets—the rebel army had regrouped, and crossed the border into Queen's.[47] The regular garrison at Portarlington had not been withdrawn, and the rebels marching on that town had been routed by a party of yeomanry helped by some men of the Fifth Dragoons. But scattered rebel parties had crossed the border at numerous points, and were concealed in the rough country along the river Barrow.[48] The loyalists "dreaded much" an attack, according to a message sent by their commander on the 26th: at Portarlington he had put the place on a footing for war; at Mountmellick the cavalry had stood at their horses' heads all night. A second attack was expected that evening.[49]

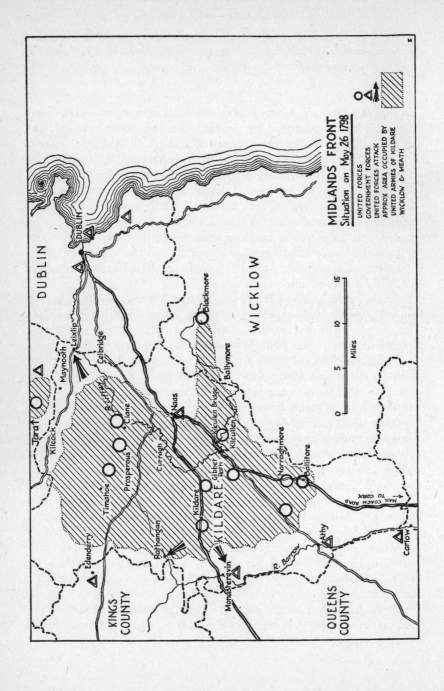

MIDLANDS FRONT
Situation on May 26 1798

UNITED FORCES
GOVERNMENT FORCES
UNITED FORCES ATTACK
APPROX AREA OCCUPIED BY
UNITED ARMIES OF KILDARE
WICKLOW & MEATH

DUBLIN

WICKLOW

KILDARE

KINGS
COUNTY

QUEENS
COUNTY

DUBLIN
Leixlip
Maynooth
Celbridge
Kilcock
Rufford
Clane
Naas
Timahoe
Prosperous
Curragh
Kildare
Rathangan
Edenderry
Monasterevin
R. Barrow
Athy
Carlow
Blackmore
Ballymore
Kilcullen Bridge
Kilcullen
Gibbet
Rath
Narraghmore
Ballitore
Jara

MAIL COACH ROAD
TO CORK

Miles
0   5   10   15

A still more dangerous situation existed on the north eastern border of the county where it marched with Dublin and Meath. On the 26th, Dublin received an urgent message from the commander of the garrison at Leixlip, Colonel Borden of the Duke of York's Highlanders, appealing for reinforcements. Three attacks had been made the previous day on the frontier towns in the area: on Kilcock in the morning, then on Leixlip and later that evening on Lucan. All three had been beaten off at severe cost to the rebels and without loss to the Government forces, yet the rebels were still on the offensive. The vast, almost trackless bog between Prosperous and the Galway road provided a secure base of operations. Kilcock and Leixlip, it was certain, would be "immediately attacked again". The town of Trim, twelve miles inside County Meath, was also threatened.[50] Already the first trickle of Kildare men were pushing out northwards to link up with the thousands of United men still unsubdued in County Meath. After being driven away from Lucan the previous evening, a party of rebels—small farmers, artificers from the local iron works and some of the Clonsilla yeomen—had crossed the Liffey into Meath and headed for the camp at Dunboyne.[51] Two hundred others had marched through Celbridge, forcing the gates of the Connollys' house at Castletown, and marched across the lawn in full view of the owners, heading for the same rendezvous.[52]

There had been no outbreak so far to the north of the county, where the vast purple bogs of Kildare merged imperceptibly with those of King's County. But from Edenderry across the border, there now came a *cri de coeur* for reinforcements. On the 26th a party, described as "five thousand Defenders", had attacked the town of Rathangan, killing both of the yeomanry officers and twenty-six of the privates. "The inhabitants of Clonbulloge, midway between this town and Rathangan, have all fled in here with their families for protection which we are ill able to give them having no military force except yeomanry." The rebels were flushed with success and "the whole country said to be up". The message ended with a desperate appeal for officers to organise the defence. Otherwise they faced "inevitable destruction".[53]

Unfortunately for the Government, there was little exaggeration in the tale of massacre. The yeomanry of Rathangan, owned by the Duke of Leinster, like so much of the county, had been commanded by the Duke's agent, a kindly old man called Thomas Spenser. He had done his best to rally the towns-people. But most of the yeomen had joined the rebels. The rest, after losing the garrison of the Cork militia stationed there, had been completely demoralised. From the roofs of their houses they could see the houses burning in the country around. Refugees flocked into the town bringing rumours of threatened massacre.[54]

About three o'clock in the morning of May 26th, a large party of rebels had entered Rathangan. No resistance was offered. Spenser was surrounded in a house where he had barricaded himself. The window shutters were broken in by some of the workmen with the butts of their muskets. Spenser surrendered, and so did his first lieutenant, a retired English officer called Moore, who had taken refuge in the home of a Quaker family. They were promised their lives if they gave up their arms to the rebels. And then, without threat or provocation, as it seemed, but simply on the blind impulse of the mob, the killing began. One by one, the Protestant men believed loyal to the Government were piked or shot: Spenser, whose mangled body was displayed as a trophy in front of his door; Moore, whose wife had lain-in three days before; six of the others who had taken refuge with the Quaker, including a boy of fourteen; a carpenter, and a shoemaker; in all nineteen men, unarmed and inoffensive, of that small town where Catholics and Protestants had seemed to live comfortably together, were now piked or shot or hacked to death. As before, the loyalists who were Catholics were allowed to pass unharmed.[55]

Despite these disasters in Kildare, and the appeals for help from the beleaguered garrisons in all the neighbouring parts of Queen's, King's and Meath, the main Government forces remained in the capital. A small detachment, it is true, was sent into Meath under the command of General Craig. But it discreetly retired before making contact with the enemy. Camden's policy was nothing if not cautious. They must remain on the defensive, he could argue, until they could guarantee the success of a counter attack. As soon as reinforcements arrived from Britain, or from the south of Ireland, they could strike. Meanwhile the army must maintain the security of the capital, the grand object of all the rebels' plans. It was a dangerous policy, because the longer they waited the greater was the risk of the fire spreading to other areas. It was also in military terms the wrong policy, as it greatly over-estimated the strength of the Meath and Kildare rebels once they had lost the first intoxicating taste of victory. Yet with a small margin of luck the policy might still have succeeded, and the rebellion died a natural death, but for two horrible tragedies, news of which now came to Dublin. They were the final part of the powder trail of Government atrocities and rebel reprisals which was to touch-off the great explosion.

On the morning of May 24th, as we saw in the previous chapter, the insurrection had spread southwards along the Cork turnpike, on the border of Kildare and Wicklow, engulfing the towns and villages at either side. Three of the Kildare towns, Kilcullen, Ballitore and Narraghmore, had fallen to the rebels. All the garrisons in Wicklow—Ballymore, Dunlavin, Stratford and Baltinglass—had beaten off the attack. But many men had been lost in the desperate fighting. At Ballymore, Captain Beevor and his garrison of about fifty regulars had barely avoided the fate of Captain Swayne and his men at Prosperous. Seven of the Ninth Dragoons had been killed in their beds; five others had been desperately wounded; and a lieutenant of the Tyrone militia had lost his life in charging the attackers.[56]

The alarm of these Wicklow garrisons was increased by the news of the rebels' treatment of other loyalists in the neighbourhood. At Ballitore they had arrested one of Lord Aldborough's yeomen, an inoffensive young man called Yeates, and piked him to death. A militia sergeant was taken at his own lodgings and despatched. Otherwise the loyalists were spared, though half dead with fear. At Narraghmore, a couple of miles to the north, the rebels had been more violent. Every Protestant's house was set on fire, and all nine of the remaining yeomen made prisoner, and three of them hacked to death.[57]

In County Carlow, to the south, the rebels were massing. Early on the morning of the 25th, the Carlow rebels had marched on the town more than a thousand strong, led by Heydon the brogue-maker. The garrison commander had received forewarning of the intended attack, and had drawn them up in full battle order: two companies of militia, several corps of yeomanry, and some of the Ninth Dragoons. Frightful slaughter had followed. The streets were choked with the bodies of the rebels and half the houses in the town had been burned. But even this did not seem to have dashed the rebels' spirits. A few hours later more then three thousand of the Carlow rebels had attacked the small town of Hacketstown, and had been beaten off with difficulty.[58]

Such were the bare facts, and to them were added wild stories of murder and treachery which were not discredited till later. And now in their rage and panic the loyalists took the law into their own hands.

At Dunlavin the small garrison led by an officer of the Wicklow militia took out twenty-eight prisoners from the gaol—nine from the Narraghmore yeomen, and the rest from the Saundersgrove corps—and executed them. These men had taken no part in the risings.[59]

Carnew, where the south western spur of the Wicklow mountains intervenes between the plains of Carlow and Wexford, was next the scene of the most appalling atrocity. Though Carnew had been the centre of disturbance for many months, the rebellion had not yet reached that area. Twenty-eight suspects were now marched out of the town prison and paraded in the ball alley. One by one, they were shot down in cold blood by a squad of yeomen and militia.[60]

We cannot tell what fatal combination of motives—what blend of fear or rage or crazy policy—drove the loyalists at either place to take such a desperate step. At Dunlavin, it is true, the victims were yeomen, and there was good reason to suspect their fidelity. All over that region, the yeomen and especially the Catholic yeomen, had gone over to the rebels. The garrison expected an attack at any moment. It is at times like this that one expects atrocities to occur. At Carnew, on the other hand, there was nothing to extenuate the shootings, nor even to explain them, except the blood feuds of class and race and religion, and the hideous nature of civil war itself. But whatever the cause, the result of the shootings was death and destruction for many thousands of men in one of the richest and most peaceful areas of Ireland.

The day after the shootings at Carnew, an express reached Dublin carrying news of disaster of completely new dimensions. The insurrection had burst out in County Wexford in great force and was spreading southwards with terrifying rapidity. A hundred men of the North Cork militia had been wiped out. Only three men and one officer had survived. That night Camden wrote to London for the sixth time in eight days that unless reinforcements were sent "immediately", and he underlined the word with his pen, he could not answer for the consequences. A speedy end to the civil war was "the only chance we have".[61]

3

The Fire Spreads South

Wexford, May 23rd–29th

Come, all you warriors, and renowned nobles,
Who once commanded brave warlike bands;
Lay down your plumes, and your golden trophies,
Give up your arms with a trembling hand,
Since Father Murphy, of the County Wexford,
Lately aroused from his sleepy dream,
To cut down cruel Saxon persecution,
And wash it away in a crimson stream,

Father Murphy of the County Wexford, 1798

ON THE Wednesday before Whitsun, the town of Wexford, third largest in the province of Leinster, found itself in festive mood. From all over the county magistrates had assembled for the quarter sessions, bringing along their wives and other ladies for the occasion. After the court closed, they took a late dinner, and trooped out along the quays to see the new wonder of the town: the seventy-five span wooden bridge across the Slaney, just built by public subscription for the huge sum of £14,000. It was midnight before the family parties set out in their carriages for the long jolting journey home.[1]

County Wexford was regarded in Ireland at this time as a moral curiosity. The Catholic peasantry were as peaceful and industrious as those of neighbouring counties were lawless and disorderly. The Protestant landlords lived on their estates, appeared contented, and were sometimes even popular. The middlemen class of both religions—the large tenants who sub-let their lands for a living—seemed to get on well together, hunting the fox and marrying into each other's families.[2]

The wealth of Wexford was derived from the corn trade, and this in turn from several striking bounties of nature. Not only was the weather warmer and drier than elsewhere. Wexford's long coast-line provided sea sand and seaweed fertiliser for the barley, and two great navigable rivers—the Barrow and the Slaney—carried the produce efficiently to the ports.[3]

Only once had the peace and prosperity of the county been seriously disturbed. In July 1793 an obscure demonstration had occurred near the town of Enniscorthy: a protest against conscription for the militia, according to some reports, an anti-tithe demonstration, according to others. (It was probably a bit of both.) After several people had been removed to the gaol in Wexford, a mob of about a thousand marched on the town to obtain their release. An officer tried to intervene and was cut down. The military fired on the mob, shot about eighty and dispersed the rest. The incident now seemed forgotten.[4]

In the last year however the war-time recession had reached Wexford. Almost overnight the bottom had dropped out of the barley trade. Granaries were bursting after the excellent harvest of 1797, when a heavy malt tax suddenly slashed the demand. Barley fell from 25s a barrel to 5s a barrel.[5] Other markets also began to fail, owing to the British financial crisis and the consequent lack of either cash or credit. The slump hit hardest, as slumps usually do, the people who could least afford a cut in their living standards. Labourers, whose regular wages during the boom had not kept pace with the soaring cost of rent and food and clothes, now found themselves without a job or only part employed. The recession threatened substantial farmers and middlemen who happened to have taken farms on unprecedently high rents a year or two before.[6] The ripples spread even to some of the proprietors of land and the established church. Tithe proctors found it harder to collect the tithes, and agents to collect rent. There were abatements, even bankruptcies.

One must not exaggerate the recession, and its effect on the public mind in Wexford. The landless labourers of the corn counties of southern England were suffering from chronic low wages and under-employment at this time. There was a war-time slump in a number of British industries.[7] And there was no more unrest *there* than usual. But it seems that in Wexford on the outer rim of the British economy, the fluctuations of price and cost were especially violent, and the crisis in confidence particularly severe.[8]

All this could only favour the United party. Although most of the county seemed peaceful enough on the surface, it was clear to many of the fifty-odd local magistrates who effectively ruled the county, that all was not well. In March a seditious paper had been sent to a respectable merchant of the town by an unknown hand; his business associate, the United leader Oliver Bond, was suspected.[9] At the assizes in April the crown solicitor, Thomas Kemmis, reported that "the Juries here are Quite Different from Those of Wicklow, and though this country appears Quiet yet I think it is in a bad state, from the great Number of those United Irishmen which are in this country, and I understand this town is the worst part of the country."[10] Up on the Carlow side of the county there were stories of United emissaries, nightly meetings, and of trees being cut for pike-handles. However, there were no raids for arms and the local magistrate, the Reverend Mr. Colclough, was "confident matters are exaggerated".[11]

A month later one of the leading authorities in the Enniscorthy area reported that the most serious conspiracy was on foot. The Protestant Bishop of Ferns, Dr. Eusebius Cleaver, wrote on May 8th to warn the Government that "the Business of Seduction goes on with increasing Facility and Success, that by much the greater part of the militia, Multi-tudes of the Yeomen—and all servants both male and female are secured." The new United strategy, according to the Bishop's source, was not to wait for a French invasion, but to go ahead with the universal rising "as soon as the Spring business shall be at an end". The immediate aim was to "massacre and pillage all Protestants and others attached to the Present Constitution". In due course they would "establish Popery and root out effectively the Protestant religion in the Island".[12]

All classes of Catholics were in the plot, according to Dr. Cleaver. Attempts by Catholic priests to establish the loyalty of themselves and their flocks by publicising loyal addresses in the newspapers were to be disregarded as either "imposed on them by their landlords" or as "ad-mitted by priests without the knowledge of their flocks for the purpose of blinding and deceiving Government". As for the Protestant gentry sup-posed to be implicated, Dr. Cleaver gave no credit to these suspicions. It was a common policy of the people to claim the support of respectable men "as a bait for the seduction of the lower classes". The Protestants they claimed as friends were simply the "gentlemen who from Indolence or Timidity make no exertion against them".[13]

What were his fellow loyalists to make of this strange story of Dr. Cleaver's? In Wexford and Enniscorthy, at any rate, the authorities showed no sign of taking it very seriously. Their counter-measures were nothing compared to those adopted in Kildare, the Midlands and Dublin. No request was sent to the Government to reinforce the feeble garrisons of militia in the towns. No troops were marched in to live there, as in enemy country. Magistrates simply went to the chapels and appealed to people to return to loyalty. Priests, Catholic bishops and Catholic landlords united in this appeal. In these districts no one was flogged or tortured. Already the proclaiming of the whole county as a disturbed area at the end of April seem to have brought the people to their senses. Of their own accord people pledged their loyalty by taking the oath of allegiance. They flocked to the magistrates to hand in their pikes. They even revealed the names of the United party leaders, and some of these fled while others were arrested. By May 23rd the magistrates could assemble at the Wexford quarter sessions confident that by their mild measures they had weathered the storm. After pardoning two men, sentenced according to the Insurrection Act, they announced that there would be ten more days for handing in arms before stricter measures were adopted.[14]

In fact the magistrates knew very little about the United party in Wexford. It was later to emerge that the party had derived unusual prestige and encouragement from three members of the landed gentry. The most important was Protestant—Bagenal Harvey of Bargay Castle. Two were Catholic—a young squire called Edward Fitzgerald of New Park and a doctor called John Colclough of Ballyteigue.[15] How far they really accepted the aims of their fellow revolutionaries it is difficult to know. Bagenal Harvey, a popular landlord of some £1,000 a year, certainly seems to have been, philosophically speaking, a republican. According to one of McNally's spy reports sent to Pitt three years before, Harvey had been repeatedly chairman of the Dublin Society of United Irishmen before it was proscribed. "His intellectual powers are not strong," Pitt had been told, "his person rather diminutive, very plain countenance but if he has not the strength he has the heart of a Hercules." Harvey's radical stance in Dublin politics had involved him in a duel which he had won "with astonishing coolness".[16] All three men, Harvey, Fitzgerald and Colclough, were believed to be radicals and were correspondingly suspect to the ruling families of County Wexford. Relations were probably exacerbated by the election contest of the previous year and by the current disarming campaign in which they had refused to co-operate. But while the political aims of the three men remained unknown or obscure to the Government party in Wexford, they were not playing, it now seems, an active part in organising the county.

Like many Irish radicals they regarded a revolution as inevitable, and let their names be used to assist it, yet did not for the moment step forward to shape its course.

So much then for the situation in the centre and south of County

Wexford: both the United movement and its adversaries were relatively inactive.[17]

The situation for both sides was entirely different in the northern frontier land of the county. It was here that despite the stationing of a small company of the North Cork militia at Gorey, outrages had been common since the previous autumn, and the position was deteriorating. Assassination of informers made it impossible to detect the extent of the conspiracy. For loyalists it was a terrifying situation, in which all the elements of the struggle in Wicklow and Kildare and the other disturbed parts of Ireland seemed to be present in their most extreme form. No rents were being paid, and the people clearly expected an immediate revolution. The yeomanry were riddled with disaffection. Many Catholics had resigned from their corps, leaving the more liberal gentry, who had encouraged Catholics to join, without any means of self-defence. There was undoubtedly a fifth column in their midst. But how to deal with this conspiracy that overwhelmed them on every side? To even the most fair-minded person it must have been clear that the ordinary process of the law was powerless to deal with the situation, and some much more drastic cure was unavoidable. But *what* expedient when they knew so little of the organisation of the Party against them. Faced with this appalling threat, and neither supported nor disciplined by a regular garrison, the gentry on the Wexford-Wicklow border resorted to reckless tactics—a campaign of terror.[18]

In fact, it was later to emerge the driving force behind the United party of this borderland of Wexford and Wicklow was a group of Catholic farmers, traders and small businessmen. The leading organiser was a farmer called Robert Graham of Coolgreany, a mile or two from the border. His two closest neighbours had joined the baronial committee. The first, a miller called Howlet, was to be deputed to organise the neighbouring barony of Ballaghkeen. The second, a Protestant from the North, Anthony Perry of Inch, who had married a local Catholic farmer's daughter, was nominated to the county committee. Graham, working with that celebrated emissary from the Leinster Executive, Putnam McCabe, had tried to galvanise the southern baronies into arming for the struggle. But after two visits to the South he failed to persuade Harvey, Colclough or Fitzgerald to step forward.[19]

Before he could put the county organisation on a regular footing, the fatal arrests of the Leinster Executive had taken place. Graham himself

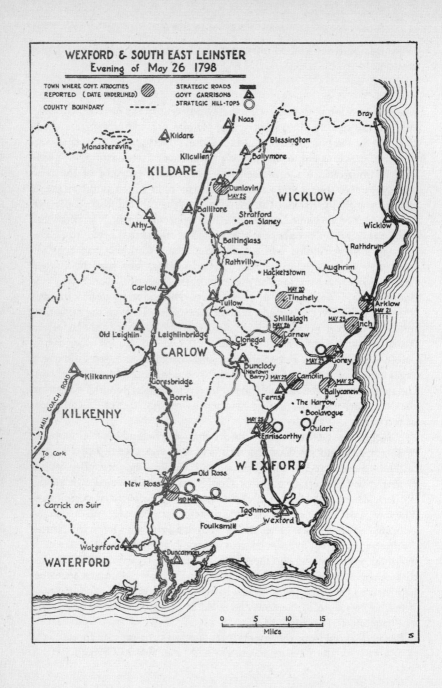

WEXFORD & SOUTH EAST LEINSTER
Evening of May 26 1798

TOWN WHERE GOVT. ATROCITIES
REPORTED (DATE UNDERLINED)
COUNTY BOUNDARY

STRATEGIC ROADS
GOVT GARRISONS
STRATEGIC HILL-TOPS

Bray

Monasterevin

Kildare

Kilcullen

Naas

Blessington

Ballymore

KILDARE

Dunlavin
MAY 25

WICKLOW

Ballitore

Athy

Stratford
on Slaney

Wicklow

Rathdrum

Baltinglass

Rathvilly

Hacketstown

Aughrim

Carlow

Tullow

MAY 20
Tinahely

Shillelagh
MAY 26
Carnew

MAY 23

Arklow
MAY 21

Old Leighlin

Leighlinbridge

CARLOW

Clonegal

Inch

Kilkenny

Goresbridge

Borris

Bunclody
(Newtown
Barry)

MAY 25

Camolin

Gorey

MAY 25

KILKENNY

Ferns

The Harrow

Ballycanew

To Cork

Carrick on Suir

Boolavogue

Oulart

MAY 25
Enniscorthy

Old Ross

WEXFORD

New Ross

MID MAY

Taghmon

Foulksmill

Wexford

Waterford

Duncannon

WATERFORD

0   5   10   15
Miles

was late and so escaped arrest, but the isolation from Dublin and the disarming of Wicklow both now checked the movement. At its apogee it had only extended to a few thousand men in these northern baronies. The mild measures of the authorities now endangered the whole organisation. Graham and his fellows became increasingly desperate.

In most respects, as we have seen, the development of Wexford's United party was much on the same lines as others in the province—Kildare's, Carlow's or Wicklow's. A smattering of Catholic and Protestant gentry gave prestige but little practical help. The heart of the movement were the Catholic *middle* class, business and professional men at the one end of the social scale, farmers and artisans at the other. All shared the optimistic belief that the revolution would give them the direct political power they still lacked, without disturbing, even in the short term, the economic position they had established in the county. But how to ensure this, how to control that undisciplined mass of small farmers and labourers, whose grievances were of so much more fundamental and bitter a character, being concerned with the very struggle to earn enough to eat and to clothe their families? To this dilemma the weak and hesitant leaders of the Wexford-Wicklow border had responded by a reckless propaganda campaign.

Reports began to circulate warning people that the Orangemen were planning a pogrom of the entire Catholic population.[20] The story, strange enough in a place where the Catholics outnumbered Protestants by thirty to one, should have been doubly absurd in Wexford where there were few or no Orangemen. But the people were already prepared to believe it. A bogus "Orangeman's Oath" had been circulated in Dublin in which every loyal Orangeman was to be "ready at a moment's warning to burn all the chapels and meeting-houses in the city and county".[21] The Orange bogey had also been exploited, as we have seen, in Cox's inflammatory broadsheet, the *Union Star* which had enjoyed wide distribution. Rumours had spread to many parts of the south that every Protestant was an Orangeman, and every Orangeman had sworn to wade up to his knees in Catholic blood.[22]

What distinguished Wexford was that such stories were officially encouraged by the party's leaders. Myles Byrne, one of Robert Graham's cousins, went out with a group of fellow farmers one night and actually impersonated a group of Orangemen. Next day some villagers near Gorey were prepared to swear to an attempted attack by Orange raiders. Byrne later claimed that his aim was to impress upon the rank and file the need for discipline against an unscrupulous enemy.[23] But in the long run, of course, exploiting the Orange bogey was a reckless policy among the credulous and half-disciplined peasantry of the district. Only the actual spark was now lacking to ignite them in an uncontrollable explosion.

In fact the nearest Wexford came to having an Orange party was a group of irregulars led by Hunter Gowan of Mount Nebo. Gowan, as we saw, was a *pied noir* who had started his life as a professional outlaw hunter. In the disturbed and mountainous borderland of the counties, where family and religious feuds were endemic, he now employed an irregular gang of Protestants called the Black Mob to control the area. These thugs had been incorporated as supplementary yeomen after the proclaiming of the county in April, and together with a few other loyalists had been enrolled in unofficial Orange Lodges.[24]

The official Orange Order had now built up its membership in Ireland since its foundation in 1795, to a total approaching one hundred thousand men, the great majority of them in Ulster. Their published aims were, supposedly respectable. They aimed to preserve the triple foundations of the Protestant establishment in Ireland—Church, Crown and Constitution —won by their ancestors of the Williamite wars a hundred years before. Their leaders were Ulster grandees like Lord Cavan and Dublin politicians like John Claudius Beresford. The liberals disapproved of them on principle, as a revival from the bad old days of race and class hatred. The Government was frightened of them, although it could not afford to offend such powerful champions of the *status quo*. But in Wexford, at any rate, they had established no official lodge and, outwardly, had no standing though this did not make their influence less pernicious.[25]

A few days before the magistrates met in the town of Wexford to proffer the olive branch to the rest of the county, their colleagues on the Wexford-Wicklow border began a campaign of terror. On Sunday May 20th the Tinahely magistrate, Mr. Morton, ordered eleven men out of their houses in the village and accused them of having been sworn into the United army. They all denied it. Two were "well flogged", in Morton's words "the others looking on", and soon they all confessed to the plot and showed where they had hidden their pikes. As the flogging campaign spread through the district, the magistrates pressed home their advantage. People fled from their homes, which were burned as a warning to the rest. Hundreds surrendered, "going on their knees", according to Mr. Morton, "praying for the king and cursing all United Irishmen". By the end of that week the United organisation in the frontier district appeared to be disintegrating, and the people were now "the most humble creatures alive".[26]

The next area to be cleared was the eastern frontier land adjoining the substantial Wicklow town of Arklow. For some months the authorities had suspected this was the underground army's headquarters for organising the borderland. But despite the presence of the regular garrison little progress had been made in detecting and breaking the conspiracy. Then on May 21st one of the Arklow leaders, alarmed perhaps by the new ruthlessness of the magistrates, made a clean breast of his part in the business, and gave the names of his associates, dramatically confirming the authorities' suspicions. Two other Arklow leaders, Philip O'Neill and Garrett Graham, were now at the mercy of the magistrates. Both their fathers were well-to-do Catholic businessmen whose property would be hostage for their sons' conduct. O'Neill surrendered himself to save the family property from being burned and his father from imprisonment. Graham broke with the movement and waited miserably to be arrested.[27]

After O'Neill's surrender, the trail led southwards into northern Wexford. Anthony Perry, the only Protestant seriously involved, was rounded up on May 23rd, and brought to the garrison town of Gorey for interrogation. The soldiers there gave him a "pitch-cap"—a frightful form of torture said to have been invented by a militia sergeant called Tom-the-Devil. Pitch was rubbed on the victim's head, gunpowder added and the mixture set fire to. Under this torture, Perry made a confession of all his seditious activities since he had been sworn a United Irishman by Matt Dowling, his solicitor in Dublin, a year before: of the party meetings in his own barn at Inch and in Thomas Howlet's mill and Moses Kehoe's house at Castletown; of the choosing of men by numbers thrown into a hat, of his own selection as delegate for the county, and of Robert Graham's two abortive journeys to Edward Fitzgerald and Bagenal Harvey in the south. After this remarkable confession, which exposed no less than twenty-two members of the United party in Wicklow and Wexford, Perry agreed to help as a prosecuting witness. He was then released on bail, in return for what the magistrates called "a candid acknowledgment and useful information".[28]

Perry's revelations spurred on the loyalists to a still more feverish hunt for the conspirators and their hidden arms. "Such exertions never were known," wrote Mr. Morton of Tinahely of that week's flogging. To add to the Black Mob of Hunter Gowan, a second group of amateur Croppyhunters was formed, under the name of the "True Blues". Night and day the frightful work went on, as army, yeomanry and volunteers interrogated suspects, especially blacksmiths, burned houses and despatched their prisoners to the overcrowded prisons at Carnew, Gorey and beyond. The hunt was now spreading well south of the Wicklow border. On May 23rd, according to Morton's report, "Twenty-one smiths and principals in that Infernal United Business" were sent off from Camolin to prison.[29] "I trust in God we will soon pull down the Cropys," wrote the postmaster at Arklow the next day. "We put on pitched caps on some of them—there is a great many of the vilins Run Away."[30]

By Friday May 25th the Croppy-hunt had reached the villages of Camolin and Ballycanew. The sixty-odd members of the local yeomanry were not yet on permanent duty, and their sabres and carbines had only arrived from Dublin a few days before. But busy work was now found for the corps, escorting parties of prisoners on the roads south, patrolling the neighbourhood, burning haggards and destroying the homes of wanted men. Whether they took any suspects and flogged them is not recorded. But if they showed more self-restraint than the reckless magistrates of the borderland, it was now too late for this lesson to be heeded.[31]

A wave of hysteria was sweeping southwards to the peasantry of central Wexford, fed by tales of atrocity some of which were only too well authenticated. Hunter Gowan, it was said, had marched into the town of Gorey with the amputated finger of one of his victims stuck on the point of his sword. The trophy was then used to stir the punch at an Orange orgy at the local inn. There were reports of wanton murders by gangs of Orangemen and of tortures cheerfully inflicted by Archibald Jacob, the Enniscorthy magistrate, who now went out on his rounds with an executioner in train, complete with hanging rope and cat-o'-nine-tails. In Enniscorthy he had hanged a man and then dragged his body backwards and forwards through the marketplace. At Ballaghkeen he had flogged a man to death and threatened the same treatment to anyone who was caught absent from his house. There was even the story of a wandering hermit at New Ross who had been tortured in the barrack yard. They had half-hanged him three times, and flogged him four times and all to no purpose. He had been found with two Catholic prayer books—regarded as evidence enough he had been sworn as a member of the conspiracy.[32]

So terrified were people of being flogged that those who had no hidden pikes looked about desperately for some to surrender. How could he confess to what he didn't know, a labourer asked Mr. Gordon, the clergyman from near Gorey, and how could he surrender the pike he had not yet been issued with? He was told that he would not be touched if he stayed quietly at home. But the thought of the cat-o'-nine-tails preyed on his mind. He could neither eat nor sleep. On Friday, according to Gordon's account, the man"fell on his face and expired in a little grave by my house".[33]

That Friday night the mass hysteria reached a crescendo. Whole villages were emptied as the people fled out into the fields to escape the Orangemen they believed were planning to burn the roofs over them. If educated Catholics like Thomas Cloney, who lived at Moneyhore, a place not yet visited by the military, honestly believed that there was now to be an indiscriminate massacre of Catholics, how much more terrifying was it to the ignorant peasantry of the neighbourhood. "No one slept in their homes," he wrote, "the very whistling of the birds seemed to report the approach of the enemy." Half dead with fright, people dragged their furniture out of their houses and spent the night in the ditches beside them. It was like a scene from the Apocalypse: women wailed, children shrieked, men prayed for deliverance, or else swore vengeance on their enemies.[34] To heighten the fever, atrocity stories were deliberately circulated by some reckless members of the United party, confirming the people's fear of the coming pogrom. At dead of night a horseman galloped through the village of Oulart shouting, "Get up, get up and fight, or you will be burned or butchered."[35]

Goaded on by either side, the people still hung back from the abyss. But for how long? In a few places the landlords were still trusted and they did their best to check the hysteria; in more cases it was the Catholic priests who retained some authority over the people. In the last few weeks many priests had helped to persuade their flocks to renounce their plans for insurrection and surrender their pikes. At this moment of hysteria the people turned to them once again, and even now catastrophe might have been avoided. Most of the priests, no doubt, told the people not to believe absurd stories of massacre, but instead to return quietly to their homes and trust to the good intentions of the Government.[36]

The two exceptions were the curates of two villages where the Camolin cavalry were now attempting to disarm the people; Father John Murphy of Boulavogue and Father Michael Murphy of Ballycanew.

Father John described as "about 45 years old, light complexioned, bald pated, and about 5 feet 9 inches high", must have seemed a typical country curate of his period. Son of a local farmer, he had been educated at the local "hedge school"—the only sort of education for most Catholic children of that period. After deciding to become a priest he had been sent to the seminary at Seville in Spain, where he was ordained. And in due course he found himself back in Wexford as curate at Boulavogue, with several hundred souls under his care.[37] During the preceding weeks he had co-operated, with thirteen other priests and more than seven thousand parishioners, in drawing up a testimonial of loyalty to the Government. They pledged their "unalterable attachment to his Sacred Majesty George the Third". They assured their Protestant brethren of their utmost abhorrence of "seditious and levelling principles". They even offered a reward for the arrest of the "wicked and designing" persons who were spreading rumours that the Catholics were planning a rising.[38]

Father Michael Murphy came from much the same background. A course at the Irish college at Bordeaux had been cut short by the French Revolution, on which he had returned to Wexford. In the previous weeks he, too, had advertised in the press the devotion to the Government of himself and his flock.[39]

Whether this show of loyalty at that period was genuine is impossible to guess. Neither of these men, at any rate, was now prepared to resist the popular tide running in the opposite direction. For days they had heard the ghastly tales of torture and massacre. The yeomanry had now arrived in person, and were apparently acting the part expected of them.[40]

It was the afternoon of Saturday May 26th. As the priests hesitated, two extraordinary pieces of intelligence swept through the villages of north Wexford.

The first was the news of two terrible atrocities. At Dunlavin, as we have already seen, the panic-struck garrison had taken out their prisoners on Friday and shot them. On Saturday morning a drunken mob of loyalists at Carnew had taken twenty-eight prisoners from the old castle and executed them in a ball-alley. To the Wexford men, it seemed there was now an official policy of extermination.[41]

The second piece of news was still more extraordinary, though it was what all the United men had been hoping for. Wild rumours of the storming of Naas and Carlow, of the capture of Ballitore and Kilcullen and most of County Kildare, had at last reached Wexford.[42] Father Michael was still undecided, but it was enough for Father John. In this feverish state of affairs, with the people intoxicated by the thought of success, as much as they were thrown into hysteria by the fear of torture, the insurgents could restrain themselves no longer, and Father John agreed to lead the campaign of resistance. But what could they achieve with a handful of men, many of whom had surrendered their arms, unless help speedily arrived from elsewhere?

About eight o'clock that evening, a patrol from the Camolin yeomanry, under the command of the local gentlemen, Lieutenant Bookey and Mr. John Donovan, were sent to search for arms at the farm of a man called Boyne about a mile south west of the small village of the Harrow. Between the village and Boyne's farm they found the road blocked by a party of Father John's farmers armed with pikes. According to one account Bookey and Donovan forced their way through the road-block but were then left to their fate by the rest of the cavalry.[43] According to another account, Bookey rashly harangued the mob, who outnumbered his men by about two to one, to try to persuade them to surrender their arms.[44] Bookey and Donovan, at any rate, were brought down in a shower of bullets and stones, and then finished off by the pikemen. The rest of the party galloped back to Ferns with the news of the outrage. As darkness fell parties of yeomen poured out of Ferns and Enniscorthy bent on avenging Bookey's death by shooting anyone they suspected of being responsible.[45]

Meanwhile Father John, no doubt amazed with the ease with which his half-armed men had despatched the over-confident cavalry, wasted no time on aimless revenge. If his aim was to raise the county, his most pressing need was arms. A party was accordingly sent to raid Lord Mountnorris's house at Camolin where the Camolin cavalry had deposited the captured arms. Fortunately for him, Lord Mountnorris had not yet arrived from Dublin to take command; the rebels plundered the empty house, recovered a great store of captured arms and some of the yeomen's own carbines, and entertained themselves in Lord Mountnorris's cellar.[46] Elsewhere that night's raids for arms were swift and ruthless. About midnight Bookey's house was burned to the ground; his two servants narrowly escaped with their lives.[47] An hour or two later the glebe-house of Mr. Burrowes, the Protestant clergyman and brother of a prominent liberal of Oulart, where several Protestants had taken refuge, was surrounded by five hundred rebels, who proceeded to lay siege to it. After a feeble defence, some sort of parley began, in which Mr. Burrowes offered to surrender his party's arms. In the confusion he was shot down, and the rebels then piked seven of his parishioners who had tried to defend the house, including Mr. Burrowes' sixteen year old son. The women and children, about half a dozen in number, were spared.[48]

The whole country to the south east of Ferns now seemed to be burning. Near Ballyadams, a man was woken by the barking of dogs and sound of firing. He counted more than seventeen houses on fire around him: all of them belonged to Protestants.[49] "This morning at dawn," wrote a Camolin cavalry officer "the country presented a frightful appearance—

houses in flames on every side, and loyal families flying into Ferns for protection."[50]

The yeomen added to the blaze. First they burnt Father John's house at Tincurry, then his chapel at Boulavogue, His vestments and personal papers, wrapped in a bundle and hidden in the garden, were brought back as loot. Two other yeomanry detachments had joined the Camolin corps, and together they made a broad sweep through the county, burned a hundred and seventy houses of suspects and probably shot as many of the peasantry.[51] Meanwhile, well disciplined detachments of militia from the Arklow and Wexford garrisons were converging on the rebels from north and south. By the afternoon of that day, Whit Sunday, Father John's party was apparently surrounded. He had taken his stand at Oulart Hill, the highest point of the ridge running across the middle of the county. Oulart was already conspicuous for the flames from the burning of Mr. Burrowes' glebe-house. As the loyalists streamed into the garrison town, the peasantry fled to the protection of Father John's camp at Oulart. A few extra guns had been procured, which a party had seized from another clergyman, Mr. Turner of Ballingale, after killing him and five of his parishioners. Some wild-fowlers from the coast had also joined them and, a still more useful addition, two of the yeomanry from near Oulart, Morgan Byrne and Edward Roche. Otherwise Father John's party, though nearly a thousand stronger, was still exceedingly ill-equipped to meet a force of regular troops.[52]

In the town of Wexford, the garrison's headquarters about fifteen miles to the south, people knew nothing of these events. Since the magistrates had met for the quarter sessions on Wednesday, little had been achieved— except the alarming discovery from Perry's confession that Bagenal Harvey of Bargay Castle and Edward Fitzgerald of New Park were United leaders. In fact both seemed by now to have abandoned all hope of the rising. Fitzgerald spent all that Saturday at New Park helping the local magistrate issue certificates of protection. To get one of these a man needed some arms to surrender. The demand for pikes for this purpose so far outpaced supply that people were bidding a premium of ten times their real value.[53] Fear of being without a protection was increased by eye-witness accounts of a flogging near Gorey. Next morning, the victim's neighbours reported it was "as though a pig had been killed there".[54]

As a magistrate, Bagenal Harvey himself issued protections and himself accepted the surrender of arms. On Saturday evening he brought them for safe-keeping to Wexford, only to be himself arrested and put in the town gaol on the order of the sheriff. During the night Fitzgerald was brought in to join him, and the third gentleman implicated, Dr. John Colclough, followed soon after.[55]

Despite these successes, some of the loyalists at Wexford were still disturbed by their situation. On Saturday the first accounts of the Kildare rising reached the town. Closer to hand there were ominous signs. Mrs. Jane Adams, a Protestant lady who lived just outside the town, has left us a full account of the events of these weeks. On Saturday she wrote: "The country wears a most alarming appearance. My father laughs at the idea of danger; but I strongly suspect we are surrounded by rebels and spies. Yesterday a rather genteel looking man came up the lawn to me, and said he wished much to have the pleasure of instructing a few young ladies in geography, and begged I would allow him to teach my family. I told him my daughters were too young, and that I did not think he was likely to get any pupils in the neighbourhood. This day as I was walking in the shrubbery near the road, I looked out on hearing a number of horses and saw the same young man under an escort going to gaol . . . there was found upon him a plan of all our houses, the names and number of the inhabitants, and a copy of Paine's *Age of Reason*."[56]

Next day on the morning of Whit Sunday, news of the Oulart rising began to reach Wexford. People who had treated the Kildare news lightly, or even welcomed it as it meant the conspiracy had at last been forced into the open, now learnt the rebels were only twenty miles to the north. Rumours exaggerated the danger. One clergyman told his congregation that they must hurry over the communion service as the church might be surrounded at any moment: on his way there that morning he had seen smiths openly at work forging pikes. An express was supposed to have arrived with the news that seven thousand rebels were within three miles of the town. People were reported to be trying to take ship for England; they included the family of the High Sheriff, Mr. Perceval. But most people remained calm.[57] Wexford was a walled town, easy to defend, and the garrison comprised a strong detachment of the North Cork militia, with additional yeomanry, under Colonel Foote, a veteran of the American war.[58]

Before mid-day the drum beat to arms and the garrision mustered outside the barrack. Although it was noticed with disquiet that the great bulk of the yeomanry were absent—some had in fact deserted to the insurgents —the North Cork militia were eager to get to grips with the "banditti". In due course, a hundred and nine strong, they marched out towards

Oulart, with an escort of nineteen yeomen cavalry. The day was exceedingly hot, and the road led through heavy sand.[59]

After several hours the soldiers reached a village called Ballinamonabeg where there was a public house whose owner had recently surrendered a pike. After helping themselves liberally to beer and spirits, they set fire to the building. Someone suggested burning the nearby Catholic chapel, but this proposal was rejected by the officers, on considering that almost half of the nineteen yeomen and the great majority of the North Cork militia were themselves Catholics.[60] About mid-afternoon they breasted Boula-boy ridge to find Father John's pikemen drawn up in a commanding position on Oulart Hill across the shallow valley ahead of them.

Colonel Foote knew enough about military matters to see the danger of a frontal attack. Even with seasoned troops it would have been a risky undertaking for men to charge up that stony hill at an enemy ten times their number, unless their force was properly supported by artillery. As it was, his infantry, the North Cork militia, were raw conscripts from one of the poorest and most backward parts of the country. Their natural way of fighting was in the rough and ready manner of the pub and the fairground. In the last few weeks they had acquired a little experience of burning and looting, and even the occasional murder. But their ideas of regular warfare, like those of most of the Irish militia, must have been limited to the figures of the parade ground. Of marksmanship and of tactics they were ignorant. Worst of all, they were so undisciplined, that it would have been a heart-breaking task to teach them. It was men like these that Abercromby had described in his famous outburst as "formidable to everyone but the enemy".[61]

Across the Oulart valley Father John's party waited in silence. There were women and boys among them, and many of them had never seen a redcoat. Breathlessly they gazed on the hundred militia men below. The sight was understandably alarming. Many of their number were ill-armed; even the more experienced of them had never seen a house on fire until the preceding night.

As the United forces began to melt away, their leaders made desperate efforts to rally them: Father John in his black cassock, the two ex-yeomen, Edward Roche and Morgan Byrne, in their scarlet regimentals. "Shame, shame!" Byrne is reported to have shouted as he rode up and down the line. "Are you afraid of the redcoats? Look at this," and he tore open his scarlet jacket. "If you met them there below in a fair, man for man, would their caps and red coats frighten you?" The desertions were halted, but as much by the fear of the cavalry that had meanwhile surrounded the hill, as through the eloquence of Mr. Byrne. There were now only five hundred men in the rebel force. Below them a party of soldiers, hoping to tempt them to leave their position, had set fire to some cabins in the village. The insurgents stayed obstinately on the hill.[62]

While Byrne had been trying to rally one side, Colonel Foote was striving as valiantly to restrain the other. His own view was that the rebels were too strong to be attacked; indeed he needed a reinforcement of forty men from Wexford to secure his own retreat. This was too much for the Irish gentlemen in his command, after the scenes of desolation they had witnessed that morning, and too much for their men, many of whom were still warm with drink. The cry went up, "We can beat the enemy out of the field." For a moment Colonel Foote's back was turned, as he wrote out a message for reinforcements. The next moment he looked up, and saw a sight as strange and terrible as any in war.[63]

Without his permission Major Lombard, the second in command, had given the order to charge. A hundred men surged across the valley and up the stony hillside. To make better speed they had stripped off their heavy military boots and ran barefoot. Long before they reached the first of the enemy marksmen, they began firing wild volleys into the air. In vain Colonel Foote tried to recall them. As he galloped up the hill, his officers and men—two majors, three lieutenants, an ensign and a hundred and three militia men—were swallowed up before his eyes.

A few were shot down at fifteen yards range by the fifty-odd men with guns and blunderbusses who had formed the enemy's first line of defence. But most were beaten and hacked to death with pikes and scythes and spades and pitchforks—and even stones from the hillside—by the desperate men waiting close to the summit. The carnage was so sudden and so complete that few of the soldiers even tried to escape. These were rounded up one by one by the peasants, though they waved their missals and cried out they "were Catholics too". No quarter was given to them, or to the wounded. Even the drummer, who had been left behind drunk by the pub they had burnt, was taken and piked.[64]

Two hours later the people saw Colonel Foote, a sergeant and two privates ride back across the bridge into Wexford. At first they were too dazed to explain what had happened, and indeed the truth was hard to grasp. They were the sole survivors of all that force.[65]

Bad as the disaster was in military terms—the town of Wexford was now virtually without a garrison—its effect on morale was still more serious.

As the news spread through the town, the unfortunate wives and children of the dead men ran "screaming through the streets". There were violent recriminations against the cavalry for deserting the militia, and equally violent moves to lynch the United Irish prisoners in the town gaol, who included Bagenal Harvey and Edward Fitzgerald.[66] "Every moment becomes more frightful," wrote Mrs. Adams that evening.[67] The townsmen were pressed into service as a home guard. The thatch was stripped off some of the cabins, as a precaution against fire. Refugees crowded into the town including "women of fortune, half-dressed, some having neither shoes nor stockings with their children on their backs".[68]

Ripples of panic spread in all directions. Refugees poured into Gorey, to the north, where the thirty men of the North Cork who made up the meagre garrison were in two minds whether to abandon the town, or to try to defend it. With evident misgivings they had built barricades with carts and wagons across the town's single main street, and stationed some irregulars in the windows overlooking the route the enemy would take. The arrival of reinforcements from Arklow coincided with the news of the regiment's disaster at Oulart and the town was promptly abandoned.[69]

Mr. Gordon, the Protestant clergyman, has described the confusion that followed the sudden order to retreat. Without the least foundation the loyalists believed that the enemy were approaching rapidly; terrified people ran in all directions, harnessing up their horses for flight. Soon the road northwards was filled with a train of cars loaded with women and children, while other women, carrying children on their backs, followed on foot. It was exceptionally hot and dry. People coughed and choked in the clouds of dust raised by the carts. Behind them, according to Gordon, Gorey presented a macabre appearance. A woman ran through the streets shrieking with mad laughter; an abandoned pack of hounds yelped mournfully; and six prisoners, shot by the garrison, lay writhing in the main street.

At Arklow the refugees found a little comfort. The garrison commander at first refused anyone admittance, then agreed to admit the better class of refugees, including Mr. Gordon, for a short respite. All the loyalists' arms were confiscated and burned. One man who objected to this, the church clerk from Camolin, was shot by the guard. That night the mass of Gorey loyalists, exhausted and panic-stricken found asylum under the hedges beside the road.[70]

The immediate threat, however, was not to Gorey, but to the much larger town of Enniscorthy. After his dazzling victory Father John's army, increasing every moment, moved north to Camolin; and then turned west to Ferns on the Enniscorthy road. Nearby a second rising had taken place that morning, led by the other Father Murphy, Father Michael Murphy of Ballycanew. They had been dispersed by the local corps of cavalry, which had retreated into the garrison town of Enniscorthy,[71] after shooting a number of stragglers. The remnants of this party were now able to link up with the main body of men from Oulart.

Early next morning, which was Whit Monday, Father John's army marched into Ferns. They found the town had been abandoned by the garrison the previous day. One of the few Protestants to stay behind was a Quaker rope merchant, who had been assured of his safety by a United friend, and took comfort, as he said, "like Gideon . . . in the Midianites camp". His house was soon filled by the insurgents who met him and his family with "caresses and marks of friendship", and declared that "they would fight for them and protect them and put them in their bosoms". Their only request was for food, and indeed they seemed to be "in extreme want of something to eat". Some of them no doubt, had eaten nothing since the rising began two nights before. The rope merchant gladly gave them some food which he had prepared for loyalist refugees. They had special respect for him, it turned out, because a few days before he had refused to sell the militia some rope for hanging United men.[72]

The insurgents were less respectful towards the abandoned homes of loyalists—including the elegant palace of Dr. Cleaver, the Protestant bishop. "An undisciplined and ungovernable multitude" poured through the town, gutting the houses of the people they considered Orangemen. They burst into the Bishop's palace, helped themselves from his cellar, ripped the vellum off the books in the library to use it as saddle covers, ransacked the palace and left it a smoking ruin.[73]

To the garrison of Enniscorthy, seven miles away to the east, the burning of Ferns confirmed their fears that they would be the next to be attacked.

For two days now they had observed the progress of the enemy to the east. On Saturday they had heard the first garbled reports of the rising: a girl had galloped into the town with the news of a massacre at Scarawalsh. The drum then beat to arms, and the yeomen marched round the main squares singing "God Save the King" and other loyal tunes. On Sunday they learnt of the piking of Lieutenant Bookey. All that day refugees had poured into the town with tales of burnings and massacres, including the destruction of their own comrades at Oulart. The garrison's alarm was heightened by the thought that some of the refugees might be enemy agents, and a few were arrested. That night, as some of the loyalist refugees were sitting down to dinner, they heard a bustle in the street, and found a man hanged from a ladder. His name was Murphy and he was supposed to have been implicated in Bookey's death. It was not clear on whose orders he had been hanged.[74]

By Monday morning the garrison commander, Captain Snowe, had organised the defence of the town. His total force was comparatively large: eighty of the North Cork militia, and two hundred from three local corps of yeomanry. To these were added on Monday morning a number of volunteers in civilian clothes. The total garrison probably exceeded four hundred. But how to dispose them against a force ten or twenty times more numerous?[75]

Snowe's plan was probably as good as circumstances allowed. In the Middle Ages the town has been a natural fortress dominating a strategic crossing of the Slaney. But by 1798 it sprawled across either bank of the river, offering numerous avenues through which an attacker could force an entry.[76] Snowe stationed his men at the two main ones: Captain Cornock and the Enniscorthy infantry at the Duffrey Gate to the north west, his own militia men at the bridge to the south east. The rest of the soldiers occupied two central strong points—the marketplace and the castle, while the civilian volunteers took their stand in the windows of the houses along the street, from which they were supposed to fire down on the attackers.[77]

Snowe had anticipated that the enemy would divide their forces in two columns and attack simultaneously from either bank of the river, which was low and easy to ford, owing to the unusually dry weather. At about one o'clock the men from the outposts galloped in with the news that the rebel army was advancing in one immense body on the Duffrey Gate to the north west. Even if there was time to concentrate his men at the point of attack, Snowe could have few illusions of his chances of success.[78]

The Wexford insurgent forces were not only far more numerous than any other local army in the rebellion. They were led by men of a completely different calibre—who had an insight into tactics and military organisation. Maddened by the stories of Government atrocities, and spurred on by their own successes against regular troops, they had become, in a matter of two days, a most formidable adversary. One more victory, they knew, and the whole of the south east would be theirs. It was only another step to the capital itself. With this prize so close to their grasp, who could wonder at the reckless courage with which they fought.

Two things, Snowe must have recognised, could save Enniscorthy from the rebels. First, some cannon to break up the waves of attackers with grape-shot. So scarce was ordnance in the Irish army that none had yet been issued to any of the four militia garrisons in the county.[79] Second, superior discipline could make up for lack of numbers. But scant reliance could be placed on the gentlemen of the yeomanry who were perfect amateurs, even if the militia should, for once, behave themselves.

By the efforts of its own garrison, then, Enniscorthy could not be expected to hold out long against the rebels. But how long would it take the Government to send a powerful and disciplined army to the rescue?

4

English Imbecility, Irish Ferocity

Dublin and surrounding counties, May 26th–29th

Believe me, we are in a very poor way. Strange indiscipline in the Troops, perfect incapacity in most of the officers. The Government itself may be considered as proceeding from an union of English imbecility with Irish ferocity . . .

Lord Wycombe to Lord Holland, June 8, 1798

ON SATURDAY the 26th, the day that Father John first raised his standard at Oulart, the fortunes of the Government seemed to have reached their nadir.

They had abandoned to the United army the whole county of Kildare, except for the border towns. They had thus lost control of the strategic roads to the South—those to Cork and Limerick. They had allowed a large force of rebels to blockade a third strategic road, running to the north west by way of County Meath. And still they felt too weak to mount any serious counter-attack. Camden believed, it appears, that the real object of the rebel offensive was the capital itself. Until the Dublin garrison was reinforced from somewhere—from the North, the South or from Britain—he dared not let them far out of his sight.

On Saturday, however, the counter-attack began more or less by accident, and the results were astonishingly successful.

The United army in Meath was established astride the Navan road a few miles north of the village of Dunshaughlin. Their camp was on the summit of a hill, visible for miles around from the flat, fertile plains of Meath. Not only would it make an excellent rallying point. Its stone walls and grassy banks could give good protection against small arms, though not of course against artillery. Still more important, perhaps, the place had once played a dominant part in Ireland's national history, and could bring a glow of patriotic pride to the pikemen fighting to restore their country's independence.[1] It was Tara, the seat of the High Kings of Ireland.

Apart from this happy choice of camp site, the United leaders had made little headway in organising their huge, motley army. On paper they were, of course, organised already according to the United system: a colonel for each barony of the county, a captain for each parish within the barony and so on, with an adjutant-general in overall command. But on paper they were also to have been only one part of the combined forces of the Midlands, aided and assisted by their friends in the militia and yeomanry. "On the arrival of your friends," their instructions had run, "the Standard is to be erected on Tara Hill, where two pieces of cannon are to be placed."[2] The standard was flying all right, but where were the friends and the two pieces of cannon?

In truth the great army at Tara Hill, though Dublin might quail at its name, had lost the initiative after the first heady days of the rising, when the Tree of Liberty had been placed at Dunshaughlin, and their leaders had neither the military insight, nor the organising ability to regain it. On Friday, however, they had received useful reinforcements from Kildare, men armed with guns taken from the ironworks at Lucan. It was one of their number—the son of the local innkeeper—who now took the supreme command of the eight thousand men with green cockades swarming over the hilltop.[3]

In the skirmishes two days before they had seized two important prizes: the baggage of two companies of a Scotch Fencible regiment that included thirty-three sets of arms and upwards of nine thousand ball cartridges, and ten Highlanders who were guarding them. These arms were now distributed, and the Highlanders were forced, at bayonet point to drill the men in their use. Three pairs of green colours were set up. And forty camp fires blazed on the hillside, producing immense quantities of boiled mutton and other plundered delicacies. By Saturday the United army felt ready for anything, and a provocative message was sent to the local magnate, Lord Fingall, challenging the royal forces to attack them.[4]

Lord Fingall was a rich Catholic landlord, and no less loyal to the Government for that. The friends and tenants who comprised his troop of yeomanry had watched helplessly while the rebels plundered the countryside. On Saturday, however, three companies of Scotch Fencibles had appeared, and began to organise the yeomanry for the counter-attack. Strange to say the Fencibles' commander, a certain Captain Blanche, had no instructions of any sort from the Government. He was not intimidated by the huge rebel army that had sent General Craig, the commander of the Dublin garrison, with twelve pieces of artillery, scurrying back into the capital. At any rate, he was determined to search out and destroy the rebels who had stolen his regiment's baggage.[5]

About six o'clock in the evening, Captain Blanche, with a total of three hundred Fencibles and yeomanry, and a 6-pounder, toiled up the hill towards the enemy's stronghold beside the churchyard on the summit. The place seemed black with rebels. The enemy had extended their line across the grassy courtyard between two royal tumuli that effectively foiled a direct attack by the Government forces. They seemed in good spirits. Upon the approach of Blanche and his men they "put their hats on their pikes, the entire length of the line, and gave three cheers". Their commander was dressed in the white uniform of the Kildare militia, from which he had absconded, though he was popularly believed to be a French officer. He advanced from the army and made "a very pompous salute" before returning "with great precipitation".[6]

Blanche decided upon an oblique attack. The yeomanry were to attack from the flanks, while the 6-pounder played on their centre. Until dusk the battle was hotly contested. "On approaching the churchyard gate," he later reported, "we met with the most daring and obstinate resistance . . . At one period as the King's troops did not gain the least advantage . . . and finding the men's ammunition almost expended, and our situation getting still more critical, I found it absolutely necessary to make one decisive effort by charging the rebels which was gallantly executed by the Grenadiers."[7]

Despite this desperate charge, the battle remained in doubt, as the yeoman cavalry who were supposed to mark the enemy's right flank had unaccountably disappeared. (In due course a court martial caught up with them). In the confusion of the moment the 6-pounder nearly fell to the enemy. But in their eagerness to seize it they exposed themselves beyond the walls and earthworks and then, in Blanche's words, the cannon "returned their cordial invitation, which crowned our operations with a complete victory".

Despite losing thirteen men killed and twenty-eight wounded—about an eighth of all their force—it was indeed a heartening result for the Fencibles, and yeomanry. Next morning, 350 rebels were found dead on the battlefield, together with immense numbers of pikes, muskets, fowling pieces, swords, spits and reaping hooks. To crown it all Blanche succeeded in recovering almost all the baggage and ammunition boxes stolen from his regiment three days before except for the actual cartridges expended in the action.

Strategically, too, the battle proved an almost unqualified success. True, some stragglers were reported to have crossed over into Kildare where they linked up with a group of guerrilla fighters encamped in an island on the bog. But in Meath itself, and the North Midlands, the rebels were, at a single stroke, completely dispersed; a fire-break between North and South created; the road to the North re-opened; and the threat from this source to the capital removed.

The news of this victory was not, however, an unqualified blessing for the Government. That all this could be achieved by a couple of companies of Highlanders and a few local yeomanry was not, of course, lost on their detractors. As usual, the ultras were baying for blood: summary executions in Dublin, exemplary punishment in the field. Even the Government staunchest supporter, Lord Clare, found the military policy "inexplicable".[8] After completely routing the rebels at Kilcullen Bridge, General Dundas had retreated to Naas for some reason best known to himself, thus allowing the rebels to seize most of the County Kildare, and virtually blockade the capital. And still there was no news of a counter-attack.

The truth was that, with a hostile Parliament at his back, and at his side a general in whom he could put no trust, Camden had left it to the men in the field to crush the rebels as best they could. The outcome was the usual muddle and confusion and a grave risk of once again exacerbating the situation.

In the last four days the man chiefly responsible for the strategy of tackling the rebels had been General Sir Ralph Dundas, Commander of the Midland district. His exaggerated fear of the enemy's military strength, leading to his precipitate retreat to Naas had proved a costly error. But Dundas, unsuited as he was to the job in that way, had also insight into the situation that was rare for an Irish general of this period. He must have recognised that most of the Kildare rebels had been caught up in the affair almost by accident; that they now found themselves in a blind alley, with little prospect of making it a national rising; that a small minority had been responsible for the murders, and the rest were now suddenly sick of the whole business. In short, Dundas was ready to impose a surrender in Kildare on generous terms. For the Government it would be politic as well as humane: not only to avoid the horrors of a protracted guerrilla war so close to the capital, but also to free a large army for service in quelling the rising elsewhere.

The Kildare rebels had four strategic camps, each of them in a suitably conspicuous place: at Knockallen Hill, commanding the Liffey bridge at Kilcullen; at Gibbet Rath astride the Cork and Limerick road across the Curragh; at Timahoe on the edge of the great Bog of Allen; and at Blackmore Hill on the flank of the Wicklow mountains astride the border.[9] From the first of these, the camp at Knockallen Hill, a deputation now reached General Dundas, offering surrender in exchange for complete pardon. Dundas's civil reply to this encouraged the rebels to try and improve on these terms. "We have deep grievances," one source quoted them as saying, "which we are well able to redress, but we can forgive and forget, and if Lord Edward Fitzgerald and our other friends are set at liberty we will lay down our arms."[10] In a different version of this affair, from one of their own side, they demanded an assurance that the Government would abandon the policy of free quarters and house burning and restore all confiscated property.

When news of these remarkable proceedings reached Camden on Sunday he sent for his aide-de-camp, Colonel Walpole, to refuse this "arrogant" offer pointblank. The only offer he could accept was submission, and the surrender of their leaders. Later that day he sent down the Commander-in-Chief himself to impose these terms.[11] But fortunately for the rebels Dundas had already committed himself to their submitting on more generous lines. Next day Lake found himself forced to acquiesce in a general surrender in which Dundas himself, attended by only two dragoons, climbed to the summit of the hill and personally received the surrender of the three thousand men there. Dundas took off his hat, thanked the rebels for their sensible behaviour, and assured them of protection. The pikes and guns were deposited in an enormous pile—as high as the Royal Exchange according to one of the rebels. And then, under the baleful eye of three regiments of infantry with four pieces of cannon, the entire rebel army, leaders and all, were allowed to disperse to their homes.[12]

Dundas's act of clemency, outrageous as it may have seemed to the Hawks in Dublin, was a brilliant stroke to help restore the people's confidence in the Government. Next day he began to arrange a similar surrender from the larger camp on the Curragh.[13] But before anything could be concluded, an appalling tragedy had intervened to blast all hopes of a quick end to rebellion in the Midlands.

For six days now the whole province of Munster and other parts of the south west had been cut off from all communication with the capital. At first it was not clear what had happened, then reports of the rising began to arrive. The alarm increased to panic. In Cork they feared an insurrection. Characteristically, the various local commanders proved incapable of acting together. The commander of the southern district, General Sir James Stewart, had been on the verge of a nervous breakdown for some time. General John, later Sir John, Moore who was now summoned to his headquarters found it in a state of hopeless "confusion and indecision".

No plan could be co-ordinated for self-defence, let alone for the re-opening of the road to the North.[14]

On Sunday, however, the Limerick commander, General Sir James Duff, had decided to act on his own accord. Leaving the yeomanry to guard the country, he organised a flying column of sixty dragoons, about 350 militia and six field pieces. He commandeered cars for the infantry, and by forced marches covered the hundred-odd miles in the remarkably short space of two days and nights. On Tuesday morning his relief column galloped into the smoking ruins of Kildare town.[15]

Various outrages had been committed there by the rebels including the killing of several loyalists, but there was one which touched Duff's men particularly closely. A seventeen-year-old officer, Lieutenant William Gifford, had been found by the rebels in the mail coach from Limerick on the first day of the rising, and piked to death. By an unfortunate chance he was the son of a popular captain in the Dublin militia which made up Duff's principal force. Determined to "make a dreadful example of the rebels", as their commander put it, they marched grimly on towards the rebel camp on the Curragh.[16]

Meanwhile, unknown to Duff, the Curragh rebels had begun to make terms with Dundas. The Protestant clergyman of Kildare, who was in the rebels' hands, was one of the intermediaries. An enormous gathering, perhaps six thousand strong, had assembled with their arms at a prehistoric fort called Gibbet Rath. An express was sent to warn Duff's force of the impending surrender. A few minutes more, and the business would have been over. But just at that moment the rebels found Duff's army advancing in full cry upon their rear.

What exactly happened next in the tragedy remains disputed. Duff claimed that he sent on some yeomen to tell the people that they would not be hurt if they laid down their arms. Unfortunately the rebels fired on this party, and from that moment they were attacked on all sides. "Nothing could stop," Duff admitted rather lamely, "the Rage of the troops."[17]

A ghastly scene followed. Several thousand people, many unarmed, and huddled together on a great plain without a scrap of cover were set upon by an infuriated pack of militia and dragoons. Three hundred and fifty were cut down in the massacre, with virtually no loss to the army. In their enthusiasm for this task, the Dublin militia even mistook Kildare's Protestant clergyman for a Catholic priest and were preparing to hang him with a chain from one of the cannons, when the colonel, who happened to be his brother-in-law, pointed out the mistake.[18] The ordinary peasantry were less fortunate in their relatives. Their bodies lay on the hillside gashed with sabres and piled up where they had fallen. That night women came out from Kildare and turned over the bodies one by one to find their sons and husbands.[19]

On reaching Dublin, General Duff found himself the hero of the city. His embarrassment at this rôle, however, was nothing to the Government's. The military results of the massacre were to disperse the Kildare rebels and reverse the process of pacification. Politically, the action was equally damaging. The ultras singled out Duff's action for praise. At the same time Dundas's act of clemency was ridiculed in private and denounced in public. "It is impossible for me to state to you in adequate terms the rage which now prevails against Dundas," wrote Beresford to Auckland on the day after the massacre, "and through him against Government. The most wanton murders are being committed . . . on the one hand the cry is for instant trial and execution, and on the other no steps are taken."

Once again Camden found, to add to his other troubles, a political crisis on his hands. The ultra-loyalist party got up a motion in parliament which, by praising Duff, in effect censored the Government, Despite the usual honeyed words from Lord Castlereagh, the loyalists refused to be reassured. Camden wrote to Pitt: the people were literally "mad with fury" against the rebels.

His own policy, as he defined it in another letter to London, was to try to arrange a surrender without "compromising the dignity of Government or irritating the feelings of the country". What a hopeless task this was he did not conceal from himself. The country, that is the loyal minority, was "scarcely to be satisfied with anything short of extirpation" of the other three-quarters of the population.[20] As usual the political crisis robbed Camden of what little energy he possessed. Without any coherent plan for a counter-attack, the Government found the rebellion passing into its second week.

Meanwhile the other commanders in the Midlands, left to their own devices, were tackling the same problem more delicately than Duff, but the results were equally disastrous.

At Ballitore, the prospects for negotiations had seemed unusually favourable. Apart from the wanton shooting of a militia sergeant and a yeomanry lieutenant, the insurgents had respected the terms on which the loyalists had surrendered the village to them: security for "persons and property". This humanity was due to the popularity and perhaps influence of the Quaker colony in the village. And it was natural that they should now play an important part in persuading the people to make their peace with the Government.

The garrison commander at Athy, five miles to the west, was Colonel Campbell, the man who first put up the triangle outside his barracks and made flogging official policy. On Saturday he received a message from Abraham Shackleton, Ballitore's Quaker schoolmaster, to say that the people offered unconditional surrender: they acknowledged their error and wished to return to their duty. Campbell's reply was reasonable enough. He would accept the offer, provided all their arms were deposited on a hill nearby by six o'clock that evening.[21]

In Ballitore, meanwhile, the tide of popular feeling was running against Shackleton and the agreement to surrender. Part of the trouble was that the parish priest, who had earlier proved his humanity by trying to beg the life of a prisoner whom the rebels shot, was now confused and undecided. According to Shackleton he "appeared all the day of wavering counsels, sometimes *before* us, persuading the people to surrender, and at other times *apart*, haranguing them to opposite measures". Worse, after Shackleton had taken the insurgent leaders and closeted them in an upper room where they seemed to incline to a treaty, some "hot spirits" addressed the people to opposite effect. When Shackleton appeared at an upper window "to enforce the mild offers of Government" a man called Whelan, a "a turbulent man with a blunderbuss", actually threatened him with "his mischievious engine". Eventually the people made a new proposal to Colonel Campbell: they would send six respectable men as hostages. It was nearly midnight before they received Campbell's reply. The hostages must be sent before morning. Otherwise the army would treat them without mercy.

The situation was already confused and difficult enough—the lives of many hundreds of people depended on the restraint of the leaders on either side—when a completely new danger emerged. In the fog of war, the commander of the Carlow garrison, eight miles to the south, had heard nothing of the arrangements with Colonel Campbell. At three o'clock on the morning of Whit Sunday, Shackleton was roused by the parish priest with the news that the army was at hand. "The people fled and dispersed," Shackleton later reported "on every hand so that if hostages were then in time it would be hard to collect them, and still harder to concentrate the wavering resolutions of the people." As for the priest he was "in great dismay. He requested to borrow my coat, but when I went for it he was gone."[22]

The soldiers from Carlow, it turned out, had been instructed to treat every man as a rebel. First they bombarded Narraghmore—the nearby mansion of the liberal member for the county, Colonel Keating, whose sister was supposed to have fought with the rebels. In the event they only killed an old loyalist hiding in the house. Before they reached Ballitore one of the Quakers, called John Bewley, managed to explain their situation, and showed them Campbell's letter. "It happened well for you, gentlemen," said the major in command of the party, "or I should have shot you every man."[23]

But in the meanwhile Colonel Campbell's ultimatum had expired and he had decided to make an example of the town. Hardly had the Carlow troops marched out of Ballitore when, as in some ghastly charade, the Athy troops marched in from the opposite direction. Mrs. Leadbetter has described what followed:

> "I though the bitterness of death was past, settled my parlour and got the cows milked when behold another party headed by Colonel Campbell came in. Ah, they came breathing vengeance . . . cannon accompanied them! To see cannon in Ballitore! . . . I ran upstairs to my children whom I had in the room over the dairy. The Currough was now on fire, the crash of breaking windows could be heard and the trumpet sounded. Just then it was said the doctor was shot. I ran out into the room, and beheld him lying on his back, his arms extended and his life flown: then terrour and distress seized me . . . the tumult now ceased. The trumpet sounded again. I suppose a retreat. We awoke as from a terrible dream."[24]

Abraham Shackleton was eye-witness of the same events from his house further up the village street. "In a few minutes this dreadful scene opened and closed, and they passed on. It resembled the operation of lightning— fierce and terrible, and over in a moment." Shackleton was fortunate, for the Quakers, whose loyalty even Colonel Campbell could not doubt, were given official protection. One of their houses, it is true, was plundered; in another pans and jugs were dashed from the kitchen table, and windows broken; but by and large they escaped the soldiers. Virtually everyone else was assumed to be guilty. Most of the houses were burnt to the ground. Those that they left standing were stripped and looted. Many people were shot or were hacked to death—including the village doctor whom Mrs. Leadbeater had found dead by her door. (His crime was to act mediator with the rebels.) Having made an example of the town, the troops returned cheerfully to Athy, wrecking two more villages on the way. That night the pigs, snuffling blood, wandered through the streets of Ballitore strewn with broken glass and earthenware and the mangled bodies of the inhabitants.[25]

While Colonel Campbell dealt so briskly with Ballitore, the real rebels were still a force to be reckoned with. In the north west of Kildare they had advanced to Rathangan and now threatened the ill-defended garrison towns in neighbouring King's County. A squadron of eighty of the Seventh Dragoons, despatched from Tullamore, proved quite inadequate to dislodge them. At their first attack they lost three men and two horses.[26] At the second, despite reinforcements from a local yeomanry, they lost six men and nine horses. The rebels conducted the defence with skill. They cut down the cavalry, massed in the narrow streets, with concentrated musket fire from the windows, and then used the fallen horses as barricades.[27] After the action the bodies of the dead were mutilated, and one of the dead horses hacked about by hysterical peasants shouting, according to a loyalist story of the period, "Take that, Protestant."[28] (No doubt the rebels told similar tales about the loyalists.)

Ironically, disaster to the Government would have been averted if there had been the least co-ordination between the various commanding officers. Marching on Rathangan at that very moment from the opposite direction was a substantial number of the City of Cork militia, who had left Dublin the previous night. It is not at all clear who sent them. Perhaps, like the captain of the Scotch Fencibles in Meath, their colonel had launched a private vendetta against the rebels who had killed so many of his men at Prosperous, including his relative, Captain Swayne. The expedition, at any rate, was provided with the essential means of success: a pair of battalion guns.[28]

A couple of hours after the Seventh Dragoons had been routed, the new column marched into the town, to find parts of it firmly barricaded with chains drawn across the street. After the second discharge of the cannon, the rebels were seen to fly in all directions. A cavalry charge was then ordered by the colonel which, according to his official report, was executed "with the greatest spirit and judgment". No prisoners, he reported drily. About fifty or sixty people were shot or sabred.[29]

In short, the re-capture of Rathangan followed much the same ghastly pattern as Ballitore's; the rebel leaders were dispersed, and numbers of innocent people were assumed to be rebels and shot out of hand. Crude and confused as it was, however, the counter-attack in the Midlands did seem to be achieving its immediate object: to drive the rebels out of the

Midlands and restore the control of the Government. The campaign concluded with a successful attack on the rebel camp about Blessington, where Dundas's troops killed many rebels and even re-captured a number of Wilton carpets plundered from the neighbouring gentry and used to make tents.

But for Camden and his advisers in Dublin there was no respite from their critics, despite these victories in the field. To succeed they must make the country safe for its loyal inhabitants—a task delicate enough in any circumstances, and how much more so after the reckless campaign of pacification.

All over Kildare and Wicklow—in every bog and on every mountain—there lurked the remnants of the men they had beaten. Contemptible they might seem, viewed as an army. But as rebels and outlaws, burning with a greater sense of injustice than before, and driven to even harsher acts to keep alive, they still represented a grave threat to the Government. "From the first breaking out of the rebellion to this hour, I would have advised a continual attack upon the rebels, instead of which we have ... suffered the scoundrels to feed upon the fat of the land," wrote one of the Government's milder critics.[30] It was understandable that loyalists, whose homes and lives were risked, should feel this way. But what they were asking of Camden was in effect a policy of extermination. And for this operation, even if Camden had agreed, there were clearly not enough troops in the whole British Empire.

The alternative, then, must be some form of compromise with the rebels. But for this, even if the loyalists had agreed, the Government did not find the opportunity.

A threat from a new source, that could well over-shadow all previous disasters, now loomed above the harassed men at the Castle.

In all the demoralising weeks since the turn of the year, as the underground movement passed into open insurrection, and the insurrection into a furious civil war, one solitary source of comfort had remained for the Government. The North, where the movement had originated, had remained calm and loyal.

Camden, characteristically, refused to believe that there was any real change of heart. The rest of the Government, though encouraged by the apparent loyalty, found it hard to explain the phenomenon. Had the severity of the previous year's campaign for disarming really taught the rebels a permanent lesson? Even its heartiest advocate, General Lake, did not think so. "The flame is smothered, but not extinguished," he had reported in January.[31] Was it, then, that the northern republicans had become disillusioned with France since that country's recent diplomatic breach with its old ally, America, and its brutal treatment of its new acquisition, the Swiss democracy? This was an attractive theory, to which Lord Clare and others inclined.[32] Yet it could hardly explain the behaviour of an uneducated peasantry. Was it, on the other hand, the fact that in the South the rebels had discriminated against the Protestants. Was it this that had deterred the dissenters and other Protestants of the North? "The Popish tinge in the rebellion" was partly responsible, according to Edward Cooke. Yet he still found the quiet "unaccountable".[33] Or was it, as Beresford believed, the Orangemen, the fifty thousand and more loyalists who had sworn to defend the Protestant King and Constitution, who had over-awed the United army?[34] In one sense, however, the Orangemen were less important in the North, where they were a reality, than in the South where they were the bogeymen of Catholic fancy. For some of the North's contingents of Orangemen had been disarmed by the Government as a dangerous faction, and were correspondingly weak and disorganised.[35]

Whatever the reason, the North was still loyal, and while it remained so "all will go yet", as Cooke put it.[36] This was the position on Whit Monday. Two days later he reported anxiously that there was a "buzz" in the North.[37] The same day news arrived from an unimpeachable source that, just as Camden had feared, there was no change of heart in the North. Not only was the province still organised. The Executive had just met to coordinate plans for general rebellion.[38]

5

Ulster Stirs

Ulster and Leinster, May 29th–June 8th

From France, now see LIBERTY'S TREE
Its branches wide extending
The Swine to it for shelter run
Full fast they are assembling . . .

Freedom Triumphant

THE NEWS that the North was about to rise came from a man who should know—the man actually entrusted by the United movement with the job of starting the revolution in the North. The name of this highly important member of the Castle spy service was Nicholas Magin a young Catholic farmer of Saintfield, who had been elected a colonel of the revolutionary army of County Down, and in due course penetrated to the provincial Directory. (He is not to be confused with the only other Government agent in a similar position—the Mag*an* who had exposed the Dublin Directory's plan a fortnight before.) Perhaps Magin, like so many other agents of this period, had originally been blackmailed into the Government's service. For the last eighteen months he had proved loyal and efficient, and on their part the Government paid him well.[1]

Magin's report of an imminent rising was all the more shocking because recently he had been so definite about the enfeebled state of the northern organisation. No meeting of the Ulster Directory had taken place since May 10th, and there appeared to be no contingency plan by the Ulster executive to co-ordinate North and South. Nor, when it came, had the southern rising apparently shaken the inertia of the northern leaders. At any rate no emergency meeting had been called to consider it either at local or provincial level.[2]

Then on May 29th, according to Magin's latest report, at a routine meeting of the provincial committee, the mood had suddenly changed.

A young man called Thomas Bashford had denounced the Ulster Executive for "betraying the people both of Leinster and Ulster". They had completely failed to carry out Ulster's part in the agreed national plan for a rising—to call the provincial delegates together, to tell the adjutants-general to prepare each county for mobilisation, and to give the signal for the rising, when the burning of the coach from Dublin showed the moment had come. "Denounce and vote them out of office," concluded Bashford and "take some speedy and vigorous measures" to help their friends in the South.[3]

The new executive's plan, according to Magin, was that the two counties closest to Belfast and best armed and organised—Down and Antrim—should serve as the trigger for the Ulster rising, much as the four counties around Dublin had been deputed to begin the rising in the South.

It was still uncertain whether the Antrim colonels would agree that their army was strong enough. But, if they did, the colonels of the Down army had voted to join them.[4]

Such was the reported situation on June 2nd, three days before Magin's intelligence reached Camden in Dublin. It confirmed, of course, Camden's gloomiest predictions. Unless the rebellion in the South was "instantly suppressed", Camden wrote in a covering note sent with a copy of Magin's report despatched to London, it would undoubtedly spread north, and a general rebellion was inevitable. Camden, however, remained characteristically inert in the face of the new danger. Terrified of alienating the Protestants of the North,[5] he delayed sending instructions to arrest Magin's colleagues on the provincial Directory. Even the new Ulster executive listed by him were left to raise the North unhampered.

In fact, Magin had, if anything, underestimated the danger. He did not, it seems, fully appreciate the reckless mood of the new Executive. For a year the old northern leaders had been debating whether or not to rise without French assistance and had watched the chances slip through their hands. Now they had been pushed aside by younger and more violent men: John Hughes,[6] a bankrupt bookseller from Belfast; Dickey, a Crumlin attorney;[7] and Henry Joy McCracken, a prosperous young cotton manufacturer.

It was McCracken, young as he was, who provided a link with the great days when Belfast had been the political centre of the United Irish movement. In 1791, Tone and his friends had established there the first United Society in Ireland. McCracken had joined soon after, and had become a personal friend of Tone's. Shortly before Tone had left for America, they had made a pilgrimage to Macart's Fort, a picturesque hill-site near Belfast, and there they had sworn a solemn oath to liberate their country.

Since those heady days, McCracken had shared the vicissitudes of the Ulster movement. Unity between Catholic and Presbyterian had been undermined by the endemic land-war in the North. This sectarian feud had culminated in the persecution and expulsion of many Catholics from Armagh. Still, the Ulster United movement had been the best organised in the country until 1797, when the Government had launched a savage campaign to disarm it.

McCracken himself was a remarkable man—in many ways the most attractive of all the original United brotherhood in Ireland. He displayed none of the defects of the others; the amiable fecklessness of Lord Edward, the impossible arrogance of Arthur O'Connor, or the stern self-righteousness of Thomas Addis Emmet. By birth a Presbyterian and by temperament a crusader, he had taken at once to the new philosophy of liberty and equality. His own ideas were at first homely and strictly practical; he had successfully established the first Sunday School in Belfast —open to scholars of all religious views. In due course he joined the United movement, and identified himself, as few of the movement's leaders did, with a demand for social justice. For him political and religious liberty, and national independence itself, were only means to that end. This, together with his personal magnetism, his diplomatic skill and this obvious enthusiasm, had suddenly thrust him into the front of the movement in the North, where all such qualities were so sadly absent.[8]

But could anyone create an effective army from a movement stricken by the sudden desertion of almost all its leaders?

Little is known of McCracken's feelings at this period, except what emerges from a note written to his sister in early May in which he speaks of the brutal disarming of Kildare. Since then the tantalising news of the United army's successes and the agonising news of the counter-attack had reached the North. In what mood of desperate hope McCracken planned the northern rising can only be surmised. By June 6th, at any rate, he had rallied to his standard the twenty-five Antrim regiments numbering perhaps twelve thousand men. As many again were expected from County Down, and perhaps half that number from Tyrone and Armagh. Arms were hurriedly dug up from hiding places: pikes and muskets and an old brass cannon from Volunteer days. Uniforms were issued: regimental scarlet with a green cockade for officers, working clothes and a green hatband for the men. Late on Wednesday messengers slipped away with a final word for County Down. Next morning the rising would begin with a combined attack on Antrim. As the strategic centre of the province, Antrim was an important prize in itself. It would also provide them with arms and hostages; it was the day of the monthly meeting of magistrates in the town. And it was only a couple of hours march from Belfast.[9]

McCracken completed his preparations by drafting a proclamation. "Tomorrow we march on Antrim," he wrote to one of his colonels, "drive the garrison of Randalstown before you, and haste to form a junction with the Commander-in-Chief, Henry J. McCracken. The First Year of Liberty. Sixth of June 1798."[10]

It was dawn before General Nugent, the Commander of the northern garrison, first heard of these plans. His informant was, of course, Nicholas Magin of Saintfield.[11] His urgent warning had been somehow delayed. Already the United armies were on the march. In the mist of a June morning they swung along to the tune of "The Marseillaise" and a workingmen's song called "The Swineish Multitude":

> "Hail ye friends united here,
> In virtue's sacred ties!
> May you like self keep clear
> Of pensioners and spies,
> May you by Bastille ne'er appalled
> See Nature's right renewed
> Nor longer unavenged be called
> The Swineish Multitude."[12]

In Ulster there was no warning of the impending storm. In every village the bleach greens were white with linen; business had never seemed better; and people worked cheerfully in the fields where the young corn crops basked in the best spring in living memory.[13]

In Wexford, two hundred miles to the south, the weather was no less kind. But Wexford loyalists had no doubts of the catastrophe that now threatened them.

Enniscorthy, second town in the county, had fallen to the rebels. The incredible news reached Wexford on Whit Monday. At first it seemed that every Protestant of the town had been massacred and the great pall of smoke visible from sixteen miles away seemed to confirm this. But after several hours the refugees began to pour in—"Persons of first fortunes in that part of the country," as an eye-witness described them, "covered with dust and blood, with their infants in their arms and their wives clinging behind them . . . women who, but a few hours before, were in possession of every comfort life could afford." The refugees brought wild tales of murder and pillage in the capture of Enniscorthy.[14] For once there was little exaggeration.

That morning Captain Snowe, Enniscorthy's commander, and his little garrison of eighty militia, and three hundred yeomen and volunteers, had been grimly waiting for reinforcements, as rebels massed on the hills to the north east of the town. They had waited in vain. About one o'clock a "black cloud" of rebels, that a man who had fought in America estimated at nine to ten thousand strong, advanced in a shapeless mass towards the Duffrey Gate, the weakest point in the loyalist defences.[15]

Captain Snowe, as we saw earlier, had expected the main attack from the opposite direction, the bridge across the Slaney that led to the eastern suburbs of the town, and commanded the Wexford road. His best troops were here, the eighty men of the North Cork militia under his personal command. The officer in charge at the Duffrey Gate was Captain Cornock, the totally inexperienced commander of the local yeomanry.

His little band now formed up in open fields beyond the gate and awaited the charge. With a good curricle gun this position would have been weak enough. As it was, they were cut down by the first volley from the advancing rebels, who by contrast had wisely taken cover from fire behind the massive banks and ditches characteristic of the Wexford countryside. Three of the officers—a third of the total officers in the garrison—were wounded, two of them mortally. Nearly half the supplementary yeomen were killed or wounded. The survivors fell back into the town, and sent an S.O.S. to Captain Snowe. The confusion was increased by a number of cattle and runaway horses that galloped ahead of the rebels, maddened by the heat and noise of the firing, according to their design. As no reinforcements arrived from Captain Snowe, or from their own colleagues in the cavalry, the yeomanry continued to retreat till they reached the market place. Here they lost a fourth officer, shot dead by a sniper in the upper window of an apothecary's. The rest were engaged in a desperate hand-to-hand battle in the street.[16]

Meanwhile Captain Snowe had his own troubles. Just as he had set off to the relief of the beleaguered yeomanry, he heard that a party of rebels was attacking the bridge, now undefended. In running back through the streets he lost a sergeant and a private to snipers, and reached the bridge just in time to catch the enemy in the act of crossing. "My men fired away thirty Rounds," he later reported, "in less than fifteen minutes."[17] But even such prodigies did not necessarily achieve the desired results. According to a loyalist who was on the bridge that day, Captain Snowe's men "would not even take time to discriminate between friends and foe". In the heat and smoke many shots were fired at a party of loyalists in civilian clothes who were seen "running down the Barrack lane towards the bridge with outstretched hands". At the same time the excited militiamen were continually exposing themselves to rebel fire, standing up above the cover of the bridge's stone parapet. In this way and by a reckless charge, the posse of the North Cork lost about a quarter of its number.[18]

Is it any wonder that many of the garrison behaved rashly on this extraordinary occasion? After all, most were soldiers only in name, untrained in marksmanship, let alone in battle. It is more remarkable that men were found to stand the continued charges of an enemy at least twenty times more numerous than they. Still more remarkable were the skill and courage of their opponents. Till now the Wexford campaign had been a string of raids and skirmishes. Even their victory at Oulart was an affair of a few minutes. Here at Enniscorthy Father John's troops acted like experienced soldiers, time after time braving the musket-fire, till they were under the enemy's guard, when the short range made the pike a ferocious weapon. Their errors, like those of their opponents, were the result of a crazy undiscriminating courage—bare hands against a bayonet, or the loaded muzzle of a musket. Afterwards the loyalists said they were like men intoxicated, but whether with whiskey or the prospect of success, or both, no one could say.[19]

By mid-afternoon the garrison had lost over a hundred men, and half the town was on fire. Captain Snowe's men made two costly charges across the bridge and dislodged the enemy who were massing below Vinegar Hill. A desperate rush up from the market-place cleared the streets as far as the Duffrey Gate. But they recognised that they had won only a breathing space. At four o'clock the garrison drum sounded the retreat, and the survivors staggered back along the only road still open to them— the road to Wexford. Captain Snowe later denied that the retreat was disorderly or precipitate. The loyalists of the town reported differently. The garrison had left behind to their fate large numbers of women and children, some ran hysterically into the river Slaney, waded across and took refuge in the woods, where they lay all night "petrified with horror at hearing shots constantly fired, the shouts of the rebels, and the groans of the dying". Many more were trapped in the burning town.[20]

Among the more fortunate was the family of the local magistrate, the Rev. Thomas Handcock. After his yeomanry unit had fled, he forced his way back into the town, and hammered wildly on the door of his house,

where he found his wife, three young children, a maid and a terrified
drummer boy in hiding. He dragged them out, hustled them along the
burning streets, just as the rebels pushed into the town. The fugitives
pushed their way across bodies heaped up in the roads, and somehow
managed to catch up with the rear-guard of the army. Some of the soldiers
gallantly gave the women lifts on their horses, but were less considerate to
the people they passed in the fields. In the general hysteria the yeomanry
"shot at every country fellow they saw". Handcock tried to restrain them
—if only because it might endanger their own lives.[21] Elsewhere in the
refugee column the officers, terrified of capture, tore off their epaulettes to
pass as privates.[22]

Despite this appalling disaster at Enniscorthy and the unnerving sight of
the refugees, the Wexford garrison did not by any means despair. Their
weak forces of yeomanry and the survivors of the North Cork militia had
been reinforced by other yeomanry corps from the county, and two
hundred of the Donegal militia from a large base at Duncannon. The
garrison was now over a thousand strong, including several hundred
civilian volunteers, and had acquired that essential weapon of defence—a
6-pounder. Still more heartening, the Donegal brought news that General
Fawcett with a contingent of regulars, and two of the latest howitzers,
was marching to their rescue.[23]

A veteran soldier serving with the yeomanry corps, Lieutenant-Colonel
Jonas Watson, now took charge of the defence of the city. Wexford, like
Enniscorthy, was still virtually a walled town, with central avenues termin-
ating in ancient gateways.[24] Access to the eastern side of the city could
only be gained by sea or by the new wooden bridge across the Slaney. To
strengthen the ancient gateways, Colonel Watson added barricades—
rough walls of masonry with a make-shift timber door to let the cavalry
patrols and vedettes pass by. Loyalists were given muskets, scouts sent out
to reconnoitre. Ruthless precautions were taken against fire, whether
started by the attackers or by a fifth column within the town. Bakers were
forbidden to heat their ovens, and all thatched houses within the walled
town were stripped of their roofs.[25]

Meanwhile General Fawcett had reached Taghmon—about twelve
miles to the west—where he waited for the main relief column to
catch up with him. For some reason which has never been explained,
the party with the howitzers, consisting of about seventy men of
the Meath militia and eighteen gunners of the Royal Irish Artillery,

overtook the general, and pushed on without him towards Wexford.[26]

About four miles from Wexford, the road from Taghmon passes below the crest of an outcrop known as the Three Rocks. In the gathering darkness the Meath militia and the howitzers pressed on towards the town. Several times they had stopped to question the country people, and each time they were reassured: the rebels were far away. As they reached the Three Rocks they saw the trap, but too late. A wave of pikemen rode down a hill and engulfed the column. When it receded, that company of Meath militia, like the North Corks three days before, had ceased to exist. A few prisoners were taken—some gunners whom the rebels took to be Catholics—but all seventy of the militia were shot and hacked to death, except for an officer and a couple of men who brought the news back to Fawcett at Taghmon.[27]

This disaster was followed by another whose result was still more serious. At first light on Wednesday, the garrison sallied out from Wexford to link up with the expected relief column. Colonel Watson led the men towards the Three Rocks. Although they retreated in time to avoid ambush, Watson himself fell in the first encounter, and his fall brought consternation to the entire garrison.

For three days Watson's energy had inspired the townspeople. But now the despairing mood of the refugees, intensified by the news of the disaster to the Meath militia, had spread to the garrison itself. Consternation turned to panic as it became clear that General Fawcett believed the rebels now too strong to risk an engagement, and had withdrawn the relief expedition hastily to Duncannon.[28]

At a hurried council of war, Colonel Maxwell, the Donegal militia's commander, still held out against evacuation. People pointed out that food was running low; others said that the Catholics in the town would go over to the rebels in the event of an attack, as they had done in Enniscorthy; already someone had set on fire part of the bridge across the Slaney. At this point, with the soldiers on the verge of mutiny, the garrison committed a culminating act of folly.

To buy time while they made their escape, they turned to the two gentlemen believed to be United Irish leaders—Bagenal Harvey and Edward Fitzgerald of New Park—lodged in the town gaol. Letters from both these men and the magistrates were sent to the rebels suing for terms.[29] The magistrates' letter gave the rebels an intoxicating new sense of power. But still more important, Harvey's letter gave the rebellion a new status. No longer need the rebels feel they were a country mob, led by a couple of country curates, in an obscure vendetta with the local magistrates. Harvey was not only the social equal of their opponents, a man of education and influence in the county, a landlord of a couple of thousand a year. He was also a national figure in the United Irish movement, or so they thought, a link between them and Lord Edward and the Executive.

No man felt this more keenly than Harvey himself—and was terrified by the prospect.[30] Whatever his philosophical views on revolution, it appears he had absolutely no military ambition. He well knew his rôle if he was caught up in that great wave—a sword thrust in his hand, and a green cockade in his hat, and chief command of a mob twenty thousand strong.

In the meantime the officers of the garrison had lost the last vestige of authority. Along the road to the west some yeomanry were in full flight, pursued by their officers. Captain Snowe, the man who had rallied the Enniscorthy garrison, was shocked to find that the North Cork were just as bad as the yeomanry. In defiance of orders they jumped over the barricade at the west gate and fled after them. He caught them up, he later reported, and "succeeded in keeping them together on the retreat, and preventing every species of Depredation and Violence". Other officers left their men to their own devices, and their retreat was marked by a trail of burning farms and haggards, and country people shot as they worked in the fields.[31]

It was now beyond any one man's power to restore discipline in evacuation, let alone rally the garrison for the town's defence. Reluctantly Colonel Maxwell, the garrison's new commander, followed his retreating army, and left the townspeople to fend for themselves.[32]

Their situation was daunting indeed. Large numbers of loyalists had already been evacuated by sea the previous evening on board the town's fishing fleet. But for many of them safety was not to be bought, even at the price—as much as twelve guineas a head for the trip to Waterford or Wales. The fishermen, who were mostly Catholic and sympathetic to the rebels, were in no mood to hurry. In the morning the wretched passengers found themselves still within sight of land. Handcock, the resourceful clergyman from near Enniscorthy, forced some sailors to weigh anchor at pistol point.[33] But many ships put back to harbour as soon as they saw the large green rebel flag hoisted above the barrack on the quay-side. The captain of a collier, a sea-dog called Thomas Dixon, was in fact a rebel commander, and personally put his passengers under arrest. The men were lodged in the hopelessly overcrowded gaol, and the women and children confined in houses in the town, in one case more than twenty in a small room.[34]

One of Captain Dixon's passengers, a Mrs. Brownrigg, has left an account of their ill-omened voyage. With her two young children she had boarded the ship on Tuesday night, expecting to sail for Wales next day.

"Great God! What a night that was. The Horns of the Rebels I heard very plainly, for the ship just lay about half way from Ferry Bank and Wexford . . . at the first dawn of day, May the thirtieth, the Bridge was set on fire from the Ferry Bank side; all our crew were or pretended to be asleep. I woke them and if I doubted their principles before could no longer doubt them. A wonderful scene of confusion now ensued. Boats of every description put off from the shore, and our ship and every other in the harbour was filled with women and children, some naked, several that had been in Enniscorthy the day before entirely frantic . . . All this time, of course, the Rebels were advancing and increasing in numbers. I sat watching the cavalry on the Quay. They began to disperse shortly after Mr. Lyster came on shore, kissed his hands earnestly to me, lifted them to heaven and went off . . . as soon as the army had gone off Captain Dixon got into his boat avowedly to join them, and saying he would *try* what he could do to save our lives in a manner that showed he had little to hope. We were then I suppose, about forty women and children put into the hold of the ship on Coals with which it was loaded, and sat expecting immediate death."[35]

The town of Wexford was now completely at the mercy of the rebel force whose discipline, as was only to be expected, was no better than that of the army they had beaten. To one of the loyalists they seemed little better than "savages", and the violence was all the more terrifying for being apparently mindless. The streets were thick with armed men firing random shots. A woman ran past, "brandishing the sheath of a sword".[36] Another loyalist, whose account of his sufferings was to have a powerful impact on Protestant opinion that summer, has left a more detailed account of the scene as the victorious rebels marched into the town.

"We passed through crowds of rebels, who were in the most disorderly state, without the least appearance of discipline. They had no kind of uniform but were most of them in the dress of labourers, white bands round their hats and green cockades being the only marks by which they were distinguished. They made a most fantastic appearance, many having decorated themselves with parts of the apparel of ladies, found in houses they had plundered. Some wore ladies' hats and feathers, others, caps, bonnets and tippets. From the military they had routed they had collected some clothing which added to the motley show. Their arms consisted chiefly of pikes of an enormous length, the handles of many being sixteen or eighteen feet long. Some carried rusty muskets. They were accompanied by a number of women shouting and huzzaing for the Croppies and crying, Who now dare say 'Croppies, lie down?' "37

That the long dreaded day, when the French Revolution would spread to Ireland, had now arrived, was all too clear to the gentlefolk of Wexford. They found their own tradespeople, their hatters and tailors, their coachmen and boatmen and shopkeepers, the solid and dependable foundations of the old social order, were their masters in the new. Abjectly, they applied to them for help, appealing to common humanity, or recalling their own acts of generosity in the past. Many, at some personal risk, helped the supplicants. Mrs. Dixon, the wife of the collier's captain, was touched by a small child of one of the refugees, warned her to destroy any papers that would betray she was a Protestant, and helped her to the quay. She was then taken by a friendly boatman to a "safe house"—one belonging to the local doctor. A chandler gave sanctuary to twenty-six refugee women, despite threats that the house would be burnt down for entertaining "orangewomen". By and large, the women and children were not in fact molested. Any man, however, suspected of disloyalty to the new regime was immediately imprisoned—which meant, in practice, most of the Protestant men of all classes. Catholics, on the other hand, were able to claim a sort of neutrality.38

Two catechisms were used to detect subversives, a conventional religious one, and a new style creed from the United Irish presses. The town shoeblack, now a United captain, went round interrogating prisoners.

"Question: What have you got in your hand?
Answer: A green bough.
Question: Where did it first grow?
Answer: In America.
Question: Where did it bud?
Answer: In France.
Question: Where are you going to plant it?
Answer: In the crown of Great Britain."39

Meanwhile a second and much larger relief column was at last marching towards Wexford on the direct orders of the Castle.

The Castle strategy, as we saw, gave first priority to the protection of

Dublin, and the second to the clearance of the rebels from the Midlands. However, by the 29th, Lake had sent 250 men under General Loftus to drive southwards into Wicklow, and at the end of the month instructed him to link up with a reinforcement he was sending and continue the advance into County Wexford. Dismayed as the Castle was at the news from Wexford, they had not, of course, yet heard of the fall of Wexford, nor had they grasped the formidable strength and morale of their opponents.

Loftus's reinforcement from Dublin, it turned out, consisted of about four hundred men and three pieces of artillery under the command of the Viceroy's personal aide, Colonel Walpole. How this courtier got the command at such a critical moment remains a mystery. Though a young man of spirit, he seems to have had no qualifications beyond a desire to prove himself in battle. At their first meeting Loftus listened aghast as the young man told him that he supposed "he would attack the rebels next morning, and that he hoped he would afterwards march, or permit him to march, to Enniscorthy, and after having taken that town to proceed to Wexford".[40]

Meanwhile other detachments were also moving southward. Lord Ancram with 250 of the King's County militia and eighty of his own Midlothian Dragoons were now poised at Newtownbarry on the Carlow border, and two more companies were ready at Carnew on the Wicklow side. Loftus ordered both these reinforcements to help him encircle the rebels advance guard who were somewhere near Ballymore Hill and now threatening the garrison at Gorey. As for Walpole, he was firmly told that, whatever his former position at the Castle, he must now obey his military superior and join the attack on Ballymore. It would be suicide to march on Enniscorthy and Wexford without first crushing the resistance to the north.[41]

There were two ways to reach Ballymore from Gorey, the coast road to the east, going by way of Ballycanew, and a short cut inland across a country of high banks and thorn hedges. Loftus was to take the coast road, Walpole to take the short cut with strict instructions to keep in line with him, and to send word if he made contact with the enemy. The Carnew detachment was ordered to cover Walpole's right, while Lord Ancram's force, marching from the west, would complete the encircling movement. Guides, and no doubt hampers of food, were to be provided by the local gentry.

About nine o'clock on the morning of June 4th, the two columns left Gorey and soon after, according to plan, Loftus watched Walpole's party diverge from his and march away up to the short cut to Ballymore, led by their colonel, resplendent in scarlet and mounted on a grey horse. Despite misgivings he had had to entrust him with twice his own force and three all-important pieces of artillery. Walpole apart, the plan must have looked sensible enough. One group or another could flush out the rebels, who must either stand and fi·ht, or be driven back south to the main rebel force.

But once again, the Government troops had hopelessly underestimated the strength of the tiger they were hunting.

Six hours later, a captain of the Ancient Britons galloped into Dublin with grim news for the Viceroy. Colonel Walpole, his aide and a personal friend of long standing, had walked straight into an ambush. Most of his men had been killed or wounded; Walpole himself had fallen early in the contest. The survivors had fled back across the frontier into County Wicklow, abandoning the strategic town of Gorey.[42]

The full story, as it emerged, confirmed Loftus' worst fears. In defiance of his orders, Walpole had pushed on towards the rebel position. The other officers had tried to remonstrate with him. It was common prudence to send out patrols, already parties of rebels could be seen hovering at their flanks. Time and again the officers had begged him to send an express to Loftus. His only concern was that the rebels should not escape him. At length the doomed column reached the part of the road that ran between high banks crowned with thick hedges. The rebels were well posted behind these natural defences and in a few moments Walpole's column, like the North Cork at Oulart and the Meath at the Three Rocks, had been swallowed up in a wave of infuriated pikemen and musketeers. The survivors included two prominent politicians—Colonel Sir Watkin Williams-Wynn from Wales and Colonel Cope of the Armagh—and, more significant, Captain Armstrong who would be the chief witness in any future treason trial. But all three pieces of artillery and most of their equipment had been abandoned to the enemy.[43]

The news of Walpole's loss, coming as it did after the disaster of the Meath militia and the fall of Wexford itself, affected the Castle in different ways. Lake was burning to go down in person to crush the rising, but was forbidden by Camden to leave the capital. Walpole's folly, though privately admitted, was tactfully kept from the public. In general, the Castle claimed to take some comfort from the knowledge that the rebels themselves had not shown themselves particularly brilliant. "They only win from our ill-conduct," as Edward Cooke put it.[12]

Beneath the jaunty façade, however, even Cooke and Castlereagh were now desperately worried by the course of the war. Walpole's fiasco was not only psychologically damaging. It gave the rebels back the initiative on a broad strategic front. With the greatest difficulty General Loftus had extricated himself and retreated far to the north. The Arklow garrison, though, still clung to their post, and the other two strategic towns, New Ross on the Slaney and Newtownbarry on the Barrow, were supposed to be still in Government hands. But without a doubt the rebels would try to break into the neighbouring counties and in due course march on Dublin. The question then, as Cooke saw it, was simply this: could they be contained for the ten days or so until reinforcements arrived from Britain?[45]

As the Castle waited on tenterhooks for reports of an attack on New Ross or Arklow, the long dreaded message arrived from General Nugent in Belfast. Taking courage from the South, the northern rising had begun.[46] McCracken's army was marching on Belfast: his pikemen were only fifteen miles from the provincial capital, the second city in the kingdom.

But even this was nothing to the chilling news that reached Lord Castlereagh just then from the Government in London. After months of delays and difficulties Bonaparte had at last gathered together his great armada and set sail from Toulon on May 19th. His destination was understood to be Ireland[47]

III

Revolution

1

The Green Bough Of Liberty

Wexford, May 30th–June 5th

It was early, early in the spring
When small birds tune, and thrushes sing,
Changing their note from tree to tree
And the song they sung was old Ireland free.

The Croppy Boy, 1798

IN THE town of Wexford the establishment of the first Irish republic was being celebrated in a weird sort of carnival. The huge, leaderless army—fifteen thousand or more—milled about in the narrow streets, cheerfully searching for whiskey and other sources of entertainment.[1] A pack of women followed and a motley group of musicians. One or two men wore regular uniforms. Dick Monk, the town shoeblack, had somehow acquired an elegant green jacket with pantaloons to match and a white ostrich feather in his green helmet. The rest wore green cockades or white bands round their hats. Otherwise they presented a less soldierly appearance. For many nights they had slept out on the heather, and their ordinary working clothes, the smock and breeches of the Irish labourer, were now all in tatters.[2]

One can well imagine the feelings of the ordinary townsfolk as this immense peasant army took possession of Wexford. The loyalists included some of the most respectable gentry in the county: Mrs. Ogle, the wife of one of the members for the county, Colonel Le Hunte of the local yeomanry, Dr. Jacob, the mayor, and Dr. Caulfield, the Catholic bishop. What could any of them now expect from such a mob of country people? Some of the leaders might talk of liberating Ireland and display the motto *"Erin go Bragh"* (Ireland For Ever) in gold letters on their hats. But the people clearly wanted a complete revolution. Already the ominous words "Liberty and Equality" were appearing in the town, and loyalists heard their servants mutter that now it was "their turn to be master".[3] As the abyss opened up before them the better class of people, Catholic as well as Protestant, even those who might have been sympathetic to the republican cause, felt a sudden solidarity. Outwardly, however, they did their best to conciliate the mob. Every window in Wexford was hurriedly decked with green flags or green branches of trees. Most doors had a placard saying "Liberty" in large capitals. Gentlewomen tore up their petticoats to make suitable emblems, and even the most die-hard loyalists found themselves waving a green handkerchief to the triumphant rebels.[4]

Strange to say, that first night of the Irish Republic passed in comparative calm. Despite the provocative behaviour of the garrison, who had promised to surrender the town to them intact, and had promptly fled with all the arms and ammunition, the rebels did not retaliate. One loyalist, it is true, was left writhing on the bridge of the gaol, mortally wounded by a pikeman in the first confused moments of the occupation. The wretched man was the brother of James Boyd, one of the members for the county, whose attempts to prevent the rising had made him highly unpopular with the people.[5] Apart from this there was hardly more disturbance in the streets that night than in time of peace. Vast numbers of the insurgents had left the town to search out their relations in the county around. The rest were understandably exhausted after their various privations—and the hilarious day's celebrations.[6]

Next day as the United forces flowed back into the town and there was every prospect of further confusion, the need for some form of leadership began to assert itself over the minds of the people. The two Catholic gentlemen originally sent to the republican camp as emissaries from the garrison—John Colclough of Ballyteigue and Edward Fitzgerald of New Park—now found themselves pushed to the fore and appointed colonels. As for their general, the obvious choice was Bagenal Harvey. No matter he was a Protestant and a landlord. He had been the inspiration of the United movement in Wexford, and was in the confidence of the Dublin executive. For this he had been imprisoned by the Government. The people rushed to the gaol and released Harvey.[7] Still covered in soot after his attempt to conceal himself in a chimney,[8] he was restored in triumph to his lodgings in the town and appointed Commander-in-Chief by popular acclamation. Together the three men began the daunting task of trying to impose some sort of order on their lawless army.

Their immediate task was to try to protect the town and the townspeople from further outrage. A retired British officer, Captain Matthew Keogh, was made military governor. Keogh had probably not been enrolled in the United movement, but his radical sympathies were well known. In the army he had performed the unusual feat of rising from the ranks. He had then retired on half-pay and married a respectable widow in the town of Wexford. He was now fifty-four years old: a distinguished looking figure with his white hair swept up and tied with a bow.[9] With the help of the respectable townspeople, Keogh divided the town into wards and organised a rough and ready company to protect each one. These men in their turn appointed their own officers. Despite their unkempt appearance and their unconventional weapons—for at this stage the rebels had to make do with pitchforks and rusty scythes instead of regular pikes—Keogh's new home-guard was a more or less disciplined body. Night and morning a regular parade was held on the Customs' House Quay. Guards were struck and relieved, and a suitably democratic password and counter-sign were given out.[10]

Meanwhile Bagenal Harvey and the other leaders had formed a kind of committee of public safety for the town. Dr. Jacob, who had been mayor before the occupation, was persuaded to serve. Whatever their misgivings, other Protestants collaborated: for example, Mr. Richards, the magistrate whom the garrison had sent earlier to the rebel camps to plead for terms, and Mr. Cornelius Grogan, an elderly gentleman of £8,000 a year.[11] Of all that committee, Grogan was the most incongruous member. On their march to Wexford the rebels had carried him off from his seat, Johnstown Castle, and more or less forced him to accompany them into Wexford. He was known as a friend to the Catholic cause and a good landlord, but he was shy and retiring and had spent much of his life in his study, where he had made a hobby of building curious mechanical contrivances. Now over sixty and racked with gout, he found himself swept into Wexford with a pike at his back.[12]

Harvey and this committee more or less succeeded in their first task—to prevent indiscriminate plunder. Looting of food supplies was being carried on by self-styled commissaries on the pretext of supplying the public needs. A special sub-committee of twelve respectable townspeople was created to regulate the food supply. They threw themselves manfully into the task: some of the plunder they even restored to its owners; mutton and flour were requisitioned from the country and a system of rationing begun which authorised all householders to draw food supplies from the public depôts free of charge on production of a ration-card. Money itself seemed to have vanished with the revolution. Coins were hoarded, while paper money was treated with derision; people lit their pipes with the pound notes carrying the Government's stamp, while others used them as wadding for their muskets.[13]

Harvey's second task—to protect the loyalists—proved harder. The active United men had excellent reasons to hate the magistrates. Many innocent people had also suffered in the reckless process of disarming, and many hundreds had lost friends and relations in the savage fighting of the last few days, including women and children murdered by the retreating soldiery. To the actual crimes of the Government forces were added the stories of Orange atrocities spread by United agents before the rising. Small wonder that an influential party among the rebels was bent on retaliation. For the moment Harvey and the committee maintained a precarious ascendancy over this party. As a concession to popular feeling, they allowed several prominent loyalists to be thrown into prison. In fact it was probably the safest place for them. Still, the prospect was hardly inviting for the prisoners: two hundred and more confined in the suffocating heat of the town gaol, so cramped for space that there was no room to set down a chair, and left to subsist on the odd loaves of bread or scraps that the gaoler cared to throw them. Outside in the street the mob talked openly of "punishing the Protestants".[14]

As well as Harvey and Keogh there was one other man with much influence over the rebels. This was the Catholic bishop, Dr. Caulfield. Like the rest of the Catholic hierarchy of that period his own political views were impeccably conservative; and he had even written to Rome, as we have seen, to denounce the godless republican spirit among his flock.[15] He was not, however, identified in any way with the Irish Government, and the rebels were somewhat awed by his spiritual authority. He was thus able to save many Protestants who appealed to him for help. "From morning to night," as he later recalled it, he was busy "writing, speaking and pleading for them to procure protection from the chiefs of the insurrection . . . our houses were constantly thronged, and every place filled with the people."[16] To intercede for Protestants was an act of some courage. As he explained to one of the refugees, "The People could not be described, that in reality the Devil was roaring among them . . . that they would make it a religious War which would ruin them."[17] Fortunately for the bishop, none of the priests involved in the rising was at this time in Wexford. He had suspended one priest suspected of Uniting. As for Father Philip Roche, who was to be the mainstay of the whole crusade, he had reprimanded him for "debauchery".[18]

Meanwhile the United forces, too, were preoccupied with protecting themselves against attack. Their first concern was the dearth of proper weapons. Like the United forces of the Midlands, the Wexford men had lost many of their best pikes and guns in the Government's disarming campaign of the previous month. Apart from the few hundred guns they had subsequently captured from the military, their army had had to rely on pitchforks, scythes and other makeshift weapons. At least they could now be properly equipped with pikes. All the forges in town and country were set to work making pike blades, every suitable piece of timber was requisitioned for pike handles. Night and day the hammers of smiths and carpenters could be heard; the Bull-Ring became an open-air factory at the centre of the town of Wexford.[19]

On the coast other defence preparations were set in hand. Four oyster boats were commandeered, fitted out in the harbour as patrol boats with a crew of twenty-five, and sent to cruise in the bay. Three old pieces of cannon were mounted at Rosslare fort, commanding the harbour mouth, and some half derelict sloops were prepared as blockships. If the British navy dared to show its head, the sloops could be scuttled to trap the invaders in the channel.[20]

These naval preparations paid an unexpectedly swift dividend to the republican army. The patrol boats intercepted a number of coasters carrying provisions to Dublin, and were thus able to provide a useful supply of oats and potatoes to the town. A more flamboyant prize was provided by the capture of one of the great Irish grandees, Lord Kingsborough. He had apparently chartered a small boat at Wicklow and sailed down the coast to rejoin his regiment at Wexford, not realising, of course, that the town was in rebel hands. Lord Kingsborough was undoubtedly somewhat impulsive. He was the son of Lord Kingston, and had been accused of helping him murder his daughter's seducer. He might now serve as a hostage, if he was accepted as a prisoner of war. But of this there was more than a little doubt. Lord Kingsborough was the Colonel of the North Cork militia, a regiment well known in Wexford for the way they had tortured and murdered their prisoners. For the time being, he was sent to join the beleaguered gentry in the town gaol and the other makeshift prisons around the town.[21]

It was now June 3rd, the fourth day of the rebel occupation. For many of the prisoners hopes of a speedy release were being replaced by the very understandable fear of being taken out and murdered. It was clear that Dr. Caulfield and the others were losing ground in their attempts to protect the loyalists. All Protestants were regarded by the mob as Orangemen, unless they could prove it otherwise, and as Orangemen they deserved the same fate as they were said to have been planning for Catholics—extermination. Catholics were given the benefit of the doubt, unless they had proved their disloyalty to the Cause. In vain, Dr. Caulfield and the other priests tried to mediate, urging Christian charity and mercy to their persecutors. This was Orange talk, as Dr. Caulfield was told to his face. Any more of this, and his house would be pulled down and "his head knocked off".[22]

In desperation many of the threatened Protestants begged to be allowed to be received into the Catholic Church. The rebels actively encouraged conversions: "If you will go home and turn Christians," they would say, "you will be safe enough." Catholic family retainers implored their Protestant masters and mistresses to ask the parish priest to christen them as it would be "the saving of them all".[23] Many Protestants were in fact received. A large procession accompanied Mrs. Le Hunte, the wife of the local yeomanry colonel, as she went to the Catholic chapel, formally renounced her religion and was re-christened.[24] The priests themselves were naturally embarrassed by this sudden flood of converts. Apart from the doubtful nature of the conversions, from the theological point of view, they ran the risk of appearing to sanction the violent prejudice against the Protestants who would not conform. For there were still some who said firmly they would be better dead than Catholic. In the event, the Wexford priests were split: some gave "conditional" baptism to those who claimed, often with the wildest improbability, that some technical error had been made by the Protestant minister at the original baptism; others hesitated to accept new converts; others welcomed them on the grounds that it was inhuman to refuse the wretched captives anything that might pacify their captors.[25]

While this dilemma remained unresolved, the first ritual execution of prisoners took place at Wexford. Though the victims were in fact Catholics, the macabre events were hardly re-assuring for Protestants— one of the condemned men had been a Crown witness against a Catholic priest, and on his evidence, perhaps perjured, the priest had been sent off for transportation the day before the rising. There were no official instructions now for the execution. It was done, it seems, simply as an act of personal vengeance by one of the rebel captains, Dixon the ship-master, who happened to be a relation of the priest. His victim was shot in the Bull-Ring and his body thrown into the river.

The other condemned man, who had also been a Crown witness, was treated with more ceremony. A solemn procession of more than a thousand men marched out across the bridge; pikemen in a hollow square, a man with a black flag, and a military band of fifes and drums who struck up the Death March. When the place of execution was reached—a strand about a mile and a half from the town—the whole procession knelt down.

For five minutes they prayed, leaning on their arms. Then the firing squad composed of three Protestant prisoners, forced to act executioner, was given the order. After several mishaps the wretched man was eventually dispatched.

To conclude the ceremony, a song in honour of the new international brotherhood—"God Save the Rights of Man"—was sung to the tune of "God Save the King".[26]

Meanwhile, Bagenal Harvey had left Wexford and personally assumed control of the main republican army in the field. It is far from clear why he took this bold step. Neither the beleaguered townspeople, nor he himself had anything to gain by his abandoning Wexford. He had already persuaded the bulk of the insurgents to leave the town. Now they were preparing to march to the west, where only one garrison, New Ross, barred the way to County Waterford. Harvey, however, was hardly the man to lead them. He had no military experience, no real fellow-feeling with the people, nor, what was still more vital in a revolution, a burning belief in himself and the rightness of his cause. On the contrary he seems to have been sickened by the turn of events, and longed to make his peace with the Government. Perhaps he now thought he could achieve better terms for himself and the people as commander in the field. Or perhaps his aim was simply to try to prevent outrage against Protestants. In either case he was to be sadly disappointed.[27]

At first, the camp at the Three Rocks a mile or two to the west of the town of Wexford had been the scene of the wildest riot and confusion. It was the same at the great camp at Vinegar Hill, near Enniscorthy. A Liberty Tree was erected; there was dancing to the tune of the "Carmagnole"; and drunken songs in honour of the new republic.

Precious days had been lost while the revolutionary leaders were trying to impose some sort of order. At length about half their forces had been sent north, in two contingents, each commanded by local men. The northern contingent under Anthony Perry and Edward Fitzgerald was now marching towards the frontier of County Wicklow. After their brilliantly successful ambush of Colonel Walpole and General Loftus' hasty retreat on June 4th, the frontier town of Arklow, and the road to Dublin itself, now lay open to them. A second contingent, under a local priest called Father Kearns, were marched north west to the strategic garrison town of Newtownbarry on the border of Wicklow and Carlow. They had captured the town for a while, but their victory celebrations had been cut short by a counter-attack, and they had been dispersed after heavy loss. Two of their leaders were reported killed in battle—priests fighting in their priestly vestments.[28]

It remained for Bagenal Harvey to lead the third and largest contingent on the march against New Ross. Despite the two precious days lost in re-organising the army after the capture of Wexford, Harvey had every prospect of success. In numbers the strength of his army was quite over-whelming—at least twenty times as numerous as the New Ross garrison. As they marched along the dusty road to the west, the republican army presented a terrifying spectacle of military might—mile after mile of soldiers "moving with slow but irresistible progress", as the fleeing loyal-ists saw it, "like an immense body of lava".[29] Close up the spectacle, though still awe-inspiring, was less soldierly. It was a whole countryside in motion, an army of country people complete with village women, all swept up by the same convulsion. A few priests marched along with their parish-ioners, some armed with pikes, others with crucifixes,[30] women carried the bedding and the cooking pots; there were quantities of beer and mutton, and whiskey by the barrel. When the procession halted, it was like a country fair; when it marched, it was like a terrifying sort of pilgrimage.[31]

On the second day after leaving the Three Rocks, the army reached Carrickbyrne Hill, within a few hours march of New Ross, and here it wasted two more precious days. The delay would have been extraordinary had the revolutionary army been organised along regular lines. As it was, it only illustrated the precarious ascendancy of its leaders. At last Harvey, Father Roche and the others got the army moving again, after forming a makeshift prison for the loyalist prisoners in a large barn at a place called Scullabogue. On Tuesday night, they set up their camp at Corbet Hill looking down on the towers and turrets of New Ross in the river valley a mile below.

That night Harvey held a council of war and drew a rough plan of battle: they would launch a simultaneous attack on three sides of the town. Nothing was done, however, to fill in the details so as to concert the plan with the leaders of each detachment.[32] Harvey was not the man to advise his pikemen on the new tactics for street fighting, to warn them how devastating cannon could be against them, nor to instruct their own gunners on how to handle the howitzers captured from General Fawcett at the Three Rocks. Even the overriding strategic importance of the assault was not made clear to the army—to cut off the Government's supply route to the great military base of Waterford, and to force open the communication with tens of thousands of their friends believed ready to rise in the South and West.

Instead, the usual atmosphere of cheerful confusion and bickering prevailed. Several thousand men, including John Henry Colclough's contingent, left their camp to return home. Other leaders spent the night in feasting. Harvey and the few who stood aloof were miserably aware, no doubt, that if they carried the day, it would be by sheer weight of numbers and courage alone. And what horrors even victory would entail. On impulse, Harvey dashed off a note to General Johnson urging a speedy surrender. In it he candidly admitted that the Wexford forces could "not be controlled if they meet resistance". Only by surrendering could Johnson save the town "from rapine and plunder to the ruin of the innocent". Harvey gave the letter to his aide—a young gentleman farmer styled Citizen Furlong. He galloped away downhill to the gates of New Ross, waving a white handkerchief as a flag of truce.[33]

Meanwhile, General Johnson had done his best to exploit the three days' breathing space provided by the rebels' delays at Carrickbyrne.

New Ross seemed at first sight tailor-made for a siege, what with its imposing town walls, its five great gates and its nine picturesque flanking towers. In fact the medieval fortifications had been partly dismantled after the town's surrender to Cromwell;[34] more recently the gates like those in Wexford, seem to have been widened for traffic. Moreover, the town was dominated by the high ground where the rebels had pitched their camp; its protective banks and ditches swept down to within a few hundred yards of the gate, and the narrow cobbled lanes in the town itself led down invitingly to the river.[35] All told, the dice were heavily loaded in favour of the attackers.

Despite this, General Johnson was still fairly confident. He was an Irish Protestant and displayed some characteristic traits of that settler society: he was brave and not without energy, but stubborn, touchy and unimaginative.[36] In the American war he had served under Cornwallis without distinction. Since the beginning of the present war his career had been prosaic in the extreme; he had spent five years organising the recruitment in Ireland of soldiers for British regiments.[37] Suddenly restored to active service, he now found himself in charge of the largest garrison in Ireland, outside Dublin and Belfast.

After reconnoitring the ground, Johnson decided that the main attack would come from the east, directly below the enemy's camp. He did not,

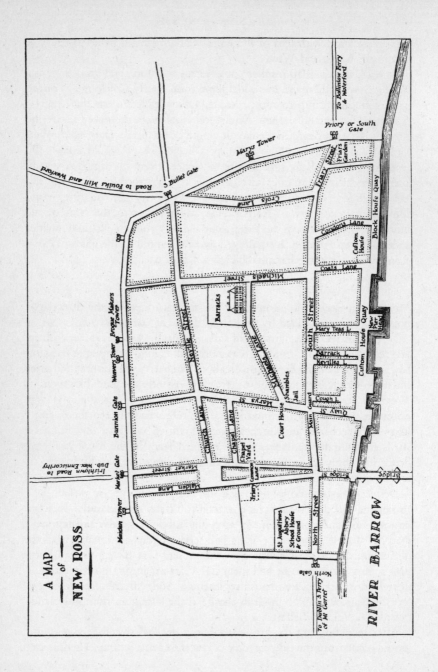

A MAP
of
NEW ROSS

RIVER BARROW

it is clear, credit the enemy's commander with much imagination or ability.[38] After all, the enemy had thrown away their strategic advantage by their delays. As for their striking successes at Oulart, Enniscorthy and the rest, they had yet to meet a large properly disciplined force. Johnson was not alone in this optimistic vein of thought. He had one man of great ability on his staff—Colonel Robert Craufurd, the man who was to win a brilliant reputation with the Light Brigade in the Peninsula. Craufurd saw no reason to be afraid of the rebels: disciplined troops, properly led and properly supported by artillery, would always win against an irregular force, however large.[39]

That evening the garrison's morale, cheered by Johnson's energy, rose still further. A large contingent of the Dublin militia, led by their colonel, Lord Mountjoy, marched into the town. Lord Mountjoy was a great landed proprietor and most popular with the militia, who were largely Catholic; as Luke Gardiner, thirty years earlier, he had successfully proposed the first Catholic Relief Act. Although exhausted by their march, the reinforcements brought the garrison's total to more than two thousand, and, equally important, raised the total number of artillery to more than six pieces.[40]

Johnson now disposed his troops to parry the anticipated attack from the east. He set his forward position outside the east gate, known as the Three Bullet Gate, directly below the enemy's camp. Here he positioned a flank battalion of regulars and militia, covered by two pieces of artillery. Outside the north gate, called the Bishop's Gate, he created a second defensive position. Already some trenches had been dug; a gang of a hundred labourers had been set to work with pick and shovel superintended by civilian volunteers. Inside the town the rest of the infantry and artillery were established around a series of strong points: the barracks, the marketplace, the Main Guard beside the gaol, and the vital wooden bridge across the river at their back.[41]

Finally Johnson took care to guard against the disasters that had attended previous engagements with the rebels. First the cavalry were ordered to stay in reserve on the quay. Johnson had no doubt heard of the devastating advantage of the rebels' long pike against the short cavalry sabre, how the pikemen could stand up to the Dragoons at full gallop, taking the shock on their ten-foot long pikes, and then piking the reeling horses and their riders. Second, the civilian volunteers, or "glorymen", were disarmed.[42] Officially it was for their own safety; they wore no uniform and could be taken for rebels. In fact, Johnson must have realised they were a danger to everyone. Even if the New Ross townspeople were all as loyal as they claimed, theirs was too reckless a brand of loyalty for such a moment. Stripped of their muskets and firelocks, the glorymen were confined to their houses, or joined the mass of the townspeople streaming back across the bridge into the safety of County Kilkenny.

It was now just before dawn on Tuesday, June 5th—a day that was to prove momentous in Irish history. All night the garrison had lain upon their arms. They must have watched the rebels' camp fires blaze out from the black mass of the hillside above them. They must have heard the sound of pipes and the irregular throb of drums, as music drifted down into the valley. Twenty times their superior in numbers, the rebels were already celebrating their victory. As the camp fires faded, the garrison waited beside their narrow trenches, half concealed by the crumbling battlements of the town wall.

A defeat that day, as Johnson and his staff knew, could be catastrophic for the Government: the whole South of Ireland might be set ablaze; it might even be the signal for total insurrection. But if it was rash to risk defeat, it was unthinkable to withdraw; New Ross guarded the main crossing of the river, and its retention kept the rebels more or less sealed off from the rest of Ireland. Johnson's mood may seem over confident, as events turned out. But he held grimly to his belief in the superiority of discipline in a contest with irregulars, however numerous. That and the artillery must carry the day.

In the half light of daybreak, the pickets saw a horseman galloping down towards them from the rebels' lines. Perhaps he was challenged, perhaps he was not; the guards did not take any chances, at any rate, and the rider fell riddled with gunshot. It was Citizen Furlong; in his pocket they found the message from Harvey, urging them to surrender or face instant destruction.

A few minutes later, several thousand rebels, enraged by Furlong's treatment, firing indiscriminately from their muskets and blunderbusses, waving their pikes and screaming contempt for the enemy, swept down from Corbet Hill and threw themselves against the weak line of redcoats dug in beside the Three Bullet Gate.[43]

Twenty-five miles away to the west, the beleaguered loyalists of Wexford waited in trepidation for news of the battle. A hundred miles to the north, Camden and the Castle were no less anxious. But while all eyes were turned to New Ross, a ghastly scene was being enacted at Scullabogue which was to leave a still more indelible mark on Irish history than the battle now raging.

The loyalists imprisoned at Scullabogue had been lodged in an empty house and adjoining barn belonging to a gentleman called Captain King. The barn was a small narrow building of wood and thatch with thick stone walls. Into this had been thrust more than a hundred prisoners—nearly two hundred according to one account—including about twenty women and children. The great majority were, of course, Protestant, though there were some Catholics who had fallen foul of the rebels, some family servants who would not quit their masters, the wife of a militia man, and an old musician whom they accused of playing a loyal tune on his bagpipes.[44]

Soon after the first attack on New Ross, a messenger reached Scullabogue with a wild story that the King's soldiers were butchering rebel soldiers; and that orders had now been given to kill loyalist prisoners in retaliation. The rebel captain in charge of the prisoners refused, unless directly ordered by the general. Another order came, to the same effect, and again received the same refusal. Then a third order, supposedly issued by a priest, and the guards could no longer be restrained.

One group hauled out the prisoners from the house. After taking off their coats and uttering a short prayer, they began the work of execution. The prisoners were made to kneel down and were shot four at a time while the next four were being lined up; countrywomen rushed forward regardless of risk to strip the bodies and take their valuables. All told, thirty-five men were shot on the lawn at Scullabogue, each fusillade provoking a cheer from the rebel guards, according to a loyalist who somehow survived.[45]

Meanwhile a second group of rebels were dealing with the families in the barn. Someone had already put a ladder to the walls and set fire to the thatched roof. In their terror of being burnt or suffocated the wretched people inside apparently tried to push open the heavy door at the back. The guards rushed to the door, hacking at their hands and fingers; the door was jammed shut again. By weight of numbers, the prisoners again forced the door open—to be again thrust back by pikes. One two-year old child actually crept under the door and lay unobserved by the house, till someone spotted the wretched creature and ran it through with his pike.[46]

At last the business was over, the screams faded into silence and the flames died away. In the ruins of the barn they found over a hundred charred bodies, families huddled together and still standing upright for want of space.

For several days, the guards were occupied turning over the bodies to look for coins or other valuables.[47]

2

"She's Stopt, Boys, She's Stopt!"

New Ross and North Wexford, June 5th–8th

Enniscorthy's in flames, and old Wexford is won,
And the Barrow tomorrow we cross,
On a hill o'er the town we have planted a gun
That will batter the gateways of Ross!
All the Forth men and Bargy men will march o'er the heath
With brave Harvey to lead on the van;
But foremost of all in the grim Gap of Death
Will be Kelly, the Boy from Killanne!

Kelly of Killane

ABOUT HALF PAST six on the morning of June 5th, James Alexander, a schoolmaster who lived in the town of New Ross was woken by the distant sound of gunfire. "Detached volleys" they seemed to him. He had once served with the colours in America. They were followed by "some very heavy running fires of musketry, drowned at some periods by the roaring of the cannon". He decided to investigate. His experiences, as he later described them, give a graphic idea of the strange, confused events of that momentous day.[1]

Dressed in his ordinary clothes and quite unarmed, he set off down the main street in the direction of the gunfire. He assumed, of course, that the fighting was outside the town. After all, the main body of the garrison must be between him and the rebels. He passed one group of soldiers: about fifteen men of the Donegal militia and a pair of swivel guns stationed at the Main Guard beside the courthouse. Otherwise the streets were deserted. In the distance he heard volleys of musket fire and in the intervals the faint sound of cheering. He went on more slowly, keeping close into the curved wall of the street.

Suddenly, he heard voices and the rattling of what he took to be cannon wheels close ahead of him. There were five or six shots; then two, four, about a dozen and then a minute of heavy firing. A deafening crash, as a cannon went off just ahead, followed by a "fearful shout" and a "triumph-ant huzza" in answer. He crept forward just as a party of rebels came into view, "stalking down the street in attitudes not unlike my own". As he tried to retreat, he saw a second piece of artillery—a 9-pounder nick-named "Grumbling Bess"—trundled out across the road by some of the garrison behind him. Alexander squeezed himself into the shelter of a bow-window, while the opposing sides stayed just out of sight of each other. For some time there was a "shy kind of firing", as musket balls bounced harmlessly off the concave side of the street. Then, as if by com-mon consent, both sides faced each other. The next moment, Alexander heard a "dreadful explosion", and the grapeshot scored the pavement by his feet, and ricochetted upwards. The cannon blew numbers of the rebels "off their legs". The rest retreated down the street, and it became a matter of hand to hand fighting—sword against sword and bayonet against pike.[2]

The scene Alexander witnessed was now repeating itself in a dozen parts of the town. What on earth had gone wrong with the garrison's defences for the United forces to have broken through into the very centre of the town?

About six-thirty, just when Alexander was woken, General Johnson was superintending the defence of the Three Bullet Gate. At first he had no cause for alarm: the rebels had driven in the outposts, but were then held in check by the flank battalions firing from the safety of their trenches. They had failed in their attempt to repeat the old Irish tactic that had triumphed at Enniscorthy the week before: of throwing the defenders into disorder by driving a herd of cattle into their lines. Here at New Ross, the black cattle had swerved to the side, diverted perhaps by the trenches across the mouth of the gate. Apart from this, the attack displayed no great sense of tactics.[3] With obstinate courage, the pikemen threw themselves against the one place where the defences were strong. The Market Gate at the east was lightly guarded, while two other gates—the Priory Gate to the south west and the North Gate—were hardly defended at all.

Then about seven o'clock Johnson and his staff saw something incredible was taking place. Inch by inch, the defences at the Three Bullet Gate were being battered down. First the soldiers of the flank battalion were pushed back inside the Gate, and the rebel musketmen captured the trenches. Then with these trenches used to give covering fire, a column of pikemen charged forward. The defenders fought back as long as they could.[4] One soldier was seen standing to the last on a wall, firing shot after shot regard-less of danger until he was finally tumbled head over heels back into a burning cabin.[5] Quite suddenly the defences gave way, several hundred attackers swept through the gate and charged downhill into the town.

To experienced soldiers like Johnson and Crauford, the courage displayed by this untrained army of peasants was "extraordinary". It had never entered their heads that the rebels could fight like veterans, covering their attack with accurate fire, and charging time and again right up to the guns. "I never saw any troops attack with more enthusiasm and bravery than the Rebels did," Craufurd was to confess later to a friend.[6] However he might explain this courage—religious enthusiasm, or whiskey —there was not a moment to lose to parry the attack. Johnson sent off his acting aide, a yeoman in a brass helmet called McCormick, to bring up reinforcements to seal the gap in the town's defences.[7]

Meanwhile on the United side, events had taken the commanders equally by surprise. One can imagine Harvey's feelings as he watched his herald of peace, Citizen Furlong, shot down by Johnson's outposts. What hope was there now of controlling the men burning to avenge Furlong's death? As a concession, Harvey sent a popular young man called John Kelly, with a company of eight hundred Bantry men to drive in Johnson's outposts. They had strict instructions not to attack the town itself. Harvey still held to the original plan of attack: simultaneous assault on three gates, by the three main divisions of the army. Kelly was on no account to attack the Three Bullet Gate until the other two divisions were in position.[8]

We do not know if Kelly turned a blind eye to his instructions or whether he simply could not hold back his men. Kelly's company, at any rate, swept on triumphantly into the town, followed by another company led by a man called Thomas Cloney. Their first objective was to get arms. As luck would have it, the barracks was close to the gate, and lightly defended. It was soon taken and its contents—precious muskets and still more precious ammunition—distributed amongst the rebels. Kelly, however, was wounded in the thigh during the action, and completely disabled, a serious loss to an army so desperately short of leaders.[9]

As Kelly lay wounded in the street, his men split into two columns. One vanished into the smoke, while the other charged downhill towards the church, and continued towards the strong point of the Main Guard. It was here James Alexander saw them cut down by grapeshot. After a confused struggle, the survivors regained the outside of the town.

Meanwhile Harvey's other two divisions to left and right had been disconcerted by Kelly's pre-emptive attack. In the general confusion some of their men joined the central body, but the majority panicked and fled. The huge army of twenty thousand or more that had camped on Corbet Hill the night before was now reduced to ten thousand or less. As the survivors of Kelly's party re-appeared outside the town, Harvey's troops continued to melt away before his eyes: some fleeing to their homes, nearby, others as far as Wexford with every kind of story to account for their precipitate flight.[10]

Johnson had regained the initiative, and without a doubt the day would now have been his, but for one fatal blunder.

Below the town, in the safety of the quays, were a small number of cavalry—about fifty of a Scottish Fencible regiment and as many of the Fourth and Fifth Dragoons. Johnson had planned, quite correctly, to keep these back in reserve. Again and again the lesson of this rebellion had been clear: cavalry were useless against pikemen if they held their ground. But, somehow, part of these cavalry were now ordered to leave the quays and moved forward to support the defence at Three Bullet Gate. It is not clear if Johnson himself gave the order. Perhaps he did, believing the rebels were fleeing in hopeless disorder, or perhaps his orders were misunderstood in the confusion of the battle. The Dragoons, at any rate, rode out into the open space in front of the Three Bullet Gate. The pikemen turned.[11]

In a few minutes, the Dragoons' commanding officer and twenty-eight of his men were piked to death. As they lay there a girl called Doyle, who was a wood-cutter's daughter, went up to each mangled body and removed the cartridge box with a slash of her bill-hook.[12]

To complete the disaster for the Government, the commanding officer of the Dublin militia, Colonel Lord Mountjoy, had for some reason ridden out on his charger towards the rebel lines. According to one account, his aim was to try to persuade the people to surrender. He was struck down and lay wounded by the gate, to be finished off at length by a pikeman.[13]

These sudden successes gave an immediate tonic to the United army's morale. With a wild cheer, they returned to the attack. Many of the defenders were caught in the mêlée. One officer, Captain Irvine of the artillery, whose horse had fallen on him, managed to catch the traces of a runaway horse and so was dragged into the town. Johnson himself had his horse shot under him, but jumped clear. For the second time that morning, the garrison were rolled back through the Three Bullet Gate.[14]

The confusion that followed has been described by a field surgeon who was an eye-witness of these events. "Such a scene," he wrote, "perhaps never before happened in any country. Cavalry, infantry, men, women and children, like a torrent running towards the bridge and pikemen and musketeers shouting after them."[15]

Down on the quays, James Alexander heard the firing approach nearer and nearer. Looking out of the window he saw flames rising from a row of cabins opposite the churchyard. Then, one by one, the thatched roofs of the cabins nearby caught fire: first Church Lane, then the Brogue-maker's Lane, then Michael Street and finally Main Street. From the same direction he heard running volleys of musketry, "as rapid and even as the long roll of the drum". Sometimes they were drowned by the roar of cannon or by sudden bursts of fire from another quarter. But the United forces were driving deeper into the town, of that there was no doubt. The noise was now universal. Even the cheering of the victors was almost inaudible. The centre of the battle seemed to be Main Street. Alexander watched fascinated as a four-storey house with a slate roof was set on fire. Gradually the roar of small arms and cannon blotted out the screams of the men— rebels, apparently—trapped inside.[16]

The pikemen had in fact pushed right into the town as far as the Main Guard—the strong point that had proved too much for them at the first assault. They ran down the narrow streets, one holding a taper to the dry eaves of the thatch, another spreading the flames with a pike. Soon half the town was burning. But they still could not capture the Main Guard, where the two ships' guns served by Sergeant Hamilton and the Donegal militia swept the vital crossroads leading to the bridge.[17]

A few yards up the road was an alleyway called Bakehouse Lane, opposite which lived an old loyalist called Dowsley. After each charge, a party of twenty to thirty rebels would slip into this alleyway to prime and reload, safe from the cannon. But none of them ever came out again (people said after the battle) except to be dragged out feet first and thrown into the river. Dowsley had three friends in his house, as well as two sons, a brother, and an old soldier to charge their muskets. After the battle, the dead lay by the house up to the sills of the windows.[18]

Apart from the Main Guard, and a strong point manned by the Clare militia at the Market Gate, only Johnson's own position between the Three Bullet Gate and the eastern wall was still holding out. All morning, Johnson had been in the thick of the battle, three times having a horse shot under him. His aide, McCormick, the man in the brass helmet, led a charmed life that day; finding himself alone, he cut his way to freedom

through a hundred men. He was sent back once again to find reinforcements. But neither of the officers he met—one with a cannon, the other
with a troop of cavalry—were prepared to join their general. At Mc-
Cormick's news, they fled rapidly back across the bridge.

At the Three Bullet Gate, Johnson waited in vain. Then, in desperation he galloped off to look for help himself. He found a stream of
soldiers pouring back across the bridge, including most of the Dublin and
the other militia regiments. Still worse, some earlier fugitives had met on
the road a large contingent of the Roscommon regiment, marching from
Waterford to the relief of the town. In their panic the fugitives, officers as
well as men, persuaded the relief column that the day was lost. They, too,
were soon in full retreat.[19]

Meanwhile, in Johnson's absence, the resistance at the Three Bullet
Gate had collapsed, within a few minutes. It was now about mid-day.
Except for a dozen men with Hamilton at the Main Guard, old Dowsley
and his seven men at Bakehouse Lane, and a small party with Vandeleur at
the Market Gate, New Ross had been abandoned by its garrison.[20]

One other loyalist, it is true, remained. James Alexander was still in his
house on the quays. Since his return from his brush with the rebels that
morning, he had helped distribute refreshments for Hamilton and his
artillery men. The men's faces were scorched by the firing, their teeth and
mouths quite black. Now they broke the news to Alexander. The rest of
the town was in rebel hands. They themselves must soon go under—if not
in the battle, in the fire that was now raging in most parts of the town.[21]

Meanwhile the United army, having snatched victory from defeat with
that sudden, extraordinary display of courage, as suddenly let the prize
drop.

For seven hours they had charged and counter-charged in the gross
heat of that June day. Many were wounded, but had fought on regard-
less; some of their wounds were half-healed after previous actions; all of
them were covered in dust and sweat, the soot of the burning cabins, and
the black powder from the cannon. Now flesh and blood could fight no
more. Quite suddenly the victorious army dissolved into knots of haggard
men hunting for food and spirits, flinging themselves to the ground in
their exhaustion, or curling up on a bed in a deserted cabin still spared by
the flames.[22]

In normal warfare, of course, fresh troops are kept in reserve for such a
moment. In the United army, it had proved impossible to make arrangements of that sort. "All was disorder and confusion and . . . want of judgement on the part of our Chiefs," as one rebel later regarded it.[23] In fact

Harvey seems to have lost all contact with the battle. Instead of pressing home his advantage, he stayed back at the Three Bullet Gate. No one proposed outflanking the two weak points still holding out in the town. No one pointed out that, when the men recovered their strength, victory would still be within their grasp provided they took one single precaution. That was to burn down the wooden bridge to prevent a counter-attack.

Across the bridge, General Johnson must have observed the sudden lull in the battle, as he tried to rally his men. "Will you desert your general?" he is said to have shouted at the fugitives. "Will you desert your fellow countrymen?"[24] The appeal to patriotism seems to have succeeded where an appeal to personal loyalty failed. The army, at any rate, rallied, led by the Dublin militia, who had just learnt of the death of their commander. There was no time to be lost. They poured back across the bridge.

As the third phase of the battle opened, Harvey must have realised he had one chance of throwing back the counter-attack. Somehow he must bring up his own cannon. In the confusion of the attack, the two howitzers, captured at the Three Rocks from General Fawcett, had not been used—except, like the brass cannon, and more than a dozen swivel guns acquired at various times, as status symbols.[25] In addition, they had captured four of the garrison's guns that morning. But what use was any of this artillery without skill and experience to go with it? Peasants could be taught in a matter of an afternoon how to handle a pike. It was a very different matter to teach them to handle a 12-pounder. Now the best that could be done was to fit up the howitzer and the cannon with a gun-crew for each.

The first was led by a young Protestant farmer, called Boxwell, who had formerly served in the Royal Irish Artillery;[26] the other by one of the artillery men captured at the Three Rocks. Both men acted bravely—in opposite ways. Boxwell fired one or two shells "with tolerable judgement", it was said by the loyalists.[27] Then he was badly wounded by his own guncrew's bungling, and, unable to stand, had himself tied to the gun till he died. The cannon served by the prisoner was taken down South Street to try to reduce the strong point at the Main Guard. With a pistol at his head the wretched man was now forced to start firing. The story was later told that after deliberately aiming too high and knocking a piece off a house close to the eaves, he turned to one of the rebels with the words, "Isn't that a fine shot?" "Yes," replied his captor, "but this a better one," and he shot the man dead with his pistol.[28]

Little by little, the counter-attack gained momentum, as the United forces were driven back, contesting every yard, to the Three Bullet Gate. They were still formidable opponents: time and again, they would charge up to the very mouth of the cannon. It was about this time that one of the most famous episodes of the battle is said to have taken place. An old man had cheerfully rushed ahead of the pikemen. Taking off his hat and wig, he thrust them up the cannon's mouth the length of his arm, calling to the others: "Blood-and-'ounds, my boys, come take her now, she's stopt, she's stopt." The next moment the gun blew him to atoms.[29]

But courage and enthusiasm could not now win the day. At last it was noticed that the pikemen's charges were becoming less vigorous. By four in the afternoon they were driven back once more to the Three Bullet Gate. By six, all but a few had retreated to their camp in a state of complete exhaustion.[30]

Harvey and a handful of men remained by the town wall—some of them too dazed or too drunk to take in what had happened. Among the latter was a group of respectable land-jobbers who had set up their post early in the action under the shelter of a high ditch and launched a fearless attack on a barrel of port-wine. From time to time they would stagger to their feet and enquire "How goes the day, boys." But they had never deserted their post for long.[31]

It is not hard to imagine Harvey's feelings at this moment. Defeat into victory—back to defeat once again—and now the tragedy had collapsed into farce. Harvey mounted his horse to ride to the camp. He was accosted by the wood-cutter's daughter, the girl who had hacked off the cavalry-men's cartridge boxes with her bill-hook. She was now seated astride one of the captured cannons. How *could* he go off, she enquired, and leave this "dear little cannon" behind. Shame on the men if they wouldn't help her remove it to safety. Eventually three men were persuaded to help her drag it off to the camp.[32]

Harvey plodded on. Beside him, one of his colonels, Thomas Cloney, had fallen asleep on his horse. It stopped to graze at the ditch. Harvey proceeded alone. Behind them the approaches to the town were now deserted, as the day of horror ended in the calm of a June evening.[33]

But in the town itself, the work of the soldiers had only just begun.

"Formidable to everyone but the enemy," Abercromby's epigram did not seem so wide of the mark. The same men who had deserted Johnson at the moment of danger now returned to claim the wages of victory.[34] Shops were ransacked without a pretext. One soldier made off with cases of port and claret; others staggered away under the weight of a ham. Empty houses were stripped of all their valuables. In all, far more property was lost and damaged *after* the rebels had left than during their occupation. Only one civilian was public-spirited (or rash) enough to try to stop the orgy of plunder. He was shot out of hand by the looters.[35]

Parties of drunken soldiers were now roaring down the streets, cheerfully letting off their muskets at anything that offered a target. Some found nothing better to shoot at than dead bodies—or the pigs that had already started to feed on them. But others succeeded in hunting down the croppies sheltering in the cabins that had so far escaped the fire. There was nothing new in this practice of shooting wounded after a battle; in the heat of the moment, it was regularly practised on both sides. But in the town of New Ross it added a new horror to the streets already choked with mangled bodies and cleft skulls. Many of the victims were merely suspects, who had the misfortune to live in houses that had been occupied by the rebels; some were probably loyalists trapped in houses burnt by the soldiers, or mistaken for rebel soldiers because they wore civilian clothes. The soldiers, as a loyalist remarked, "thought no more of shooting any man in coloured clothes that day, than of shooting a dog".[36]

General Johnson and his staff deplored these scenes. But how could they call off their men? "The carnage was shocking," wrote Major Vesey, the man who had taken over the Dublin militia after Mountjoy's death, "as no quarter was given, the soldiers were too much exasperated and could not be stopped."[37] Johnson had ordered all firing to cease, as soon as the men had discharged their loaded guns. The reckless firing continued; one ball nearly killed Sir James Foulis, the Commander of the Midlothian Fencible Cavalry. He drily remarked that it was "the fourth time I had like to be shot by my own friends".[38]

Eventually Johnson restored some sort of discipline and the firing ceased. Looting continued for some days afterwards, until that in turn was swiftly ended; a drummer of the Donegal militia, caught red-handed with some plunder, was hanged from a tree in the churchyard.[39]

The most gruesome postscript to the battle remained: the rebel dead. In the exceptional heat they lay where they had fallen. For several days they remained one of the sights of the town. Respectable Protestants went to view the huge piles of bodies, each heap marking some phase in the ebb and flow of the battle; the largest heaps were, of course, by the Three Bullet Gate and the Main Guard.[40] Most of the rebels, it was noticed, wore Catholic scapulars around their necks—small leather wallets with a suitable religious text inside. It was said and believed in the town that they included one prayer "to wade up to the knees in Protestant blood".[41]

General Johnson had first to dispose of his own dead—ninety-one men in all. Lord Mountjoy's remains were despatched with his faithful horse and other accoutrements for a ceremonial funeral in Dublin.[42] Humbler men were buried in the graveyard near the Main Guard. Then Johnson deputed James Alexander, as one of the more competent loyalists, to dispose of the rebels. He found it an exacting task. "The rebel carcases lay in the streets unburied for three or four days; some perforated over and over with musket balls, or the bayonet; some hacked with swords; some mangled and torn with grapeshot, and worse still with *pigs*, some of which I have seen eating the brains out of the cloven skulls and gnawing the flesh about the raw wounds! Many rebels were reduced to ashes . . . and many partly burned and partly roasted." The pigs had been shot too and then burnt in turn, so that it was hard to tell between them and the roast bodies of rebels.[43]

Eventually, with the help of a pioneer corps of more than a hundred civilians, Alexander disposed of most of the bodies in an old gravel pit by the town wall. The rest were tipped into the river, to be carried down to the sea by the tide. No one will ever know how many rebels died in the battle or, later, of their wounds. One eye-witness claimed that sixty-two cart-loads were thrown into the river in addition to 3,400 buried in the mass grave.[44] Alexander, who should have known, gives a rather lower estimate: 2,600 in all, including 1,010 bodies counted dead in the streets. Though several cartloads of quicklime were thrown into the grave before it was filled, the townspeople were afraid of an outbreak of plague.[45]

Beside their dead, the rebel army had left behind a vast and diverse armoury; nineteen field guns of all types, shot of every size, a quantity of muskets, an immense number of pikes, as well as the usual green standards of liberty.[46] These, too, were suitably disposed of, apparently, by Alexander's volunteers. The guns and muskets were useful enough, but what happened to the rest is not clear: probably the pikes, as on other occasions were melted down for horseshoes, and some of the standards of liberty sent off to Dublin for Cooke's museum at the Castle.

With these pressing tasks complete, James Alexander found time to inspect the scene of the republican camp at Corbet Hill. All along the way were "old tattered garments and wretched brogues which the fugitives threw away in their flight, many broken bottles also; some stained with wine, and a little whiskey diluted with rain". The house on the hill which Bagenal Harvey had made his headquarters was quite intact. True, there were bloodstains in the parlour where the wounded had rolled and tumbled on the carpet; and the heads of the fire-irons had been cut off to make bullets. But apart from this, and quantities of empty bottles about the place, Alexander could see no sign of the great army which had once camped here.

Going down from the pure air of Corbet Hill, Alexander could smell the stench of those two and a half thousand bodies under their pall of quicklime.[47]

The survivors of the United army, meanwhile, had re-established their camp at Carrickbyrne, and here Bagenal Harvey was once again brooding on his wretched position as their Commander-in-Chief. The massacre at Scullabogue was the last straw. Cloney, one of the few he could trust, found him in the morning after the battle wringing his hands over the murders. "God knows," he wrote miserably, "where this business will end."[48] How could he control these desperadoes who would gladly kill him if he stood in their way? Yet what hope was there of any mercy from the Government? One way or the other, Harvey saw little chance of his surviving the next few weeks. He issued a last solemn proclamation to his army: he would give a reward for the discovery of those guilty of the massacre; and any serious breach of discipline would be punishable by death.[49] But Harvey's days as Commander-in-Chief were now over, he returned despondently to Wexford to try what he could do for the imprisoned loyalists: command of the United armies in the field had now passed to the hands of men of sterner stuff.

Father Philip Roche, the new leader of the republican forces at Carrickbyrne was a huge boisterous curate from mid-Wexford the same Father Roche whom the bishop had reprimanded for debauchery. He does not appear to have been a man of unusual military talent or understanding.[50] But his size and strength, together with his authority as a priest, gave him a firm hold over the more wayward insurgents, while his enthusiasm and courage stirred others to extraordinary feats of arms. He had also grasped the cardinal principles of strategy for insurgents: mobility and surprise. Though weakened by defeat and by further desertions, Roche's army still kept the initiative. While General Johnson was digging in for a second assault, a raiding party was sent down to harass his supply line along the Barrow.[51]

The party was led by the gallant Cloney, and soon captured a gunboat in the estuary a few miles from Duncannon Fort. This little victory did wonders for morale, especially as they found many official dispatches, private letters and newspapers on board. The official dispatches must have confirmed that General Johnson was still very much on the defensive. The private letters were gallantly forwarded to their destinations unopened. As for the newspapers, the wild tales of Government victories and rebel disasters appealed to the rebels' sense of humour;[52] like most people they were more amused than angry to read their own obituaries. It must have been flattering, too, to feel so feared.

A few days later Cloney was sent up to Borris to lead a second raiding party. This time the object was to capture the arms and ammunition from the substantial garrison here on the borders of Carlow. The garrison had fortified the mansion of the local landlord, Mr. Kavanagh. Cloney was sorry to be one of the party, because the Kavanaghs had always been good landlords; Cloney's family had been their tenants for generations. In fact, Kavanagh came from one of the great Gaelic families of Ireland; he could trace his descent in a direct line from McMurrough the last King of Leinster. Still, like so many other men of property, Protestant or Catholic, he was actively supporting the Government. In a war of this sort, there was no room for neutrality. Cloney set off with several hundred men and a small howitzer to batter down the walls. If all went well the insurrection might spread into County Carlow. At any rate the Wexford army, once properly armed, could make a second assault on New Ross.[53]

It was however in the northern army—or the Gorey division, as it had become—that hopes of the United army's victory now chiefly depended. And there the ambush of Colonel Walpole a few days before, and the hasty retreat of General Loftus that it had precipitated, had presented them with a dazzling opportunity. Loftus had abandoned not only Gorey on the northern frontier of County Wexford, but the three main towns in south Wicklow—Carnew, Tinahely and Arklow. The first two were mountain towns of no great strategic importance, but Arklow on the coastal strip would be a golden prize, holding as it did, the key to the march northwards. Only one garrison town of any size, Wicklow, barred the way between Arklow and the capital itself.

On Thursday, June 6th, one of the United colonels wrote to a confederate in Dublin. "Great events are ripening . . . we shall have an army of brave republicans, one hundred thousand strong, with fourteen pieces of cannon on Tuesday before Dublin; your heart will beat high at the news. You will rise with a proportionable force."[54]

The army moved north on the following day—in fact they mustered fewer than twenty thousand fighting men. But, with their swarm of camp followers, they were certainly a formidable total. The men came from every part of the county and beyond: the pikemen of Scarawalsh and Ballaghkeen who had first raised the United standard at Oulart, the marksmen from Shelmalier with the long-barrelled wild-fowler's rifle; and the musketeers from the northern borderland, including a thousand eager Wicklow men. Their leaders presented an equally varied spectacle: some swaggered along dressed à la revolutionnaire, with a pistol at the belt and a green sprig in their hats; others rode along in a more gentlemanly fashion, as though they were out for a morning's hunting. The most senior colonels were a priest, Father Michael Murphy, and two gentlemen, Anthony Perry of Inch, and Billy Byrne of Ballymanus. But no one had overall command. In theory Bagenal Harvey was the Commander-in-Chief of the United forces of Wexford; but in practice his command, weak as it was at Ross, had never extended to the Gorey division. His successor, Father Philip Roche, was equally isolated from them.[55]

The organisation of this immense army had seemed at first simple. It was left to the local leaders to arrange food for their men, to find them billets for the night, and to impose discipline as best they could. None of these jobs had proved too difficult, even if things seemed outwardly chaotic. It was a citizen army; the men had elected their captains, who in turn had chosen their colonels: both officers and men were correspondingly easy-going. No one had seemed to worry if bread was often short or unobtainable; they killed some fat cattle from some loyalist gentleman's demesne. True, it was often difficult to preserve the meat, so hot was the weather; the surplus had to be left behind to rot when they set off on the march. But the exceptional heat more than compensated in other ways; it was the summer of the century: people could sleep out on the ground without covering, and suffer no ill-effects; billets were unnecessary. As regards discipline, the officers of the Gorey division were no more successful in controlling their men than their colleagues in the New Ross division. Still, there were not too many disputes or defections, even if more whiskey was drunk than could be justified on grounds of health.[56]

Nonetheless the lack of a commanding officer, it was becoming apparent, was the army's gravest handicap. The two great defects of the United army—in arms and strategy—could be directly traced to this.

In the first place, no one had any responsibility for servicing and repairing the huge number of firelocks captured at various times in the last fortnight. Many had been broken then, or had since gone out of order; others had become fouled with constant firing of their makeshift black powder; or needed adjustment to their flints and locks. Except for the Shelmalier men, who thoroughly understood fire-arms, the United men were country people who had spent their life working with ordinary country tools—spades and forks and harrows. For many of them a musket was a glamorous new acquisition, a promise of their new place in the society that would follow the revolution. Who cared if its barrel was cracked, the flint worn out, or the lock rusted up? People still preferred a useless musket to a good pike. Not that all the pikes were still serviceable by any means. Many had been broken or twisted in the violent events of the last fortnight and needed urgent repairs by a blacksmith.[57]

All this was apparent to the more intelligent of the Gorey division's officers, but they could no nothing to put things right. It needed organising ability of the most outstanding sort to set up military repair depôts and military forges; to enlist carpenters and smiths; and enforce repair of damaged muskets and the captured cannons.

It was the same with regard to their powder and ammunition. With no high command, and communications between the divided United forces proving so difficult, only one small barrel of powder could be procured from Wexford, to be shared out among thousands of musketeers and riflemen. This powder had to be distributed in loose form; there was no time to pack it properly into paper cartridges. The result was inevitable: untrained musketeers were at special disadvantage compared to trained men, because it took them longer to load and fire; now the gap would be still further widened. There was the same sort of muddle in the arrangements made for the United forces' precious pieces of artillery.[58]

But none of these defects could compare to the complete absence of any agreed strategy for the United armies. It was easy to talk of being outside the gates of Dublin on Tuesday with a hundred thousand brave republicans. But how to plan the advance? How to co-ordinate with the brother armies of Wicklow? How to outwit an army sent to block their passage? The truth was that the "United" army was seriously divided on strategy, as it was on everything that mattered most. The rifts between the rebel leaders at Gorey were not due simply to personalities—nor indeed to the absence of a commanding officer. At root was the fact that their army was not supposed to be more than a *Wexford* army;[59] that is, it was an alliance of local forces that had answered the call for national revolution. No one could deny they had achieved their task far beyond expectations. "All Europe must admire," as their own general put it, "and posterity will read with astonishment the heroic acts achieved by people strangers to military tactics."[60] It was perfectly true. Their success in the county was astounding considering their handicaps. But what was the next step now that Wexford was theirs? No word of guidance, not a whisper of encouragement came from the National Executive in Dublin. In fact, nothing at all had been heard of them since several days before the rising. And despite the reported republican victories in Kildare, Carlow and Meath, no liaison had been established with any of these forces. It was this isolation and their unpreparedness for an independent rôle that was the root cause of their weakness.[61] Now Father John Murphy warned them not to leave the safety of their own county of Wexford. The Wicklow leaders were eager to press on to Wicklow but no further. It was thus a minority who, as we have seen, believed in the necessity of marching immediately on Dublin.[62]

In the event the northern army wasted precious days at its camp at Gorey, just as the New Ross division had wasted time at the Three Rocks and Carrickbyrne. Then on June 7th it marched north—but to Carnew, not Arklow, diverted by the Carnew men who had a private score to settle with those responsible for the murders there a fortnight before. Two days later, the army at last resumed its march. In the meantime, they learnt to their dismay, Arklow had been reoccupied by Government forces.[63]

Even this was not too great a setback. Arklow, like New Ross, stood with its back to a river—in its case, the River Avoca which flowed into the sea not far to the east. At the best of times the river was shallow. In the present extraordinary drought, it could easily be forded a few miles above the town. A glance at the map showed, that after by-passing Arklow, the forces could return to the main road without too much difficulty. One of the junior United leaders pressed the overwhelming advantage of this strategy: if the Arklow garrison gave chase, they could be cut off in some mountain pass, and meanwhile their comrades among the Arklow townspeople could take the town for them.

But after all the delays and misgivings, the United leaders were not the men for a brilliant stroke of this sort. They had already issued orders for a frontal attack on Arklow, and the orders must be adhered to.

After one final delay at Coolgreany, where the officers had greatest difficulty in detaching their men from a wine and spirit store, the army at last came in sight of Arklow.[64]

At the same moment, they were sighted by the garrison, who were drawn up on parade, more or less unprepared for the attack. One of them wrote later that he first saw thousands "appear on the tops of ditches, forming one great irregular circular line from the Gorey road ... to the Sand Banks near the sea as thick as they could stand". The rebels put their hats on their pikes and gave a wild cheer. Then they rushed on "like madmen" waving the green flag inscribed "Liberty or Death".[65]

3

Ulster Will Fight

Dublin and the North, June 9th–13th

Were you at the battle of Ballynahinch,
When the country arose to stand their defence,
And the army all gathered to prove their overthrow,
When commanded by that hero called General Munroe ...

Munroe took to the mountains, his men took the field,
They swore that to tyrants they never would yield;
We fought them four hours, and beat them to and fro,
When commanded by that hero called General Munroe.

General Munroe, 1798

AT THE Castle they faced the third week of the rebellion in a mood of
almost unqualified gloom.

They were fighting for the first time on two fronts—North and South—
and under the imminent threat of invasion from France. Of the latter they
had heard no more news. Nor was the report from the North more than a
bare outline of events: General Nugent so far had only reported that the
rebels attacking Antrim had been beaten off. They could only hope for the
best, though their information was that Antrim's rising was merely the
first blow in a general insurrection of the North.[1]

In Wexford, as Lord Clare remarked, the situation remained "critical".[2]
It was some comfort, of course, to hear that the expected attack on New
Ross had been parried, and the rebels' drive to the West halted for the
time being. At the same time the whole character of the war had become
still more alarming. Who were these peasants who could stand up to
twelve hours of continuous fighting, who could charge time and time
again into the cannon's mouth, and then had only missed victory by a
hair's breadth? "Rely on it," as Castlereagh wrote to Pelham in England,
"there never was in any country so formidable an effort on the part of the
people."[3] "The organising of this Treason is universal," wrote Camden,

"and the formidable numbers in which the rebels assemble oblige all those who have not the good fortune to escape, to join them." Already the rebel armies appeared to include the population of Wexford and most of the four adjoining counties of Kildare, Wicklow, Kilkenny and Carlow.[4]

Strategically, the Castle felt their hands were completely tied until help could come from England. There was even a rebel army organised in the capital, or so Lord Clare, not normally an alarmist, was now firmly convinced. "If the garrison was forced out," he wrote despairingly to Auckland, "to meet an invading army from this side of Wexford, they would probably on their return, find the metropolis in possession of its own . . . rebels."[5] If this was the view of Camden's most senior minister, imagine his feelings at the prospect of the rebels' march north towards the capital. The news had just arrived of the expected attack on Arklow. In desperation they had requisitioned every spare coach in the capital to send a reinforcement of 300 Fencibles post haste to General Needham.[6] Now they could only wait for the outcome of what might well be the decisive battle of the war.

In this anguish, Camden wrote one more of his long bitter complaints to London. Where, oh where were the soldiers from England? Unless they poured an "immense" force into Ireland immediately, the country was lost.[7]

Camden's bitterness about the reinforcements was perfectly understandable. He had asked for 10,000 men; that was no less than Abercromby had said was the minimum to defend the country. Portland had promised 4,000. And now on June 9th, over a fortnight after the rebellion had begun, not a single soldier had landed. It turned out that even the first contingent—300 men of the 100th Regiment—had not left Portsmouth till June 3rd, and by some incredible chance the ship had been sent in error to Dublin not Waterford. As for the rest of the 3,700, some were cavalry, almost useless in this type of campaign, and none would reach Ireland for at least another week. The bulk of them were still struggling towards the ports of embarkation. By the time they disembarked in Ireland, all would be decided one way or the other.[8]

Camden's anguished appeals arrived in London two days later and Pitt and Portland were finally convinced of the necessity of sending 10,000 men. But before these arrangements could take effect, the situation in Ireland had deteriorated once more.

Two days after Antrim had risen, Down decided to follow suit, and by

June 11th the whole north-eastern side of Ulster was on fire with revolution.

"Army of Ulster, tomorrow we march on Antrim; drive the garrison before you and haste to form a junction with your Commander-in-Chief." McCracken's proclamation struck a confident note. But his mood must have been quite the reverse as his troops assembled at their battle stations in the early hours of the morning of June 6th. How much could this make-shift army achieve by weight of numbers alone? Their blows must be swift and simultaneous. That was the plan. But how to co-ordinate all parts of that scattered underground army, so that each detachment knew the part it must play, and the time to play it?

In the chaotic aftermath to the resignation and arrests of so many of his colleagues, McCracken had not been able to fill the gaps in the organisation. Many corps had been left leaderless and isolated. Others were without proper arms or provisions. Even that cannon, the brass cannon from Volunteer days, the symbolic link with the early phase of the independence movement, had not been properly mounted. A crude cradle had been made from a freshly felled piece of timber, and the gun itself mounted on an ordinary farmer's cart. One or two shots, and then it would probably be disabled by its own recoil.[9]

Still, McCracken did not need to pin his faith on pitched battles. His plan, as we saw, was for a double explosion—a simultaneous rising in both Antrim and Down—which in turn would spark off the risings in the rest of the province. It was a plan that might be achieved almost without a shot: each village could be occupied by its local United corps, each town by the people from the area, and so on; in each case the garrisons would be outnumbered by twenty to thirty times their number of United men; their own militia could be depended on to defect; and, as each garrison fell, the movement would snowball, both in men and arms. If it now sounds ingenuous, one must recall that McCracken, like the other United leaders, like Neilson and Sheares and Emmet, in fact every active leader except Lord Edward, had never heard a shot fired in anger. McCracken did, however, have one guiding principle that marked him out from a Jacobin like John Sheares. He was a gentle, idealistic man, and determined that the rising in the North, at any rate, would not be disgraced by a counter-terror in the name of liberty. And to this principle he remained true in all the horrors of the succeeding week.

The town of Antrim lies at the strategic centre of Ulster, astride the main road between Derry and Belfast. To attack it successfully, they must cut it off from the other garrisons. First they must secure the surrounding

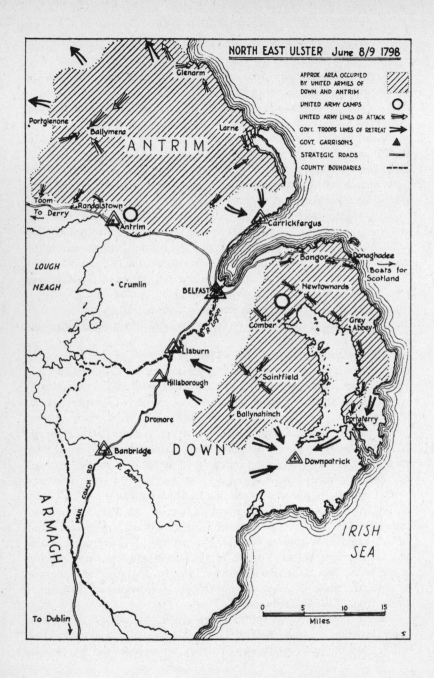

NORTH EAST ULSTER June 8/9 1798

APPROX. AREA OCCUPIED
BY UNITED ARMIES OF
DOWN AND ANTRIM

UNITED ARMY CAMPS

UNITED ARMY LINES OF ATTACK

GOVT. TROOPS LINES OF RETREAT

GOVT. GARRISONS

STRATEGIC ROADS

COUNTY BOUNDARIES

Glenarm

Portglenone

Ballymena

ANTRIM

Larne

Toom

To Derry

Randalstown

Antrim

Carrickfergus

LOUGH

NEAGH

Crumlin

BELFAST

R. Lagan

Bangor

Donaghadee

Boats for
Scotland

Newtownards

Comber

Grey
Abbey

Lisburn

Hillsborough

Saintfield

Dromore

Ballynahinch

Portaferry

DOWN

Banbridge

R. Bann

Downpatrick

MAIL COACH RD.

ARMAGH

IRISH
SEA

0   5   10   15

Miles

To Dublin

S

towns and villages, Toome, to the west, commanding the bridge across the Bann on the frontier with Derry; and Randalstown on the same road but to the north; Crumlin to the south, the most direct link with County Down; and Templepatrick on the road to Belfast itself. The latter was, of course, the most vital road to secure against counter-attack, as Belfast was the largest military base in Ireland after Dublin. But it could be assumed that they would be preoccupied at that time. The strategic centre in County Down, corresponding to Antrim, was Ballynahinch, and this was to be attacked at the same time as Antrim. Meanwhile the other towns would be occupied by the respective contingents in each army.

Such were the plans, hastily drawn up in the last few days, and hard enough to execute in any event. With green colours flying, McCracken and his column marched to the rendezvous at Donegore Hill above Antrim, and waited for the moment. He could not yet know, of course, that the Adjutant-General and Colonel of County Down had been arrested a few hours before, and that General Nugent, forewarned by Magin the informer, was sending reinforcements post-haste to Antrim. It was already clear, however, that plans had partly miscarried. Many of the contingents were missing from their place: particularly, it seems, the Catholic corps originally known as Defenders, who had only been partly assimilated into the United movement.[10] Five thousand had promised to assemble that day at Antrim—nearly half the total United army.[11] It is strange that the Catholics, of all people, had deserted the movement at this time. Those tales of atrocities in Wexford were calculated to affect them least; they had the least to lose, and the most to gain in the case of revolution. There are various possible explanations: perhaps they mistrusted their better-off Protestant neighbours, or perhaps they were cowed by the rise of the local Orangemen. Certainly, their absence reflected the partial disintegration of the movement.[12]

Still, McCracken's army at Donegore Hill mustered at least three thousand and with every hour more rallied to the standard. From Donegore Hill, 800 feet up above the Antrim valley, McCracken must have seen further encouraging signs. Smoke was rising from the market house at Randalstown to the west, while to the north east there was the sound of gunfire from the direction of Larne.

At Randalstown, as it turned out, all had gone like clockwork. A mixed force of Defenders and United men, flying both sets of colours on their pikeshafts, had surrounded the town about dawn. Most of the men were ordinary working people from the surrounding parishes. But they included Samuel Orr, brother of the celebrated William Orr, executed the previous year and now revered as a martyr. Samuel Orr led the party to attack the market house; after sheaves of straw were put under the arches and set fire to, the garrison of yeomen surrendered without a fight. For once the rules of ordinary warfare were respected. Orr took the prisoners and placed them in safety on an island nearby. He then divided his forces into three: one division was left to garrison Randalstown; another marched off westwards to break down the stone bridge at Toome, a task they only achieved after fourteen hours' work with pick and crowbar; the third and largest marched off, as arranged, to join McCracken.[13]

To the north, fighting had been going on in Larne since two o'clock in the morning. Despite ominous signs of the rising, the commander of the local Fencible corps had not exerted himself to make the least preparations for defence, and slept as usual in his lodgings in the town. No one saw the United force as they lined up in a sheltered field below the town. By the time the soldiers and yeomanry sallied out, they were ready in ambush, killed three and wounded another two almost without loss to themselves, and drove back the rest to the shelter of the barrack.

For the next few hours, the battle ebbed and flowed in the streets. Many of the townspeople, perhaps a majority, were sympathetic to the rising: the loyalists barricaded themselves in their houses, or fled down to the little port of Larne. Eventually the garrison managed to get an S.O.S. to the neighbouring garrison of Carrickfergus and were promptly told to evacuate the town. Meanwhile, the force that had attacked Larne had linked up with other local contingents. Some, no doubt, came from Glenarm to the north where the garrison had taken refuge in the medieval castle of the local magnate, Lord Antrim. Taking some prominent prisoners with them—good in any future exchange—the combined forces marched southwards down the glen to Antrim.[14]

About ten miles to the north west of Donegore Hill, but hidden by a long ridge of heather-covered mountain, is the county's second strategic centre, Ballymena. In its turn it was attacked by a United force led by some musketeers who had apparently kept their arms from Volunteer days. The garrison of yeomen and loyalists retreated to the marketplace, and were smoked out by the same method as at Randalstown. All were taken prisoner, including one of the county magistrates called McClaverty. A committee of public safety was then established in the town. In contrast to the wild scenes in the South, the northern United men acted with notable restraint. The shops of some loyalists were broken open, it is true, and the contents distributed. Otherwise the revolution was swift and virtually painless.[15] The only signs of the new régime were the green flag on the church steeple and a couple of dozen yeomen locked in a kind of black hole below one of the captured buildings.[16]

By evening, virtually all other parts of the county, except around Belfast and Carrickfergus, had been captured by United forces. But meanwhile mistakes had been made by McCracken's army at Antrim that were to turn all these other victories to dust.

About two o'clock, McCracken and about six thousand cheering United men marched into the town from the east. Antrim was still vulnerable enough. The garrison numbered about seventy light dragoons, fifty yeomen infantry led by Lord Massereene and about thirty civilian volunteers. These had occupied two strong-points: the market house and Lord Massereene's castle beyond. The other main buildings were undefended: the church, midway along the main street, and the Presbyterian meeting-house at the nearer end. McCracken sent one party to converge on the church from the north. His column would advance down the main street. As for the market house, this was to be attacked by Samuel Orr's detachment advancing from Randalstown.[17]

Astonishingly, McCracken seems to have had no fears about reinforcements for the garrison: no roadblocks were set up along the road from Belfast, nor along that from the great camp at Blaris across the border in County Down. He could not have known, of course, that his plans were now well-known to General Nugent; quite apart from Magin's information, Nugent had now been sent copies of McCracken's stirring proclamation by two of McCracken's trusted colonels.[18] He relied completely on his allies in County Down to carry out their part of arrangements. In fact, there had been no rising of any sort in that county, owing to the confusion caused by their general's arrest. By ill-luck, Crumlin, the town to the east of Antrim that should have blocked the road from Blaris, was one of the few still left in Government hands.[19]

And so it turned out that at the precise moment that McCracken's forces stormed into the town from the east, the vanguard of a strong body of reinforcements from Blaris galloped in from the opposite direction: about a hundred and fifty of the 22nd Light Dragoons with a couple of curricle guns.

At first McCracken's army won the advantage. Once again a cavalry troop made the fatal mistake of charging head-on against a United column, and paid the price with a third of their number killed and wounded. Some were brought down by the old brass cannon from Templepatrick, manned by a weaver called Burns, who fired a strange concoction of grape-shot—fifty musket bullets wrapped up in a silk stocking. In the mêlée, the curricle guns were abandoned by the garrison. But soon McCracken's cannon was disabled, and the attackers pinned down by a party of defenders dug in at the castle garden.

All now depended on Samuel Orr, and the party from Randalstown. As they marched into the town, they were met by the troop of retreating Dragoons. Somehow, the sight unnerved them: the retreat was mistaken for a pursuit. In a moment Orr's men had scattered. No one could rally them. And soon the panic spread to McCracken's men.[20]

Half an hour later the main body of reinforcements arrived: Colonel Durham from Belfast with more Dragoons and 250 militia men, and Colonel Clavering with the rest of the men and two of the latest 5-inch howitzers. Neither took any chances. Clavering remained outside the town, Durham bombarded it for half an hour with his howitzer before entering. But the battle was already over. Except for a small party of United men still holding out in the churchyard, famous in later years as the "Spartan Band", McCracken's whole army had fled.[21]

That evening the victors celebrated in the usual brutal fashion. Suspected rebels—often loyalists trying to escape—were hunted down and shot. Prisoners were as soon disposed of, together with the wounded found in the gardens behind the houses. Their bodies were removed in carts to be dumped in a sandpit nearby. The numbers were moderate compared to those at New Ross—three hundred at most.[22] The story is told of how a cartload of dead and dying arrived at the sandpit, and a yeoman officer called out, "Where the devil did these rascals come from?" A poor wretch raised a blood-stained head and feebly answered: "I come frae Bally-boley." He was buried with the rest.[23]

On the loyalist side the casualties were light—not more than sixty killed and wounded—but they included one of the great Irish magnates, Lord O'Neill. As Governor of the county, he had called a magistrates' meeting that day in the town. By ill-luck he had never received Nugent's warning of the rising. So he found himself alone in the street as the rebels marched in—an old man with a pistol, trapped between the opposing armies. There are various accounts of how he fell. Some say he was set upon by his own lodge-keeper;[24] others claim that the rebels would have let him pass had he not fired on them. He fell, at any rate, a few yards from Lord Massereene's gate, mortally wounded by a pike thrust in the back.[25]

In Dublin, when they heard the news, people recalled that both these victims of popular fury—Lord O'Neill at Antrim and Lord Mountjoy at New Ross—had led the struggle for the rights of the people. Both had favoured Catholic emancipation. To some loyalists it seemed poetic justice that they were the first to fall.

Despite his overwhelming victory at Antrim, General Nugent was left with a daunting task. Most of County Antrim, the richest in the province, was in rebel hands. Somehow he must crush the rising before it spread to the neighbouring County Down. Already these parts were stirring: pikes were being sharpened, it was reported, and small bodies of people were collecting on hill-tops overlooking the principal towns. Everything tended to confirm Magin's forecast of a concerted plan.

Nugent's dilemma was remarkably similar to General Dundas' a fort-night before in Kildare. His main forces were guarding Belfast on the east coast—several thousand men were stationed there and at Blaris camp nearby. The rising in the immediate ring around the city had failed, and the rebels were on the defensive. But how to muster troops enough for an attack without risking a rising within the city of Belfast itself? If he sent too few and they had to retreat, then the revolution would spread like a prairie fire into the western counties of Derry and Tyrone, just as it had spread southwards into Carlow, Wicklow and Wexford after General Dundas' disastrous retreat from Kilcullen. If he sent too many, and there was a rebel rising within Belfast, they might as well abandon all hope for the North. If he did nothing, and waited for reinforcements from Scotland, Down would rise unchecked, and things would be as bad as ever.[26]

Nugent seems to have been a humane man like Dundas, but with an altogether surer touch. In contrast to his blundering predecessor, General Lake, he had conciliated opinion in Belfast,[27] and his tact had earned him what years of bullying had failed to produce—the four cannons hidden since Volunteer days and forming the main armament of the United army.[28] (The fifth had not been surrendered. This was the brass cannon used by McCracken at Antrim.)

In addition about four hundred stand of arms had been discovered—though not without some flogging of suspects. The city now remained quiet and outwardly loyal. A great change had undoubtedly come over the place where the United Irish movement had been founded seven years before—Belfast, that nest of republicans where people had celebrated the execution of Louis XVI by a grand illumination. The previous week the city was again illuminated, and bonfires lit on the neighbouring hills, but this time it had been to celebrate King George III's official birthday.

How far was there any real change of heart? Nugent had no sure means of judging. The loyalists felt more sure of themselves: that was clear from the astonishing growth of the Orange Movement. Of the actual United men in Belfast, many must have been cowed by the show of military strength—the curfews and the courts martial, the searches for hidden arms—which had now been maintained continuously since the outbreak of the rebellion.[29] As for their sympathies, many had surely dropped their flirtation with the revolution after the events of the last fortnight. The Belfast papers had carried terrifying reports of the religious war in Kildare and Wexford: of killing and looting by the peasant mobs, of priests leading them to war in a religious frenzy, and of the Protestants being forcibly baptised to avoid death.[30] If these were the fruits of liberty, better to support the Constitution. This must be at last apparent to all men of property, Catholics as well as Protestants.

It was to this property instinct, keenest in the rich eastern counties of Ulster, that Nugent now decided to appeal in his policy towards the Antrim rebels. Colonel Clavering, who had already received overtures from the rebels, was authorised to grant an amnesty. Clavering's proclamation was a brilliant piece of bluff. If all prisoners were surrendered and all arms piled on the high road between Randalstown and Antrim, he would "molest no one in the county". But if these terms were not instantly accepted, he assured them "most positively" that "he would set fire and totally destroy the towns of Antrim, Randalstown and every town, village and farmhouse with the stock and cattle in this county and put every one to the sword without any form of tryal whatever". Negotiations were conducted by one of two magistrates called McClaverty who had been carried off by the rebels.[31] And on the release of prisoners by both sides, the rebellion fizzled out in Antrim as suddenly as it had begun.

That such terms were expedient as well as humane was immediately obvious. For at the very moment the Antrim rising collapsed, the Down rising began.

Strategically, everything was back in the melting-pot. It was now too dangerous, Nugent believed, to move either troops from Tyrone or Derry into Antrim and Down. At all costs he must stop the rising spreading to the West, as Derry included the best port for a French fleet to make a landing; there were no suitable ports on the east coast.[32] But how on earth had Nugent, despite Magin's warning, failed to prevent this new disaster?

Magin, as we saw, had been promoted colonel of the United army, and on his information, the general, Dickson, and all the colonels had been arrested two nights before. In fact, the organisation, though shattered by arrests and desertions, was still afloat. Once again, the pattern of the Kildare rising was repeating itself. In the short term, the arrests had increased the danger; appeals to reason were less likely to be heeded now the moderate leaders had been removed. The army of Ulster might be mortally wounded, but it was still a most formidable adversary. This was the situation, and it disposed Nugent to adapt a strategy of extreme caution.[33]

First, he must prevent the enemy winning any sort of advantage. He would have to withdraw all his artillery garrisons, and concentrate on defending the strategic towns in each county. Apart from Downpatrick, he would have to abandon the whole east of County Down to the rebels, including the rich Ards peninsula. He would try and hold the line of the Dublin road on the western side of the county: the line from Belfast to Newry by way of Lisburn, Hillsborough and Banbridge. Until reinforcements arrived, it was the best he could manage. He could keep the communications open with Dublin, and block any move by the rebels to reanimate. On the other hand, he had allowed a large rebel force to concentrate only ten miles to the east of Belfast. He had also abandoned to their fate hundreds of loyalist families in eastern Down, including that of Lord Castlereagh himself, whose father, Lord Londonderry, and seven brothers and sisters lived at Mount Stewart in the centre of the threatened Ards peninsula.

Scrabo Hill near Newtownards is a few hundred feet high, but in that flat landscape is visible for miles around: from the flax fields on the western shores of Strangford Lough, to the luxuriant woods of Mount Stewart to the east.

Early on that Thursday morning, when McCracken was marching on Antrim, a schoolmaster called Fox had climbed Scrabo Hill. He expected to find his division of the United army massing on the summit. Not a man appeared. Below him he could see the lights blazing in the barracks of Newtownards, and he surmised, correctly it seems, that the garrison had been warned of the attack.[34]

Next day he met the only official representative of the Down High Command to survive the arrests. There seemed only two alternatives: to try to build a new organisation, or to force their way through to County Antrim, now known to be in the hands of the United army.

But while they argued, a message came that acted "like lightning" on the company. The men of Saintfield and Kill to the west were already up. Promising every support, Fox and another man set off on horseback to raise the neighbouring towns—Bangor and Donaghadee. That night they made an assault on Newtownards with 300 men who had collected, but the first attempt ended in a ludicrous rebuff. In the darkness the two parts of the little army mistook their comrades for the enemy, threw down their arms and fled in disorder. When they plucked up courage to return, they learnt that the garrison had been evacuated some hours before.

It was now late on Sunday, "Pike Sunday" as it later came to be called. The victors had just retired to Scrabo Hill, when a message arrived directing them to march to Saintfield. At this, the men began to complain loudly, according to Fox. "I was torn by a thousand vexations—which no person but one who may have been in my situation can understand or feel—however, after much flattery, I got them to begin to march off by companies and it was eleven o'clock before the rere marched off the hill." At sunrise, they reached Saintfield, where the rest of the United army of Down had now made their headquarters. There were no arrangements to receive them. Under protest, they camped for the night in the main street.[35]

The people had chosen as their Commander-in-Chief a young draper from Lisburn called Henry Monroe. By that strange chance which can make the most fervent nationalists of people of immigrant stock, Monroe was a Protestant from Scotland. The head of the local freemason's lodge, he had had no position in the United army.[36] He now found himself tackling almost single-handed the task of making some military sense of this insubordinate army of 7,000 men.

By contrast to Wexford, where the people had dragged their protesting leaders into battle, in Ulster it was the people who protested against the rashness of the enterprise. There was good reason for this. In Down and Antrim, military government had been kept more or less under control. Some of the leaders might feel too far committed to draw back; their only alternative to the rising was to escape to France or emigrate to America. In either case they must abandon their homes and businesses. But for the ordinary working people, their best hope of prosperity was to stay quietly at home. Already, this was clear from the rising in Antrim, where the threat of house-burning had prevented many United men joining their units, and had even brought others hastily back home. In Down, too, this lesson was now being exploited.[37] On Sunday General Nugent had issued a proclamation almost identical to Clavering's: they must liberate their prisoners and return to their allegiance. Otherwise the army would be let loose to wreck "indiscriminate vengeance" on them.[38]

For Monroe and Fox and the other leaders, the fear of being abandoned by their men was now a very real one. The rising had begun, they well knew, in the least promising circumstances. For some reason to do with subaltern officers, the careful timing of the original general orders had not been communicated to individual divisions. In theory, the arrest of the colonels of a battalion should not have crippled the movement; the next in rank was supposed to step forward and take up the organisation. But the intellectuals who had devised the system had miscalculated the effect of the arrests on such a volatile people "The arrest of a colonel threw the whole battalion into disorder," Fox complained; the result was that "Instead of the forces meeting at any point in collected and organised bodies, they met rather by accident than design; and they were in no better order than a country mob."[39]

On Monday, the Ards division was sent forward to Ballynahinch where they pitched their camp at Montalto, Lord Moira's elegant demesne. Moira was the great Whig magnate who had done more to expose the misgovernment of Ireland than anyone. Fortunately for him, he was in London as the rebels shinned over the park wall, and began to requisition his cattle and other stock for the use of the citizen army. Some help was also given voluntarily. Messengers had gone out to all the surrounding country to find provisions and persuade more men to join them. The women of Ballynahinch hastily prepared oatcakes and salt beef; these were carried in procession to the rebel camp. But, as for reinforcements, they failed miserably. The men of Ballynahinch were as wary of the United army as of the Government. They were all for an independent republic, and for liberty and equality too, if they meant abolishing tithes and taxes. But was there any real hope of success? The men of Ballynahinch retired to the satety of the Slieve Croob and the mountains beyond.[40]

In the camp, the army's spirits began to revive as they settled down for the second day in Lord Moira's demesne. The weather remained glorious. People lay down in the shade of the great oaks. Parties of ladies were conducted on a tour of the camp, and were proudly shown the various types of pike and cannon: steel pikes with an extra hook to cut through a horseman's bridle or even drag him from the saddle, small swivel guns mounted on common carts. In fact the arms themselves were no improvement on the Wexford army's. Only the more respectable class of person had a musket; the rest had pikes, battered old swords and pitchforks; powder and ball were, as always, desperately short. But in contrast to the scenes at Wexford, the atmosphere at Montalto was sober, almost dull. People wore their Sunday best decorously embellished with green. One had a sprig of green laurel, another a green ribbon in his buttonhole. The United officers were to be seen moving down the ranks chatting with their men. Most of them had green belts or green coats to distinguish them and many displayed a patriotic token given them by wives and sweethearts— an Irish harp entwined with a shamrock instead of a crown, the lion and the unicorn lying in disarray or the French cap of liberty.[41]

Monroe had now brought the rest of the Down army to Montalto. Behind the scenes the leaders were divided on what strategy to adopt.

All the north east part of the county was theirs—including the whole of the Ards peninsula. They had set up four military camps—at Ballyna-hinch, Saintfield, Newtownards and Kilgobbin—and makeshift garrisons at other places. Some sort of revolutionary administration had begun to emerge. They had succeeded in preventing outrages to loyalists and their property. At Newtownards, for example, the committee of public safety had made a formal order to requisition cattle and meal from Mount Stewart, in the absence of its owner, Lord Londonderry, who had re-treated with his yeomanry on the evacuation of the town.[42] (His six children had escaped to Donaghadee). Nothing else had been touched, though one of the estate workers had been heard swearing that "he intended to live in Lord Londonderry's house next week".[43]

But were they yet strong enough or well disciplined enough to face regular troops in open battle? Monroe was apparently eager to show their strength. After all, it could be argued they would not retain the initiative for long. And unless they had some sort of military success, they had no chance of rallying the waverers to their side. Fox, on the other hand, believed that it was vital to have more time to drill the men in elementary tactics. So far he had hardly done more than take the men's names in each local corps, and appoint officers where there were vacancies.[44]

At this point, another serious split emerged: between the Catholic Defenders and the rest. For probably the same reasons as at Antrim, the main body of Catholics had shrunk back from the abyss. Those that had come were resentful of Monroe's overall command. According to one account, they even accused Monroe of trying to establish a Presbyterian state.[45]

But while these troubles remained unsolved, the United army saw what they had long dreaded—away to the north west a line of burning houses and farms as the Government troops marched towards them to "wreck indiscriminate vengence", according to the terms of the proclamation. Ahead of them the country people fled in terror. Beds, clothing, flitches of ham, casks of butter, chairs, tables, in short everything that could be moved was carried away with them to be hidden under hedges or in bogholes or wherever would least excite suspicion. Meanwhile a second column of troops was sighted marching from Downpatrick presumably to attack them from the rear.[46]

For three days, Nugent had stuck to his policy of leaving the initiative to the rebels while he summoned up his strength for a decisive blow against them. It was a calculated risk that seemed to have succeeded. In the interval the last embers of the rising in the glens of Antrim had been stamped out, and so had a new disturbance on the borders of Derry.

In Belfast, the preparations for a siege made on the first day of the rising —cannon on all the avenues of the city and at the Laggan bridge to the east—had been succeeded by a vigorous curfew. Every shop was shut, all civilians had to stay indoors, sentinels were posted in every street. Extra volunteers had been enrolled as supplementary yeomen, armed with some of the 5,000 stand of arms that had just arrived from Dublin.[47] By Tuesday morning, with no further response to his offer of amnesty, Nugent sent some English Fencibles and about one hundred Irish militia to Comber where he could cut off the rebels' only line of retreat to the Ards; while Colonel Stewart, the Commander at Downpatrick, was ordered to bring his Scotch Fencibles to meet the main army under Nugent at Ballynahinch. By cutting the Belfast garrison to the bone, Nugent had himself mustered a force of about 1,500 men including half a dozen 6-pounders and two howitzers. The combined operation left the rebels with only one line of retreat—to the mountains in the rear, where they could be mopped up in due course.

On the march from Belfast, Nugent found nothing to oppose him, except a broken bridge on the near side of Saintfield. When he reached Saintfield itself, he found the town abandoned by almost all the inhabitants, and many were said to have joined the rebels. He ordered the town to be burnt, and marched grimly on towards Ballynahinch.[48]

He found that the rebels had stationed their front line on Windmill Hill, to the Saintfield side of the town. They were soon dislodged by a charge of Stewart's Scotch Fencibles, leaving one man behind whom the soldiers promptly hanged from the sails of the windmill. A protracted cannonade followed. Nugent was taking no chances. His troops were exhausted by forced marches, and the weather remained uncommonly hot. As darkness fell, the explosive shells from the new howitzers crashed down on the slate roofs of the houses in the town, sending up showers of sparks, or thumped into the fields beyond doing little damage, though one solitary shell crashed through the roof of Lord Moira's house.[49] The bombardment ended about ten o'clock. Nugent decided to attack at dawn if the rebels had not fled during the night.

In fact, at the sight of these ferocious preparations, the last ties holding Monroe's army together had begun to dissolve. The officers were still wrangling about tactics. One group thought their best hope lay in a night attack. Monroe rejected this, rightly perhaps, for such an unwieldy and ill-disciplined force. But the disputes and rivalries were too much for the men. As the night wore on, hundreds of men could be heard making off across the fields towards their homes, while their captains shouted ineffectually at the runaways.[50] According to one account, 2,000 Catholics from the parish of Loughistand fell away in a body.[51] Certainly large numbers deserted with their arms, leaving Monroe and the rest in a still more critical position.

Monroe's only hope was, clearly, in the strength of his massed companies of pikemen. On the open hill-side, they would be cut down in swathes by the artillery, but in the streets of the town, they could exploit weight of numbers—still in their favour, despite desertions—and their long iron pikes. Accordingly, Monroe sent some of his best pikemen down into the town as soon as it was light. They found that the Irish militia's advance had degenerated, as so often in this campaign, into plundering and looting. And soon they began to drive the militia back, killing and wounding about thirty of them; the dead included their commander.[52]

But this success in the centre was rapidly overshadowed by a serious reverse on the flank. Colonel Stewart had been sent with the Scotch Fencibles and two guns to carry the camp at Montalto. After driving in their outposts he approached within two hundred yards of the main body, and pounded away at their ranks with grape-shot. Time and again they charged with pike and musket; and still they could not get under Stewart's guard, being "blown from the mouth of the cannon like chaff", as an eye-witness described it.[53] Perhaps they lacked the fanaticism of the Wexford men. Certainly Stewart's Scotch Fencibles and local yeomanry were steadier, and better commanded than the garrisons at Enniscorthy and New Ross.

About seven o'clock in the morning, after a couple of hours of heavy fighting, onlookers on a neighbouring hill-top heard the shrieks and yells and the wild cheering fade as the rebels began to throw down their arms and run.[54] Nugent's army pressed almost unopposed into the town, and the cavalry relentlessly turned defeat into rout. Most of the rebels' casualties were suffered, it appears, at this time: terrified men shot down in open country, or cut down by the Dragoons in Lord Moira's woods.

When it was all over, and the army had returned to Belfast, leaving the town of Ballynahinch a smoking ruin, local loyalists came out to inspect the battlefield. One of them, the steward of the Bishop of Dromore, counted seventeen dead bodies and took away a couple of bloodstained pikes "for to be put along with your lordship's other curiosities".[55] Later the Bishop acquired the white plume Monroe had worn on his helmet. The official tally of captured arms was 1,236 guns, pikes, pistols and swords;[56] and some cannonballs embossed with a harp. No one knew how many rebels had been killed, but it was assumed about four hundred. The bodies lay unburied in the deserted streets of Ballynahinch, like those at New Ross a week before, food for the local pigs.[57] Other victims of the battle were taken away at night and buried by their relations. Among these was a young girl called Betsy Gray, who was later to be famous for her part that day. She had fought beside her brother and lover, and they had stayed by her in the retreat, although they could have outridden their pursuers; all three were shot down by the yeomanry.[58]

Two other sad relics of the short-lived Republic of Ulster were found on the battlefield. One was a half-illiterate note written on the morning of the battle by Monroe. "Worthy citizens," it ran, "we have had some small ray enforcement . . . I hope the Defenders have rallied to you. The citizens are all in choice spirits longing for action. Health and Respect."[59]

They also found the bodies of two beautiful women fantastically dressed in green silk, who had carried the rebel standards. They had been known as the Goddess of Liberty and the Goddess of Reason, and were apparently the town prostitutes.[60]

4

A Drastic Solution

London, May 28th–June 22nd

What plaintive sounds strike on my ear!
  They're Erin's deep-ton'd piteous groans,
Her harp, attuned to sorrow drear,
  In broken numbers joins her moans.
In doleful groups around her stand
  Her manly sons (her greatest pride),
In mourning deep, for by the hand
  Of ruthless villains Edward died.

Edward, 1798

IN LONDON, the parliamentary session dragged on; there were reports about dockyards and victualling, transports and stationery.[1] Pitt, the Prime Minister, was in failing health after the nervous excitement of the previous week,[2] culminating in his duel with Tierney, and took little part. He knew that the crisis in Ireland was likely to stir Fox and the Opposition to renew their attack on his Irish policy, and he treated this threat with his usual disdain. But his own mind was also focused on Ireland, and, ill as he was, the crisis had forced him to take a momentous decision.[3]

He would make a clean break with the old system of governing Ireland. The new system was not, of course, to be the sort of Jacobinical nonsense the Opposition were pressing for. That sort of appeasement would be an invitation to the French to take over the country. It would be the final solution combining "practicality" with "propriety".[4] The rebellion had proved the Irish Government bankrupt in every sense. Ireland could neither pay for itself nor defend itself. If Ireland could not, then England must take over the burden.

The first task was to remove Camden. The rising hysteria of his letters showed he was not fit for his present office, let alone the great political challenge ahead. Fortunately he had offered to resign twice recently, suggesting a military viceroy was needed. On June 10th the cabinet received a dispatch from Camden referring again to this offer. Lake was perfectly inadequate as Commander-in-Chief; why not combine both jobs in one?[5] Pitt did not lose a moment. Lord Cornwallis had already been sounded.[6] The same morning the King wrote to Windsor himself proposing Cornwallis.[7]

Home affairs in general were left to Pitt's uninspiring colleague, the Duke of Portland, the leader of the Whig part of the coalition. Despite the bogey of invasion that summer, he could flatter himself that the country's self-confidence seemed to be rising to the occasion. Reports of flat-bottomed barges ready at Dunkirk, Calais and the other invasion ports had only worked up the volunteers to a new pitch of patriotism. The total was now 150,000 with one corps, it was claimed, consisting entirely of clergymen.[8] £15,000,000 was expected at the Treasury for the war loan, and one and a half more from voluntary contributions, led by the grudging royal contribution of £20,000.[9] Yet if there was any war fever, it was not noticeable when a good-humoured crowd, reckoned at one hundred thousand, turned out in early June for that favourite spectator sport—a public execution. In this case there was the novelty that the victims, three forgers, were to be despatched, according to the press, by "the new contrivance of the drop."[10]

Holiday-makers also assembled on Penenden Heath a couple of days later to watch the despatch by more traditional methods of an Irish Catholic priest. It was Father Quigley, the United Irishman, tried with Arthur O'Connor the month before. Quigley, who was undoubtedly guilty of conspiring with France, died with apparent indifference to his fate. After making his devotions, and protesting his innocence in a lengthy speech to the crowd, he took out a penknife and calmly set about peeling an orange. People said he did this to show he could have cut his own throat, but was not afraid to be hanged. After his execution, his head was removed by a surgeon and held up to the crowd: "Behold the head of a traitor." The rest of the ritual—the drawing and quartering—was omitted by gracious permission of His Majesty.[11]

Apart from Father Quigley's execution, Ireland made little impact on English life that summer. True, the war bulletins from Dublin Castle were reprinted in the English papers, suitably edited by the Government.[12] Yet had they been printed in full they would have caused little stir. Few British troops had yet been committed to that theatre of war, and they had suffered next to no casualties. For most Englishmen, Ireland remained a closed book,[13] and its current disturbances were no more alarming than a rebellion in some distant part of Africa.

The Duke of Portland, however, and the authorities were increasingly aware of one unfortunate repercussion of the Irish rebellion in England. They had been warned by the Castle to expect some refugees. "All our women are running off," wrote Lees.[14] "I am sorry the ladies are leaving us," was the comment of that urbane bachelor, Edward Cooke.[15] But no one had foreseen that the trickle of refugees after the outbreak in May would so rapidly become a flood. The eruption in the North had turned fear to panic. From Belfast they fled to Scotland: the families of generals like General Nugent, half the bishop's bench, Lord Castlereagh's brothers and sisters and so on.[16] The refugees from Dublin included the Viceroy's own wife. (This was supposed to be kept secret, but Castlereagh's wife blurted out the news one night in Merrion Square).[17] By every packet they fled, and the ports of England became camps for Irish refugees for the first time since the rebellion of 1641.

People did their best to cope with the flood. One refugee in Anglesey wrote in late May: "Holyhead has never cut so respectable a figure . . . every house above the rank of hovel was fitted for the reception of the Emigrées."[18] But in early June, the authorities had lost control of the situation in many coastal areas of England, Wales and Scotland. In Galloway, it was reported that "the Town of Port Patrick is so crowded with fugitives from Ireland that people cannot shelter and the prohibition of communication with Ireland has reduced them at Stranraer to be nearly starving".[19] Still worse was the situation in south west Wales, which bore the brunt of the Wexford and Wicklow refugees. Some were only temporarily embarrassed for money, as the critical shortage of specie in Ireland had prevented them taking any along with them. But many others were actually destitute after leaving their homes and possessions in the hands of the rebels. At Milford the distress of refugees, "mostly of the genteeler sort" according to the papers, was particularly acute.[20]

To complicate the relief problem, it turned out that not all the refugees were loyalists. A boat load of forty from Northern Ireland landed on the Isle of Man, of which some were found to have battle wounds; twenty-seven in all were shipped back to Ireland as United Irishmen.[21] Other suspects were rounded up at Whitehaven on the coast of Cumberland, after landing in a pleasure boat. The most spectacular arrest had been made a few weeks earlier by the authorities here when William Sampson, the United Irish leader, had been found disguised as a woman, after someone had spotted him shaving. In the fever of the moment many Irish loyalists were now treated as suspects, particularly those who had failed to obtain passports in their haste to escape.[22]

Meanwhile Fox and the Opposition in London were also concerned with the problems of Irish refugees and of two in particular: Henry Grattan, the leader of the Irish Opposition, and Lady Edward Fitzgerald, wife of the leader of the Irish rebels.

Grattan's predicament was an odd one: he needed asylum from the loyalists. Many conservative Irishmen regarded him as the troublemaker who had egged on the rebellion. At the end of April he had happened to go to London to give evidence for O'Connor in his trial for High Treason. Fortunately for him the trial dragged on until mid-May. Before he could return he learnt from his wife that a party of Wicklow yeomen had already paid one visit to his house at Tinnehinch, beaten up his steward, and threatened to hang the French tutor. As a result the whole household had been forced to take refuge with relations in Dublin; they were warned by a friend that they might be killed if they returned. With some difficulty the family managed to get passports and took lodgings at Llanrwst at North Wales.[23]

Meanwhile Grattan had stayed in London, and was himself arrested by Bow Street runners and taken away for questioning by the Duke of Portland and the rest of the Privy Council. With him were arrested the son of another celebrated Irish whig—John Philpot Curran—and the owner of the house, Valentine Lawless, the son and heir of Lord Cloncurry.[24] It turned out that Lawless had written a letter supposedly implicating Grattan in the United Irish conspiracy: it referred to "Little Henry" having subscribed £50 to the fund for the defence of Father Quigley. In fact the Henry in question was an obscure squire from County Kildare.[25] After Lawless had explained this, Grattan was released with an apology, and set off to take up exile with his family in North Wales.

While this little episode was taking place, Fox and the Whigs learnt news of a tragedy involving Lady Edward Fitzgerald, and indeed touching many of their families personally.

On June 7th the Duke of Richmond heard from his sister, Lady Louisa Connolly, that their nephew, Lord Edward Fitzgerald, had died of his wounds in Newgate, Dublin three days before. The news was all the more distressing as he had been thought to be recovering.[26] All the family's efforts had been concentrated on trying to obtain a postponement of the trial till the fury of the rebellion had abated. His mother, the Duchess of

Leinster, had hurried to see the Prince of Wales and the Duke of York; both were decidedly sympathetic.[27] Indeed the Prince of Wales wrote to say that there was "nothing in the world he would not attempt" to help the Duchess in her distress; every opportunity would be given "poor Lord Edward" to get a fair trial; a postponement would both enable him to prepare himself better for the ordeal, and give people in Ireland time to recover "their usual tone, so absolutely necessary to the firm administration of justice". All this, said the Prince, could be passed on in the strictest confidence to Lord Clare. He would have liked to have done more for "poor Lord Edward" but he was afraid that would "do more harm than good".[28]

While his sister appealed to the two princes, the Duke of Richmond had had an audience with their father, George III. He had told the King that Pitt had given him permission to appeal to the Irish Viceroy for a postponement, and the King appeared "very feeling".[29]

Meanwhile Lord Edward's cousin, Charles James Fox, had offered to go to Dublin himself, if it would help Lord Edward's defence, though he was afraid that, his own reputation being what it was, it might not count in favour of "dear, dear Edward". In the event the family decided that his mother, the Duchess of Leinster, with her youngest children, his step-father, Mr. Ogilvie, and two of his favourite sisters, Lady Lucy and Lady Sophia, should go to Ireland to intercede for him. On the road to Holyhead they were overtaken by a messenger with the news that all was over.[30]

Their first pangs of grief were not relieved by the harrowing story told by his brother, Lord Henry. He had returned to London after seeing him in Newgate a few hours before he died. He accused the Irish Government, and Lord Camden in particular, of being responsible. "Amongst you," he declared in a letter to Camden, "your ill-treatment has murdered my brother, as much as if you had put a pistol to his head . . . to his grave in madness you would pursue him—to his grave you persecuted him." No relations or family servants had been allowed near him as he lay there mortally wounded. Time and again Lord Henry had applied to be allowed to visit him, but he was fobbed off with legal excuses. Meanwhile the one man allowed near him who gave him comfort, an officer called Stone, had been sent away, leaving him "possessed as he was of the tenderness of a woman to all whom he loved . . . abandoned, most barbarously neglected". Finally, two days before he died, the Government had allowed one of the United Irishmen captured near Dublin to be hanged from the balcony close to his window. Lord Edward heard the noise. "He asked, eagerly, 'What noise is that?' And certainly in some manner or other he knew it; for . . . from that time he lost his senses: most part of the night he was raving mad; a keeper from a madhouse was necessary."[31]

Hysterical with grief, Lord Henry shut himself up in Stratford Place. Others members of Lord Edward's family took the news nearly as hard: his eldest brother, the Duke of Leinster, was "often crying"; the Duke's own state was the more pitiful because his wife was in the last stage of a long illness; his cousin, Cecilia Lock, had hysterics which it was feared would bring on a premature confinement; his sisters gave way to the most alarming transports of grief; his wife, Pamela, was as well as could be expected, though she had had violent hysterics and was in a state of nervous collapse. But within a day or two the family became more resigned to their loss, and left London for Goodwood where the Duke of Richmond had offered sanctuary for all his Irish relations.[32] Here they were calmed by a long letter from Lord Edward's aunt, Lady Louisa Connolly, who had actually accompanied Lord Henry on his visit to his brother and gave an account of his last days very different from Lord Henry's.

In fact the Irish Government, despite the preoccupations of civil war and the very real possibility that an attempt would be made to rescue the United army's Commander-in-Chief, had leant over backwards to be fair to him. He had been given the best room in Newgate—a sort of peer's suite just vacated by Lord Aldborough, confined for insulting the Lord Chancellor. Here he was attended by three excellent doctors: the state surgeon, George Stewart, and a doctor, well-known to the family, called Lindsay and another called Gamet. At first he seemed better—but the doctors were unable to extract the balls from his chest, and the wounds went septic, in the exceptionally hot weather. He was much affected by the news of the death of Captain Ryan, whom he had mortally wounded in resisting arrest, and still more so by the execution of Clinch.[33] An unfortunate feature of the principal room in Newgate was that it was on the same level and only a few yards from the balcony above the main door from which prisoners were hanged.

If the Government had been heartless to Lord Edward, it was only in one respect, in refusing to let his relations visit him. But when it was obvious he was in great danger, Lord Clare had defied the ban and taken Lady Louisa and Lord Henry to the prison in his own carriage. The pathetic scene has often been described. Lord Edward at first recognised them both and embraced them warmly. But he soon became half-delirious, rambled on about the plans for the attack on Dublin, and said several times: "I knew it must come to this and we must all go."[34] The visitors left him, and a couple of hours later he died. Next day Lady

Louisa wrote a long account of the business to her brother the Duke, that was published, but one strangely moving detail of the deathbed scene has since come to light. Lord Henry and Lady Louisa had somehow managed to control their feelings as they sat beside Lord Edward. But Lord Clare, the iron Lord Chancellor, "cried like a woman when he saw him dying".[35]

A couple of nights later Lord Edward had been hastily buried in the Fitzgerald family vault at St. Werburgh's. Ill-luck dogged even the funeral. Passions ran so high among the loyalists that Lord Castlereagh had arranged for the funeral to take place about midnight, with only a handful of mourners to attend the coach. But the city was under the strictest curfew and the orders never reached the guard. The funeral was stopped by patrols several times on the way from Newgate; the burial did not take place till two in the morning; and the mourners were unable to leave the church until a pass was brought them. It was dawn before Lady Louisa's ordeal was over. She returned to Castletown with a few last relics—his little grey cloak, the watch and chain that he had hung around his neck, and a locket of his hair (to be sent to Lord Henry in England).[36]

The Duke of Richmond, a member of the right wing of the Whig Party with whom he had served in Pitt's cabinet, was now in retirement in Goodwood, amusing himself with his farm and the race course.[37] He was delighted to be able to take his unfortunate Irish relations under his wing. The Duke's first reaction to the news of Lord Edward's death— "a more generous and goodhearted soul I believe never existed"[38]—had now given way to a cooler view. Tragic as the circumstances were, his death was providential for him and his family. The real aims of the United Irish were beginning to emerge. The Duke was convinced "that he had got so entangled with the people he was connected with and His head was so turned by them" that sooner or later he would have "brought on Misery and Disgrace to his family, which indeed his Death alone has I fear now prevented". Privately the Duke observed that his nephew had a weak mind and a weaker character, though he still conceded "his intentions, however misled they might have been, to be good".[39] He had not forgotten the time six years before when he had persuaded Pitt and the King to give Lord Edward a second chance in the army, only to find Lord Edward had broken his word to him, and rejoined the violent anti-Government party in the Irish Parliament.

The chief sufferer in the tragedy was, of course, Lady Edward, and for her the Duke and the whole family declared they would do everything possible. They refused to believe the stories that she had contributed to

Edward's downfall. Lady Louisa, in particular, rallied to her defence in a long sisterly letter to the Duke—"Poor dear unhappy Lady Edward" combined "good religious principles" and "great firmness of mind" with being "lively, merry and engaging". Indeed she had such a "taste for the world that I often thought her more calculated for Aristocratic than Democratic principles". Yet such was her devotion to her husband that "she would have preferred living in a Hut with him, to all the Palaces upon Earth". As for the violent prejudice against her in Ireland for supposedly having converted poor Edward to French principles, people wronged her. Of course she knew her husband's political opinions and, adoring him as she did, accepted them. But far from leading him on, she did her best to discourage him. "More than once have I seen her listen with pleasure to the little opposite arguments that I have held with him." In fact, when she returned from the continent the previous year she had seemed more decided than ever in lamenting revolutions. "How could I think of such things without horror," she had told Lady Louisa one day, "after losing everything dear to me in the French Revolution." If she had been guilty of anything it was during the two harrowing months when her husband had been on the run in Dublin, and she had told some "plausible story" to protect him. But, "where is the wife to be found that would not do so? And how detestable to do otherwise".[40]

The Duke's view was similar, though more briefly put. She was "an amiable good little creature". Yet though he gladly took her under his protection, he had to admit he was "much embarrassed by what to do about poor Lady Edward."[41] She had been expelled by the Irish Government because of her supposed complicity in the plot, and the English Government was no more enthusiastic about her. Perhaps it would be better for everyone if she retired to some neutral place like Hamburg. And so it was arranged. Later that year she left England to go to stay with an old school-friend, a certain Mrs. Mathiesen, at Hamburg. Her three children, the youngest of which had been born a day or two after Lord Edward's arrest, were left behind to be brought up by their doting grandmother, the Dowager Duchess of Leinster. Although she was to live till 1831, Pamela never saw her son again.[42]

While Richmond was resolving these "embarrassing" family questions, the other wing of the Whig party, led by Fox, was preparing to launch a new attack on Pitt's Irish policy. The circumstances of Lord Edward's death were not to be raised in Parliament. Some of the more passionate Whigs, Lord Holland for example, shared Lord Henry's view that he had been persecuted by the Government.[43] But the general feeling was to keep out of trouble, while the facts were uncertain. Some, no doubt, had already begun to have cold feet about the way they had rushed to the defence of Lord Edward's friend, Arthur O'Connor. Instead, the Opposition decided to attack on a broad front: the rebellion was the result of Pitt's "tyranny", and the Administration must be censured accordingly.

The first debate on the rebellion was held on June 15th in the Lords, on the motion of Lord Edward's brother, the Duke of Leinster. Though beaten by fifty-one votes to eighteen, the Opposition could feel they had won a moral victory. The rebellion, Lord Moira said, was not the result of a Jacobin conspiracy, but arose from "immediate & local outrage to the feelings of the lower classes".[44]

The Foxite Whigs had in theory given up Opposition as a bad job in the middle of the previous year. With the exception of the redoubtable Tierney, who had duelled with Pitt the fortnight before, they were now rarely seen in Parliament. Their distaste for active politics was understandable enough. All three planks in their platform—parliamentary reform, Catholic relief and an end to the war—were extremely unpopular in the unreformed Parliament. Even if they had won a majority, this would not bring Pitt's Government down, unless he lost the King's support. But now this Irish rebellion, confirming their gloomiest forecasts, seemed to throw a new, hard light on the evil system they had opposed so long. For the moment their political appetite was restored. Even Fox, the most passionate advocate of the secession, was prepared to put aside his Greek verses, and his mistress in St. Anne's Hill, to return at last to Westminster.

Before the main debate on Ireland in the Commons, scheduled for the 22nd of that month, a secret meeting was to be held in Lord Holland's house to discuss strategy with the Prince of Wales.[45] The Prince's position was, at this moment, a particularly delicate one. He had always been embarrassed for money—when he had married three years ago, he had owed the tidy sum of £600,000—but now his creditors were pressing for £40,000 in hard cash.[46] Perhaps there was some way he could intervene, some motion he could propose in the Lords without offending Pitt and the King too much? Grey certainly believed that he should throw his weight into the scales. It might be the last hope of saving Ireland's wavering loyalty for the Crown. At the same time, Grey warned the Prince of Wales that if he was too clearly identified with the peace party in Parliament, it might cost him the throne. The King had strong views on the war. If the worst came to the worst, he could arrange to have him cut out of the succession.[47]

At Windsor that spring and early summer the sun had shone with the same extraordinary brilliance as in the other parts of the Three Kingdoms, burnishing the ancient towers and turrets, and the new Italianate rooms of the King's suite. But the King remained his old self, moody and difficult, full of barely concealed resentment at his son's reckless extravagance, his ministers' errors in letting this "once firm nation" be repeatedly humiliated by France, and the "outrageous" disloyalty of some of his subjects.[48]

His Irish subjects were now, naturally enough, very much in his mind. He had never been to that kingdom, nor had he ever expressed a wish to: it had given him nothing but trouble during the ten years since his recovery from his illness. At the time he had strongly disapproved of Pitt's policy of giving the vote to the Catholics, and events had proved him right. However, it was not too late for a radical change in their policy towards Ireland. Conservative as he was in most respects, the King would not oppose any change necessary to safeguard that great constitution "which has been the admiration of ages".[49]

At the end of May, the King heard the news of Pitt's duel with Tierney, which had only increased his ill-humour. "I trust what has happened will never be repeated," he wrote sternly to the Prime Minister. Was he so obsessed with his personal honour, that he had forgotten what was "due to his country"?[50] Pitt's duel was followed by a short illness—a flare up of an old stomach complaint—and he was away from court during the next critical days. In his absence, the King learnt of the Irish crisis; the atrocities in Kildare, the spread of the rebellion to Wexford, and the culminating disasters at Oulart, Enniscorthy and Wexford. Finally, in early June, the King heard that his Viceroy, Lord Camden, could not answer for the consequences unless "massive" reinforcements were sent immediately.[51] The King despondently agreed, adding that he trusted that, "As the sword is drawn it be not returned to the sheath until the whole country has submitted without conditions. The making of any compromise would be perfect destruction."[52]

A week later, as Camden continued to bombard England with appeals, the King was asked to authorise a second, much larger contingent of rein-forcements. Once again he agreed, even if it left the country in a "very naked state". Nothing but "the greatest necessity" could justify it. But the crisis over the reinforcements brought home to the King the facts of life concerning Ireland. It would never be at peace unless it was properly governed; in theory it was governed by his ministers, acting through his Viceroy; but the present Viceroy was "too agitated" and "totally under the controul of the Irish Privy Councillors". It was their rashness that had led to the military disasters. If this was allowed to continue, they would "by degrees teach the Irish Rebels to fight".[53]

Next day he learnt from Pitt, who had now recovered, that changes of the most drastic nature were to be made. Lord Cornwallis, the veteran of the American war, was to go to Ireland. His instructions were twofold. First, he must win the war. Second, he must impose the settlement that both the King and his ministers had long regarded as the ultimate solution of the Irish problem—to unite it with England.[54]

The King replied that he was "pleased" with the news. But he added a line that was to be most ominous for the future, indeed which ensured that, as far as the King could get his way, there would be no peace in Ireland for more than a century to come. "Lord Cornwallis must clearly understand that no indulgence can be granted to Catholics further than has been I am afraid inadvisedly done in former sessions."[55]

In fact the King's objections to giving Catholics the same political rights as Protestants was not mere bigotry. It was centred on a strange belief, shared by many of Pitt's cabinet, that this political concession would undermine the Established Church and so, indirectly, the safety of the State.[56] This view ignored the fact that there was no Church Establishment in Scotland or Canada and neither had suffered political disaster. Pitt's own view, that of liberals in both political parties and in both countries, was that the Union of the two Parliaments would remove the last rational obstacle to full emancipation. The Catholic majority in Ireland could not abuse their political power in a United Parliament where the overall majority would be Protestant. Pitt had not, however, decided whether it was expedient to combine the two measures, or postpone emancipation till that dangerous anachronism, the Irish Parliament, had been safely merged with Westminster.[57]

Whatever his misgivings about the King's attitude to Catholics, Pitt had no doubts about the inability of the present Irish Government to rule Ireland. On military grounds alone, the arguments were overwhelming. How could they tolerate a system that had forced the resignation of Abercromby for daring to criticise the Irish army—criticisms that were only too rapidly justified by events? For Pitt, the Abercromby crisis seems to have been the last straw. He had begun active discussions, at any rate, with his inner cabinet shortly after Abercromby's recall in April.[58]

Most of these discussions were considered too confidential to be committed to paper. But we know that Pitt and his confidants agreed with the King that the Irish Privy Council or cabinet lay at the root of the problem.

This was the "fatal" innovation, as Lord Carlisle, an ex-viceroy, called it —"the tormenting thorn" in the side of the Viceroy that had bedevilled all attempts to govern Ireland either by coercion or conciliation. "Ireland cannot be saved, if you permit an hour longer, almost, the military defence of that country to depend on the tactical dictates of Chancellors, Speakers of the House of Commons etc."[59] Carlisle himself does not seem to have been fully in the secret, but the argument led naturally to the Union. For if the King's "friends" in Ireland were a tyrannical junto, who else was there to co-operate with in Ireland? Certainly not their open enemies in the Dublin Parliament, the Grattanites, or the rebellious nationalists in the country.

But when would the time be ripe? Pitt agreed with the King that they "must not lose the present moment of terror for frightening the supporters of the Castle into a Union".[60] Everything that had occurred had only confirmed the urgency of the measure—including the report of Bonaparte's plan to invade Ireland. As Pitt put it, they must strain every nerve "to make use of the few weeks left before his reaching Ireland (if he ever comes)".[61]

Cornwallis' first task, of course, was to win the war—not an easy one, considering the known character of the Irish army and the unknown intentions of the French. His instructions from the British Government were not particularly helpful. He was restricted to using the three battalions of the Guards in a supporting rôle; they were part of Britain's last line of defence, and must not be risked in an actual battle overseas.[62] Otherwise he was more or less free to put down the rebellion in his own way. True, the old Irish hands were never slow with advice—especially that touchy political king-maker, magnate and ex-viceroy, the Marquis of Buckingham. "Bucky", as his friends called him, was a mine of information about the Wexford tides—the effect of a landing in force on the beach would be "very decisive" and the English canals. ("It is *certain* that by the canals you could have them deposited at Liverpool on the fifth day.") What was more, Bucky was pestering the Government to be allowed to go to Ireland in person, at the head of his regiment of militia. "I have no military ardour," he explained modestly. "My time of life and my habits put aside any nonsense of that sort." But he would gladly go to help Pitt out of his "difficulties".[63] In the crisis, with less than ten thousand regular infantry left in the whole of Great Britain,[64] Pitt accepted the offer; and in due course Cornwallis was informed of his good fortune.

One crucial question remained uncertain when Cornwallis left for Ireland—Bonaparte and his mysterious armada. Could he really be heading for Ireland, and if he was, would Nelson, who had been sent after him into the Mediterranean, succeed in stopping him?

All the British secret service could report was that the Toulon fleet had sailed on May 19th with twelve sail of the line[65]—three less than Nelson's. There was absolutely no clue to its destination, except one extraordinary spy report written in late March describing the "scientific" nature of Bonaparte's expedition. He had enrolled teams of "chemists, physicians, mathematicians, archaeologists, naturalists and artists",[66] a distinctly odd choice of party to invade Ireland. It did, however, appear that this strange expedition was absorbing all the Directory's naval energies. None of the invasion ports along the channel coast had any fleet of any sort. There were a few ships at Rochefort and Brest, but in no state to sail, with no troops ready to embark.[67] So England itself was in no immediate danger, and, if Ireland was, it would all depend on Nelson.

It was now the third week of June. After an audience with the King, Cornwallis had posted to Parkgate where he embarked for Dublin. Pitt, still weak from his illness, was left to repel the Foxites' second attack on his Irish policy. The motion was debated in secret, as it affected national security; it appears to have been a damp squib. There were the same accusations of torture, as earlier in the year, and the same cries for a change of Government. But the war in Ireland had rallied the country behind Pitt, and he won one of his largest majorities—204 to 62.[68] Parliament cheerfully disbanded for the four month summer holiday; Fox to his mistress at St. Anne's; the Hollands, Erskine and Lauderdale to a pictures-que tour of Scotland; and Sheridan to his garret near Covent Garden. The Prince of Wales was politely told, no doubt to his relief, his help was not required. It would be "misconstrued" by the Irish loyalists.[69]

At Hollwood, his country estate near Bromley, Pitt's health continued to improve. He was drinking less, and spent the mornings in bed. To visitors he chatted about the pleasures of landscape gardens—and the "bigoted fury" of the Irish Protestants.[70] Cornwallis would beat the rebels, of that Pitt had little doubt. But would the loyalists be as easily vanquished? For the moment, Pitt's plan for Ireland was not to be divulged in that country. On the contrary, it was officially announced that Lord Cornwallis would carry on precisely the same system of government as before.[71]

5

The Relief Of Wexford

Dublin and Wexford, June 16th–22nd

At the siege of Ross did my father fall,
And at Gorey my loving brothers all,
I alone am left of my name and race,
I will go to Wexford and take their place,

The Croppy Boy

IN DUBLIN, the Castle was awaiting with some foreboding the arrival of
the new Viceroy. Cooke was upset by Camden's abrupt recall, and afraid
that it would be seized by their political enemies as confirmation of the
charges against the administration. "Explain and explain and explain how
we can till we tire ourselves," he wrote on June 16th, "we shall never
persuade others of the real Motive."[1] Camden himself felt the manner of
his recall "a strange proceeding". Though he had himself offered to
resign, he now confessed that he "would have been very glad to have seen
this storm quelled during my residence here".[2] In turn, he wrote to Pitt,
his brother Lord Chatham, and Pelham, begging for a post in the British
cabinet, "as a mark of confidence" in him. And Elliot, the Irish Under
Secretary then in London to plead for reinforcements, was instructed to
urge the same to his friends in "confidential situations".[3]

In general, the Castle could now see little military point in the change.
For the war in Wexford had, quite unexpectedly, taken a decided turn for
the better; some optimists believed it might even be over before Cornwallis
took office.

The turning point in the South seemed to have been reached when the
rebels attacked Arklow, the Wicklow town commanding the route to
Dublin. At first the battle had followed much the same alarming pattern
as at New Ross four days before. Two large disorderly columns of rebels,
reported to be 19,000 strong, armed with pikes and urged on by priests,

had attacked the garrison dug into a very strong position on the edge of the town. In the face of a heavy fire of grape-shot from five pieces of artillery the rebel columns flung themselves repeatedly at the Government lines. "Their perseverance was surprising," reported General Needham, the garrison commander, "and their efforts to take the guns on our right were most daring, advancing even to the muzzles, where they fell in great numbers."[4] Just as at New Ross, some of the pikemen managed to break through the line, and part of the town was soon ablaze. Once again, the Government's cavalry galloped off rashly in pursuit of some pikemen and lost a number of their men. All this was too much for part of the garrison, who began to talk of retreat. Some even fled across the bridge to the north of the town.

On the rebel side, however, the lack of gunners to man their artillery effectively was just as keenly felt as at New Ross. And although Father Murphy personally led the attacks on Needham's crucial right flank, the United commanders showed the same kind of blind faith in weight of numbers to carry them to victory. It was a mass attack at the precise point where Needham had anticipated it. Moreover, in contrast to Johnson's predicament at New Ross, Needham had received a reliable reinforcement of British Fencibles shortly before the battle, and had stationed them on the crucial right flank.[5] After two and a half hours of bombardment, the attackers broke and fled, leaving two or three hundred bodies on the field, with the usual sad relics: the battered pikes and pitchforks, the green flags inscribed "Liberty or Death" and the Catholic texts folded in the leather scapulars. The rebels' losses would have been heavier if Needham, afraid of exhausting the artillery's ammunition, had not given the order to cease fire. As it was, they were able to retreat with nine cart-loads of wounded back to Gorey, their most forward position in County Wexford.[6] According to some prisoners it was really a tactical retreat. Once they had replenished their ammunition they would renew the attack with treble the numbers.[7]

Reports of this victory had reached the Castle at the height of the crisis caused by the northern rising, and Camden was in his blackest mood. Taken with the rest of the news from the war fronts, it merely confirmed, he said, the "awful situation" of the country. It would only need a small French force to make these immense peasant armies, inflamed with religious enthusiasm, almost invincible. Yet how were they to tackle the rebels? If they attacked too soon they risked another defeat; if too late, they risked losing the capital.[8] Castlereagh too was hardly disposed to be cheerful. "The rebellion in Wexford," he wrote on June 13th, "has disappointed all my speculations. I had not a conception that Insurgents could remain together and act in such Numbers."[9]

But the third week of the rebellion ended, and there were no further accounts of rebel attacks. The northern rising collapsed. In Wexford, the rebellion seemed to be at last burning itself out, and the initiative returning to Government.

General Lake's plan for the counter-attack had been simplicity itself. Like beaters at a pheasant shoot, they would drive the rebels towards Enniscorthy at the centre of the county, and, after recapturing this strategic town, press on south to Wexford itself. However, after the alarming success of the rebels in pushing north to Gorey, on the Wicklow frontier, the plan had to be slightly modified. There were to have been five columns converging on Enniscorthy. Meanwhile, as planned, General Johnson, the victor of New Ross, would attack from the west. As Commander-in-Chief, Lake was personally to go down from Dublin to take command— his first action in the field since the outbreak of the rebellion. The combined armies would total over ten thousand.[10]

With this plan of operations, General Lake sent out an important cautionary note. They must remain on the defensive until the word was given for the line to advance.[11] Everything would depend on co-ordination. At all costs they must stop the rebel armies slipping through the net. On one important point, however, Lake was strangely silent. He made no mention of any steps to rescue the several hundred loyalists who must have fallen into rebel hands in the town of Wexford—including Lord Kingsborough, the colonel of the North Cork militia and Mrs. Ogle, the wife of the county member.

The reason for this omission was, quite simply, that the Government knew remarkably little about the situation in occupied Wexford. Only two prisoners had succeeded in escaping: Captain Philip Hay (the brother of Edward Hay who was to be the main Catholic historian of the rebellion) and a man called Robert Edwards. Hay had said nothing about the prisoners.[12] Edwards' report was fuller, and regarded as important enough to be sent to Portland in London. It gave plenty of harrowing details: how the garrison had tried to link up with the relief expedition and both had been abjectly defeated; how white and green flags had been run up all over the town as the rebel army swept in almost unopposed; how the rebels had liberated all the prisoners in the gaol, including Bagenal Harvey and Edward Fitzgerald; and how one of their first acts had been to shoot two yeomen who had fought against them at Enniscorthy. But Edwards had left Wexford on May 31st, the day after its capture.[13] Since then there were only the vaguest accounts of the proceedings in the town. They could only hope for the best, although the conduct of the rebels in other parts of the country was hardly reassuring.

The Government's first priority, then, was to destroy the rebels in the field, and by June 14th this aim seemed already within their grasp. As their five columns took up their positions, the rebels made no attempt to break out of the net—except one half-hearted thrust to the north west.

As we saw earlier, Father Philip Roche, after he had replaced Harvey as Commander-in-Chief, had detached Cloney's corps from the New Ross division and sent him to raid the small town of Borris on the Carlow frontier. The garrison, less than thirty men of the Donegal militia, beat them off without too much difficulty. On their part, the Government forces made one offensive move during this lull—a naval action at Fethard at the mouth of the Barrow. The gunboats *Louisa* and *Pakenham*, called after the popular Lieutenant-General of the Ordnance and his wife, gallantly set fire to thirteen empty fishing smacks and totally destroyed them. They also bombarded a potato store in the town. After this great naval victory, they returned safely to Duncannon.[14]

By the 15th, the Castle heard that everything was ready for the counter-attack—bar the reinforcements, which somehow were still missing. It was partly the fault of the exceptionally fine weather. There was little or no wind, and that, of course, meant no ships could reach them from Britain.[15] (If Bonaparte had set sail for Ireland, the same, fortunately, must apply to him.) The reinforcements were not to be used directly, but were no less essential. The Dublin contingent—about eight hundred of the British 100th Regiment—would reinforce that garrison and allow General Lake to take his detachment of the Irish army south to Wexford. Quite apart from the danger within the capital, Camden and Lake were still alarmed by the threat to Dublin posed by the couple of thousand rebels who had formed a camp in the Kildare bogs to the west. There were also fears of an attack from the guerrillas who had camped with impunity fifteen miles south of the capital in the Wicklow mountains.[16]

On the 16th, the Castle was still waiting on tenterhooks for reinforcements.[17] Castlereagh gloomily observed that the moral was clear: "With French assistance the People could have carried the country before a Regiment from the other side found its way to our assistance." The lesson would not be lost on either the Irish rebels or their French associates.[18] And then, on the evening of the 16th, at long last the reinforcements sailed into Dublin Bay. Next day, Lake set off to the South. There would be three days to wait, and then, in Lake's pretty phrase, they would give those "rascals a drubbing".[19]

"GOD save the PEOPLE!" ran the proclamations. "WE THE PEOPLE associated and united for the purpose of procuring our just rights, and being determined to protect the persons and properties of those of all religious persuasions who have not oppressed us, and who are willing in both heart and hand to join our glorious cause . . ."

"In the moment of triumph my Countrymen," proclaimed their general, "let not your Victories be tarnished with any Wanton Acts of Cruelty: many of those unfortunate men now in prison were not your enemies from principle . . . neither let a difference in religious sentiment cause a difference among the PEOPLE."[20]

. As the third week of the Wexford Republic opened, Keogh and his committee of public safety still held a precarious ascendancy over the mob.

But the appeals to the glorious cause—to Liberty and Equality and Fraternity—underlined their own dilemma. How to find time to heal those violent divisions of class and religion? Every day some new tale of Government atrocities reached the rabble of pikemen hanging about in the streets. Some were unfortunately true.[21]

The troops at New Ross had hanged and shot every straggler they found. The mob were naturally eager to retaliate on the prisoners in the town gaol. How to pacify them? One safe concession was to announce that the four most notorious magistrates—Hunter Gowan, Hawtrey White, James Boyd and Archibald Jacob—were to be tried before the "Tribunal of the People". In fact, all four had made their escape to Duncannon. To keep their people out of mischief, the committee also tried to involve them more closely in the town's administration. Some ordinary working men were elected to serve on the numerous sub-committees— the salt sub-committee, the tobacco sub-committee and so on. This social experiment was, in a way, a success. According to Hay, it taught them "the trouble and vexation of which they had no conception until they shared in the labour . . . The common people henceforward proved less troublesome."[22]

As before, property was easier to protect than people—in the town, at any rate. People still grumbled that the committee ate better than they did, but they accepted the principle of rationing, if they sometimes went uninvited to dine at the houses of respectable citizens. Most of the plundered goods had been returned to the care of the committee.[22] (By contrast, a few miles from town, servants were unashamedly ousting their masters. Mrs. Le Hunte, wife of the local yeomanry colonel, was refused admittance by her housekeeper who told her "that she had a good deal of impudence to expect it".[23] And when Mrs. Adams of Summerseat reproved some rebels for riding over her lawn, they replied: "Faith, we ought to take care of it, for we don't know whose turn it will come to, to have it for himself."[24])

What of the people's own view? Apart from their pathological hatred of the prisoners, the mass of the people seem to have been understandably bemused by their new republic. Yet some of the more politically conscious artisans—the tailors and carpenters and shoemakers[25] from the original United movement in Wexford—had begun to think about the future. Their first aims had been local and negative—to protect themselves from the "Orange" yeomanry. But what of the ideals they had talked about in the committees—those intoxicating ideals of Paine's *Rights of Man*? To some, at least, of the Wexford men, liberty and equality were not merely slogans, nor the republic simply a way of ending taxes and rents. Their overriding aims were social, not political. They wanted to build a new society.

This, at any rate, is the message of a Wexford catechism of this date. "I believe in a revolution founded on the rights of man, in the natural and imprescriptable right of *all* Irish citizens to all the land." They would abolish the privileged orders "who consider the people as an inferior and degraded mass, only made for their amusement or convenience, to dig, plow or enlist whatever the tyrant's amusement". Who cared if trade collapsed? "Our miserable and confined commerce is calculated rather to injure the poor . . . our exports are necessaries of life taken from them who labour, and our imports luxuries to pamper the idle." In fact a new egalitarianism had begun to develop at Wexford, far more revolutionary than the ideas for separatism and political reform favoured by lawyers like Wolfe Tone and Emmet and export merchants like Oliver Bond.[26]

But meanwhile, people's attention was focused on one overwhelming question. What had happened to the other United armies supposed to have captured Dublin? For a fortnight, ever since the first wild news of the risings in the Midlands, they had been cut off from the world. Their leaders did their best to reassure them: stories of setbacks for the United army were clumsy lies designed to spread panic. William Kearney, the gaoler had specific news to the contrary. "I suppose you know," he explained one day, "the park near Dublin is full of our encampments, *we*

suffer no provisions into the city, *our* army possessing themselves of everything that comes near it; they have the canals, and have stopped the
entrance to the shipping."[27] Still wilder rumours circulated: the people
had risen in England as well as Ireland. Keogh did not deny these stories.
Tight-lipped, he continued to conduct his usual parade in the heat of the
day—his green cocked hat, trimmed with lace, invisible behind the forest
of pikemen.[28]

If the committee of public safety remained outwardly calm, this could
hardly be said for the wretched prisoners confined in the town. There
were nearly three hundred of them: most of them in the sweltering heat
of the gaol; others in the barrack and others again in the verminous hulks
in the harbour; a few soldiers, including Lord Kingsborough, were lucky
enough to be under house arrest. All these prisoners believed, with some
reason, that many of the people would like to murder them. Their minds
had been further inflamed by recent reports of atrocity. The question was:
would the mob find leaders to make this possible?[29]

Acting a strangely equivocal rôle in the town were the two Dixons:
the sea-captain and his wife, who was still dressed in her captured green
riding-habit. At times, they seemed reasonable enough. Yet one day Mrs.
Dixon had appeared in the streets of Wexford carrying a pair of orange
silk fire-screens. She announced to the mob an important discovery: at
last she had found the place where the Orangemen held their lodge, and
here were their colours. The firescreens came from the drawing-room of
Colonel Le Hunte and had been embroidered in orange—the fashionable
colour a few years before—with allegorical figures. And this, said Mrs.
Dixon, triumphantly pointing to the anchor below the figure of Hope, is
a red-hot anchor for burning Catholics. And before they are burned, she
added, pointing to the blindfold figure of Justice, their eyes are put out.[30]

The people understood it all. In a frenzy, they rushed to the place where
Colonel Le Hunte was lodged, half stripped him, beat him about the face,
tore his hair, and had half killed him when a Wexford priest called Father
Broe happened to pass. Somehow he managed to drag him to the safety
of the gaol. Inside, the prisoners heard the hysterical shouts and the violent
knockings on the gates. Their feelings can be imagined as Colonel Le
Hunte was carried in, wounded by two pike thrusts in the back, and
pushed into the condemned cell. Outside, the mob screamed for his blood.
It was a scene, one hysterical prisoner later confessed, out of the French
Revolution. Whether they were really in such danger was not clear. At

any rate, the mob dispersed as soon as it was given the true explanation of the firescreen.[31]

A day or two later, it was the turn of the other colonel, Lord Kingsborough, to receive a visit from the ingenious Captain Dixon and his wife. Someone had now discovered some real Orange relics: a commission for the North Cork militia to found a lodge in the town, and a pitch-cap for torturing prisoners. Someone, probably the Dixons, spread the news. In a moment, the mob appeared outside the Cape of Good Hope, Lord Kingsborough's lodging on the quayside, waving the pitch-cap on a pike and roaring for vengeance. This time, it was Edward Hay, the Catholic historian, who came to the rescue. Did the people have anything personally against the man? Had they forgotten that he had surrendered as a prisoner of war? The people must respect the terms they had imposed. Meanwhile a kindhearted bystander managed to throw the hated emblem over the quay. For the moment, the mob's attention was distracted, and Lord Kingsborough was hurried away to a place of safety—a half water-logged prison hulk in the harbour—until the hysteria subsided.[32]

These narrow escapes, and the constant threat of the mob breaking into the gaol, so preyed on the minds of some prisoners that one of them actually lost his reason. He was a clergyman called Owens, and his sister, Mrs. Adams, has left a harrowing account of the scenes when she visited the prison. When she arrived, he was roaring abuse at his captors. "Oh, my God, the dead bodies of thy servants have they given to the fowls of the air, and the flesh of thy saints to the beasts of the land. Oh, let the vengeance of thy servants' blood that is shed be openly shewed upon the heathen in thy sight." He stood there, an Old Testament figure, at the prison grating, without shoes or stockings, his hair shaved to his skull and bleeding where a pitch-cap had been stuck on by his captors.[33]

His distraught sister climbed up and handed him fruit through the bars. He assured her: "Don't be afraid, Jenny. I have sent an express to Lord Castlereagh, and to the Bishop of Ferns, and I have desired one of them to buy a harp for dear Susan." And he leant forward to try and kiss his niece through the bars. Then something reminded him of his friend, the Reverend Samuel Haydon who had been piked at Oulart, and he began shouting: "Haydon, Haydon—excellent man! These villains have murdered him."[34]

By the 13th, the prisoners believed that the mob would shortly make a direct attack on the gaol. Lord Kingsborough, now back in the Cape of Good Hope, was allowed by his captors to circulate a message to the other imprisoned loyalists. All prisoners were, in effect, hostages. Could they not persuade the Government to make an exchange of prisoners? It so happened that the idea of negotiating terms of some sort had also occurred to the leaders of the various camps—Carrickbyrne, Lacken Hill and Vinegar Hill—where the United leaders were finding it still harder to control the people. Agreement in principle was reached by the prisoners' committee and their captors. But how to persuade the people? One step was to try to bind them by some new moral commitment to obey their leaders. With this aim in mind, Lord Kingsborough himself suggested that the people took again the famous illegal oath devised by Wolfe Tone and his friends seven years before: "In the awful presence of God, I, A. B., do voluntarily declare that I will persevere in endeavouring to form a brotherhood of affection among *Irishmen* of every religious persuasion . . ." Accordingly, the new republican press in Wexford reprinted the oath and it was distributed to be taken by all the people, "in the most public and solemn manner".[35]

A further attempt was also made to reshape the government of the Wexford Republic. The system of *ad hoc* committees with popular representation was too top heavy and disorganised to handle these delicate negotiations with the Government. A provisional council was established called "The Council appointed to manage the affairs of the people of the County of Wexford", with Harvey as its president. Later its membership was to be formally ratified by popular vote in the different camps.[36] A document was drawn up, duly signed by Lord Kingsborough, addressed to the Viceroy in the name of all the prisoners: they had been properly treated as prisoners of war, and they hoped the Government's prisoners would be treated as well, otherwise they faced "inevitable destruction".[37] Late on the evening of the 14th, a lieutenant of the North Cork called Bourke set out on this mission, accompanied by one of the United officers. He was to go via Vinegar Hill to the nearest Government outpost.

Within a few hours, Bourke returned having narrowly escaped with his life. Someone had galloped ahead of them to turn the Enniscorthy people's mind against the scheme—apparently the work, once again, of Captain Dixon. The prisoners were, understandably, worked up to a new pitch of alarm. Who could now doubt the will of the people to murder them, with Dixon's aid?[38]

The next three days passed in mounting hysteria for both the inhabitants of Wexford and their prisoners. The mob made some sort of attack on the gaol. By good fortune, two of the dozen or so Catholic priests in Wexford at this time happened to reach the gaol in time to drive off the people. Crowds again gathered outside Lord Kingsborough's lodgings, and tried to break in.[39] To add to this, there was a new source of danger to the prisoners—indirectly the result of the Government's own victories. Refugees were pouring into the town from the country to the west and north with fresh tales of atrocities. In fact, the progress of the army towards them could be clearly seen from the Three Rocks above the town, marked by a line of burning houses and hayricks, and columns of country people carrying their belongings and dragging their children. Meanwhile warships had been reported to be hovering around the coast, and gunboats had taken up their station outside the estuary.[40]

On the eve of the 19th the New Ross division of the United army itself appeared at the Three Rocks in hardly better order than the refugees. Its commander, Father Philip Roche staggered into Wexford. (Owing to his exhaustion that night, according to Hay, "less drink than usual" made him "very much intoxicated".) Beneath this boisterous manner, he had always acted humanely towards loyalists, and despite his present state he was now prepared to do his best for them at Wexford. A few hours later the drum beat to arms. All the pikemen and gunmen were ordered to join Father Roche at the Three Rocks camp. The town was to be left to the prisoners, their guards and the various non-combatants including the priests and the Council itself.[41]

It was now the morning of the 20th. At Enniscorthy, twenty miles to the north west, some ten thousand Government troops were taking up their positions to surround the Vinegar Hill camp. To the west Sir John Moore, as he was to become, was pushing forward with 2,000 troops including one of the first British regiments to land; they were guided by some of the local yeomen whose wives and brothers were imprisoned in Wexford.[42]

But in Wexford, as in a nightmare, the loyalists saw Captain Dixon ride through the streets, booted and spurred, up to the gates of the gaol, leading a vast mob of country people who had retreated in disorder from General Needham's army to the north.

Only one member of the committee cared to intervene—Edward Hay. In desperation, he tried to arrange a makeshift trial for the prisoners, and made the seven men on the tribunal swear an oath "not to be guided by public prejudice". By a majority of four to three they voted the first batch of prisoners not guilty. But after they had left, Captain Dixon plied the people with whiskey.[43] Then he took two of the prisoners, including an English wood-carver who later published an account of his ordeal,[44] and persuaded them to make "a full confession" of the Orange plot at Wexford in return for their own lives. The news turned the people to a frenzy.[45]

At first the plan was to deal with the prisoners there and then. But Mrs. Dixon pointed out that they should allow the people on the bridge "the pleasure of seeing them". About two o'clock the first batch of prisoners were hustled down the street to the Customs House Quay beside the great wooden bridge across the estuary, led by a man carrying a black flag with a red cross on it. Here Dixon set up a popular tribunal of his own in a small billiard room. Each prisoner was charged and unless he could prove that he had helped the people by some worthy action, he was to receive sentence of death. Charges ranged from house-burnings to accusations of keeping a wife away from Mass. The chief prosecutor was Dixon. The mob was judge. Inexorably the nightmare continued.[46]

From a window on the quayside a loyalist woman could see the Government frigates. Below her she heard screams. The crowd, many of whom were women, seemed to kneel in prayer. From the tribunal someone counted the numbers in a loud voice, as each victim was led out and told to kneel down on the gaily decorated bridge.[47]

Nothing could save them now—except the Catholic priests of the town. A mile away, cut off behind the high walls of his palace, the Catholic bishop, Dr. Caulfield, was dining with another priest, unaware of the catastrophe.[48]

For two hours, the ghastly ritual continued. Ninety-seven of the prisoners lay dead on the bridge or in the water below, their backs and stomachs ripped open by the pikes of the executioners. And then, about five o'clock, as the last three men of a batch were told to kneel down, they heard a stir in the crowd. Father Corrin had just returned from a visit to the country and immediately hurried down to the bridge to try to stop the massacre. At almost the same moment, General Edward Roche, who had heard of the massacre from Hay, galloped up and ordered them to beat to arms. The Vinegar Hill camp was beset, and every able-bodied man was needed to defend it. The pikemen marched away immediately, and the mob of spectators dispersed. Soon there was no one on the bridge except the three prisoners, still kneeling on the blood-stained planks, unable to take in what had happened. Then their gaolers returned and took them back to prison.[49]

That night and early next morning, the surviving prisoners managed to get word to the committee and both agreed on a common front in their desperate situation. Keogh and the committee were almost as alarmed for their own safety as the prisoners were for theirs. For it was now clear that the Government forces were closing in on Wexford. At nightfall, part of the Ross division retreated into the town. And early next morning the cannon could be heard thundering at Enniscorthy—fifteen miles to the west.[50]

The plan was that Lord Kingsborough would take possession of Wexford in the name of the King, on condition of protection for the town and its inhabitants, except those actually guilty of murder. Three pairs of emissaries, one for each of the armies encircling Wexford, would take this news to Government. Accordingly, Lord Kingsborough put on the regimentals of a militia colonel, and after some argument, Keogh was persuaded to surrender his sword. Lord Kingsborough drafted a remarkably diplomatic letter: "The People here have treated their prisoners with great humanity and I believe will return to their allegiance with the greatest satisfaction."[51] Then the emissaries rode away on their perilous mission, through the retreating rebel army towards the Government lines.

The loyalists were left between hope and despair. Would Lake accept the surrender? If he did, would relief arrive too late? The people appeared to accept the surrender, yet there was still Dixon to contend with. At the gaol the prisoners were bluntly told that night: "Neither man, woman or child of the Protestants should be left alive."[52]

Vinegar Hill—the large pudding-shaped mound outside Enniscorthy where the rebels had made their central camp—is some eighty miles south of Dublin, taking the road to the west of the mountains. With good horses a man could reach it in a day. But the Government armies, 10,000 strong with twenty pieces of artillery and 400 requisitioned coaches loaded with ammunition and equipment, had taken four days to encircle it; and even now, on the morning of the fifth day, General Needham had not reached his position at the appointed time. Lake did not bother to wait for him. With four other generals, he must have felt confident enough: Duff and Loftus were ready to strike from the side of the River Slaney, Johnson was poised to attack the town of Enniscorthy, and Dundas was with his own force, ready to attack on the east of the camp itself. About seven, the cannons opened up a brisk bombardment on the 20,000 wretched rebels herded together around the green standards on the summit.[53]

Lake was, as usual, utterly unsuited to the delicate situation. His aim was, apparently, military victory. He did not attempt to impose surrender first. He gave no thought to the plight of the beleaguered Wexford loyalists. It was not hard to see the risks: unless the plan was for extermination, victory might only disperse the enemy, spreading the blaze anew, with all the danger of an extended guerrilla war. Perhaps the plan *was* for a massacre. In that case it was rash indeed not to wait for Needham.[54]

For an hour, the pikemen manfully withstood the bombardment. But against the rain of grape-shot and the new explosive shells fired by the howitzers, the rebels on the summit had no protection. Like all the rebel camps, Vinegar Hill had been chosen as a rendezvous, not a strong-point. True, the musketeers found cover behind the steep banks on two sides of the hill. But on the east side the hill was exposed, and up this the cavalry soon charged almost unopposed.[55]

The fighting was fiercest in the town of Enniscorthy itself. Here the rebels had posted one of their bravest divisions of pikemen. Slowly they retreated up the cobbled streets, inflicting heavy casualties on Johnson's forces as they went. The dead numbered about twenty; and there were sixty wounded, including two of the Irish militia colonels—Lord Blayney and Colonel Vesey, Lord Mountjoy's successor in command of the Dublin militia.[56]

But soon both rebel forces broke and fled through the gap that Needham had still failed to close—Needham's Gap as people later nicknamed it —along the road to Wexford.

When the pursuit was called off, after perhaps five hundred fugitives had been cut down, Lake's army celebrated their victory in the usual style of the period. Some found bodies to make targets for sword play; others stripped the dead of clothes and valuables. The worst atrocities were committed in Enniscorthy itself. The rebels had turned one of the town houses into a makeshift hospital, and there they had made their wounded as comfortable as they could. Lake's troops captured the hospital and then set fire to it—patients and all. Next morning the bodies were still hissing in the embers.[57]

Meanwhile, Lake remained sublimely indifferent, it seemed, to the fate of the Wexford loyalists. Along the road from Wexford, past burning houses and mangled bodies of men and women at the roadside, came Edward Hay and Captain McManus, waving a white handkerchief and carrying the terms of Wexford's surrender. In due course they were taken to the Commander-in-Chief. For twelve hours they were kept waiting for a reply. Then at three next morning they were given a brief note beginning, "Lieutenant-General Lake cannot attend to any terms of surrender by rebels in arms against their sovereign." As a consolation he added that if any of the prisoners were harmed, he would annihilate the town.[58]

Fortunately for the 200 prisoners in Wexford and at least three times that number of loyalist women and children, all British generals did not act like General Lake.

General John Moore, the man who was to capture the British public's imagination by his heroism in the Peninsula, had marched from New Ross the morning before the massacre on Wexford bridge. After Father Philip Roche's force had abandoned Carrickbyrne and divided, Moore followed the southern division retreating directly towards Wexford. The forces under his command were not the soldiers he had personally trained and disciplined—but some ordinary Irish militia. Their officers were lazy and ignorant with little control over their men. On the march from Cork, their indiscipline had been "quite disgraceful". Moore now found himself in a country that was "rich and beautiful but perfectly deserted". At first the men cheerfully left the column to set fire to the houses and farms at the sides of the road. By personal exertion, Moore imposed some sort of discipline, and there were no further outrages.[59]

At a place called Foulk's Mill, the enemy were formed up in line of attack, outnumbering his little army by about five to one. He, on the other hand, had six pieces of artillery. The engagement that followed was typical of the Wexford campaign, and there is little doubt would have ended in disaster for the Government, had not Moore been the commander. As Moore later commented, his men were brave, but lacked proper officers, and had no proper training or experience of tactics. When the attack came, his centre wavered. Moore had to dismount and put himself at their head as they charged. Meanwhile, his left had broken and was retreating in disorder through a wood. Again, Moore in person had to come to the rescue. He stopped the runaways and when the moment came, "I took off my hat, put my horse into a trot, gave a huzza and got them to make a push. The tide immediately turned; we drove the rebels before us, and killed a great many."[60]

Moore's instructions from Lake were to halt at Taghmon, well short of Wexford. Next morning, as the guns thundered at Vinegar Hill, Moore's army were met by the second pair of emissaries from Wexford. Moore immediately grasped what Lake had ignored: the loyalists' predicament. He decided, contrary to orders, to march to the relief of the town. It was a calculated risk. He had just received reinforcements—two regiments under Lord Dalhousie, the first of the long-awaited British reinforcements that had landed a day or two before at Waterford. But his force might still be outnumbered by ten to one, and there was serious risk of ambush. Through his field glasses, Moore could see crowds of armed men at the

Three Rocks commanding the road ahead. He sent out a flanking party. Fortunately, the armed men dispersed. As they approached the town itself, Moore saw the flames of burning houses and crowds of people running in every direction. Moore halted the main army and sent 200 British regulars into the town.[61] Ahead of them galloped a dozen Wexford yeomen, hardly daring to hope they would find any of their relations alive.[62]

Day and night the loyalists had lived in the shadow of a violent death, and still that fate seemed inescapable. The rebels Moore had beaten poured into the town vowing vengeance on all the Protestants. The mob surrounded Lord Kingsborough's house. The loyalists prepared themselves for a general massacre.[63]

And then that nightmare faded into an impossible dream. About five o'clock that afternoon, Mrs. Brownrigg who had watched the loyalists piked to death on the bridge the previous day, was sitting at the same window. "The rebels were settling themselves as before on the bridge, and sending a boat to the Prison Ship, when, conceive my astonishment, when I saw them all begin to run. I flew downstairs to tell Doctor Jacob. He came to the window. It was no Illusion. Run they did in such confusion that I am amazed numbers were not trampled to death." There was a general cry, "The Army are come."[64] And so they fled, five thousand men perhaps, tearing off their green cockades and tossing away their pikes like chaff, fleeing before a dozen yeomen, and a couple of hundred British regulars. Far ahead of the other fugitives was a man on a white horse. It was, people said later, the resourceful Captain Dixon.[65]

Wild scenes followed as the prisoners were released from the various gaols. "Nothing but kissing and embracing. Most of the men cried violently," was the account of one loyalist lady.[66] "At the windows of several of the houses," wrote one of the rescuers, "were to be seen ladies who were prisoners crying, others deliriously laughing, and more shrieking with joy."[67] Meanwhile Lord Kingsborough, conspicuous from his scarlet regimentals and Keogh's surrendered sword, emerged from the Cape of Good Hope to receive the army in the name of the loyalists.[68] Even General Moore, that professional fighting man, found the scenes "most affecting". He reflected that his work that day had been "one of the most pleasing services that could fall to the lot of an officer". He had just heard of the massacre on the bridge, and had been assured by the survivors that "it was intended to have shot the rest that evening if I had not come on".[69]

In the town, all traces of the Wexford Republic now disappeared with amazing speed. The green boughs were stripped from the windows, and the notices for "LIBERTY and EQUALITY" were hastily torn from the doors. It was the twenty-sixth day of Liberty, according to the republican calendar, as the green standards vanished from the church steeple above the town.[70]

To protect the town from his own troops, Moore kept the Irish militia in camp outside, and left the British regulars to patrol within. Next morning, General Lake marched in triumph into the town, and took up his quarters in Keogh's house.[71] In his official reports to the Viceroy, he described with self-satisfaction how he carried the rebel camp at Vinegar Hill, and recaptured in turn both Enniscorthy and Wexford. He added that he had started the "very painful task" of trying the leaders who would, if condemned, be executed very soon, for nothing but "severe examples can get the better of this rebellion". And he concluded: "The cruelties these wretches have committed would astonish you."[72]

What Lake did not mention, and was incapable of recognising, was that his own block-headed pursuit of military victory and insistence on "severe examples" had dispersed, not extinguished, the Wexford rebellion.

Despairing of terms, the rebels streamed north from the town past the burnt-out farms and dead refugees at the roadside, one army making for the place where they could ford the Barrow and break out into Carlow, the other heading for the fastnesses of the Wicklow mountains, but both still trapped in the vicious circle of atrocity and reprisal.

IV
Olive Branch

1

"Murder Is Their Pastime"

Dublin and Leinster, June 22nd–July 21st

The Rebellion was a sad thing. For many a poor Innocent man was killed by villains on both sides, for Orangemen and United Men . . . destroy poor Ireland and between these rogues all Honest men suffer. But Lord Cornwallis has saved Ireland.

From an anonymous letter to a Kildare magistrate in the summer of 1798

IN DUBLIN it rained. The extraordinary weather of the last seven weeks seemed to have broken at last, as the state procession of Privy Councillors, gentlemen ushers, axe bearers and the rest followed Lord Camden to the quayside. Otherwise nothing marred his send-off in the viceregal yacht *Dorset*.[1] It had been a different story on his arrival three years before. In protest against the sacking of Lord Fitzwilliam, crowds had blocked the streets, and Camden had been hustled into the Castle by a back way; the Chancellor had been mobbed, and nearly murdered; John Beresford had drawn his pistol and fired at the crowd.[2] Today, only loyalists flanked the streets. One of them, John Lees of the Post Office, has left a description of the scene: "No man ever left this Country possessing so perfectly the Affection, Esteem and Love of the people—I saw him a mile beyond the Light House, and took my leave of him under a discharge of twenty one guns from my own Barge—I love the man—a worthier never existed."[3]

Le Roi est mort. Vive Le Roi. The new Viceroy, Lord Cornwallis, had slipped into Dublin two days earlier, by the ordinary packet boat.[4]

Cornwallis was the same man who, twenty years before, had been one of the principal actors in the last great colonial tragedy—in America. After surrendering to George Washington at Yorktown, Cornwallis had returned to England on parole. As strategist and negotiator he had won a reputation for himself, which was more than could be said for many British generals who had fought in America. When peace came, he was appointed by Pitt, on the fall of Warren Hastings, to the combined job of

Commander-in-Chief and Chief Governor of India, where he had served for six years. Recently he had had further political experiences; he had served in Pitt's cabinet as Master of the Ordnance. At fifty-nine he was now in indifferent health, and looked older than he was, if we can judge by the portraits of the period. Still, to Pitt and his party in Britain he seemed uniquely qualified, both as a soldier and a statesman, to bring peace to Ireland.[5]

Cornwallis himself was hardly enthusiastic about the appointment. "You are too good to me, to wish to place me in so easy a situation," he had remarked in March, when the business was first mooted.[6] Now he had arrived, he wrote home: "The life of a Lord Lieutenant of Ireland comes up to my idea of perfect misery," adding half seriously that he even wished he were back in Bengal.[7] Yet Cornwallis had a powerful sense of duty. "If I can accomplish," as he put it, "the great object of consolidating the British Empire I shall be sufficiently repaid."[8]

Characteristically, the new Viceroy made no effort to conform to the seedy magnificence of Castle life. Instead he set up his headquarters at the humbler and more private viceregal lodge in Phoenix Park. Here he lived the life of an ordinary general. One of his British officers has left this account of the new viceregal style, surely the most austere of any Irish ruler until the present day. He breakfasted early and immediately afterwards "retires with his secretary . . . he continues to do business and to write till two or three o'clock, when he gets on horseback and rides till six." After dinner, he spent the evening chatting with his family, and usually retired about eleven. The man himself was as unpretentious as his style of living. "He has held the greatest situations his country affords without their having in any degree affected the simplicity of his character or manners . . . perhaps the effect of his always having felt himself superior."[9]

Poor weak, despondent Lord Camden—no one could accuse him of feeling that.

Before he left London, Cornwallis had agreed with Pitt and Portland, it seems, the priorities to put Ireland in better shape to receive the threatened French invasion. His immediate task, of course, was military: to impose discipline on the army, and surrender on the rebels. But hardly less urgent was the political task, cut short by the war, of exposing the conspiracy, and thus restoring confidence in the Government.

The first reactions of the men in the Castle and the friends of Government in Parliament were hardly auspicious. Edward Cooke was still grumbling about the indecent speed of Camden's removal, and the strange "manoevre" which had made it necessary.[10] Beresford whispered about the Viceroy's well known soft spot for the Catholics, and said that if the Viceroy tried to impose these opinions on Ireland he "could not account for the consequences".[11]

Cornwallis had a simple, soldierly attitude to people of this sort; he completely ignored them. The old cabinet of Speaker Foster, Beresford, Clare and the rest was simply not consulted. Cornwallis had no wish to fall into the same trap as Camden, and it was no time for the niceties of diplomacy. The day-to-day grind of running a civil administration was left to Cooke, and the other secretaries. To manage the wild Irish Parliament was left to Lord Castlereagh. He, at least, Cornwallis found, had "abilities, temper and judgement".[12]

A few days after his swearing in came the first trial of strength in Parliament. His own official measures to regularise the English militia's service in Ireland and to vote on an immediate loan of £100,000 for the loyal victims of the war passed easily enough. But the Commons' address of welcome gave them a chance to speak their mind. For once the rage of the loyalists was not directed against their fellow Irishmen. Instead they chose to launch violent attacks on the British Whigs, like Moira, Fox and Holland for suggesting in the British Parliament the week before that the Irish Government was the cause of the Irish rebellion.[13] Although the indignation was genuine enough, the political purpose was clear: to warn Cornwallis against a change from the "firm" policies of his predecessor.

In his first official report to Portland, Cornwallis commented drily that Camden would tell them all they wanted to know about the present state of Ireland. He himself "would not enter into a discussion of the subject until I am better prepared".[14] In fact after a week in Ireland he already knew the worst. "The violence of our friends," he confessed in a private letter that week, "and their folly in making it a religious war, added to the ferocity of our troops who delight in murder, most powerfully counteract all plans of conciliation."[15]

In the space of a week Lake's rough and ready methods of "pacification" had multiplied the war and spread it across the three adjoining counties.

His belief in letting loose the army to handle the situation in their own way had done much, as we have seen, to provoke the rising. Now it achieved the almost impossible feat of creating new adversaries for the Government out of the shattered armies of Wexford.

It was a situation, admittedly, that would have taxed a much more imaginative mind than Lake's. The loyalists in Wexford had seen both their homes destroyed and nearly five hundred of their number murdered, including women and children. Many of them, particularly those in the yeomanry, were now burning for revenge. The Irish army shared this feeling, partly because they felt so completely identified with the loyalists, and partly because they too had seen prisoners murdered. Whatever Lake did, there were bound to be reprisals by loyalists and soldiers. Martial law is a blunt instrument and inevitably the innocent suffer. But the worse these abuses, the longer the war must continue. What was essential was for every effort to be made to restore discipline on the army, to correct abuses, and to win the confidence of the ordinary people who had never been committed to the conspiracy. Lake issued no instructions. So the army cheerfully continued their practice of "butchering without discrimination", as Cornwallis called it, "any man in a brown coat ... found within several miles of the field of action".[16]

Ironically, these reprisals at last fulfilled the stories of "Orange" atrocities that had originally stirred up the Wexford rebellion. Only one Catholic chapel had been burnt before the day of the rising. By the end of the summer no less then sixteen had been destroyed in this county alone.[17] In Gorey before the outbreak there had been one or two isolated cases of flogging.[18] Now Hunter Gowan scoured the country looking for rebel fugitives, recklessly shooting suspects and burning houses.[19] Moore, by his own account, did succeed in preventing the yeomen taking revenge on the local people. He explained to them that it was "to their interest that the past should be forgotten". If they had information against anyone, he would be prosecuted according to the law. If they took the law into their own hands, the country would revert once again to anarchy. Eventually, by force of character and threat of punishment, Moore persuaded the yeomen that it would be imprudent to disobey.[20] In most areas, however, Lake's policy was triumphant. West of Enniscorthy nearly two hundred country people were murdered, according to Cloney.[21] Over the whole country perhaps ten or twenty times that number must have perished at this period, many of whom had not the slightest connection with the events that had provoked the reprisals. Around Wexford where there had been no incidents of any sort before the outbreak some German mercenary Dragoons led by Colonel Hompesch had an orgy of looting and rape. It was the same wherever the military went—except for the places where commanders like Moore took special measures to prevent it.[22]

This reckless policy to the innocent reduced the chances of a quick surrender by the people who had actually been involved. And here again Lake achieved the difficult feat of exacerbating the problem.

The situation was an unusual one. Many thousands of rebels—perhaps half of the 40,000 who had, at one time or another, joined in the rebellion —assumed that Lord Kingsborough's terms for surrendering Wexford had been endorsed by Lake. As a result they had left the two Wexford armies and were awaiting official protections. The remaining rebels in arms, including the men like Perry and Fitzgerald who had organised the United movement, were more skeptical of the Government's good faith. But the effective Commander-in-Chief, Father Philip Roche, decided to try to negotiate. He rode back to Wexford on the day of Lake's triumphal entry. The western division which he had led in person, arranged for word to be sent them if terms could be arranged.[23]

Legally, the rebel leaders were guilty of treason, unless they could prove they acted under duress. Yet there was a strong case for clemency. It was not always necessary to be too fussy about the law, as Lake himself had frequently observed. The law of treason did not take into account the peculiar origins of the Wexford rebellion. As a blood feud between two communities, it had caught up people of every class who had no wish to be involved. Some had joined the uprising to protect themselves, others their property; others had acted from altruism, others again from fear. But few had wanted it, and fewer still welcomed the brutal form it had taken.[24]

To all such considerations, Lake remained, as usual, indifferent. Only "severe examples" would serve. Pardon could be offered the "deluded" masses: the "villains" who had led them must pay the penalty in full. That was the rule, and Lake was in no mood to be soft.

Accordingly Father Roche was dragged off his horse, knocked about the face till he was hardly recognizable, tried by a summary court martial and hanged three days later on Wexford bridge.[25]

For the next few days Lake continued doggedly at this task, without discriminating against Catholic or Protestant, or taking any account of the different degrees of responsibility among the leaders. Next to be executed was another man who had surrendered himself—Matthew Keogh, the rebel governor. He was taken to the bridge along with Father Roche. He made an eloquent speech at the scaffold protesting his innocence. Moore, who happened to be present was much struck by his assertion that he had never been a United man. He got the execution postponed, and ran to see Lake—but Lake reassured him that he had proof of his having had correspondence "of the most violent and horrid kind" with the rebel chiefs.[26] Keogh was hanged, and his head stuck on a spike over the courthouse.[27]

Meanwhile, the other gentlemen caught up in the rebellion—Harvey, the Protestant, and Colclough, the Catholic—had believed that their own claims to have acted under duress would be accepted. After Wexford's surrender they simply went home to their country estates. To show his loyalty, Harvey sent an offering of some cattle to the army. When he realised the danger, he and Colclough fled to one of the Saltees Islands off the Wexford coast, taking with them in addition to Colclough's wife, a feather bed, a keg of whiskey, a tub of water, a live sheep, a crock of pickled pork, a chest of the family plate, and other comforts.[28] But their flight was somehow noticed, and a landing party, composed of some sailors and men of the Queen's regiment, was despatched in a cutter to bring them back.[29] They were found in a cave disguised as peasants, according to one account. At any rate, they and their valuables were placed under strict guard, and lodged in the gaol. At their courts martial, both Colclough and Harvey made the same kind of plea as Keogh, though they admitted having been members of the United movement for three years. Soon their heads joined Keogh's on the railings of the court house.[30]

Lake selected a third gentleman that week to make an example of—sixty-five-year old Cornelius Grogan of Johnstown Castle. Whatever could be said about the others, Grogan was undoubtedly innocent. Too old and gouty to ride a horse, the rebels had taken him under guard to New Ross. He was convicted on the evidence of a loyalist who claimed he had led the rebel divisions. His other crime was supposed to have been acting as the rebels' commissary.[31] In fact, he had only issued one warrant for food, and that under duress. Ironically, Grogan's brothers had fought bravely on the Government side. One of them had been killed in a cavalry charge during the battle of Arklow. The other, who had been wounded at New Ross, now tried to intercede for him. The case against his brother, it was claimed, had been rigged by his political enemies; Grogan himself was a liberal, and had fallen foul of the local ultras at the recent elections.[32] Lake knew better: the law must take its course. Grogan's head was sent to join the others on the court-house railings. His body was thrown into the river, where it was later rescued by one of the old man's servants, reunited with the head and buried in the family graveyard.[33]

After this display of strength—and the executions soon totalled more than a dozen, including a tanner, a grocer, and others—Lake announced that he would give the "deluded" masses a final chance of surrender. The condition was that they should bring in their arms within three days and either give up their leaders to the Government or send information of where they could be found. If they did not accept these terms he promised them "just vengeance". It would be his "indispensable duty" to destroy "every town, cottage, and farmhouse" that was found unoccupied, and put to the sword without trial every person found in arms or with arms in their possession. With that he returned to Dublin to report his successes to the new Viceroy.[34]

Wexford and Enniscorthy had fallen; their camps at Vinegar Hill, the Three Rocks and Gorey Hill, were in royal hands. Where could the surviving Wexford armies turn?

The next phase of the struggle is as inexplicable as the outbreak itself, if the Wexford war is taken in isolation. But there was another potent force still driving on the Wexford men, as well as the despair fostered by the Government's reckless policies. Paradoxically, this was hope.

For three weeks they had held their county in the name of the Republic —the Irish Republic.[35] Those of the leaders who, like Perry and Fitzgerald, had been in touch with the Dublin Executive knew of the plan, as we saw, for the inner counties to attack Dublin. Wexford's rôle was to take over the county and wait for instructions. No instructions, of course, had arrived. There were stories of the capital being blockaded by the combined armies of Wicklow, Meath and Kildare. If the leaders adopted a less credulous attitude than their followers, they knew nothing positively to disprove the stories. All they knew for certain was that the republican armies had established two large camps—one on the Meath-Kildare border and the other in the frontier of Wicklow and County Dublin. This fact, taken with the apparent helplessness of the Dublin garrison, either in attacking these camps or in sending relief to Wexford, made it possible that the stories were true, and that Wexford was still on the winning side in the national struggle.

Now, after Lake's arrival, they learnt at last the shattering truth.[36] Many of the rank and file, and those of the leaders, who had never joined the United party, now despaired of success and snatched at the chance of surrender. It was different for the others, the hard core of the United movement in Wexford and their followers. They despaired of being able to surrender; and instead clung to the hope of linking up with United armies elsewhere.[37]

For in fact there were two camps near Dublin still in republican control. Despite a series of attacks by the Government, these had still survived as bases for an attack on the capital. The Kildare camp was at Timahoe on a gravelly island in the trackless Bog of Allen. The Wicklow camp was above Blessington on the edge of the great mountain spine that runs from within a few miles of Dublin to the borders of Wexford.

The two Wexford armies now separated again—the northern army under Perry and Fitzgerald to make for the mountains, the western army led by Father John Murphy to head for the central plain. Ammunition for both armies, always chronically short, was desperately needed. To capture ammunition, they would be forced to adopt the dangerous tactic of attacking fortified posts. But the western army, at any rate, had hopes of raising the country as they went—especially the Kilkenny mining towns where the unemployed coal miners were notoriously disaffected.[38]

As an epic, the western army's march to the Midlands was unique, even in that year of wonders. Loaded with stores and wounded, their wagon train struggled up to the misty watershed that marks the border with Carlow; across the Barrow at Goresbridge, where they brushed aside the small posse supposed to block their passage; up to the watershed again and down through the hill fog into County Kilkenny: and on another thirty miles into Queen's County. Nothing could stop them. Sir Charles Asgill and 1,100 men of the Kilkenny garrison sallied out to meet them and hastily retreated to Kilkenny. Yet all their marching, all their skill and endurance were tragically wasted. The country people eyed the army of Wexford with suspicion; some fled as though they were the yeomanry. They were exhausted and short of food. They failed to capture any ammunition, despite some bitter fighting.[39] They could not get information about the movements of the enemy. On they marched, still refusing to believe the people would not rise at the sight of the standard. Only one small party joined them in all those four counties—the miners of Castlecomer. Next day they deserted, taking the Wexford men's guns along with them.[40]

At length the survivors struggled back across the Barrow, crossed the shoulder of Mount Leinster and doubled back into Wicklow. They had marched through five counties in the space of a week—and all for nothing. They found the northern army led by Perry and Fitzgerald were in little better state. Despite some ferocious reprisals against the yeomanry, and some brilliant defensive actions against the regular army, they had failed to gather new recruits or capture new stocks of ammunition. Many of their best men had been killed in the desperate ten-hour siege of the barracks at Hacketstown. Others had returned in despair to the guerrilla war in the woods near Enniscorthy.[41]

June ended and July came—wet and cold for the remnants of the Wexford army left behind in the fastnesses of the Wicklow mountains.

But the main body, and the hard core of the United army including Perry and Fitzgerald, after a brief respite had marched away. They had decided to try a second attempt to link up with the United army of Kildare, and make a last forlorn attempt to raise the 100,000 men pledged to the Cause in the counties around the capital.[42]

By the first week of July, some fresh air had begun to blow down the dusty corridors of the Castle. As a first priority, Cornwallis announced that he was determined to stamp out the practice of indiscriminate floggings and hangings by yeomen and magistrates. No punishment "under any pretence whatever" must be inflicted without confirmation by a general, after a properly constituted court martial.[43] Privately, Cornwallis had no great confidence in courts martial. "There is no law either in town or county except martial law," he wrote to a friend in England. "but you know enough of that to see all the horrors of it, even in the best administration of it, judge then how it must be conducted by Irishmen heated with passion and revenge." Still, even this was better than the "numberless murders" hourly committed by loyalists "without any process or examination whatever".[44]

At the same time Cornwallis instructed his generals to offer pardon to the rank and file of the rebel army provided they surrendered their arms and took the oath of allegiance. This offer was significantly more humane than Lake's. The ordinary people did not now have to betray their leaders as the price of pardon, nor did the army threaten collective punishment on towns and villages. Yet its results were disappointing: a majority of the rebels in arms ignored it. It began to emerge that there was little real difference between most of the leaders and the rest.[45] Cornwallis did not then flinch from the extremely bold course of a general amnesty. Leaders would be offered their lives, though they would be liable to be exiled abroad. The only exception to the amnesty would be the handful guilty of "cool and deliberate murder". But how on earth to carry this measure with Parliament and Privy Council in the present mood?

"The conversation of the principal persons of the country," wrote Cornwallis that month, in a renewed outburst at his predicament, "all tends to encourage this system of blood, and the conversation even at my table, where you will suppose I do all I can to prevent it, always turns on hanging, shooting, burning etc., etc. If a priest has been put to death the greatest joy is expressed by the whole Company."[46]

There is ample evidence that Cornwallis did not exaggerate. The blind panic that had seized the Irish loyalists when the abyss opened up before them had now turned to a ghastly confidence in repression. *"All good Protestants,"* wrote the ex-Viceroy the Marquis of Buckingham, who had just disembarked at Dublin at the head of his own county militia, now talked "with great composure" of exterminating the Catholics. It was "the only cure for the present and the only sure preventive for the future".[47] The loyalists saw a pattern in the events of their lifetime: step by step they had allowed the Catholics to be appeased and in due course brought the rebellion upon themselves. It was a view of events that had long found acceptance out in the backwoods, among the hangin', shootin' and burnin' gentlemen. And now it was the official doctrine of the Privy Council of Ireland.[48]

The hard core of the Privy Council were the cabinet—John Foster, Beresford, Toler, the Primate and others. Naturally they had not been fooled by Portland's assertion that Camden's system was to be continued as before. They could hardly fail to notice Cornwallis's aloofness from the Castle. Indeed he seemed to have set aside their own cabinet altogether. This was too much for the men who, in most respects, had been the real rulers of Ireland for a decade.[49] The clamour grew, as it had when Foster had hatched the successful plot to unseat Abercromby. "The business of Wexford has been shamefully handled," whispered Colonel Ross. "Time will tell."[50] The new pardon was "a million times worse than Dundas's business". Another of the central figures in the Abercromby plot, Lord Kingsborough, took up the cry. He was smarting against the Government's "cavalier" treatment of his proposal for Wexford's surrender. He found no difficulty in adopting a violent anti-Government line. "His X," he told a crony, "thinks he may domineer here as in India." A cabal was got up to thwart the Viceroy in Parliament. Perhaps they might even send him packing.[51]

It was a critical moment for the Viceroy and those Castle secretaries like Castlereagh and Elliot, who shared his liberal feelings. Bucky, the ex-Viceroy, commiserated with Cornwallis but could offer no comfort. He had "not a conception of the creed of persecution preached by both sects as indispensable to the peace of the country".[52] At this point rescue came to Cornwallis from an unexpected quarter: the Chancellor. As senior law officer his help was vital. But what gave Clare peculiar political weight in this case was the fact that Clare had been consistently the most articulate (and often the most violent) spokesman against concessions for Catholics. Now he deserted his cabinet colleagues and let it be known that he heartily approved of the amnesty.[53]

In fact Clare acted without inconsistency. Time had not softened his prejudices against Catholics. He still believed that giving Catholics the same voting rights as Protestants had been folly and madness.[54] He deeply distrusted the British cabinet's reported new "Popish plans".[55] But Clare, despite his adjectives, had a statesman's view of events. He believed that Ireland's place, like Scotland's, was in union with Britain. He thought that given a breathing space they could repair the damage of the past decade. And he had no doubt that the real enemy of the Constitution was not Catholicism, degraded and dangerous as it was, but the new godless ideology sweeping Europe—Jacobinism. "It is a Jacobin conspiracy with popish instruments," Lord Castlereagh had said, shortly after the outbreak of the rebellion.[56] "That deep-laid conspiracy to revolutionise Ireland on the principles of France," Cornwallis called it, "by men who had no thought of religion but to destroy it," the plot "for the most dreadful of all evils, a Jacobin revolution".[57] Clare's own view coincided exactly, and as Lord Chancellor he now intended to see that Ireland recognised it.[58]

Once formed, the new partnership flourished. At first Cornwallis had looked with some amazement on the Chancellor. Could this be the same man who was regarded by English liberals as the embodiment of all that was most reactionary in Ireland? By July Cornwallis was describing him as "much the most right-minded man among us".[59] Together they now planned a triple dose of bromide to satisfy everyone: they would settle the rebels with the amnesty, the loyalists with a series of treason trials, and the opposition with a parliamentary enquiry into the rebellion. But first they must find a way of ending the guerrilla war in Wicklow and Kildare. For nothing gave the loyalists a better pretext for violence than the Government's inexplicable failure to cope with these elusive insurgents in the bogs barely twenty miles from Dublin.[60]

A whole series of expeditions had been sent against the Kildare army, and each in turn had apparently won the final victory. On June 20th a party of 2,000 had been crushed near Kilcock; other parties had been broken and dispersed at Prosperous to the south, and Edenderry to the west.[61] Yet the Government's army, as Lord Edward's aunt, Lady Sarah Napier said, was "like a young dog in a rabbit warren, here and there, flying from spot to spot, and catching little or nothing".[62] Somehow the rebels always reappeared, to attack Lord Leitrim's house near Celbridge, to murder Lord Harberton's dairy maids and to terrorise the entire county.[63] "Protection" for the rebels, one Kildare loyalist snorted—how could the Government talk of protection when they could not even protect "their own soldiers if they go half a mile out of their garrisons".[64]

By July 11th, matters had reached a head. There were impertinent attacks on the Athlone and Galway mail coaches whose route via Mullingar ran to the north of the rebel camp.[65] And there was the even more serious threat that the fugitives from Wexford, who were being smoked out of the mountains by Lake's army, might join up with their fellows in the bog.[66]

On a gravelly island in the centre of the great Bog of Allen was the village of Timahoe. Today there is hardly a house left standing, but at this period it was a village of a few hundred inhabitants. Here, surrounded by a sodden desert of peat, was the stronghold of the Kildare rebels, under the command of the colonel of the northern army, William Aylmer of Painstown. Like most of the other gentry sworn into the United movement—like Esmond Kyan, and his cousin Esmonde, like John Colclough and his brother-in-law Edward Fitzgerald, like both the Byrne brothers—William Aylmer was the son of a Catholic squire and connected by birth and marriage with other Catholic revolutionaries.[67] In the camp at Timahoe were two of his connexions, Ware and Luby. All were from the northern barony of Kildare which, according to Lord Edward's master-plan, should have taken part in the combined attack on Dublin. In fact they had risen two days late—and almost immediately retired to the bog.[68]

Aylmer's camp in Kildare, like the Wexford camps, had its share of desperadoes. There were the men there who had burnt Captain Swayne in a barrel, piked the Duke of Leinster's elderly agent and hacked to death a dozen loyalists in Rathangan. None of them could hope for much sympathy from the Government.[69] There were also some deserters from the army, who had no political cause to be there, but presumably believed that life as an outlaw could hardly be worse than life as a soldier.[70] And there were a few ordinary fugitives from justice, honest highwaymen and burglars who must have taken a temporary refuge with the United army for the sake of a square meal. But by and large the Kildare men were better disciplined than the Wexford men. They were the same sort of people—young farmers, and artisans, and they had the same sort of grievances—rents, taxes and so on. But these were not felt so personally, nor influenced by the sectarian bitterness of Wexford. They had also been better drilled and organised by Lord Edward, and the emissaries from Dublin, and they had been instructed over a period of years that only by self-restraint could the country be theirs.[71]

For these reasons Aylmer and his fellow colonels, Ware and Luby, found themselves in a stronger position than men like Bagenal Harvey in Wexford. True, four Protestant prisoners had been roughly handled— and two had been shot, apparently after a revolutionary court martial. But by degrees Aylmer had imposed firmer authority on his men. A Dublin barber, who had been kidnapped and taken to Timahoe to shave the United army's officers, was well treated; in fact after the shave Aylmer tipped him a shilling.[72] A still more interesting prize to have fallen into their hands was the clergyman son of General Eustace. He had gone to visit some family property at Robertstown on the Grand Canal, and had been surprised by one of United outposts. After sternly warning him that he would be tried by court martial if he had ill-treated either his tenants or labourers, they took him to Aylmer's headquarters at Timahoe. Here he was courteously treated, and returned to Dublin with the news that some of the leaders would surrender if they could only be sure of their lives.[73]

The fact was that after holding out for a month Aylmer's army had achieved only one of its aims: to stay alive. Originally, it seems, Aylmer and the other leaders of this barony had thought of escaping from Ireland, but when the ports were closed against them, they had seen no alternative but to follow the other baronies that had already risen.[74] After fighting with the Prosperous and Rathangan divisions, they had formed a camp of at least three thousand. They had kept alive by raiding the neighbouring villages for food, and moving rapidly out of the way whenever the army lumbered after them. But at best it was a stalemate: there had been no useful reinforcements from Meath or Wicklow, no instructions from Dublin as to what to do next and, of course, none of the all-important aid from France. After the fall of Prosperous in late June, their situation had become increasingly desperate.

By early July Aylmer sent a message to his father to see if he could arrange terms of surrender. By good fortune the Marquis of Buckingham happened to be an old acquaintance of the family. Bucky in turn passed on the message to Cornwallis. But before any terms could be agreed, a dramatic change in their situation occurred.[75]

On July 10th the Wexford and Wicklow forces suddenly appeared on the scene. Apart from their leaders—Perry, and Fitzgerald, Father Kearns and Garrett Byrne—they looked wretched.[76] It turned out that, despite a successful attack on the mail coaches at Kill earlier that day, they had still not enough ammunition or other supplies for themselves. To Aylmer and his corps the condition of their long-lost allies from Wexford must have been a crushing disappointment—and no doubt it was reciprocated. Still, their arrival brought the size of the United army to over four thousand—

vastly more than any Government troops in the locality. Yet numerical strength also had its weaknesses. One of the reasons for leaving the Whelp Rock camp above Blessington, had been the failure of that barren plateau to support such a large population of insurgents.[77] The same applied for twice that number in the bogs of Kildare.

After some wrangling the armies split up again almost immediately: the Wexford and Wicklow men to march northwards, the Kildare men to remain to try to negotiate surrender. One of the Wexford leaders, Edward Fitzgerald, threw in his lot with Aylmer, and a few of the more militant Kildare men marched away with the others.[78] But once again the hopes of forming a real provincial army out of different county forces had proved a mirage.

On they marched, the survivors of the Wexford Republic, still refusing to believe that the Midlands would not rally to the standard. Were these counties round Dublin not the ones that had been best organized by the great men of the Executive? Desperate for ammunition they attacked a fortified house at Clonard, and were beaten off by twenty-seven yeomen.[79] On they went through Meath, and across the Boyne into Louth, and still no-one came to join them—not even women to bring them food or help the wounded. And all the way the yeomanry and regulars were yapping at their heels, wearing them down, and cutting off stragglers, till the army of 2,000 had degenerated to a few hundred pikemen with broken pikes and musketmen with no ammunition, desperate for food and shelter.[80]

Ten days later, two men—Anthony Perry and Father Kearns— struggled back towards the bogs of Kildare. It was two months to a day since the Liberty standard had first been unfurled in the midnight raids in Kildare. Since then the wild message had been carried by their armies through eight counties of Leinster—300 miles from Kildare and back.

The same day the surrender of the last of the United armies in the field was made official. Five thousand pikes and firelocks were handed in at Timahoe, together with cattle, sheep and horses, and some other plunder. The rank and file received protection. The leaders, including Aylmer and Fitzgerald, were taken in five carriages to be examined at the Castle, the first captured leaders since the outbreak of the rebellion to avoid the gallows. By ill-luck Perry and Father Kearns returned too late. They fell into the hands of some yeomanry, and were hanged at Edenderry.[81]

In Dublin, both Edward Fitzgerald and the Kildare men complained to Cooke of their "betrayal" by the Executive. They had been assured that all Ireland would rise on May 23rd. Edward Cooke found Aylmer "a conceited boy".[82] In the meantime a great change had come over Ireland.

In the teeth of the hangin'-shootin'-and-burnin' gentlemen, Cornwallis had pushed his amnesty through Parliament. It was now up to the thousands of wretched fugitives in all parts of the country to put their faith in the Government and give themselves up.

2

The French Are On The Sea

The four provinces, July 21st–August 24th

The French are on the Sea, says the Shan Van Vocht;
The French are on the Sea, says the Shan Van Vocht;
The French are in the Bay, they'll be here without delay
And the Orange will decay, says the Shan Van Vocht

The Shan Van Vocht

As CORNWALLIS's general pardon began to take effect, and the rebels emerged from their hiding-places to collect their written protection slips, and return home, even the loyalists could see some sense in the scheme. Quite simply, there were no prisons left to put them in: and it would have been a tedious job to hang and shoot half the nation.

Already the prison system had more or less collapsed under its burden. Irish prisons, like other Irish institutions, sometimes had fine facades. Inside they were ramshackle beyond belief. For half a century the scandal of Dublin prisons had been a well-worn theme of Parliamentary debates.[1] Ten years before, John Howard, the great prison reformer, had reported that the Dublin prisons were some of the worst in Europe. At Newgate there were no proper drains or baths. The Marshalsea was dirty and over-crowded. At the New Prison the water supply had failed. There was no bedding; the floors were of stone; there was no attempt to separate the young offenders from the old, the women from the men, or the sick from the healthy. He saw boys from nine to twelve shut up with "the most daring offenders", and women lying on the flags "with a very little straw worn to dust". There was no shortage, however, of whiskey; and deaths were reported from "intoxication and fighting" as well as from gaol fever.[2]

But overcrowding, damp cells, bad drains and bad company were not the chief complaints of Dublin prisoners. Gaolers obtained their jobs through some influential patron, and were then more or less left to their own devices; the pay was small and often in arrears; as a result they tended to behave more like businessmen than civil servants. Some were merely incompetent, but a number were openly extortionate. If these defects were characteristic of the whole rickety Irish administration, they took their most extreme form in the gaols. To squeeze the most income from their position, gaolers created a series of "optional" privileges. For example, in the Black Dog, as the Marshalshea was known, there were twelve rooms, some of them mere closets, others large enough for several beds. For the privilege of sharing a bed with three or four other prisoners they had to pay a shilling, otherwise they were thrown into the "Nunnery"—a dungeon for prostitutes below street level, with no light except what came in from the sewer carrying the filth from the prison. Prisoners also had to pay for drink, at one time 2s.2d. for the "penny pot" of liquor whether they wanted it or not. And when it was time for their release the gaolers insisted on a tip of a shilling; or the gates remained shut against them.[3]

These anachronisms were not confined to the great civil prisons of Dublin. Each county had its own gaol and its own gentleman to regulate it; in practice most gaolers were left to do as they liked. The gaol at Kilkenny, one of the richest counties, had been the subject of repeated remonstrances to Parliament by the official inspector.[4] "The Principal Apartment for Felons is a Dungeon fourteen feet underground without Flue to carry off the Smoke, air and light admitted only thro' one grate which is level with the Street . . . to enter this cavern you must descend thro' a large trap door by a long ladder which when opened what with putrid air, Sulphurous vapour peculiar to the coal of this country, the rattling of chains, the confused voices and execrations of the Prisoners below, whose bodies can scarcely be distinguished in this gloomy Vault, strike the imagination with all the miseries which the Damm'd endure in Hell."[5]

If Kilkenny was an extreme case, the main provincial gaols—at Limerick, Cork and Galway—were all officially recognised to be beyond repair. New gaols however did not always fulfil reformers' hopes. The one at Clonmel had no proper water supply owing to the "jobbing spirit too prevalent in Ireland", according to the official inspector. At Cork the new gaol had already taken years to build and it was not half complete, he reported, owing to fraud by the contractor on a scale unusual even for Irish gaol-builders.[6]

Like their Dublin colleagues, the officials at county gaols did what they could to eke out their incomes. At Limerick it was the practice to chain up the vagrants or tie them to logs; for a fee the beadle would agree to untie them. In the Leinster circuit, it was "*a usual occurrence*" according to the inspector, for gaolers to keep prisoners longer than their sentences in order to exact fees. The prisoners were also at the mercy of other officials. The baker was paid whether or not he brought men the right measure of bread, and so could starve them with impunity, unless the grand jury were unusually vigilant.[7]

Such were the gaols of Ireland—hardly a tribute to eighteenth century enlightenment. All that could be said was that in peace time their facilities were not always overtaxed; in Carlow, for example, there had not been a prisoner sentenced on a capital charge for the seventeen years before 1797.[8] But now there was war, and how could they survive the avalanche?

Cornwallis' first step was to call for a series of reports on the prisons and their wretched inmates. In Dublin the eighty-two state prisoners arrested at Bond's in March, or in the round-up that followed, had been installed in the main Dublin prisons: Kilmainham, the New Prison, Newgate and the Bridewell.[9] Aylmer and the thirteen other Kildare prisoners had been lodged in the Royal Exchange—a coffee-house requisitioned as a yeomanry barrack.[10] But the mass of ordinary prisoners brought into Dublin after the outbreak of the rebellion found no such comfortable accommodation. Some had been lodged in the Provost, a military prison for deserters, consisting of two cells twenty-four feet by twenty feet, half sunk in the ground, and wretchedly damp and ill-ventilated. According to the doctor in charge it was dangerous for more than fifty prisoners. Now there were 150 "crowded together in a very miserable and uncomfortable state and without the smallest accommodation for the relief of the sick". The doctor warned the authorities that fever would break out unless the overcrowding was immediately relieved.[11] The bulk of the Dublin prisoners were shipped off on one of the half dozen tenders or so in Dublin Bay, like the *Lively*, the *Mary*, the *William James*, the *Alexander*, and the *Columbine* and so on—no less ill-ventilated and overcrowded than the Prevost, but easier to guard.[12]

Despite these miserable conditions, it emerged that there was one compensation for the Dublin prisoners. When their case came up for trial by court martial, they had some chance of a fair hearing. Under the eye of the Commander-in-Chief, the courts martial had been run more or less according to statute. The majority of prisoners tried in the weeks after the outbreak had been discharged as not guilty. Still more significantly, less than a dozen prisoners in the entire region were to be executed by order of court martial in this period. In general, the Dublin garrison could claim to be doing their best in difficult circumstances.[13]

Unfortunately, this could not be said for the garrisons which had taken over the administration of justice in other areas. It was not a question of prison conditions, though in many cases they were more wretched, over-crowding still worse, and the defects in the prison system more acute than Dublin, it was quite simply that the Irish army had been free to administer justice as they liked—that army whose "favourite pastime", according to Cornwallis' own view, was murder.[14]

Cornwallis, of course, had no responsibility for what had been done. Like the rest of this year's horrors, it was Camden's, if not Pitt's. The policy, such as it was, was Lake's: a deliberate policy of "giving the Irish army its head". In the five weeks between the outbreak of the rebellion and Cornwallis' assumption of command, Lake had issued one clear in-struction to his generals: take "summary" means to crush the rebellion.[15] The result had been inevitable in an army with so little connection between the links in the chain of command. The local garrisons comprised the county militia and the local yeomanry; officers and men, they shared the same reckless spirit as the other Irish loyalists, and there had been little to stop them gratifying it.

Even the bare facts about this five-week purge before his arrival were impossible for Cornwallis to establish. No official records could be com-pleted; some generals had characteristically lost the records of the courts martial, if they had ever had them. The incomplete records still surviving gave a total of 106 death sentences passed on United Irishmen that year and of 268 to be transported. (In fact the real total of executions might be at least twice that number, and to them must be added the cases where there were executions without even a pretence of trial.)[16]

In some cases the commanding officers were doing their best to correct abuses, and in a few, like General John Moore's, they were efficient as well as humane. But generally, the standard of justice was no better than could be expected from the victorious minority in a civil war.

To Cornwallis, unusually sensitive for an experienced military man, the official reports from the garrisons only added to his feelings of wretched-ness.

A ghastly kind of pattern emerges. In each area where there had been any fighting or signs of rebellion, a more or less systematic campaign had been mounted to discover the leaders. The garrison had assumed, usually correctly, that great numbers of men had been sworn into the movement in their area. Once they had got the name of one of them, he could give them the names of his fellow committee men, and so by degrees they would get to the heart of the conspiracy. And now, with a wretched irony, those tales of reckless floggings in the Midlands, which had done so much to precipitate the rebellion, had at length become a reality. For there was no way, bar torture, of extracting information from many of the suspects; promise of freedom would not affect people liable to be murdered by their own friends if they peached.

It was an inhuman policy, because many of the people flogged, and even some of those executed, knew nothing of the military organisation— and would not have taken part if they had. It was also reckless, from the loyalists' point of view, as it made the most incompetent revolutionary into a martyr. But in the short term it certainly succeeded in crushing all hope of resistance to the Government.[17]

That Cornwallis did not exaggerate the horrors is made abundantly clear by the records of the South Midlands region under the command of Sir Charles Asgill, that are unusually complete. They are also corroborated by the accounts left by some of the victims.[18]

Strange to say, Sir Charles had himself once been condemned to death by a military court. As a young officer in America he had been taken as a hostage for the life of an American prisoner in British hands, but eventually pardoned.[19] He now had the power of life and death over the population of three counties—Kilkenny, Queen's and Carlow—and proved as insensitive and negligent as Lake. When someone wrote to the Government protesting about reckless punishments at Mountmellick he replied that he had complete confidence in the local commander. If he had a fault it was "being too lenient for the present time". This was in a small town where no rising had taken place and twelve men had been executed—ten of them from a single parish; only one was a "captain"; many others had been flogged, and numbers ordered for transportation; and the local commander was preparing to arrest other "noted villains concerned in the United business".[20] Already the result, it was reported by the Maryborough landlord, Wellesley-Pole, was that 200 prisoners crowded the gaol, and gaol fever was expected.[21]

It was the same story in County Carlow, where the local garrisons at Carlow and Leighlinbridge were allowed to flog large numbers of men to extort confessions. Carlow was the place where the local United party's main attack on the town had ended in fiasco: nearly seven hundred had been killed that night, shot down on the street or trapped in the burning town, without the loss of a single loyalist.[22] Now the garrison was determined to make an example of the leaders. Nearly a hundred were flogged and fourteen executed. Yet only one or two, it later turned out, could be called leaders in the full sense of the word; of the rest, some knew about the plot but had opposed it, others were only nominally sworn into the organisation,[23] and one of them—a liberal baronet called Sir Edward Crosbie—was framed, like Cornelius Grogan, by his political opponents.[24] Much the same applied in Leighlinbridge where half a dozen were executed in a few days on the information of friends or enemies or on the assumption of their guilt from their stoicism under torture.[25]

In only one other area do the legalised atrocities that followed the outbreak of the rebellion stand out in as clear relief—in Tipperary. Like the counties on its northern border under Asgill's command, Tipperary had been little disturbed; so little, in fact, that there were virtually no troops there, and justice was dispensed by the local High Sheriff, Thomas Judkin Fitzgerald.[26]

Fitzgerald (who happened to be Beresford's brother-in-law) was later prosecuted for his part in these events, and the main facts were not in dispute. The man himself was a parody of the more extreme kind of loyalist: brave and energetic, but arrogant and reckless to a degree verging on insanity. While the rebellion was still raging in the neighbouring parts of Wexford, he rode through Tipperary like an avenging demon, haranguing the people in Irish for hours at a time, making them kneel down and pray for the King, pardoning them if they confessed their crimes, and flogging them if they had no crimes to confess.[27]

At his trial in 1799 Fitzgerald was to claim that only by "cutting off their heads" could some people be made to talk. There was laughter in court. The terrible thing was that Fitzgerald was not joking. His judicial policy, as summed up by the judge in his own case, reads like a speech of the Red Queen's: sentence first, then execution, then trial.

To avoid the lash, one of his victims had accused a French professor at Clonmel of being a United officer; in fact he was a respectable Protestant of unimpeachable loyalty. Fitzgerald seized the professor by the hair, dragged him to the ground, kicked him and cut him across the forehead with his sword; then he had him stripped to the waist, and tied to a ladder, and ordered him fifty lashes. A major from the garrison came up and asked Fitzgerald why the man was being flogged. Here is the evidence, said the Sheriff, and he handed the officer a note in French; he did not understand the language himself, he added, but he could assure the major that he would find ample evidence there to justify flogging the scoundrel to death. The major, who did read French, explained that the note was a harmless one. The Sheriff ordered fifty more lashes for the professor, and part of his bowels could be seen protruding from the wounds. His waist-band was cut, and a further fifty lashes were added. And then, leaving the wretched man hanging from the ladder, the Sheriff went to find a firing squad to finish him off. They were not to be found, and the professor survived in the town gaol where he was left for a week without medical help. Others were less fortunate.

Strange to say, it was the Presbyterian North that suffered most executions (according to official statistics, at any rate). Thirty-four people were executed, thirteen in Lord Castlereagh's home town of Newtownards. None of these was a Catholic, as far as is known. The United generals were hunted down and hanged—McCracken betrayed by an associate, Monroe captured by some Orangemen in a potato ridge. A trio of rebel heads soon decorated the railings of the Belfast courthouse (McCracken himself was hanged but not decapitated, and his body was given to his sister for burial).[28]

The redeeming feature of these ghastly episodes is that in many areas there were officers and gentlemen who did not accept the need for severity. General John Moore avoided holding any courts martial at all.[29] General Dundas in Kildare remitted most of the death sentences to trans-portation.[30] At Birr, Sir Laurence Parsons wrote to protest against the flogging to death of a man by two magistrates.[31] And in a large part of Connaught the gentry, according to Lord Altamont, "disapproved of the measure entirely and having any one opinion upon it will not cooperate in the execution of it".[32]

Yet for every loyalist in the threatened areas of Carlow, Kilkenny and Queen's County who disapproved of severity, there were a hundred who felt that the policy was lenient to a fault. "This country would have been in the same situation with Wexford," declared one loyalist, but for Sir Charles Asgill's "activity and exertion". It was proposed to present him with a ceremonial sword. He was "humanity personified".[33]

Meanwhile, Cornwallis had received from the Castle a prison report of a very different nature from the one supplied by the generals. Inside the great Dublin prisons the National Executive of the United movement and the rest of the eighty-two state prisoners complained bitterly of their treatment. The normal arrangement for gentlemen prisoners was for food to be supplied from outside. In the case of the state prisoners the Government had arranged to supply them from an eating house across the road; chicken and boiled mutton were allowed, with one bottle of port and two bottles of porter.[34] But since one prisoner had made a daring escape from the prison privy, orders had been given for them to be confined to their quarters. They found this constricting and wrote frequently to Mr. Cooke to tell him that gentlemen expected better treatment.[35]

The great majority of the state prisoners in Kilmainham, Newgate, and the Bridewell were in no danger from ordinary process of law, as Cooke gloomily reported. As we saw, the arrests in March of the fourteen members of the Executive in Bond's had failed to produce the evidence for a civil conviction. True, one witness had subsequently agreed to come forward and prosecute. That was Thomas Reynolds, the Kildare delegate appointed by Lord Edward to attend that fatal meeting which he then betrayed to the Government. But Reynolds' evidence of the arrangements for the meeting was sufficient to commit three at most—Oliver Bond, his secretary McCann, and the Wicklow delegate, William Byrne. With the possible exception of Neilson, only two others could be prosecuted, Henry and John Sheares, who had been arrested before the rebellion on the information of that free-thinking militia officer, Captain Armstrong. For some reason, Captain Armstrong had later been sent to fight in Wexford, but was still available as a witness, fortunately for the Government, despite being wounded in the ambush where Walpole lost his life.

In the circumstances Cornwallis had two choices—to try these five and abandon hope of prosecuting all the rest of those chiefly responsible for the rebellion, or to use other methods to bring them to justice. Edward Cooke had originally tended to the second, and so had other Government advisers.[37] But Cornwallis was not the man to allow "severity beyond the law". In mid-July he authorised the Castle to proceed as best they could with the treason trials in the civil courts.

The Sheares brothers, the last to be arrested, were the first to be tried, and the result delighted the Castle.

The trial itself was a macabre one. For some reason it continued throughout the night; the courtroom was lit by guttering candles, and thronged with violent loyalists who made no secret of their sympathies. The judge, Lord Carleton, was an old friend of the Sheares family, and even rumoured to be their guardian.[38]

At midnight the defence counsel, John Philpot Curran and Plunket, perhaps the two most famous barristers Ireland has ever produced, rose to defend their clients. The only chance was to discredit Armstrong. He had admitted having been introduced to the Sheares brothers through his habit of buying left-wing political pamphlets. How could they believe the word of this man, asked Curran; his ideas were taken from "that abominable abomination of abominations, Thomas Paine's *Age of Reason*"? They might as well have the witness swear on that book as on the Bible. He was an atheist, and a Painite, and had blasphemed against God and King. Nothing was sacred to him—the ties of family or the loyalty of friends. With the baseness of an informer, he had wormed himself into the households of his victims, he had even dandled the children on his knee. "He saw the scene and smiled at it, contemplating the havoc he was to make of all that family".[39]

To the Castle's relief Captain Armstrong stood up well to the battering of the great advocate. True, he made admissions that would have been damaging before another sort of jury. Yet in his brutal way he managed to score off Curran in one of the sallies:

> Armstrong: "We met three men with green cockades—one we shot, another we hanged, and the third we flogged and made a guide of."
>
> Curran: "Which did you make a guide of?"
>
> Armstrong: "The one that was neither shot nor hanged."[40]

Curran could not shake his story that the Sheares brothers had taken a leading part in the plan for the triple attack on Dublin, and had asked him to enrol in the plot the embittered Catholics in his regiment. The Crown's case was immensely strengthened by John Sheares' captured manifesto concluding "Vengeance, Irishmen, vengeance on your oppressors". The only issue was how far the less active brother, Henry Sheares, was actually implicated. It took the jury seventeen minutes to decide both were guilty.[41]

Next day, the executions were to be held at Dublin's Newgate. Desperate attempts were now made by the friends of Henry Sheares to obtain a reprieve from the Castle. Lord Clare was sympathetic. Henry was not the stuff conspirators were made of; he had broken down and wept in court; besides he had now agreed to "any conditions" if he was restored to "his beloved family"; he might even make important disclosures. Jonah Barrington, the intermediary, hurried to Newgate with the news but because of Cooke's security arrangements was refused admission. He dashed back to the Castle, and returned with the necessary papers—only to see the executioner holding up his friend's head, with the words, "Here is the head of a traitor."[42]

The Sheares' executions had a no less macabre postscript. Two nights before he died, John Sheares had written a long, moving letter to his sister. It began "The troublesome scene of life . . . is nearly closed, and the hand that now traces these lines will, in a day or two, be no longer capable of communicating . . . the sentiments of his heart."[43] After the execution the heads and bodies were placed together in the vaults below the church of St. Michan's near the prison. In the peculiar atmosphere of the place, the coffins soon crumbled away. Twenty years later Curran's son visited the place and was shown the severed heads, trunks and "the hand that once traced those lines" not yet mouldered into dust.[44]

For the Castle, the second batch of treason trials proved as heartening as the first. This time their key witness was Thomas Reynolds. Curran denounced him with a ferocity striking even in that period: "Are you then prepared, in a case of life and death, of honor and infamy to credit a vile informer, the perjurer of a hundred oaths, a wretch whom pride, honour and religion cannot bind . . ." He accused him of swindling a blind neighbour, robbing his mother, and even poisoning his mother-in-law[45]— the lady who had also been mother-in-law to Theobald Wolfe Tone. But, once again, the Crown witness cut a good figure in the eyes of the jury. Loyalists saw nothing wrong in Reynolds' agreement to betray the conspiracy to murder them all in their beds—even if he had been well compensated for his information. In turn, the three members of the Leinster Directory were found guilty—McCann, Byrne and Oliver Bond.[46]

As their colleagues were led out to the scaffold, the feelings of the rest of the state prisoners may be imagined. For years they had dared the Government to prosecute, but their façade of constitutionalism had proved impenetrable. Now, a week or two after the collapse of the insurrection, the bluff had been called. How much more did the Government know? Who else had agreed to turn King's evidence?

In Newgate and in other prisons urgent meetings were arranged by the gentlemen prisoners. After McCann's execution on July 24th, a round robin was signed putting a very remarkable offer to the Government. Without implicating individuals they would agree to give *full* details of the United movement in Ireland and of its links with allies overseas. In return they should all be allowed to emigrate.[47] It was, as McNevin put it, "the best service" they could perform, "to save the country from the cold-blooded slaughter of its best, its bravest, its most enlightened defenders".[48]

Neilson, next on the list to be tried, found no reason to disagree. Holding out a clenched fist to a Castle official, Mr. Alexander, he declared: "I hold in my hand every muscle, sinew ... of the internal organisation of the United Irishmen." Then, gradually opening his fist, he added: "I will make it as plain as the palm of my Hand." Neilson's dramatic gesture impressed Alexander for its frankness, if not for "rhetorick or logick". The round robin was presented to the Castle on the day appointed for the fourth execution—Byrne's.[49]

Such was the situation on July 26th, as the Castle reported to Cornwallis. For Cornwallis, of course, the proposition was extraordinarily tempting. Of the three principal officials at the Castle, Cooke was "strongly in favour", so were Elliot and Lord Castlereagh, and Cornwallis felt that the information would be worth more than the lives of twenty men like Bond.[50] Kilwarden and the other law officers, however, thought to be moderates by Irish standards, opposed even a stay of execution to examine the offer more carefully. They could not answer for the behaviour of judges and juries "if persons so convicted were pardoned". The effects on public opinion would also, they insisted, be disastrous. Unfortunately for Cornwallis his ally, Lord Clare, the senior law officer, was away ill at his country estate.

In the circumstances Cornwallis felt no choice but to let the law take its course.[51] Byrne was having breakfast with the other gentlemen prisoners at Newgate, together with some of their wives, when he was called out of the room. The gaoler told him their proposition was unacceptable. A few moments later he was led out to the scaffold.[52]

Next day it was Bond's turn for execution. The small minority of prisoners who had refused to sign the first round robin, including Arthur O'Connor and William Sampson, frantically added their signatures, and the terms were made more specific.[53] At the Castle, Cooke was still more strongly in favour of accepting. To Pelham in England he described the arguments:

"Let me state the Case. There were between 70 and 80 state prisoners. There had been four capital Trials and Convictions and Executions. The Treason in its Extent was proved most completely and satisfactorily. Justice was restored. Example was made. It was to be feared that many Executions would raise Criminals into martyrs. A loophole was to be opened for United Irishmen to escape thro'. They wanted a Pretext for returning to Loyalty. Clemency was the fairest pretext— it was impossible to have 74 Trials at Bar supposing our Proofs to be complete—If our proofs failed in any case, and they were likely to fail in Neilson's, the Rebels gained a Triumph.—But what was the justification for Government when all the Capital Traitors, Emmet, O'Connor, McNevin etc. were to come forward, confess themselves conspirators and traitors and engaged for above two years in a correspondence with France. What an overthrow would such a confession be to all the Lord Moiras, Mr. Foxes, Duke of Bedfords, Judge Bullers, Maidstone Juries etc."[54]

Cornwallis agreed with this, but how to carry their own supporters, let alone the general public? As Cornwallis gloomily remarked, their minds were "now in such a state that nothing but blood will satisfy them".[55] Already there was an outcry in Dublin at the prospect of negotiation. The yeomen threatened to resign. John Foster, the Speaker and leader of the ultras in Parliament, was reported to be "frantically against it";[56] Jonah Barrington, with characteristic inconsistency, was preparing a public onslaught on the Government for their weakness, a few days after he had privately tried to save Henry Sheares.[57]

At this critical moment Lord Clare, the Chancellor, returned from his country estate to Cornwallis' rescue. Reactionaries often carry more weight than liberals when they turn their hand to liberal measures. Lord Clare announced that it would be "inexcusable" to reject the offer—and declared it in Parliament, too. The outcry died down, and the pact was signed between the seventy-eight surviving prisoners and the Government.[58]

The "Kilmainham Deputies", as Cooke whimsically referred to the five representatives—Emmet, McNevin, O'Connor, Bond and Neilson—were as good as their word. A week later they produced a forty page memoir of their plans for revolution. The extent of the Government's triumph was apparent. There was little new to them in the document, though it was reassuring to have their spy reports confirmed. But here were the authors of the conspiracy freely confessing to all the charges that they and their Whig champions in England and Ireland had so long denied.[59]

In the tragi-comic history of revolution, few documents can read with such an engaging frankness as this memoir, and its counterpart in the replies that the state prisoners made to the secret committee of the Lords and Commons. To the United Executive the idea of a Catholic conspiracy was perfectly laughable. They were all Protestants and free-thinkers, except for Dr. McNevin, and when McNevin was asked for his views on the Catholic church he replied: "For my part I would as soon establish the Mahometon as the Popish religion."[60]

When asked what their followers felt about Catholic emancipation, Bond replied: "I believe that the mass of the people do not care a feather for Catholic emancipation, neither did they care for Parliamentary reform till it was explained to them as leading to other objects they looked to ... principally the abolition of tythes." (He added disarmingly, that if they were abolished "the people, on taking new leases, would be obliged to pay more in proportion for lands than the value they now pay for tythes".)[61]

The real aim, they cheerfully admitted, of the United Irish movement was to set up an independent republic on democratic principles. Socially as well as politically the country would be revolutionised. They would nationalise the property of anyone above a certain rank who opposed the revolution (though there would be maintenance grants for wives and children). The people would have a new status, and a higher standard of living. As for the economic programme, Emmet and his friends foresaw no permanent damage to the Irish economy by separation from England. True, the first years of independence would be difficult, especially if Britain used her navy to impose a blockade. But Ireland's natural resources were greater than Britain's, and she would soon stand on her own feet. Even the coal imports from Britain could be dispensed with, when the canals opened up the rich turf deposits of the interior.[62]

Such were their aims, they freely admitted, and all talk of constitutional redress of grievances were "mere pretence".[63] They were equally frank about their methods. Physical force was the only way of achieving independence. This had been finally agreed in 1796. A military alliance was established with Britain's enemy, France, in the same year. Thus they had begun to organise the secret revolutionary army a year before the first military steps were taken to counteract it. At first everything had gone in their favour. The Government's clumsy attempts to suppress them had only stiffened resistance and widened the appeal of the movement. But everything depended on French assistance at the right moment. The Bantry armada had sailed too early. And now the French had left things too late. After they themselves had been arrested, the new Executive had made fatal errors of strategy. Instead of waiting for the French, or at least making it a general insurrection, they had let it go off at half cock, as a result of the military severities in Kildare.[64]

"That deep-laid conspiracy to revolutionise Ireland on French principles," Cornwallis had called it.[65] And now they had made a clean breast of it. At one stroke the state prisoners' revelations resolved a whole series of problems for the new Viceroy. The barefaced plan to exploit Catholic grievances for their own ends, the bogus constitutionalism that had hood-winked the English Whigs, the exposure of these would hardly endear the United leaders to either of the Party's allies. And the traitors themselves could be safely disposed of. As the secret committee prepared its devast-ating report, Cornwallis wrote, in his first cheerful report to London, that they had won a "complete triumph".[66]

In other ways they seemed to be making headway. To calm the loyalists, Cornwallis decided on one concession. An act of attainder was to be passed on the estate of Lord Edward Fitzgerald whom Reynolds' evidence had proved to be "the great author and contriver of all the mischief and treason that has cost so many lives". Predictably, the plan was unpopular with the Leinster clan in England, but Cornwallis was deaf to their appeals. It would have been an insult to the feelings of the loyal not to proceed.[67] In fact, the attainder was a fairly harmless exercise in public relations. It was discreetly arranged that Lord Edward's step-father, Mr. Ogilvie, should take over the estate and administer it for Lady Edward and her children.[68] More heavily penalised were the relations of Cornelius Grogan who together with Bagenal Harvey, had been included in the attainder for the sake of appearances. Grogan had been convicted of high treason it was true—but on evidence of the most doubtful nature. Both his brothers had fought on the loyalist side, and one had been killed in the battle at Arklow; as a result the latter's estate had technically been in-herited by Cornelius Grogan in the fortnight before his execution; so the attainder robbed the surviving brother of *both* family properties.[69] Still, the Irish Parliament cheerfully accepted the posthumous punishments of the three men.[70]

By mid-August, peace seemed at length within their grasp. Cornwallis had taken a calculated risk in offering an amnesty while there were still the remnants of guerrilla war in Wicklow, as his detractors in Parliament and elsewhere had not failed to observe. With the news that resistance in Wicklow had petered out, he was now politically on the crest of the wave.

The campaign itself, directed by General John Moore, confirmed the success of those revolutionary new weapons—elementary humanity and military discipline. Moore reported personally to Cornwallis on August 20th:

"When the troops were sent about a month ago into the county of

Wicklow, the County appeared a desert, for though the inhabitants were not all in arms they fled everywhere on the approach of the army— old men and terrified women were alone to be found in the cottages.

"The good conduct of the troops, who were kept from marauding, made to pay for everything they got, and not permitted to molest the people, together with kind treatment and encouraging language from the officers, gradually brought back the inhabitants to their houses. The proclamation and the humane interests of Government were then explained and circulated and protection offered to such as would bring in their arms.

"At this time a considerable body of Rebels in arms still haunted the mountains who threatened death and destruction to all who should take protections; and the people owned that they were afraid to take them, lest the troops should be withdrawn and leave them afterwards to the mercy of the mob. This fear diminished daily, and at last when the mob was dispersed and brought to surrender, the great forwardness appeared in everyone to get a protection—the country is now full of people at work."[71]

Moore, like Abercromby and Cornwallis, had nothing but contempt for the Irish yeomen. "I cannot but think that it was their harshness and ill-treatment," he wrote in his private diary, "that in a great measure drove the peasants to revolt." And again: "I am convinced the country would again be quiet if the gentlemen and yeomen could behave themselves with tolerable decency and prudence." He had no illusions of a permanent settlement in a country so poisoned with communual hatred. The better class of Protestant had "learnt nothing by the lesson" of the rebellion. The ordinary yeomen had "shot many after they had received protections, burned homes and committed the most unpardonable acts". At the same time he confessed that his own policy of giving them pardons must result in some of the guilty escaping and some of those with arms keeping them for another occasion.[72]

Moore's return to Dublin seemed to signify the end of the war. It had lasted almost exactly three months, and cost perhaps 25,000 lives, including those of 2,000 loyalists'.[73] The numbers engaged on either side had been vast. The official list compiled in Cornwallis' headquarters in August recorded a grand total of 129,583 captured arms: 48,109 guns, 1,756 bayonets; 4,463 pistols; 4,183 swords; 248 blunderbusses; 119 musket barrels; 106 sword blades; 22 pieces of ordnance; and 70,630 pikes.[74] Thousands of other pikes had been recovered and melted down for horseshoes. Thousands of other guns had been taken by the yeomen as the spoils of war.[75]

If the war was over, one mystery remained unsolved. What on earth had happened to the French? Bonaparte's great armada, it was now clear, was not destined for Ireland. He had sailed eastwards to Malta, and then disappeared without trace. Yet the spy reports from France still maintained an invasion was imminent. In early August, the War Office in London had received an urgent warning from Prince Bouillon, the organiser of the spy ring at the invasion ports. A fortnight before two frigates at Brest had received orders to "make every effort to put to sea and endeavour to reach the Coast of Ireland". Only violent westerly winds had prevented them. The latest spy report, dated August 3rd at Brest, had arrived in Dublin on the 20th. The fleet there now consisted of six frigates and a ship of the line, the *Hoche*, with 3,800 troops—all destined for Ireland.[76] But there was no news of any ships having beaten the British blockade of the ports, nor indeed, because of the delays in the spy reports, was there likely to be before the French arrived in person.

At Cornwallis' headquarters contingency plans were now made for some sort of French landing in the South or West. Having no confidence in his Irish troops, Cornwallis arranged to station the English and Scotch Fencibles and the British regiment of the line on the more vulnerable parts of the coast. Yeomanry were to be kept on permanent duty, and the militia were to be given a rigorous inspection.[77] Some, it was already clear, were grossly ill-equipped as well as ill-disciplined, and badly in arrears with their pay. Characteristically many of the great Irish landlords found themselves too busy for soldiering. Absentees, they farmed out their militia regiments as freely as their estates and with the same demoralising results.[78]

Now that Cornwallis had more time for politics, he could cast his mind to "the great point of ultimate settlement" as he called the Union. But he confessed he could not see "the most distant encouragement".[79] Only a handful of Irishmen were in the secret. Even the most fervent among them, like Lord Clare, saw no prospect of carrying it while the loyalists were in their present state. Yet Cornwallis believed it could only be passed while the country gentlemen were frightened enough to see the need for "sacrifices".[80] Of the Englishmen at the Castle, Elliot was sceptical of its practicability: Cooke, however, was less pessimistic, and had sent over a sketch plan for the Union, incorporating Catholic emancipation.[81] To liberals on both sides of the water, this was the overriding argument in favour of the Union. Full political rights could be given to Catholics without any risk of their abuse, as Catholic representatives would be in a minority in the new imperial Parliament. Yet Clare knew the Irish Protestants, even better than Cooke, and Clare was adamant. For a consideration, the hangin'-shootin'-and-burnin' gentlemen might sell their own political birthright to Britain. But nothing would ever induce them to sell it to help the Catholics.[82]

In this situation, Cornwallis could only report sadly to Pitt that he would "never lose sight of the Union", and he would be delighted if the moment ever arrived "when we may neither think ourselves in too much danger nor in too much security to suffer its production".[83]

It was now the third week in August, and outside Dublin the reapers were working late in the fields to gather in a bumper harvest. The whole way to Belfast "there was the greatest appearance of peace and plenty", Bishop Percy wrote to his wife.[84] Others reported that even the parts of Ireland that had witnessed the most ferocious fighting appeared to have suffered little damage to the crops; for horses and men left little mark on the ground in that extraordinary summer. (In some cases the fighting had added a macabre bonus to the harvest. On fallow land, it was said, you could see where the insurgents lay buried, as the grains of corn in their pockets had sprouted above ground.)[85]

In Belfast everything was back to normal. Nugent had even ordered his men to remove the heads of three rebel leaders stuck on pikes above the market house—a measure "highly gratifying to the inhabitants".[86] In Dublin the Chancellor, Lord Clare, gave a party in honour of Cornwallis. From all parts of the country came reports of a return to work, of a bonanza of corn and linen, with encouraging prices to match.[87]

If there was one province whose loyalty had never seemed to waver it was the province of Connaught. True, there had been odd stories of United activity: of gentlemen from Galway coming to meet their friends in Dublin and being sworn into the conspiracy, of a man peddling copies of Paine's *Age of Reason* in Westport, County Mayo,[88] and the usual *canard* of Orangemen planning to kill all the Catholics. But there was certainly no regular United organisation, and many of the reports seemed put about for reasons of private malice.[89] Grievances there were in plenty; the province was the poorest and most backward in Ireland; land hunger was endemic; no wonder there were tensions between landlord and tenant. Yet so far no serious attempt appeared to have been made to exploit the grievances politically. And the people had been accordingly left in peace by the army and magistrates.[90]

If there was one place within this province that seemed unlikely to be thrust into the mainstream of the revolution; it was Killala, thirty miles west of Sligo. In the Middle Ages, it had been an ecclesiastical centre of some significance. It was still the seat of a bishop. But the sea had receded, and the town had little now to offer except its "cathedral"—about the size of a small English parish church—and a half ruined pile known as the "castle" which the Bishop had made his home.[91]

The Bishop, Dr. Joseph Stock, who had arrived a few months earlier, was a very superior man to find in such a situation. Apart from his family connections—his wife was sister-in-law to the Primate—and his friendship with members of the London-Irish literary set like Edmund Malone,[92] he was a distinguished scholar in his own right. He had been a Fellow of Trinity College. He had translated the Book of Job from the Hebrew. He had also travelled widely on the continent and spoke fluent French.[93]

It was now August 23rd and the Bishop had arranged dinner with an unusually convivial party. The annual visitation of the diocese was to be held next day, and as there was no decent inn at Killala, the Bishop had put up the clergymen who came from a distance; accordingly, three or four were to dine with the Bishop, and so were two officers of the Carabineers stationed at Ballina, ten miles to the south.[94]

That day there had been something of a sensation in the town. The navy were rarely seen in these parts, and there in the bay three frigates were suddenly to be observed, flying British naval colours. They anchored in the next bay to Killala. It was a fine afternoon with the sea as smooth as glass. A number of small boats went to welcome them. One of them was a launch with a British officer on board; he had been fishing in the bay, and sailed across to offer some of his catch to the men-o'-war. Another was carrying the port-surveyor and two of the Bishop's sons, who had rowed out with a still more hospitable offer—an invitation to join the Bishop's dinner party.[95]

There was a pause. Then it gradually dawned on the bystanders on the shore that something very remarkable was taking place. The boats put back from the frigates, accompanied by a launch. Soldiers began to disembark on the beach—sun-tanned men, dressed in curious blue and green uniforms with white facings. They unloaded barrels of powder, crates of firelocks, and other stores. They began to distribute leaflets to the crowd.

About half past seven the Bishop and his party in the castle were just

about to join the ladies, when a terrified man burst into the room. These
people he had invited to dinner—they were certainly coming to Killala.
But the frigates were not the King's men-o'-war. Nor were the soldiers
the King's men.[96]

"Liberty, Equality, Fraternity, Union! Irishmen, You have not
forgot Bantry Bay. [ran the proclamation distributed to the crowd]
After several unsuccessfull attempts, behold Frenchmen arrived amongst
you . . . The moment of breaking your chains is arrived. Our triumphant
troops are now flying to the extremities of the earth, to tear up the roots
of the wealth and tyranny of our enemies. . . . Can there be any Irishman
base enough to seperate himself at such a happy conjuncture from the
grand interests of his country? If such there be, brave friends, let him be
chased from the Country he betrays, and let his property become the
reward of those generous men who knew how to fight and die . . .
Union! Liberty! the Irish Republic!—Such is our shout. Let us march.
Our hearts are devoted to you; our glory is in your happiness."[97]

An hour or two later a French general rode up to the castle and broke
the news to the Bishop in person. They had come to liberate them from
the "English yoke".[98]

The news that the French had arrived at last naturally sent a shudder
through the capital. It was followed by the sensational news that O'Connor,
McNevin and Emmet had flouted the "Treaty of Newgate" by planting an
advertisement in the newspapers denying reports of their confessions to
the Secret Committee.[99] The timing of this advertisement was no coinci-
dence. But two days passed and there came absolutely no sign, it seemed, of
any risings precipitated either by it or the French landing. On Friday,
Lady Sarah Napier wrote to her brother, the Duke of Richmond: "All
things considered, it seems not to have given any sensible person the least
alarm".[100] And the official reports to London confirmed that the "public
mind was perfectly tranquil".[101]

To some extent this reaction may be attributed to Cornwallis' calm
handling of the crisis. Thursday's papers carried a dignified three-line
bulletin on the landing, with the welcome news that the peasantry had
stayed loyal.[102] On Friday some of the English militia soldiers marched
through the capital on their way to the harbour of the Grand Canal where
they embarked on a fleet of canal barges for the journey to Tullamore by

that strategic waterway. It was known that forces totalling more than seven thousand men were converging on the French.[103] The same day the Viceroy and his suite rode out of the capital. Cornwallis was to lead the army in person—the first Viceroy for more than a century to take the field against a foreign enemy.[104]

Despite the withdrawal of part of its garrison, the capital remained absolutely silent. The Marquis of Buckingham, feeling "disgraced and degraded" because he and most of his regiment had been left behind to "*faire la guerre de pots de chambre*", rode about the streets each night by himself. In a three hour ride he saw not a soul except the guard.[105]

Except for Bucky, loyalists were beginning to see the comic side of the situation. What indeed could they fear from an army of 1,000 French who had landed in that remote part of Connaught? Surely this was the last place for the French to be any use to their surviving United friends. Anyway, the total number of troops in Ireland now numbered 100,000 including the yeomanry. By the end of the week, people were looking forward to a little French farce before the final curtain for the rebellion.[106]

One man, however, was not taking any chances. Cornwallis had seen enough of the Irish army and its officers to agree with Abercromby's damning verdict on them. He had also good reason to think that the Killala force was only the first instalment of a sizeable French expedition. And there was a confidential report from Mayo, that 5,000 peasantry had in fact joined the French.[107]

An hour or two before leaving for the front he wrote to Portland to warn him that more English militia reinforcements might be needed after all.[108] He also issued a stern warning to the generals assembling their forces ahead of him, especially to Hutchinson who was at Galway. On no account was he to risk any action with the French until there were sufficient troops to ensure they were beaten. With Ireland in its present state, a single check could be "fatal in its consequences".[109]

3

The Republic of Connaught

French-occupied Mayo, and France, August 1798 and before

I give you the gallant old West, boys,
Where rallied the bravest and best.
When Ireland lay broken and bleeding;
Hurrah for the men of the West!

The Men of the West

THE 1,099 officers and men who had landed at Killala were indeed only the first instalment of a sizeable French armada. They had sailed from La Rochelle on August 6th, to coincide with the sailing of a force of 3,000 men from Brest, commanded by a senior French general, Hardy, and including Wolfe Tone; there was to be a small expedition from Dunkirk; and a further 4,000 were to follow as soon as the wind, the British blockade and the French bureaucracy would allow.[1]

Their own commander was General Humbert, a typical son of the revolution. Born in Lorraine he had started his career as a dealer in goat and rabbit skins supplying the Lyons glove industry. On the outbreak of war he had been elected officer by his fellows, and risen rapidly in the new army. He had served under Kléber in the Mayence campaign, learnt the techniques of guerrilla war in La Vendée with Hoche, and sailed with him on the abortive expedition to Bantry Bay. After Hoche's death, he himself had been under a cloud. Now, a veteran of thirty-one, he was to be given a second chance of putting his and Hoche's theory to the test: that the place to attack Pitt was in Britain's soft underbelly—western Ireland.[2]

Humbert's naval colleague, Savary, had precise instructions from Paris. His three frigates—*Concorde* (44 guns), *Franchise* (44 guns), and *Médée* (38 guns)—were to dodge the British fleet by a specified detour into the Atlantic. Then they were to land on the south Donegal, Sligo, or north Mayo coast according to the direction of the wind. If attacked on landing, the sailors were to burn the boats and return to base with all speed.[3]

Humbert himself was left a fairly free hand. The object of the expedition, as defined by the Directory on July 19th, was "to convey to Ireland arms and ammunition" in order to "help the United Irish who had taken up arms to throw off the English yoke". But Hardy and Humbert were not to attempt to try to bring help to the main insurrection directly. Instead, they were to land at one of the places "where it has not been sufficiently developed to attract the British forces, and where it will certainly break out on the first favourable opportunity". The right landing place would offer little or no likelihood of British resistance, good facilities for distributing arms, and a strategic situation "for rallying to the flag all the Irish whose convictions will cause to join us at the appearance of our forces".[4]

Once he had established a base, Humbert was to try to locate Hardy. If he had already arrived, he was to place himself under his orders. If not, he was to wait for him. Whatever happened he was to act with "the greatest caution" until he had either joined Hardy or rallied a large enough number of Irishmen "for important operations". And in this case he was warned to surround himself with men "known for their devotion to the cause of Liberty", to correspond with patriot chiefs who could offer "reliable guarantees" and to concert his operations with theirs. After further cautions against spies, and instructions on setting up a press to print further copies of his proclamations, the citizen general was emphatically recommended to "respect the manners, customs and religious practices of the Irish and not to allow, in any case, any damage to . . . property". His men were to regard the United Irish as brothers, and "citizens of the world persecuted by a ferocious Government".[5]

Such were his instructions and Humbert could flatter himself as he began to unload his arms and stores at Killala that, despite a near-mutiny on board by the soldiers who demanded a month's wages in advance,[6] the first stage had gone smoothly enough. After landing one of his Irish officers, Matthew Tone, younger brother of Wolfe Tone, wrote jubilantly back to a friend in France: "The People will join us in Myriads—they throw themselves on their knees as we pass along and extend their Arms for our success. We will be Masters of Connaught in a few Days. *Erin Go Brough.*"[7]

But at Brest, the mood was anything but cheerful. By an extraordinary combination of bad luck and bad management, General Hardy's fleet had still not put to sea.

The Directory had given the same military instructions to Hardy as to

Humbert, and in addition some useful advice about setting up the Irish Republic. In the part of Ireland controlled by the United Irish, a provisional government was to be set up; each town and each county would have its own civil or military administration. Hardy was warned to be especially tactful in his handling of the new democracy. He must carefully avoid giving the impression that France had designs on Ireland. All they wanted was to establish liberty and equality in their own country. And now, the Directory concluded, Hardy must take steps to embark with all possible speed.[8]

In his reply Hardy explained that his ships were perfectly ready to sail—the *Hoche*, his 74-gun flagship, and eight frigates—but that he could do nothing till he received the 150,000 francs promised for paying the crew and soldiers, and buying stores. It took a fortnight to squeeze the francs out of the national treasury, and meanwhile Humbert's force had sailed. The next obstacle was the wind, which blew from the west for three weeks in succession. It swung to the north only to reveal the sails of forty-two British ships blockading the harbour. An attempt to run the gauntlet ended in fiasco; two frigates collided, and the whole fleet returned to Brest. On August 26th, Hardy was instructed to give up the enterprise until the equinoctial gales broke the British blockade. Worse, all idea of sending the second expedition of 4,000 men to Ireland was now abandoned. On the 23rd, Tone's ally from Bantry days, General Chérin, originally appointed the Supreme Commander, resigned in disgust; and the rest of the "Army of Ireland" dissolved, many being sent to reinforce the defences *against* invasion.[9]

For Wolfe Tone, the delays at Brest were the culmination of a crushing series of disappointments.

His misgivings earlier that year about the sincerity of Bonaparte's concern for Ireland had been only too well justified by events. After that chilly interview with the new master of France, in which Lewins and he had presented the second set of situation reports on Ireland, he himself had not seen Bonaparte again. For weeks he had hung about Paris, waiting for news, leaving negotiations to Lewins, the accredited diplomatic agent of the United Irish. In April Lewins had been received politely by the current President of the Directory, Merlin, who made the most welcome assurance that "France would never grant a peace to England on any terms, short of the independence of Ireland". On the other hand, Merlin would say nothing about either the time or place of the expedition to liberate Ireland; that was "the secret of the State". Lewins' next interview with Bonaparte himself was much less encouraging. News had now reached the Irish exiles of the round-up of the entire Leinster Directory in Bond's house in Dublin. Lewins begged Bonaparte to do something for their colleagues. Bonaparte explained that it would be mere bluff to threaten Britain, as the British well knew; intervention by France in favour of the Irish patriots at this moment could only "injure them materially"; France was not yet in a position to follow up threats with effective action.[10]

Thoroughly demoralised, Tone and Lewins both left Paris in mid-April: Tone to take up his posting as Adjutant-General on the staff of the "Army of England", stationed in Rouen, Lewins to go to Holland to look after his personal affairs. Events in Ireland, they could see in the papers—including the liberal English newspaper, the *Courier* which found its way to France—were now moving towards a crisis. After reading of the arrest of his close friend, Thomas Addis Emmet, Tone read a report that the revolution had actually broken out in Ireland. It turned out to be only a small rising in Tipperary: obviously the English Government were trying to exaggerate the danger in order to "terrify the Irish gentry out of their wits" and crush the people's spirit; though "atrociously wicked" the policy was a logical one if they were to subdue the country before the French landed. And yet Tone believed, "The spirit is, I think, too universally spread to be checked now, and the vengeance of the People, whenever the occasion presents itself, will only be the more terrible and sanguinary."[11]

Tone spent Easter in Rouen, where he had the curiosity to attend mass in the cathedral, and was subjected to a sermon comparing Christ in the tomb with Jonah in the whale: "I wonder how people can listen to such abominable nonsense." He was depressed to read a report of Napoleon's plan to take command of the Toulon expedition said to be preparing to sail for Egypt. He supposed that the object would be to restore Palestine to the Jews in exchange for certain "shekels of gold". At the end of April, he returned for a fortnight's "delicious" leave with his wife and children in Paris. There was excellent family news, at any rate: his younger brother Arthur was coming to join them, and he hoped to find him a post in the French army; after a silence of four years, his brother William had written from India to say that he had risen to be second-in-command of the Mahratta State Infantry with a salary of £750 a year, a triumph, Tone felt, for talent and courage—"The first war in India, we shall hear more of him."[12]

Meanwhile Bonaparte's intentions remained as baffling to Tone as to the British Government. But wherever else might be the man's destination, it did not seem to be Ireland. On May 19th Tone wrote: "I do not know

what to think of our expedition. It is certain that the whole left wing of
the Army of England is at this moment in full march back to the Rhine;
Buonaparte is God knows where, and the clouds seem thickening more
and more in Germany."[13] It was understood that the expedition from
Toulon and other Mediterranean ports had now been started. A week
later, the cat was out of the bag. Bonaparte had embarked with the
Toulon fleet after all, and in his address to his troops exhorted them to
sustain the glory of France in "distant" seas. "What does that mean?"
Tone asked himself. "Is he going after all to India? Will he make a short
cut to London by way of Calcutta? I begin foully to suspect it. He has all
his savants embarked with him, with their apparatus; that can hardly be
for England . . . If it be India, I wish to God I were with him; I might be
able to co-operate with Will, and perhaps be of material service." A few
days later Tone wrote to General Kilmaine formally offering his services
for an India expedition, if it would serve France. In his private diary he
recorded that the "only difficulty" was his family. He was bored to tears
with waiting, and there was "no [more] question or appearance here of an
attempt on England than of one on the Moon". For once Tone was so
carried away by the thought of his military duties that he seemed to have
forgotten Ireland.[14]

Three days before, unknown to anyone in France, the rebellion had
broken out in the counties around Dublin.

In Paris, the other Irish exiles had not given up hope so easily. One of their
difficulties in negotiating with France was that they had split, as political
exiles often do, into hostile groups. Tone's friends—Lewins, Teeling and
Orr—were now boycotting Napper Tandy and his friend, the Scottish
Jacobin Thomas Muir.[15] Tandy, they said, had put on airs: he gave out
that he was an old officer and a man of great property. In return, he had
tried to smear Lewins and Tone with abusing the confidence of the United
movement, and had actually asked a meeting of all the Irish refugees to
denounce them. Still more galling, Muir, the Scottish Jacobin, claimed to
have the authority of the Irish movement to put their case in the French
papers.[16]

Personalities apart, their wrangles were exacerbated by their isolation
from Ireland. Since McNevin had returned to Dublin the previous year
they had had no reliable channel for concerting their plans with the Irish
Directory, and their knowledge of the Irish organisation was now lament-
ably out of date.[17] Inevitably, reports of the split came to the ears of the

French. General Kilmaine, himself of Irish stock, put it bluntly: "There was nothing to be heard of amongst them, but denunciations, and if every one of them, separately, spoke truth, all the rest were rascals." And this, he added, had lowered the Irish nation in the esteem of the French Government.[18]

The news of the outbreak of the rebellion reached France in early June. Tone was still with the Army of England, his request to go to India had been politely refused; instead he was manning an artillery battery at Le Havre. In Paris, Teeling, Orr and some others drafted an appeal to the Directory to launch an immediate expedition. A force of 1,000 men with 5,000 arms should be landed on the north or north west coast where there were plenty of safe landing places, little or no army to guard them, and a people who were "exceptionally brave", though General Lake had tried to disarm them.[19] Characteristically, another very different plan was presented by Lewins: for five times as many men and arms.[20] The Directory responded by adopting a scheme still more ambitious than the second, although two months later, as we have seen, they had only succeeded in carrying out the first—by sending the 1,000 men with Humbert.

What part Tone played in all this is not clear; the last entry in his diary dates from the end of June when he returned to Paris to throw his weight behind Lewins. Tone's own view was that there was no point in sending a small expedition; though here Napper Tandy's party opposed him. Tandy declared that he had only to appear on the coast of Ireland for 30,000 to rise to meet him.[21] The Directory were most impressed by this argument—and the next month Tandy found himself being given a fast frigate of his own to put it to the test. However, such was the state of the French Ministry of Marine that Tandy was in no great danger of sailing.[22]

So the weeks passed: Tandy at Dunkirk, Tone at Brest, and both could hardly doubt that, unless Humbert achieved a miracle, the Irish revolution would be over before either of their expeditions could arrive.

Meanwhile, Humbert had consolidated the position at Killala, and began the advance into the interior, brushing aside the feeble forces opposing him.[23]

Bishop Stock, who was to write the best account of these events, found his dinner party at the castle suddenly interrupted by an astonishing scene: French officers and soldiers dragged in their arms and baggage; prisoners were interrogated; and an emergency operation performed on a grenadier wounded in a scuffle with the local yeomanry. Three hundred men had soon packed into the lower part of the castle and its outbuildings—and how admirable was their discipline. A French officer called to the Bishop's butler, on first entering the dining-room, and asked him to take charge of the spoons and glasses on the sideboard; and when the dinner guests later came to collect their belongings from the hall they found not one of the hats, whips or great coats missing.[24]

The invaders displayed equal delicacy towards the women of the household. The upper storey of the castle, where there were the library and the three principal bed-chambers, was still used by the Bishop, his wife and eleven children; and so scrupulous were the French not to disturb this female sanctuary that only once did any Frenchman dare to climb the stairs to that floor—when the officers begged leave to report a military victory of theirs that they hoped would attach the Bishop's family to the French cause.[25]

On their part, Humbert's men remained puzzled by the attitude of the respectable inhabitants. They had been briefed by the United Irish in France to expect the country to rise in arms to shake off the detested yoke of Great Britain. And just in case they needed encouragement, the Directory had officially instructed Humbert to take every possible means to foster the country's "hatred of the English name".[26] Yet despite the proclamation safeguarding property and religious freedom, only two Protestants came forward to join them, two drunks, who had promptly turned Catholic. And the Catholics themselves who flocked to join them all seemed to be ignorant peasants who could hardly be of much assistance in forming a provisional government.

The night of the landing Humbert put the problem to the Bishop. Even when he chose to act like a gentleman, Humbert was intimidating. His eye was "small and sleepy" like the "eye of a cat preparing to spring", wrote the Bishop. He offered the Bishop a place on the Connaught Directory; some of the members had already been appointed, but there was still a place for a man of the Bishop's ability and consequence if he would join in "liberating his country".[27] On the Bishop's politely declining, Humbert reverted to the roughness and violence that were natural to him—a style that he had learnt to exploit to excellent effect. As the principal inhabitant of Killala, the Bishop was instructed to produce the boats and cars necessary for unloading the heavy stores from the ships—artillery, gunpowder and so on. Despite the high prices offered, the fishermen and carriers were not to be found. In vain the Bishop protested that he had no civil authority. Humbert replied that the magistrate had fled and the Bishop must continue to arrange things, by some means or other.[28]

Next morning when neither boat nor car appeared, Humbert became furious. "He poured forth a torrent of vulgar abuse, roared, stamped, laid his hand frequently on a scimitar that battered the ground, presented a pistol at the Bishop's eldest son, and at last told the Bishop himself that he would make himself sensible he was not to be fooled with, for he would punish his disobedience by sending him to France." Time was only allowed for him to put on his hat, and he was then marched away under escort past the shocked inhabitants in the direction of the beach. The Bishop took all this in good part. As he foresaw, cars and boats were instantly produced; he himself, once out of sight of the town, was restored to his family with apologies from the French officers for Humbert's behaviour: "he was a hasty man but very good-natured."[29]

In the next two days, Humbert continued systematically to establish Killala as a base for the republic. A green flag, inscribed *Erin Go Bragh*, was mounted on the castle gate.

The Bishop, despite his proficiency in Hebrew, was weak in Irish, and someone gave him the translation—"Ireland for ever".[30]

The French explained to the populace that they were only the advance guard of 30,000 men; the rest were expected any day. Their aim was simply to make the Irish people "independent and happy". If they seemed short of ready cash, money was expected at any moment. Meanwhile, they would pay for all local supplies—meat and bread and so on—in drafts on the Directory of Connaught. The people were puzzled by this idea, as they were not in the habit of handling cheques. But the Bishop himself re-assured them: the French would take the supplies anyway, and no one would lose by accepting a receipt. For the next two or three days the French commissary was busily occupied writing drafts on the Connaught Directory that had yet to be established.[31]

If cash was lacking, the French did not stint the supply of arms and uniforms. The Frenchmen's own clothes were much the worse for wear; half of them had served with Bonaparte in Italy, and the rest with the Army of the Rhine, and bore evident marks of their privations. Yet they cheerfully handed out shiny new helmets to their allies.[32] "Patt will look droll in a helmet without any corresponding article of dress," was Matthew Tone's comment.[33] But who cared if the uniforms were odds and ends scrounged by Humbert from the magazine at La Rochelle? The Bishop, roped in as interpreter, joined in the fun:

"The coxcombry of the young clowns in their new dress; the mixture of good-humour and contempt in the countenances of the French, employed in making puppies of them; the haste of the undressed to be as fine as their neighbours, casting away their old clothes long before it came their turn to receive the new; above all, the merry activity of a handsome young fellow, a marine officer, whose business it was to consummate the vanity of the recruits by decorating them with helmets beautifully edged with spotted brown paper to look like leopard's skin, a task which he performed standing on a powder barrel, and making the helmet fit any skull, even the largest, by thumping it down with his fists, careless whether it could ever be taken off again . . ."[34]

Humbert also enjoyed the joke. "Look at these poor fellows," he told the Bishop triumphantly, "they are made, you find, of the same stuff with ourselves."[35]

When it came to arming his new allies, however, Humbert's sense of humour began to fail. Often the recruits put in their cartridges at the wrong end, and "when they stuck in the passage (as they often did) the inverted barrel was set to work against the ground, till it was bent and useless".[36] At first they were issued with balls as well as powder. The practice was not repeated after an unfortunate incident when Humbert was standing at an open window and heard a ball whistle by his ear, discharged by an awkward recruit in the yard below. Other recruits were found to have expended their powder and shot on the local ravens, prized for their quills.[37]

Still less familiar to the Irish recruits than musket and cartridge were French military rations. Accustomed all their lives to a diet of sour milk and potatoes, the recruits had no difficulty in developing an appetite for beef. One French officer complained that these Irishmen would eat more in four days, proportionately, than the whole Army of Italy in a month. He added that he had seen a recruit on receiving his week's allowance lie down on the ground and gnaw it with such vigour that he was sure it would all be gone before he rose![38]

Of course, Humbert's men did their best to respect the idiosyncracies of their new allies, as they had been instructed by the Directory. But the more they saw of them, the more they felt sorry for themselves. Their eagerness to dress up like soldiers, and their reluctance to behave like them; their indiscipline and sloth; their endless cadging and pilfering; all this was disheartening. But what were the French to make of a people who had no political interests at all, and welcomed them as crusaders who had come to "take arms for France and the Blessed Virgin"? "God help these Simpletons," said one French officer to the Bishop. "If they knew how little we care for the Pope or his religion, they would not be so hot in expecting help from us: we have just sent away *Mr. Pope* from Italy, and who knows but we may find him again in this country."[39]

Another French officer was less charitable: "Do you know what I would do with those Irish Devils, if I had a body to form out of them?" he asked the commandant. "I would pick out one third of them, and by the Lord I would shoot the rest."[40]

Before leaving, Humbert collected up supplies for his march. The Bishop's larder and cellar, his corn, potatoes and cattle, the nine horses from his stables, and the six belonging to the guests, they were all commandeered. In all, the Bishop reckoned that he lost £600 worth of belongings. Still, he reflected that it was fair to plunder *him* before taking from the poor. And he consoled himself that, by not abandoning the castle, he had saved his more valuable possessions—his classical library and his furniture.[41]

On Saturday the 25th, the day before Humbert's superiors in France finally decided to abandon hope of sending a large expedition to Ireland, Humbert advanced to Ballina. He left behind a colonel and 200 of his men, ostensibly to protect the Protestants of Killala and their property, but in fact to secure his own line of retreat.[42] In return he took away four respectable hostages—a curate, a lieutenant of the yeomanry, a custom-house official, and one of the Bishop's sons. Characteristically, Humbert let them all go home next day, after a rough night with a party of rebels in the neighbouring town of Ballina.[43]

Humbert also left one important item in the Bishop's care: the main power magazine of the expedition, totalling 280 powder barrels. This was deposited in the castle yard a few yards from the kitchen. In the best of times it would have been an embarrassment. Now, with several hundred men billeted at the castle, the Bishop feared for the worst. The people had a cheerful habit of smoking their pipes in the yard: there was also considerable danger from the kitchen grate. This was kept stoked up from early in the morning till midnight—a *ton* of coal, the Bishop calculated, was being burnt every day that month—and several times the chimney itself caught fire. Eventually, the Bishop succeeded in conveying all 280 powder barrels into various hiding-places in the garden. The French colonel agreed to the plan, not so much afraid of an explosion, as of the possibility of the powder finding its way to his Irish allies.[44]

At Ballina, ten miles to the south, Humbert continued to strengthen his military position. In the absence of any regular troops in the area, he found the yeomanry easy meat for his veterans. The day before his own arrival he had sent out a reconnaissance of 250 men under his second-in-command, Colonel Sarrazin; they had returned, after posting a patrol by the strategic bridge on the road between Ballina and Killala.[46] In due course the Ballina garrison had advanced, and lost a few men, including a clergyman volunteer called Fortescue, in the ambush. Their nerve broken, they now retreated to Foxford, abandoning Ballina to Humbert without a shot. On entering the town the French found a macabre relic left by the garrison—one of the townspeople, who had prematurely revealed his loyalty to the French and had been hanged from his own doorway an hour or two before. One of the French officers was horrified.[46] Colonel Sarrazin, is said to have kissed the face of the corpse and cried: "Voilà messieurs, thus do we honour the martyrs of your sacred cause."[47]

Humbert's instructions, as we saw, were to establish a bridge-head and then wait until Hardy's main army made its appearance—unless the Irish forces should prove strong enough for independent action. In this respect he had still made little progress. Of the five thousand odd volunteers who had been issued with arms, little more than a tenth could be formed into regular companies to fight alongside them, and the officers were peasants like the rest, who might run at the first sound of the cannon; however two gentlemen, both Catholics, had at last stepped forward to risk their lives in the cause—a magistrate's son called McDonnell, and an ex-soldier called Blake.[48] Humbert, at any rate, must remain on the defensive. If he was to follow the Directory's instructions to give Hardy a fair chance of linking up with him, he would need to lie low for up to a fortnight.

Yet perhaps those instructions could be evaded. To precipitate a rising, as he was told, meant advertising his presence. And how else except by some daring feat of arms? Humbert, at any rate, was too flamboyant a character to wait while his enemies closed in around him. He had just learnt that 3,500 regulars were advancing towards him. There was only one chance: to strike at their position at Castlebar, the county town of Mayo, while they were still off-balance.

Humbert left Ballina on the afternoon of Sunday the 26th, with 700 French infantry and cavalry and about the same number of Irish levies. From Ballina the coach road ran almost due south to Foxford and then swung south west to Castlebar. But there was another road to the west of Lough Conn, barely more than a bridle track, leading through the wildest part of the district, across a waste of bog and then over a ridge close to the peak of Mount Nephin. Humbert learnt—apparently from the parish priest of one of the local villages—that this mountain road was just passable for his column. It was quite undefended, while the strategic bridge at Foxford was blocked by a substantial garrison. Accordingly, he announced that he was to march via Foxford, and took the road for a few miles, then dodged back and continued along the mountain track.[49]

The going was so rough that the single cannon they had brought with them had to be manhandled; for this purpose some of the Irish levies were tied to the traces.[50] The twenty-five mile march lasted all night, with one halt of two hours. There was not the slightest sign of opposition. At six in the morning they saw the town walls of Castlebar ahead of them— "a tough nut to crack" as one of the officers commented, "for a little army like ours".[51] The British had thrown up trenches astride the only possible approach to the town and had brought up thirteen pieces of artillery to defend it.[52]

While the Viceroy and his suite were being carried majestically along the Grand Canal towards the front, the responsibility for defending Castlebar remained with the Connaught commander, General Hutchinson. He was the second son of the famous place-hunting Provost of Trinity, of whom Lord North had said that if the King were to give him all three kingdoms on one day he would come next day to ask for the Isle of Man as a potato garden.[53] The General was now himself a member of the Irish Parliament, but an uncharacteristic one: he believed in conciliation. For an Irish general, he was also unusually experienced, as he had served with Abercromby on the continent.[54] Still, he was totally outclassed by Humbert.

His first blunder had been to assume that the French would attack by the main road, and to fail to station even a patrol on the western approaches. Much more serious, strategically, was the risk of exposing a force little superior than the enemy's within reach of a sudden strike.[55] Yet he could hardly be expected to have anticipated the extraordinary outcome of the battle.

After stationing a garrison at Foxford, he was left with only about 1,700 troops at Castlebar, the great majority of which were Irish militia, with a small force of Scotch Fencibles, some of Lord Roden's Dragoons, a sprinkling of yeomanry, and the skeleton of one regiment of the line. Much his strongest card was his artillery—ten curricle guns and a howitzer —if properly served.[56]

Soon after his arrival at Castlebar he had sent an officer under flag of truce to Killala, ostensibly to make enquiries about a wounded officer, but in fact to reconnoitre the enemy's strength.[57] He had then decided to move forward on Sunday to the attack. An express from Cornwallis, however, arrived first. The Viceroy warned him not on any account to advance with so small a force. So he had prepared a defensive position to the north west of the town. At eleven o'clock at night General Lake, sent on post-haste by Cornwallis, reached Castlebar, and took over the command.[58] There was a moment of panic in the town when someone fired a shot in the direction of the Longford militia who were bivouacking on the green.[59]

About three a.m. a yeoman, who had been out to visit his farm, returned with a story that was greeted with incredulity: a large body of men "in blue uniforms" were marching down that wild, rocky track. About five o'clock, General Trench, the most junior of the three generals, rode out to investigate, received a few musket balls from Humbert's advance guard and returned with news that sent the garrison scurrying for their trenches.[60]

Hutchinson proved to have chosen his position well enough. Castlebar lay in a hollow, beside a small river flowing from the mountainous country to the north west; low hills protected it on either side. On one of these, called Sion Hill, the front line had been established: four curricle guns, including two manned by experienced gunners of the Royal Irish Artillery, and several hundred musketeers, mainly consisting of the Kilkenny militia, under the command of the great Kilkenny magnate, Lord Ormonde. Behind them were a second line of musketeers: Fraser Fencibles from the Highlands, with two battalion guns, and a corps of Galway yeomen. And behind these were a third line, consisting of four companies of the Longford militia, under their landlord, Lord Granard. Held back in reserve, according to practice, were the cavalry: Lord Roden's Foxhunters, some squadrons of the 6th Carabineers, and a few yeomen from the neighbourhood. There were also some gunners with the rest of the artillery, including a curricle gun (a small mobile field piece) in the marketplace—no doubt to encourage the townspeople.[61]

At eight o'clock, the French column appeared over the ridge and Lake ordered the cannonade to begin. The effective range of a musket of this period was hardly more than a hundred yards.[62] Lake's artillery had a clear field of fire of about ten times that distance. Thus, he could have every hope that the French would not reach his line before their column was broken and dispersed by grape- and canister-shot, and he could unleash his Foxhunters at them.[63]

On his part Humbert recognised his desperate situation, now that he had lost the element of surprise. His veterans, however, did not flinch. There was "no alternative to victory but death", said one of the captains.[64] The Grenadiers, led in person by Sarrazin, charged forward along the line of a ditch that only half sheltered them from the cannon balls "falling every-where like hail". Their own cannon was disabled. Unable to fire a shot in reply, with his casualties mounting, Sarrazin learnt from his aide that most of the "Irish Legion" under Blake and McDonnell had fled at the first cannon shot.[65]

It was at this moment that the Irish levies on the other side—the Irish militia—achieved what even their greatest detractors would have believed impossible.

They turned and ran, throwing down their muskets and stripping off their packs in their panic. The sudden collapse of the line left their artillery and Fencibles reeling. The Grenadiers charged the guns at bayonet-point, and carried them. A few of the rear-guard fought gallantly; later people told the story of a solitary Fraser sentinel, shooting attacker after attacker from the top of a flight of steps, till at last he was hurled from his post and his brains knocked out.[66] But who could rally the main garrison? Lord Ormonde tried. First he "begged and beseeched" them, then he "up-braided and swore at them", finally he burst into tears.[67] Lord Granard fought on alone by the bridge. But nothing could now check the wild, primitive terror that the French had inspired without firing a shot.

Landlords and tenants, generals and privates, all were now united in their eagerness to escape. On they ran, through the narrow streets of the town, and out into the country beyond. All their cannons, all their flags, all their munitions were left scattered behind them—even General Lake's luggage lay at the mercy of the invaders. Exhausted by the march of the previous night, the French soon gave up the chase. But the garrison never paused till they reached Tuam, thirty miles beyond the scene of action. Some pressed on to Athlone, covering sixty-three miles in twenty-seven hours.[68]

So ended one of the most ignominious defeats in British military history, which came to be known as the "Races of Castlebar".

4

The Race for Dublin

Connaught and Leinster, August 27th–September 30th

Erin's sons, be not faint-hearted,
Welcome, sing then "Ça Ira",
From Killala they are marching
To the tune of "Vive la".

Rouse, Hibernians, 1798

THAT DAY, August 27th, Cornwallis and his staff had disembarked from the canal at Tullamore[1] and pressed on by carriage to Athlone, the grand military rendezvous astride the Shannon. Cornwallis himself was in a miserable state; his foot was inflamed; he could only wear a sort of canvas shoe; and riding was difficult and painful. Yet he felt so uneasy about his army's situation at Athlone that he insisted on taking General John Moore and riding across to the Connaught bank of the Shannon, to see if there was a better position to be taken up there.

It turned out that Athlone, whose castle had been for hundreds of years the symbol of British power in the centre of Ireland, was perfectly incapable of defence on either bank. Only by encamping the entire army, did Cornwallis feel he could give them security, and this could not be done till the other contingents arrived in the morning. For the time being they could only place pickets, and hope for the best.[2]

During the night an express galloped into camp with the news that Cornwallis had been half expecting: a French triumph at Castlebar. Lake's despatch was abject, as well it might be. He found it "impossible to manage the militia"; their panic was "beyond description".[3] "Nothing could exceed the misconduct of the troops, with the exception of the artillery . . . and of Lord Roden's Fencibles," was Hutchinson's verdict.[4] No less shocking than their behaviour on the field was the army's behaviour after their defeat. "Their conduct," wrote Cornwallis' military secretary, "and that of the Carabineers and Frazers, in action on the retreat from

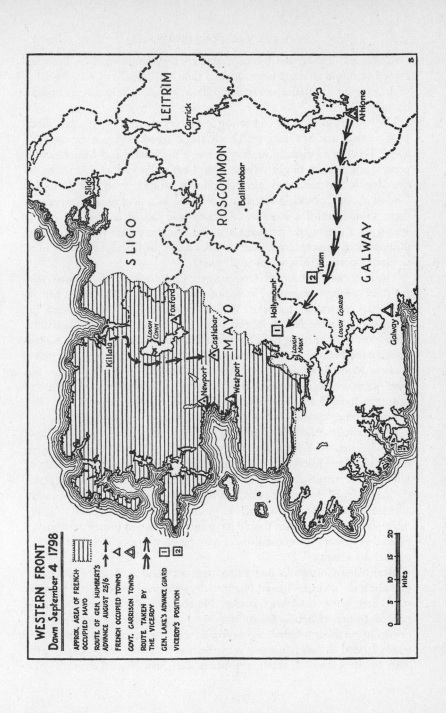

Castlebar and Tuam, and the depredations they committed on the road
exceed I am told all description. Indeed they have, I believe, raised a spirit
of discontent and disaffection which did not before exist in this part of the
country."[5]

The military losses were bad enough: 9 pieces of artillery; 53 men killed;
36 wounded; and 278 missing. The strategic repercussions were incalcul-
able.[6] There were already signs of a rising in Kildare and Meath, and a
general insurrection might follow. Still, Cornwallis had never minimised
the dangers, and remained calm.[7] In Dublin, Bucky, who had grumbled
loudest about Cornwallis's caution, declared in a panic that "never was
there so disgraceful a scene . . . Galway will fall of course." A report
spread by a deranged lieutenant asserted positively that the French had
pushed ahead and captured Tuam.[8] Once again the Irish loyalists began to
think of escorting their wives to England.

The reaction of the British Government to the news of the disaster was,
for once, prompt enough. Pitt happened to be down in Kent when he
received Cornwallis's message. Within four hours he had arranged for
massive reinforcements of British militia to be embarked immediately,
despite the most pressing need for them elsewhere.[9] Pitt was still on tenterhooks over Nelson's confrontation with Bonaparte. It appeared that a
decisive action had taken place earlier that month near Alexandria, but
there were conflicting reports about the result. Favourable or not, it had
begun to look as though India would be the next theatre of war. But
Ireland's strategic needs, for once, claimed priority.

Pitt's cabinet colleague, Lord Auckland, took the same serious view.
"In the course of twenty-four eventful years", he told Cooke, "it has
happened to me to receive many unpleasant and unexpected accounts of
military defeats and disgraces. One of the hardest strokes in that way was
the surrender of Burgoyne's army at Saratoga, but I do not think it either
affected or surprised me so much as your Castlebar catastrophe . . . If the
impression of that business should have encouraged and brought forward a
general explosion, the consequences may be very serious and God send us
a good deliverance."[10]

Meanwhile Cornwallis had halted for two days at Athlone doggedly
preparing the counter-attack. His strategy remained basically the same as
it had been before the French landed. No confidence at all could be placed
on Irish troops, especially the militia; as far as possible they must be withdrawn to garrisons where they would do the least harm; and some of the
newly landed British regiments must be hurried to the front. On August
29th he took two Scottish regiments detached from Longford—the

Sutherland and Rehy Fencibles—and pushed on to Tuam, less than forty miles from Castlebar. Here the rest of the reinforcements were waiting; and the army was divided into four brigades commanded by three British generals—Hunter, Campbell and Moore—and by Hutchinson.[11] The latter was understandably miserable about his lapse at Castlebar, though Cornwallis was soon to tell him in a fatherly way that it was "an error of judgement, which a General Officer, who has more zeal and courage than experience in the practical part of his profession, is very liable to commit".[12]

While Humbert was reported to be digging in at Castlebar, Cornwallis' forces continued to accumulate at Tuam. By September 2nd the combined forces at Tuam totalled 7,800 men, and a further 2,800 under General Taylor had retreated to Boyle. To establish such overwhelming numerical superiority, Cornwallis had cut the garrisons of Ireland as near to the bone as he dared, leaving only 1,100 regular infantry in Dublin, and hardly more in Wexford.[13] Once again, the defence of Ireland against the enemy within was left mainly to the Irish loyalists who made up the 40,000 strong yeomanry corps. If there was a second insurrection in Leinster, as the Government now thought likely, everything would depend on the energy (and restraint) of the huntin'-shootin'-and-burnin' gentry.

The longer the French survived, of course, the greater the danger of the insurrection starting up again. And there was a second, still more chilling danger. Humbert was reported to be expecting the 4,000 men of the Brest expedition any day, and this report seemed to be confirmed by his digging in at Castlebar. For both these reasons, Cornwallis was now under strong pressure, from his British generals and Irish public opinion, to act swiftly to crush the French.[14]

In Dublin, Bucky, having got over his panic after Castlebar, continued to do his best to make things difficult. He was still moaning about being left behind in Dublin; he hoped that Cornwallis would not make "the same experiment" on the commanders of the three new British militia regiments being sent over; yet if he did not, it would make his own position "if possible still more degrading". In the intervals between advising the British cabinet on these great injustices, Bucky warned them that Cornwallis' caution was "more hazardous" than prompt action. "I am confident that the French looked to another flotilla. I know that they have been, through correspondences, urging an insurrection in Dublin." Cornwallis took "a most heavy responsibility on himself by this most unaccountable delay". In case of disaster, he repeated, he himself was prepared to act as Lord Deputy in Ireland (though he would not "for any consideration" agree to hold it for more than a month.)[15]

Cornwallis was not however to be diverted, even by Bucky, from the task he had set himself. On the 4th his army of 10,000 moved ponderously forward to Hollymount. On the 5th he would attack Castlebar. That total might seem large, but it still included several thousand Irish militia and yeomanry; and the rest were the scrapings of the barrel from Scotland and England.[16] Cornwallis had naturally tried to restore discipline. After Castlebar he had issued a reprimand as outspoken as Abercromby's famous general order. Officers must assist him "in putting a stop to the licentious conduct of the troops, and in saving the wretched inhabitants from being robbed".[17] And he had no illusions about the value of his men. As he explained to General John Moore, it would be "unpardonable, for the sake of a little military or a little personal glory, to run the smallest unnecessary risk. The troops he had were bad and undisciplined . . . the least check and the country was gone."[18]

In the eight days since he had occupied Castlebar, Humbert had acted with his usual dash and determination. A young Catholic called John Moore of Moore Hall, who had studied law at the Temple and hob-nobbed with the British Whigs, was swept up by Humbert and appointed "President" of the Provisional Government of Connaught. No matter that he protested that he was not, nor wished to be, a United Irishman.[19] Humbert had not more time for such niceties at Castlebar than he had when dealing with the Bishop at Killala. Citizen Moore, it was proclaimed, would lead the twelve-man council of the Provisional Government. They would organise the militia and the joint commissariat of the French and Irish armies. All those who had received arms and uniforms and did not rejoin their army should be considered rebels; and every male between the ages of sixteen and forty must repair to the French camp "in order to march in mass against the common enemy, the tyrant of Ireland—the English; whose destruction alone can insure the independence and welfare of ancient Hibernia".[20]

Outwardly, Humbert remained on the crest of the wave. The strategic results of his victory had been dramatic. He had captured the capital of Mayo, and was now master of the whole county except for Claremorris: local risings at Westport and Newport on the coast had followed his own victory; some Irish levies had driven south to Ballinrobe; and the British had fled to the garrisons at Sligo and Boyle, abandoning Foxford and Swinford.[21] It was also encouraging to find at last some respectable Irishmen joining the movement. Citizen John Moore's father was one of the richest men in the district, having made a fortune in Malaga. The commander of a regiment of Irish levies, Colonel John Joseph McDonnell, also came from an excellent background; his father, a Catholic squire, had distinguished himself in the Volunteer movement.[22] There were two gentlemen from Ballina called Barrett; the father was a respectable apothecary, while his son had proved an active member of the yeomanry.[23] And there was Mr. Matthew Bellew, the flamboyant brother of the Catholic bishop. He came from an ancient Catholic family and had originally been educated for the priesthood, but had had a chequered military career in the Austrian and Russian service instead.[24] As he was the only military man among the gentry, Humbert cheerfully appointed him general.

At the same time, his victory brought the country people from miles around flocking to his standard. "Liberty!" they cried and "*Erin Go Bragh!*" displaying the tree of liberty and a harp without a crown.[25] It began to look as though he might, after all, achieve the recruiting target of 10,000 men he had set himself—according to proclamation.[26] To celebrate, Humbert invited the townspeople to a victory ball in the assembly rooms at Castlebar. He took the opportunity to make an announcement: he was expecting a contribution from the town of 2,000 guineas to provide the sinews of war.[27]

In this, however, Humbert's hopes were not to be realised. The cash was not in the town. (In fact the economic crisis had created a currency famine in all parts of Ireland.) Equally discouraging was the calibre of the gentlemen Humbert had relied on to provide officers for his levies. Only McDonnell proved to be a convinced friend of liberty—the kind of "patriot chief" that the Directory had instructed him to contact.[28] The rest turned out to have little or no connection with the United movement, and their motive for joining the army seemed to be to safeguard their property or indulge their love of adventure. The choice of Bellew as the general proved especially unfortunate. It emerged that he had first offered to join the yeomanry defending Castlebar, but had been rejected as a hopeless alcoholic.[29]

With officers of this sort, what hope was there of making anything of the rank and file? The recruits at Castlebar proved to be of the same exuberant type they had met at Killala. They broke into the house of the local improving landlord, Lord Lucan, and chopped up his lordship's furniture to make fuel for their cooking pots; they lit their pipes with the engravings from his lordship's picture gallery; and paraded in his lordship's fancy waistcoats. Every prominent loyalist they treated much the same: they rampaged through the house of Mr. Denis Browne, the member for the county; they gutted the wine cellars of his brother, Lord Altamont, and drove the cattle from the park; and they left the home of his cousin, Sir John Browne, an empty shell.[30]

The Protestant church in Castlebar was treated with no more respect than its parishioners. A mob broke in, destroyed a copy of the Bible, and scribbled obscene drawings on the pews. An attempt was then made to appropriate it for Catholic Mass—or so the Dean said later.[31]

To cap it all, some of the peasants began to complain that they were ill-treated by the French. It was unfair to ask them to surrender their loot; they felt discriminated against in the supply of food and lodgings; and they resented the menial task given them by French officers, some of whom were coloured men from the West Indies.[32]

After several days of this, Humbert finally lost patience. Two Irish captains were taken out and shot for mutiny. Order was restored. Humbert now realised that if the expedition was to achieve anything in Mayo, it could only be by French arms.[33] But what had happened to Hardy's troops from Brest? And why had the victory at Castlebar had absolutely no impact on the other parts of Ireland supposed to be ready to rise? Roscommon, for example, was reported to have kept intact its United organisation, commanded by Wolfe Tone's friend, Jemmy Plunket. Yet in Roscommon the people worked industriously at the harvest, apparently unconcerned at the struggle to make Ireland a nation once again.[34]

In his official dispatches that week to the Citizen Directors of France, Humbert emphasised the bright side of things. "Officers and soldiers have showed prodigies of valour," he wrote. The enemy's loss amounted to 1,800 men.[35] (In fact the total was less than three hundred.) To the Minister of Marine, however, he conceded that "slow progress" had been made in organising the Irish, as Mayo had never been disturbed; in other counties in Ireland it would have been "very different". He confessed that the Irish legion at Castlebar had fled at the first cannon shot; "I expected as much and their panic in no way deranged my operations." As for the future, he needed 2,000 more troops from France, including infantry, cavalry and artillery. "I will venture to assert," he concluded, "that in the course of a month after the arrival of this reinforcement . . . Ireland will be free."[36]

After sending these urgent dispatches to Newport, where the French courier was embarked in the disguise of an Irish sailor, Humbert decided to concentrate all his forces at Castlebar and then strike out towards Roscommon. If he could somehow give the British army the slip, he could then cross the Shannon and make rendezvous with the Ulster insurgents somewhere to the north.[37] Meanwhile the reinforcements from France might have arrived, and the combined armies could march on Dublin.

It was a desperate venture certainly, but no more so than many accomplished by the French Republic in the process of carrying the revolution into all the chief countries of Europe.

The failure of Humbert's triumph at Castlebar to precipitate risings in other parts of Ireland may seem puzzling. In one sense the weather was too good: the glorious weather that had so much assisted the establishment of the Wexford Republic had now returned keeping people everywhere busy at harvest. It is also true that the counties adjoining Mayo—Leitrim and Roscommon—formed a kind of firebreak against the spread of revolution. In Leinster, as we saw, the rebellion had spread like a prairie fire from one organised village to the next along the line of the road from Dublin. Roscommon and Leitrim, though a stronghold for the Defender movement during the last decade[38] and virtually without garrisons,[39] were too far from Dublin or Belfast to have been organised by the United men. The only man who might have succeeded in this—Jemmy Plunket, Tone's friend—had surrendered to the Government shortly before Humbert's arrival.[40]

Beyond Connaught, most of the Leinster counties had had their fill of rebellion. That strange explosive mixture of fear and euphoria was not to be recaptured, though Humbert's victories were reported uncensored in the newspapers,[41] though their garrisons had been reduced and though some of their United leaders had tried to reorganise them for a rising.[42]

In two counties of Leinster, however, the United organisation had remained all the summer like an unexploded bomb in the ground. And in both these counties the shock of Humbert's victory was now sufficient to explode it.

On the borders of Longford and Westmeath, there is a tract of downland called Fruen Hill. It is a nondescript place in itself, but nearby is the Hill of Uisneach, where the High Kings of Ireland lie buried, and it commands the same broad sweep of the central plain. About eleven o'clock on the morning of September 4th, Lord Sunderlin, the nearest landlord of any consequence, was shocked by the sight of several hundred country people assembling close to his house, armed with pikes, pitchforks, scythes and so on. Gathering numbers every moment, they marched to Fruen Hill and formed a camp there. His alarm increased when he found that only ten of his yeomanry would report for duty.[43]

At Mullingar, eight miles to the east along the Dublin road, the garrison were in the same defenceless state. Two days before, the local magistrate, Captain Rochfort, had been informed that some men had ridden through the county warning their friends to be ready to rise when the Kildare boys marched in. He had sent an urgent S.O.S. to the Government: most of the troops had been drafted from the garrison to fight with Cornwallis and Lake, and the loyalists had no arms of any sort.[44] Rochfort was a true blue magistrate, who had long believed in "severity beyond the law" for suspected United men. Ironically he had now been converted to a more conciliatory policy by his cousin, Lord Belvedere, a warm adherent of Cornwallis.[45]

About ten miles the other side of Fruen Hill was the town of Edgeworthstown, the home of the Edgeworths. That summer had been an unusually tranquil one for the family, though the storm raged around them in other parts of Leinster. Richard Lovell Edgeworth had just married again. His young bride had settled down happily among the ten children of his three earlier marriages, including the celebrated Maria.[46]

Edgeworth was certainly a queer fish to find in the bogs of Longford—and was regarded by the county as such. He made curious mechanical contrivances and had advanced ideas on education. He was a friend of Mr. Darwin and Josiah Wedgwood, and a Fellow of the Royal Society. And he disapproved of the yeomen of the local Protestant party who harassed the people in their searches for arms, and of the local magistrates who believed in severity beyond the law. In fact, he was a loyalist, too, and had formed his tenantry into a yeomanry corps, pointedly including Catholics as well as Protestants.[47] Unfortunately there was a chronic shortage of arms at the castle. Despite his appeals to his friend, Captain Pakenham, who commanded at the Ordnance, Edgeworth's corps remained unarmed.[48] Meanwhile the news of the French landing was followed by the still more alarming news of their victory at Castlebar.

On September 4th, at ten o'clock, just before Lord Sunderlin saw the rebels marching to Fruen Hill, one of Edgeworth's retainers was horrified to see twenty or thirty men with green boughs in their hats, and pikes in their hands marching towards Edgeworthstown.[49] A few days before a notice had been posted on the local chapel door warning people of a plot to massacre them.[50] The rebels now announced they were "standing there to protect themselves against the Orangemen . . . who, as they heard, were coming down to cut them to pieces".[61]

Absurd as the story was, the rebels continued to pour across from Westmeath into County Longford. Edgeworth sent word to the nearest garrison town—Longford. He was told that no help could be spared. Moment by moment the alarm increased. It was said the pikemen now numbered 300. As the family were gathering on the portico of their house, they saw an ammunition cart galloping by. It contained barrels of gunpowder to blow up the Shannon bridges before the advancing French.

A few minutes later the house was shaken by an explosion. A spark from the axle had set fire to the ammunition cart, killing the driver and several horses, and seriously wounding one of the escort, the son of Captain Rochfort of Mullingar. That afternoon the Edgeworth family reached Longford to find it packed with other refugees. Behind them the country was now reported to be in rebel hands. Every Protestant's house in Edgeworthstown had been broken into and plundered—except the Edgeworths'. Fortunately, their English house-keeper, who had been left behind, had recently lent a few shillings to a farmer to pay the rent of a flax-ground. He had appeared, pike in hand, threatened to kill anyone who set foot in the house, and reassured his benefactress: "not a twig should be touched, nor a leaf harmed". Still, panic prevailed in Longford: the French were believed to be marching that way to Dublin. And for Edgeworths' house to be spared by the rebels was a mixed blessing. In the minds of the true blue yeomanry of the town it only confirmed the stories that he was in the conspiracy.[52]

How far in fact, was the people's army in Longford and Westmeath organised at all? Clearly, some part of the United organisation which had merged with the original Defenders movement in both counties had survived the collapse of the Dublin Executive. Some of the men who now took to the field were Protestants and United men: Hans Denniston, an opulent farmer from Granard who was lieutenant in the yeomanry, and Michael Farrell who had fled from Trinity that spring with Robert Emmet.[63] Yet it was a crude enough kind of republicanism that inspired the rank and file. "May the skins of all kings make drum-heads for United Irishmen" was their toast; "to take the livings from the gentlemen, and every man to have equal riches"[54] was their oath. And once in the field, at any rate, the movement degenerated, like the Meath, Kildare and Wexford movement before it, into a war against Protestants that made a mockery of the principles of the United Irishmen.

Meanwhile Humbert was marching away towards Sligo, turning his back on the Midlands where his victories had stirred the people to revolt. And at the same time another strategic development was taking place, still more significant and equally unknown to Humbert.

On the day of the Races of Castlebar, a second expeditionary force from France had at last put to sea, and was now only two days' sail from Ireland. Its commander was Napper Tandy, the senior United Irish officer in the French army, and Tone's bitter rival. Tandy, as we saw, had boasted that he and a mere handful of French soldiers could set alight the revolution in Ireland, and the Directory had taken him at his word. With only 370 French Grenadiers (less than a third of Humbert's original force) he had embarked from Dunkirk in the corvette, *Anacréon*. What the force lacked in troops, it more than made up in supplies: guns, ball-cartridges, barrels of powder, not to speak of a vast armoury of proclamations.

"Liberty or Death" was the heading at either side of a cap of liberty and a harp. The text began: "The soldiers of the GREAT NATION have landed on your coast . . . JAMES NAPPER TANDY is at their head. He has sworn to lead them on to victory, or die . . ."

For the dare-devil commander, however, there was one comfort. The *Anacréon* was one of the fastest French ships afloat. If attacked, they should be able to show a clean pair of heels.

About the fortnight after Napper Tandy had sailed from Dunkirk, the Directory received the first dazzling dispatch from Humbert. He had landed as directed at Killala; he had brushed aside the British troops sent against him; and thousands of brave Irishmen had rallied to his standard. Since Bonaparte's departure for the east the plan to revolutionise Ireland must have appeared a forlorn hope to the Citizen Directors. But now at last it seemed worth a serious attempt. With new respect for their Irish allies, the Directory threw themselves into the task. Savary, who had brought Humbert's dispatches, was ordered to pick up 2,000 more men and return immediately to Killala. Hardy, Supreme Commander of Humbert's expedition, was told not to delay a moment longer.[56]

We can imagine how Tone's heart must have leapt at the news.[57] And for once his luck held. The wind, the British blockade, and the French Ministry of Marine—there was nothing to hinder them. On September 16th, three weeks after the brave Tandy's departure, Tone sailed after him on course for Ireland.[58] The expedition was still too small for Tone's liking. In the end, Hardy had only succeeded in embarking 2,800 men, distributed in eight frigates, a schooner, and a ship of the line. But Tone had respect for Hardy, and was glad to take the dangerous step of sailing on Hardy's ship, the *Hoche*.[59] The slowest sailer in that squadron, it would have no chance of escape if pursued by the British navy. Still, it was the flagship. It also bore the name of the Frenchman whom Tone most admired

—General Hoche who had led that last armada to Ireland two long years ago.

In the north west of Ireland, Humbert had managed, in his masterly way, to throw off his pursuers and keep the initiative. In one bound—fifty-eight miles marched in the span of a night and a day—he had reached the outskirts of Sligo. Ahead of him the garrison was almost defenceless. Its commander, Colonel Vereker, had more courage than experience. He pushed forward with his yeomanry and militia to a strategic village called Collooney. And there they stood, a few hundred rustics from Sligo and Limerick, to contest Collooney with the veterans of Bonaparte's Army of Italy.

The action that followed was to be one of the most celebrated in the whole rebellion. It earned a peerage for Vereker; he took the motto of "Collooney"; and people spoke of him as the Irish Leonidas.[60] In fact the battle was of little direct significance. After a short skirmish, a hundred of Vereker's men surrendered and were sent back to Sligo on parole, and there were about fifty casualties on each side.[61] Humbert pushed on unchecked to the north. In one sense however, Vereker *had* achieved a victory, Humbert had learnt that the Irish militia did not always run at the first shot; and with such a small force as his, he could not afford very many Collooneys.

That evening, Humbert reached Dromahair, a few miles to the north of Sligo, and his men took their first proper rest since they had left Castlebar thirty-six hours before.[62] He seemed to have been uncertain what he should do next. The prospect of attacking Sligo itself was uninviting, even if they could capture all the garrison without loss to themselves. For, as one French officer remarked, why make prisoners if they are sent back as soon as the fighting is over?[63] What Humbert's tiny force needed was allies. Yet apart from a handful of Irish militia prisoners who had joined them after Castlebar, their prisoners proved strangely loyal to the Crown, while the country people of Sligo and Leitrim did their best to keep their distance from both armies.

And then Humbert heard the news for which he had waited so long: the Midlands had risen. He abandoned the plan to head for Ulster. If there was a rising, he could still form a junction with them in the north Midlands. His new aim was to link up with the insurgents in Longford and Westmeath at Granard, and then go bald-headed for the capital.[64] He was still unaware, of course, that Napper Tandy's relief expedition was now not less than a week's sail from the west coast of Ireland.

Dumping some of his captured artillery by the wayside to make still faster progress, Humbert marched off along the Dublin road. On the night of the 6th he reached Drumkeeran near the iron-works on the west bank of Lough Allen. At mid-day on the 7th, he crossed the upper Shannon at Ballintra. By evening he was at Cloone—only a few miles from County Longford, and almost half-way to Dublin. Close at his heels came Cornwallis's cavalry.[65] It was to be a race between the Viceroy and Humbert, who could first reach Granard.

Everything now depended on the insurgents from Westmeath and Longford. Could they hold out till Humbert came to their assistance with his artillery, his arms, and above all, his irrepressible optimism?

On September 5th, the weak and demoralised garrison at Mullingar had learnt that the rebels, now about seven thousand strong, were in possession of Wilson's Hospital—a large Protestant institution astride the main road to Longford. The Mullingar commander, Colonel Blake, did not lift a finger against them.[66] From Castlepollard however, a small town several hours march to the north, a force of about a hundred local yeomanry, under their landlord, Lord Longford, boldly marched off in pursuit of the rebels. They reached the area to find the United army of Westmeath had encamped in the Hospital's demesne, having expelled the charity boys and old men who were supported there, wounded the chaplain, and siezed a quantity of arms and liquor. Lord Longford's party halted. A message had been sent to some Highlanders stationed at Cavan to come to their assistance with all speed.[67]

The Cavan garrison was commanded by a Scotsman called Major Porter, a man of sterner stuff than the commander at Mullingar. Despite the risk of an attack on Cavan, he had set off early that morning to the rescue with every man that could be spared: 250 of the local yeomanry and a hundred Argyll Fencibles with one piece of artillery. It was a daring move against an enemy reported so numerous—7,000 in Westmeath, 6,000 at Granard—in an action of such strategic importance.[68] Major Porter's instinct was, however, perfectly correct.

For this Midland rising followed the same pattern as the rising around Dublin on May 23rd, or around Belfast on June 8th. Wild rumours of success had swept the country; some of the most respectable people were supposed to be involved; they had only to rise to find the neighbouring counties would follow. They had risen accordingly. But no other counties had joined them. Few of the respectable leaders were to be found. And except for a minority bent on vengeance or plunder, the people had no idea what to do next.[69]

At Granard, it is true, the rebels made a regular attack on the town, led by an ex-yeomanry officer and his brother, Hans and Alexander Denniston. But they fled before the start of the battle, and the action was a massacre. For four hours, the garrison, reinforced by Major Porter's 250 yeomanry, shot, sabred and bayonetted their attackers. Only two men were wounded on their side. The official estimate of the rebels' losses was 400, but others put it at nearer a thousand.[70]

At Wilson's Hospital, Major Porter completed the work of destruction. Some of the rebels tried to negotiate a truce. They offered to go home if their grievances were redressed: probably they meant protection from the yeomanry and release of their fellows from prison. Thousands left the camp and returned home. The rest found themselves trapped between Major Porter's Highlanders and Lord Longford's yeomanry. About two hundred were cut down in the demesne of Wilson's Hospital; others tried to escape across a neighbouring lake and many were drowned; darkness ended the pursuit. Otherwise, as one loyalist reported, "The slaughter would have been prodigious".[71]

Late on the evening of the 7th, all that was left of the United armies of Longford and Westmeath staggered into Humbert's camp at Cloone.[72]

The net was now closing in around Humbert. On the news of his amazing march from Castlebar, Cornwallis had backed a hunch that the French might double back across the Shannon. He had divided his army into two corps: Lake's, which would hang on the enemy's rear; and his own, which would keep between Humbert and the capital. To many of his army, this had seemed an absurd manoeuvre.[73] All the evidence suggested that Humbert was either heading for Sligo and the North—or perhaps moving westwards to Killala, and the mountains of Mayo, where he could shelter until reinforcements arrived.

Now it was clear that Humbert was actually making for Dublin, Cornwallis's prudence was redeemed. Yet even now there was a danger of Humbert turning his right flank and slipping through the net. Lake's advance guard reported that Humbert continued to discard his captured cannon to make more speed: five English 6-pounders and a tumbril had been thrown over the bridge at Dromahair; three more 6-pounders and a tumbril left on the road.[74] Late on the 7th, Cornwallis learnt that they had crossed the Shannon at Ballintra, ahead of his own forces. Fortunately,

Colonel Robert Craufurd, commanding Lake's advance guard, was close behind Humbert's rear; he had prevented him destroying the bridge at Ballintra, and relentlessly wore down the stragglers. Lake's army had marched, stopping only for brief rests, four days and four nights. Cornwallis's army, too, marched on through the small hours. Early next morning, all three armies—Humbert's, Lake's and Cornwallis's—were neck and neck in the race for Dublin.[75]

That day, September 8th, the race was abruptly ended. Near a small village called Ballinamuck, just out of sight of the great moat of Granard where the United armies of Longford and Westmeath had been crushed three days earlier, Humbert turned and drew up his 850 French troops in line of battle. There could be little doubt about the outcome. Behind him at St. Johnstown (Ballinalee), Cornwallis with 5,000 men and a dozen cannon blocked the road to Dublin. Ahead were Lake's forces—nearly as strong.[76] There were murmurings from his own Grenadiers that the struggle was hopeless and they should surrender.[77] Only about a thousand of their Irish allies remained of all the thousands who had joined them.[78]

Humbert fought on, but no longer than the honour of the Great Nation demanded—half an hour of brisk fighting. And then, as he was to put it with understandable pride in his report to the Directory "After having obtained the greatest successes and made the arms of the French Republic triumph during my stay in Ireland, I have at length been obliged to submit to a superior force of 30,000 men."[79]

Lake set the seal on his victory by the pursuit of the rebels that followed the surrender of the French. The Dragoons were as usual, only too eager to make an example of the peasants, and Lake was not the man to stand in their way. True, one of the staff officers rode up to the rebel lines— Captain Pakenham, Lord Longford's uncle and Lieutenant-General of the Ordnance. "Run away, boys," he is said to have shouted, otherwise you'll all be cut down."[80] But the gesture, it seems, was too late; when Cornwallis arrived, several hundred of the Irish legion lay scattered over the battlefield and the neighbouring bogs. "'Tis incredible," a loyalist wrote, "the number of them, exclusive of the French, lay on the field ... however, we had a most glorious day."[81]

The day after the battle, Cornwallis and his staff retired to Castlepollard, where Lord Longford entertained them at his seat. General John Moore, who rode over from Ballinamuck next morning, found Cornwallis arranging the final phase of the campaign. Trench was to march westward to mop up the remnants of the Franco-Irish army at Castlebar and Killala. Moore was to take station at Moate in Westmeath, to be ready for any new crisis.[82] A message had just arrived from London that the Brest fleet— the fleet with Wolfe Tone on board—had at last sailed for Ireland.[83]

At the camp at Ballinamuck the soldiers had settled back into their military routine. One afternoon Richard Lovell Edgeworth, who was recovering from the experience of being taken for a French spy and nearly murdered by a half-crazed mob of Longford Loyalists,[84] rode out with his wife and daughter Maria to see the battlefield. "In the fields, which rise in a gentle slope," wrote Maria," about sixty bell tents were pitched, the arms all ranged on the grass; before the tents, poles with little streamers flying here and there; groups of men leading their horses to water; and others filling bottles and black pots; some cooking under the hedges; Highlanders gathering blackberries."[85]

A less edifying sight, which the Edgeworths did not see, was presented by the rebel prisoners. Some of the victors had not had the heart to kill rebels in cold blood and about ninety had been taken prisoner.[86] They were soon disposed of. Blake, the Galway fire-eater who had joined Humbert before Castlebar, was hanged from a tree, after receiving permission to rub soap on the rope to ensure himself a quick death.[87] Nine of the Longford militia deserters were hanged with him.[88] The others were taken to Longford and told to draw lots: pieces of paper with "Death" written on were put in a hat, and the draw began. People looked on with indifference, so inured were they now to slaughter.[89] One man, however, is said to have saved his life with a witty retort. Sentenced to be hanged for deserting at Castlebar, he told the court martial: "Sure, your honours, I think it's the army that was the deserters. I stayed where I was."[90]

Meanwhile, Humbert and his men were being treated with all the courtesy demanded by the conventions of war. A fleet of canal barges were fitted out at Tullamore to convey them smoothly to Dublin. Thousands of people lined the banks, curious to see the invaders. They were not disappointed, according to the *Evening Post*: "The Progress of the Captives down the Canal formed a very picturesque and interesting scene . . . The first [boat] contained the band of the Fermanagh Militia, the second the French officers and the remaining boats were occupied by the privates, amounting to near eight hundred men. Nothing could exceed the *nonchalance* and merriment with which the French bore their situation, collecting in parties . . . and singing the Marseillaise."[91]

On their arrival in Dublin, the French prisoners continued to draw large crowds of all classes. Humbert, Sarrazin and the other staff officers were lodged in the best hotel, the Mail Coach Hotel in Dawson Street (now the Hibernian). By all accounts they played up to the crowd, standing at the open windows "in a continual roar of laughter" all day, after reading a description of themselves in the local press. On their part, the Dubliners were amazed by the rich appearance of the French officers: blue coats with gilt buttons, gold epaulettes, gold vellum on their capes, and white cashmere waistcoats. Their hair was highly powdered; and far from wearing it cropped in revolutionary fashion, they all wore long queues.[92] A story of their gallantry went the rounds. After their surrender, they heard that some of the rebels had stolen General Hutchinson's horses. They immediately offered to join the British officers in the pursuit of the rascals.[93]

As for the invasion, that was a terrible mistake, the French officers assured their captors. The Irish exiles had completely deceived them about the state of Ireland. They had expected to find the people in open rebellion, or at least organised for one; they had found instead "only ragamuffins".[94] They described ruefully how their allies had treated them: queuing to get a second consignment of arms and uniforms, after hiding their first in some boghole; selling the ammunition for whiskey; and running away at the first shot. It was hard, they said, for them to endure—they who had conquered the world, to be at last beaten in an Irish bog. And now they swore they would never willingly return to a country where there was "neither wine nor discipline" and the people lived on "roots, whiskey and lying."[95]

One Irishman, however, Humbert recalled with nothing but gratitude— Dr. Stock, the Protestant Bishop. Before his departure, in an exchange of prisoners, Humbert could not resist a last Gallic flourish; he sent the Bishop a letter of thanks reprinted in the newspapers. He apologised to the milord for having disturbed his "well-deserved domestic happiness"; he left him with a very full heart; he flattered himself that the compliment was reciprocated; and he sent the kindest regards to his lady wife and his estimable family.[96]

And so, fêted by Dublin society, Humbert and his men sailed back to France.

But meanwhile in the West, the last chapter of the rebellion had yet to be written. Dr. Stock was still beleaguered by the rebels. Tone and Tandy had not yet tasted the bitterness of their homecoming.

5

The Last Day of Liberty

Mayo, September–October

I met with Napper Tandy and he took me by the hand,
Saying, how is old Ireland? and how does she stand?
She's the most distressful country that ever yet was seen;
They are hanging men and women for wearing of the green!
O wearing of the green, O wearing of the green,
My native land, I cannot stand, for wearing of the green.

The Wearing of the Green

AUTUMN HAD set in, and the Government seemed to have put aside all thought of Killala and the two hundred odd loyalists imprisoned there by the French and their allies.

Nearly a fortnight had passed since the echoes of Ballinamuck had reached that town. A young Irish officer brought the news—Major Fortescue, Lord Clermont's heir and member for Louth. He had wandered into the town, never dreaming it was still in French hands; a few days before he had left Dublin in search of his brother, the clergyman mortally wounded at the time of the French landing, and he had happened to pass Humbert and his men shortly after their surrender. The French officers and the Irish loyalists tried to keep the news secret, for fear of its effect on the insurgents. But this proved impossible, as those who had escaped the massacre, soon began to find their way back to the town.[1]

The Bishop, who kept up a lively diary to the end, was now on excellent terms with his captors—the three French officers left behind by Humbert when the main garrison was withdrawn. Charost, the commandant, was treated almost like one of the family. Though he was not a religious man, Charost took care to see no one disturbed the Bishop when he held family prayers in the library. Boudet, the second-in-command, came from Normandy, was excessively tall and rather morose, and reminded the Bishop of Don Quixote. He would recite "his wonderful exploits, delivered in measured language and with an imposing seriousness of aspect". Finally, there was Ponson, the very reverse of Boudet. "Tied to a sword as long as himself and armed with pistols, firelock and bayonet," he kept up the company's spirits with an endless roll of talk, laughter or whistling.[2]

At first the captors and captives had cheerfully sat round the fire in the Bishop's castle, sampling the choicest beef and mutton, and the rarest wines from the cellars of the neighbouring gentry. The Bishop, who was a retiring, scholarly man, found it a novel sensation to live off plunder. He soon came to accept it as the misfortune of war, and did not object when the owner of a particularly fine crate of hock, Colonel King of Ballina, was found guilty in his absence of "loyalty" and of an "obstinate adherence" to King and Constitution.[3]

Once the news of Ballinamuck had leaked out, however, even Ponson's cheery whistling could not disguise their predicament. The French officers were rapidly losing control of their allies. Despite the efforts of a young and gallant man, called Ferdy O'Donnell, who had replaced the drunken Major Bellew as generalissimo of the Irish levies, the people began to talk of "vengeance" on the Protestants. Meanwhile, they went on assiduously with the work of wrecking Protestant homes and Protestant churches. It would have almost been reassuring if their motives had been simply plunder. But the true republicans, it seemed to the Bishop, were determined on "universal levelling of conditions in order to bring on the glorious reign of equality", and far more was destroyed than was carried off as loot.[4] As the days went by, refugees poured into the town, loyalists stripped of everything they possessed, and terrified by the talk of vengeance.[5]

The French officers were tireless in their stratagems to prevent trouble. At one critical moment, Ponson broke the tension by accusing the Dean of trapping him into matrimony with a local colleen; it was also found that a good mutton dinner for the allies, without too much whiskey, worked wonders for their morale; and long hours of drill on the parade ground kept the trouble-makers out of mischief. In public, the French continued to talk of their war against their common enemy. In fact, their aim was merely to keep order until they could find some British officers to whom they could honourably surrender their swords.[6] Meanwhile, they took no chances. Eighteen trusted men were employed as bodyguard at the castle, paid by the Bishop the wage of ten pence a week. Ten carbines were kept in the French officers' bed-chambers and they slept in shifts. Eight of the Bishop's own family were issued with arms.[7] Yet despite all these precautions, the loyalists at Killala began to feel more and more like the loyalists at Wexford. Refused ammunition by the French, the rebels now armed themselves with pikes. Their leader, Ferdy O'Donnell, seemed to despair of controlling them. "We hold our lives by a thread," wrote the Bishop in his diary on the 16th, the twenty-fourth day of their captivity, and the ninth since Humbert's surrender.[8]

Meanwhile the long-awaited expedition had reached the coast—but a French one to relieve Humbert, not a British one to rescue the loyalists.

On the same day as the Bishop had written that despairing entry in his diary, Napper Tandy sailed boldly into the harbour of Rutland, on the north western extremity of Ireland. His corvette *Anacréon* had passed clean through the British naval blockade, covering the journey from Dunkirk in just over a fortnight. The *Anacréon* was chiefly, as we saw, a gun-runner. She contained arms for several thousand, a pack of artillery and other useful equipment. She had also 270 French troops and half a dozen Irish exiles, including the redoubtable Tandy who had sworn, according to his own proclamation, "to lead them on to victory or die".[9] This imposing force now disembarked and seized the post office of Rutland without firing a shot, where they were assured by some peasants that the Mayo insurrection was in full swing.[10]

By an odd chance, the postmaster at Rutland was an old friend of Napper Tandy. He told Tandy that it was all nonsense about the Mayo rising; few had in fact joined the French, and Humbert had surrendered to Cornwallis a week before; he also informed him that his Irish colleagues —McNevin, Emmet and Bond—had blown the gaff on the conspiracy in exchange for their lives. On his part Tandy answered the postmaster that the French were determined to land 20,000 men, or perish in the attempt. Meanwhile the Irish standard was hoisted and green cockades distributed. Privately, however, he confessed his astonishment at the news of Humbert's collapse.[11]

At a council of war the French officers reassured Tandy that even if Humbert had failed, this did not affect their own mission to land him and his precious cargo of arms, and to "nourish and sustain among the Irish people the spirit of liberty". And they professed to believe the word of the Irish peasantry that the rising was still in progress, rather than that of a British postmaster.[12] Tandy, however, interpreted his duty rather differently. About this time the post happened to arrive from Dublin, and the newspaper accounts confirmed the story of the postmaster.[13] Tandy went on distributing the proclamations: "Let not your friends be butchered unassisted; if they are doomed to fall in this glorious struggle, let their deaths be useful to your cause, and their bodies serve as footsteps to the temple of Irish Liberty." Then, after a nostalgic evening with the postmaster, when his wife was presented with a golden ring as a keepsake, Tandy was carried back insensible to the corvette *Anacréon*. Next morning she sailed.

And so ended the last landing of a French invasionary force on the coasts of the British Isles.[14]

At Killala, of course, the loyalists knew nothing of this interlude. They had just learnt of the relief of Castlebar by Trench's army, but so had the rebels, and as the Bishop put it, "I believe they may come here time enough to see us buried." On the 18th the pikemen at the castle gate announced that all Protestants were to be taken as hostages for the lives of their own friends imprisoned at Castlebar. Fortunately, the Bishop rose to the occasion. Ambassadors should be sent to General Trench to ensure that his prisoners were properly treated. The pikemen agreed. Dean Thompson and one of the rebels' leaders rode away on the hazardous mission. Meanwhile, Charost and the French officers sat up all night at the barricades in the castle to defend the loyalists against their allies.[15]

It turned out that General Trench knew nothing of the Killala loyalists' predicament. After rashly abusing the insurgents' ambassador, his men agreed to treat their prisoners with all possible "tenderness", and this message was to be conveyed to Killala by the two ambassadors. Privately, the general assured the Dean that he hoped to be there himself on Sunday with 1,200 men and five pieces of artillery.[16]

At three o'clock on that Saturday afternoon the Bishop was taking a turn in the castle garden with Major Fortescue, when they heard the distant rumble of cannon. Soon the flash of artillery could be seen from the Steeple Hill—the prospect point where the first Christians had built a round tower in defence against Vikings—and the alarming sign of smoke from cabins set on fire by Trench's troops advancing along the road from Ballina.[17] The loyalists were asked to go and see for themselves. "They are only a few cabins," said the Bishop, and immediately regretted it. "A poor man's cabin," came the reply, "is to him as valuable as a palace."[18] Yet strange to say, now that the moment had come, the Killala rebels did not think of reprisals—at any rate, no loyalist was touched. Many of the pikemen fled to their homes; about 800 remained determined to make a last stand in the town, under the green standard and the tricolour.[19]

It was now the day of the equinox, September 23rd, and the rain poured down, churning up the turnpike, as Trench's relief expedition lumbered towards the town. In the castle, the Bishop and the loyalists talked in whispers. After thirty-one days of captivity they were alone again. Charost had gone, though he knew it was a hopeless struggle, to organise the defence; so had Boudet and Ponson, still whistling like a cricket; the only leader left in the castle was Bellew, the drunken Major, whose habits had proved so offensive to Charost that he had locked him up "like a beast in a dark hole under the staircase". (When told the English were entering the town, he stopped calling for liquor, and retorted, "I always thought I had good luck, for now I am in a safer place than any of you.")[20] From the library window, the loyalists could see the rebels lining out along the stone walls behind the Ballina road, led by the gallant Ferdy O'Donnell. At the last moment he had come to the Bishop and begged his advice. "I think I might expect pardon," said he, "from the share I had in preserving the peace of the district. But the people would never forgive me if I did not stand by them now; and their revenge would follow me". The Bishop advised him to fight till he saw the battle turn, which would not be long, and then to escape. Mrs. Stock poured him out a glass of wine. He drank a farewell toast, and galloped away.[21]

The battle that followed was the last military action in the whole rebellion. It was no less tragic than countless others in which half-armed peasants took the field despite hopeless odds. Yet, according to the Bishop, thrust so incongruously into the front line of battle, there was a touch of chivalry—on the rebel side at least—to redeem the futility of the struggle. And in fact the ignorant peasantry of Mayo had never tarnished their cause by the dismal atrocities common in more favoured parts of Ireland.[22]

That afternoon the rain had cleared, exposing the rebels' position to the afterglow of the storm. General Trench had advanced on Ballina by the same mountain road that had given Humbert his victory nearly a month before. With a force of English and Irish militia some English Dragoons, and Scottish Fencibles, he pushed on directly towards Killala. Meanwhile a force of yeomanry and Kerry militia, commanded by their clansman and landlord picturesquely known as the White Knight, were to take the town from the rear.[23]

The attack was led by the Downshire. Ducking behind the breast of the library chimney, the Bishop watched as the musket-balls whistled and ricochetted over the castle. Despite their strong position, the rebel fire was curiously ineffective against their assailants. Only one militia man, a corporal, was seen to fall dead, and another was wounded. In general, as so often happened during the war, the rebel musketeers overcharged their guns and the shots went high.[24] However, one man with a carbine by the castle scored a direct hit on the library window. Fortunately, the loyalists had barricaded the room with beds. The slugs only slightly wounded Major Fortescue, whose curiosity had got the better of him.[25]

For half an hour the rebels made a gallant resistance, "running upon death . . . as if they were hastening to a stew". Then they broke and fled. How many were killed in the slaughter that followed will never be known. The Bishop put it at 400, Trench at 600. As usual, the troops were exasperated, and their officers could not control them. Hunted down like animals, the peasants fled into the wildest parts of Erris, and many no doubt died there of their wounds and of exposure.[26]

In a potato ridge beyond the town, the Bishop was sad to learn, Ferdy O'Donnell had been found stripped and shot. He had done his best to follow the Bishop's advice, gallantly rallying his men, till his horse was shot under him, and then escaping on foot across the fields. But weighed down by his boots and a heavy French surcoat he was soon overtaken, and pierced with a ball in his back. The Fraser that killed him reported his last words to be "I am Ferdy O'Donnell: go tell the Bishop I am shot."[27]

The end of the Mayo rising followed the usual brutal pattern, bringing death and destruction to loyalists as well as rebels. In the storming of the town a number of loyalists were shot by the military, including the son of the local magistrate. He was shouting, "God save the King" and standing at the door of his house next to the castle, when a volley of musketry cut him down.[28] Charost, after surrendering his sword with some difficulty, nearly suffered the same fate. One of the Frasers burst into the castle compound, and fired at him point blank. The ball passed under his arm and pierced one of the heavy wooden doors of the castle.[29] In spite of the exertions of Trench and his officers, their troops continued that night cheerfully shooting up the town. Some houses were perforated like a riddle; most of them had their doors and windows destroyed; the townspeople lay terrified on the floor. It was not until nightfall on the following day that the sound of musket fire died away, as the troops finally abandoned the pursuit of the defenceless rebels.[30]

Even now the Bishop and his flock found no respite. There were courts martial and hangings—Major Bellew was dragged out of the castle and despatched in the grave behind it—and the soldiers lived off the town as though it were an enemy country. The Irish militia, the Bishop found, were no different from the Irish rebels except "that they seized upon things with somewhat less of ceremony or excuse, and . . . were incomparably superior to the Irish traitors in dexterity of stealing".[31] The Bishop's own duties were still more onerous than during the French occupation: entertaining the general who insisted on playing chess (aptly enough) with the White Knight till the small hours; and supplying food and drink for the 26 men who, to the alarm of his family, acted as the garrison at the castle. Once again there was a terrifying moment when the 200 barrels of powder, left behind by Humbert and later moved to an outhouse, seemed certain to catch fire and destroy them all; fortunately the White Knight put the fire out in the nick of time.[32]

But at last the Bishop's guests took their leave. Trench and the army made a punitive raid into Erris, where they killed about fifty or sixty unresisting peasants, and returned satisfied to the Midlands.[33] The Bishop withdrew to Dublin, after making himself unpopular with the gentry by condemning these reckless punishments. He was also alarmed by the possibility of a new French landing.[34]

Mayo was left to itself. As winter came on and the Atlantic gales lashed that bleak coastline, the peasants, who had lost all they possessed, huddled together in the caves and bog-holes as famine followed in the wake of the revolution.[35]

Only chicken and boiled mutton. Only one bottle of port and two bottles of porter a day. In Dublin, the gentlemen prisoners continued to call heaven to witness their "inhuman" treatment by the Government.

6

Home-Coming

Dublin and the Three Kingdoms, October 2nd–November 19th

Si au lieu de l'expédition d'Egypte, j'eusse fait celle d'Irlande . . .
que pouvait être l'Angleterre aujourd'hui?

Napoleon, on St. Helena

IN LONDON, on the afternoon of October 2nd, the great bells of St.
Paul's began to peal, and the sound of victory, carried by church bells,
began to spread across the three kingdoms.[1] It was the news everyone had
been waiting for; yet the official report far surpassed the wildest rumours.
Nelson had annihilated Bonaparte's fleet at the mouth of the Nile without
the loss of a single British ship. "A victory more glorious or compleat is
not recorded in the annals of our navy," thundered *The Times*.[2] The mood
of the capital was hysterical. When Captain Capel, the young captain sent
overland with Nelson's despatches, reached the Admiralty, the First Lord
fell flat in the passage outside his office.[3] "Joy, Joy, Joy to you brave,
gallant, immortalized Nelson!" wrote the First Lord's wife, Lady Spencer.[4]
And the people of London, starved for so long of anything to celebrate,
were in raptures too. That night the city was all lit up; the Tower guns
fired salutes; a grand gala was held at Ranelagh; a mob blocked the streets
by the Admiralty, throwing fireworks and good humouredly forcing
gentlemen to remove their hats; and people slapped their sides at the story
of the loyal Hibernian who said, "Nothing on earth could resist us by
sea."[5]

Late that evening, after riding the 131 miles to Weymouth in the
amazing time of nine and a quarter hours, the King's messenger brought
the news to the King. His Majesty was already in high spirits. Two days
before it had been the anniversary of the defeat of the Spanish Armada,
and he assisted at a sports day for Lord Radnor's tenantry, in which he had
been much entertained by the sack race; a British frigate had arrived from
Ireland with some pikes to add to his collection of bric-à-brac. Nelson's

triumph evoked from the king "a degree of joy" that he could not "pretend to express".[6] Next morning he personally read Nelson's despatches to groups of sightseers on the esplanade, repeating the performance four times; the local troops fired a *feu de joie* on the beach; rockets were fired from the ships in the bay; and when the royal family went to the theatre that evening the manager displayed an illuminated transparency of "Britannia treading Anarchy and Rebellion under her feet".[7] Meanwhile, hour by hour, the good news was spreading across England. City after city was illuminated; the flags flew, the bells rang out, and the guns thundered; and on the morning of the 5th that shock wave of rejoicing had reached the shores of Ireland.

Dublin, the city that felt itself above all others threatened by Bonaparte, was not slow to celebrate his apparent downfall. In a sense, too, they were celebrating the end of the rebellion. That night the capital was all illuminated. To cram more candles into their windows, people used potatoes as candlesticks; the streets were crowded, according to the *Evening Post*, with "groupes singing 'God Save the King' and 'Rule Britannia'". Various devices were erected on prominent buildings—an illuminated transparency of George III on the Mansion House, and another on the Post Office of the "Brave Admiral Nelson defending with his sword the Harp and the Crown".[8] It was months since the Irish loyalists had felt such a glow of patriotism. Those gallant tars who had beaten Napoleon—nearly half of them must have been Irish. It made one proud to be part of the British Empire.

Cornwallis, and the Castle must have been as delighted as Pitt and Whitehall. At one stroke, Nelson seemed to have redrawn the map of Europe. Already a Russian fleet was approaching the Mediterranean; an alliance between the Czar and the Sultan now seemed certain. In addition, the beleagured Austrian Emperor would draw fresh courage from Bonaparte's disaster, and the King of Naples might throw in his lot with the allies. Such were the diplomatic possibilities.[9]

But the immediate military results were still more dazzling for Britain and Ireland. Bonaparte, the master of Europe only a few weeks before, was now marooned in the east; his navy was gone and presumably his army would soon follow it. For the time being the Directory must abandon all military ventures against Britain or Ireland.[10]

Meanwhile, there was still the Brest fleet to be dealt with. According to the latest information from the Admiralty, this fleet, numbering nine ships and carrying about three thousand troops, had sailed from Brest on September 16th. On the 24th Sir John Warren had put out from

Portsmouth to intercept it. He was now taking up a position with six ships in the western approaches, and four others were joining him. Behind the French fleet, Lord Bridport and a second British fleet had sealed off the port of Brest.[11] One way or the other the French would be brought to action, and then it must be assumed the bells would ring out a second time in Dublin.

For once the Castle was not to be disappointed. On October 12th, less than a week after the Nile celebrations, Sir John Warren intercepted the Brest fleet off the north coast, and after ten hours of fighting achieved a victory which, in its way, was as complete as Nelson's. Without losing a ship, he captured all but two of the French ones, with 2,500 troops on board, and the gallant Irish commander, Adjutant-General Smith, otherwise Wolfe Tone.[12]

That year the equinoctial gales raged unabated and it was nearly a month before Wolfe Tone was brought in irons to Dublin to face his trial before a military court. In the meantime, Cornwallis had lost a battle that was to prove more decisive than any of the others of that disastrous year.

Pitt and the British cabinet, encouraged by the Irish ex-cabinet that Cornwallis had dismissed, had agreed to *exclude* catholic emancipation from the terms of the Union.

Cornwallis, distracted by the aftermath of the rebellion, and with hardly a supporter among the Irish ruling class,[13] struggled to prevent this exclusion. The case for the Union on the broadest terms he believed to be just and expedient. The day after Clare's departure to London for consultations with Pitt and the Duke of Portland, he sent both of them letters strongly recommending emancipation. "I certainly wish that England, would now make a union with the Irish nation instead of making it with a party in Ireland, and although I agree with those who assert that the Catholics will not be immediately converted into good subjects, yet I am sanguine enough to hope, after the most plausible and most popular of their grievances is removed (and especially if it could be accompanied by some regulation of tythes) that we should get time to breathe, and at least check the rapid progress of discontent and disaffection."[14]

How on earth had Pitt allowed himself to be persuaded to drop the plan for emancipation? At the time, Clare claimed he was largely responsible. On his return from London in October he wrote: "They were as full of their popish projects as ever," [but now] "they are fairly inclined to give them up."[15]

Clare was no friend to the Catholics, but he does not deserve to be taken too seriously as the architect of the Union in this illiberal form. Pitt was the driving force behind it; Clare had begun, at any rate, by doubting whether it was practical on any terms at this time.[16] Clare's visit to London was influential but not decisive; for it appears that Pitt had already been persuaded to leave out emancipation *before* Clare arrived.[17]

According to a curious little minute of the two interviews Clare had with Pitt, Clare "confesses he fears nothing himself from the Catholics having *everything*, but it is impossible to carry that point in Ireland". (The minute ends: "Conclusion. Drunkeness at Bellamy's . . .")[18] Difficult as the Union would be to steer through on a narrow Protestant basis, it was totally impractical, Pitt agreed, on broader terms.[19] In addition to the almost universal opposition to be anticipated in the Irish Protestant Parliament, the great majority of his own cabinet were against making the concession to Catholics at this point.[20] Only Henry Dundas, the War Minister, was known to be unequivocally in favour, and Dundas was away at his castle in Scotland during the fatal weeks before Clare's visit.[21]

Ironically, the man more responsible than Clare was to pass into popular history as the champion of Irish rights—John Foster, the Speaker. He and his cronies, the same men who had procured Abercromby's downfall, had been intriguing with the British cabinet for several months before Clare's arrival.[22] Later, by blocking the Union proposal itself, they were to pose as patriotic Irish nationalists. What they meant by the Irish nation, can best be judged by a letter written that autumn, apparently seriously, by one of the more high-minded, Lord Roden: "I should look upon [a new] rising as a fortunate event as by that means we should have an opportunity of annihilating one or two million of inhabitants who are a disgrace to humanity . . ."[23] This was Foster's Ireland—a beleaguered nation of Protestants who felt little more identity with the Catholic masses than George Washington's America with the Red Indians.

Cornwallis made a last, forlorn attempt to change Pitt's mind. A week after Clare's departure he sent over Elliot, one of the Castle under-secretaries, to plead for immediate emancipation[24]. Pitt's argument was purely tactical: why risk defeat of both measures in the Irish Parliament, when emancipation could be safely left to the United Parliament to follow? But this argument about timing could be reversed. No one—not even Foster—could deny that the root cause of the rebellion was the alienation of a Catholic people from their Government. Why risk this alienation a moment longer than was necessary? Why wait till they extorted the measure from the United Parliament— or the Whigs were able to exploit it for their own ends? The chance to present it as a positive part of a new deal for Ireland would never recur.

By mid-November, Cornwallis had conceded defeat. "Things have now gone too far to admit of a change," he wrote to a friend on the 15th, "and the principal persons have received assurances from the English Ministers which cannot be retracted."[25] Next day the draft Articles of Union reached him; he could only lament that the clause about Members of Parliament taking the Oath of Supremacy had no longer a query attached to it. In his letters to England at that time, Cornwallis could not conceal his utter despondency. "This wretched country I am sorry to say," he wrote to his friend Ross, "is in its internal state getting worse and worse every day."[26] To his brother he confided: "You will hear much of a Union: God knows how it will turn out. Ireland cannot change for the worse, but unless religious animosities and the violence of Parties can be in some measure allayed, I do not think she can receive much benefit from any plan of Government."[27] And to Dundas, the one man in the British cabinet who appeared to share his fervour for Catholic emancipation, he admitted that he was still haunted by the thought that, if Pitt had taken it up "in a firm and decided tone in England . . . it might have been carried here".[28]

Was Cornwallis correct in thinking Catholic emancipation to be politically practicable in the Ireland of 1798?

Ireland's history has more than its share of lost opportunities, and it would be an added twist to the tragedy of the rebellion if it presented one of the greatest of them. Cornwallis, however, had greatly underestimated the practical difficulties, even on the narrow Protestant basis, of getting the Union through the Irish Parliament, as events were soon to show. Probably no amount of inducements—titles, jobs or cash—could have persuaded the Protestant Parliament to open its membership to the other nation in Ireland. Before the rebellion it might have been possible. After all, in the past they had had to accept the measures to help the Catholics imposed by the British Government; by now this amounted to the lion's share of emancipation, giving Catholics everything, franchise included, except the right to seats in Parliament and certain other high offices. But the rebellion had changed everything. At one stroke, a century's progress towards uniting the two nations in Ireland had been reversed.[29]

The aftermath of the rebellion, like the aftermath of other disasters, left the country in a state of shock. In many of the areas which had seen the most violent fighting during the rebellion communal violence flared up again that autumn. From Naas to Carlow there were nightly reports of robberies and burnings;[30] the mail coach was successfully ambushed on the main road to Waterford.[31] In the Enniscorthy area of Wexford loyalists were reported to have been hunted out of their farms by gangs of outlaws based on Killoughran woods. As a reprisal, loyalists once again took the law into their own hands.[32]

Gradually the cycle of violence worked itself out, either from sheer exhaustion on both sides, or from the people's returning confidence in the Government as Cornwallis's new policy of conciliation slowly began to take effect.

The most dramatic expression of this policy was his public rebuke to the great Ulster landlord, Lord Enniskillen, and the other officers of a court martial who had acquitted a yeoman called Wollaghan who had deliberately killed a pardoned rebel.[33] It was a test case, for the yeoman had based his defence on the orders given him by his superior, Captain Armstrong—the same Captain Armstrong of the militia who had made the quip at the Sheares' trial that he had "taken for a guide the one he neither shot nor hanged". In this case his orders had been to shoot *suspected* rebels on sight, whether or not they had been given protections, a practice that was cheerfully continued in some Irish regiments.[34] To allow Wollaghan's acquittal to go unnoticed would have made a farce of Cornwallis's policy of conciliation. Cornwallis could not reverse the verdict. But he dismissed the yeoman, dissolved the court martial, all of whose members were Irish, and banned them from sitting on a new one.[35]

The hullabaloo over this decision was hardly less than the fuss over Abercromby's famous general order. Even the so-called moderates, like Beresford's friends, were outraged. All the frustrations of their situation rushed to the surface. They compared the "severity" of Cornwallis's treatment of Lord Enniskillen with his softness in everything else; they mocked him for letting Humbert lead him such a dance, and for leaving the Killala rebels thirty days to cut the throats of the loyalists; and they accused him of now abandoning the loyalists in Wexford and Kildare. They said that this softness towards the rebels was all part of the Government's policy—to terrify people into the Union.[36] (The same was being said by the gentlemen prisoners in Newgate about the *harshness* of the Government's policy to the rebels.)[37]

Though they needed no encouragement, that mischievous ex-Viceroy,

Bucky, egged on the loyalists against Cornwallis. Pique at not being allowed to lead his regiment into battle had turned to paranoia. He was now doing his best to destroy Cornwallis in England; to his brother Lord Grenville, Foreign Secretary and Pitt's right hand man in the cabinet, he reported gleefully the Irish complaints about "unaccountable lenity"; Cornwallis had "thrown away the greatest game that ever was put into the hands of man", there was not "one grain of confidence" in his talents; he had refused to execute any rebels except where *murder is proved*; he had made enquiries about "improperly convicted" rebels on board the prison ships and released "400 of the most dangerous and desperate". It was inconceivable, he concluded, that the Union could ever be passed by a man of this sort.[38] Lord Camden, the newest ex-Viceroy, and now sitting in Pitt's cabinet, joined in the criticism of Cornwallis for being so hard on Lord Enniskillen. After all he would have been such a useful friend to help with the Union.

Cornwallis soldiered on. The rebellion, the result of gross misgovernment, had made the Union a matter of strategic necessity for both nations. But whatever form of payment he would have to use to induce the Irish Parliament to accept it—and its members were expected to drive a hard bargain—he was not prepared to pay them in floggings and executions.

Already the loss of life and property had been on a scale unknown in Ireland since the rebellion of 1641. The autumn assizes which ran parallel to the courts martial, had now greatly increased the total sentences of death and transportation. According to the figures collected by the Government the following March, eighty-one men had been executed since Cornwallis's arrival, 418 banished or transported, by sentence of court martial, while in addition "great numbers" had been sentenced at the assizes.[39] The total casualties in the rebellion, according to the Castle's estimate, was about twenty thousand of which about fifteen hundred were loyalists.[40]

In fact the death roll in the rebellion was probably much higher. Madden put the figure at 70,000, of which 20,000 were supposed to be Government troops. Contemporary evidence suggests 30,000 as the best estimate including the numerous deaths of soldiers on both sides from exposure and exhaustion, and the murders of men, women and children trapped between rival terrors.[41]

As regards property destroyed, the Government was to receive claims totalling £1,023,337 for compensation to the "suffering loyalists". The list of the most severely affected counties reflected the scale of the fighting: Wexford £515,191; Wicklow £130,379; Mayo £120,533; Kildare

£97,090; Kilkenny £27,352; Dublin £25,829; Carlow £24,854; Sligo £15,769; Antrim £17,729; Down £12,129.[42] The sufferers who were not loyalists were naturally not compensated. If they generally had less to lose, they greatly outnumbered the loyalists, so their losses must have been at least as great again.[43]

Abstract figures of this sort can only hint at the suffering caused by a war. About a dozen towns had been partially or totally destroyed: some like Kildare had been burned to the ground by the military, others like Enniscorthy and Gorey, by the rebels; most of them had been destroyed by both sides, towns like New Ross, Prosperous, Monasterevin, Antrim, Ballynahinch, Carlow and so on.[44]

"In the capital," according to one traveller, "the streets were crowded with the widows and orphans of those who had fallen in battle. In the country, I beheld villages everywhere burned and razed to the ground."[45] The newspapers of the period confirmed the picture of misery. One correspondent described visiting a woman in Wexford whose family that spring had comprised thirteen children, with two cows, three pigs and eleven acres of land. Her husband and three sons had been hanged as rebels at Wexford; two of her boys had been killed at the battle of Vinegar Hill, and three more at the battle of Arklow; all four of her daughters had joined the rebel camp and returned riddled with disease.[46]

On the loyalist side, too, whole families had been annihilated.

But as autumn turned to winter the process of reconstruction in town and country was already on foot, helped by that golden summer which had produced one of the harvests of the century.[47]

On November 8th, Wolfe Tone was escorted into Dublin, dressed in the brilliant uniform of a French colonel—blue coat and pantaloons, large gold epaulettes and tricoloured cockade—and wearing irons on the legs. With characteristic gallantry, he managed to wave to a lady of his acquaintance, one of the Beresfords.[48] Still he had no illusions of the fate in store for him.

"If we are taken," he had written in his diary two years before, as the storm lashed the armada in Bantry Bay, "my fate will not be a mild one; the best I can expect is to be shot as an *emigré rentré*, unless I have the good fortune to be killed in the action."[49] He had lived up to those words on board the *Hoche*, in the hopeless struggle with Warren's fleet, manning one of the batteries till every gun was silenced, and fighting with such desperation that the French officers said later that he seemed to court death.[50]

But he had been taken prisoner with the rest, and with his well-known face he had no chance of escaping detection. (Later on the story was told that his old Trinity friend, Sir George Hill, had given him a Judas Kiss at Letterkenny and betrayed him to the Government.[51] In fact Tone's identity had been known to the Castle even before the ship landed at Buncrana, and he himself now made no effort to conceal it.[52]) Escorted to Derry gaol, he protested that he had enlisted in the French service and was therefore entitled to be treated as a prisoner of war; it was "an indignity" against "the honour of the French army" to put him in irons.[53] But this was little more than a chivalrous gesture towards his adopted country. He soon learned of the treatment meted out to the two Irish officers in the French service who had sailed with Humbert before him, and been captured after Ballinamuck. They had made the same defence as he. They had been hanged on Arbour Hill. One was Bartholomew Teeling, the other his own brother Matthew.[54]

Early on November 10th crowds began to collect outside Dublin barracks, anxious for seats at the court martial of the celebrated Wolfe Tone. When he was brought up for trial, people were impressed by his French uniform—"fantastically decorated with lace", according to a contemporary report—and they noticed that he was not so thin and pale as when he had left the country. Understandably, he seemed agitated, but he recovered his composure after taking a glass of water.[55] After a few questions from the President, the General Loftus who had fled so ignominiously from the Wexford rebels after Walpole's ambush, Tone began to read a statement to the court. He admitted all the charges against him, and asked only one favour—a soldier's death before a firing squad.[56]

In his speech from the dock, Tone did not attempt the poetic flights that were to ensure Robert Emmet's place in the national Valhalla. He spoke with a courage and dignity of a soldier who knows that the end has come. He said that he wished to spare everyone the pain of a long trial. "What I have done has been clearly from principle and the fullest conviction of its rectitude. I wish not for mercy; I hope I am not an object of pity. I anticipate the consequence of my capture, and I am prepared for the event. The favourite object of my life has been the independence of my country, and to that object have I made every sacrifice."

He went on to claim that from his earliest years he had considered the connection with England to be the "bane of the prosperity and happiness of Ireland", and that he had done everything in his power to break it and to "raise three millions of my countrymen to the rank of citizens". He had sought the assistance of France because Ireland was too weak to achieve independence unaided. In his absence, he learned, "there had been atrocities committed on both sides", which he heartily lamented. He himself could bear no responsibility if that "generous spirit" he had tried to raise among Irishmen had degenerated, by force of circumstance or policy, into a "system of assassination". He concluded: "In the glorious race of patriotism, I have pursued the path chalked out by Washington in America ... I have done my duty and no doubt the court will do theirs, and I have only to add that a man who has thought and acted as I have done, should be armed against the fear of death."[57]

Tone's appeal to die by firing squad was sent to Cornwallis, and late the following day he learned in his cell at the Provost prison that this appeal had been rejected. Meanwhile, apparently unknown to him, some of Tone's friends at the Dublin bar had devised a scheme for a respite. The execution was fixed for one o'clock on Monday outside the New Prison.[58] An hour or so before John Philpot Curran brought a motion before the Lord Chief Justice in the King's Bench Court for an order of *habeas corpus* for the Provost Marshall, Major Sandys, to "bring up the body", of Tone.[59]

It was an ingenious argument: a military court could not have jurisdiction over a man taken prisoner at sea in the French service—not, at any rate, while the court of the King's Bench was in session. The Lord Chief Justice at this time was Lord Kilwarden—the man in whose family Tone's grandfather had been confidential servant, and who himself, as Arthur Wolfe, the Attorney General, had connived in Tone's escape to America five years before.[60]

The next step would have been Gilbertian enough, but for the fact a man's life seemed to depend on it. "Have a writ instantly prepared," said the Lord Chief Justice. "My client may die while the writ is preparing," said Curran. The Sheriff was sent post-haste to the Provost to prevent the execution and as swiftly returned with the news that the Provost Marshal had refused to accept the authority of the court. He was told to return instantly and arrest the Provost Marshal. Kilwarden and the court waited for his return in a state of agitation; Tone might still be executed in defiance of the court. The news the Sheriff brought back was sombre enough. Tone had found a different form of respite. He had cut his throat.[61]

Some months before he had set sail in the *Hoche*, he had told his wife and friends that he would never submit to the indignity of execution. To kill oneself in these circumstances was not suicide in the ordinary sense; it was simply choosing the mode of one's death. Others might think differently, but "Please God, they should never have [these] poor bones to pick."[62] Now, he lay dying in the cell in the Provost with that satisfaction at least. He had written a last letter to his wife, and another to the French Directory;[63] and then he had cut his throat with a razor, apparently left in the cell by his brother Matthew,[64] before they took him out to be hanged. Yet even now his ordeal was not over. The razor had severed his windpipe, not his jugular. When told this by a doctor, he was just able to whisper: "I find I am but a bad anatomist."[65] The Castle was not amused. Sir George Hill, one of the Beresford clan, commented grimly: "I would have sewed up his neck and finished the business."[66]

A week later, at the age of thirty-five, Tone died of his wound, and his body was given to his friends.

What is one to make of Tone: soldier of France, Irish patriot, colonial adventurer, citizen of the world? Daniel O'Connell was impossibly harsh when he described Tone and his friends as "criminals".[67] But if we take him at his own valuation in his speech from the dock—as a soldier fighting for Irish freedom—he cannot avoid some responsibility for the military catastrophe. True, he cannot be blamed for the fatal defects in the United organisation that led to the movement's degeneration into a peasant revolt. But it was his persuasiveness, his charm and his optimism about Irish unity that helped decide the French to try their luck in that quarter; and, but for the hopes of French assistance, there would have been no rebellion in Ireland.

Tone lived long enough to see his illusions of a United Ireland dispelled. The respectable Protestants who had toyed with the United Irish movement held grimly to the British connection when their property was threatened. The Presbyterian artisans, so receptive to the ideas of revolution, found it impossible in practice to make common cause with the Catholics. And the Catholics themselves were inexorably divided by class and culture.[68] The great mass of the peasantry remained united only by a common history of oppression, and when the moment came, their victories turned to dust.

Tone's posthumous achievements, however, have been great and enduring. His shining virtues—vision, humour and self-sacrifice—set alight the imagination of later nationalists. He came to personify the tradition of violent revolution in Ireland. A hundred and seventy years after his death, its successful exponents honour him as few men in Irish history are honoured. Not the least of his achievements is that, for later generations of Irishmen, he helped transform what would otherwise have been remembered as a national catastrophe into a heroic struggle of a people against their oppressors, of Irish liberty against English tyranny.

Yet, strange to say, for forty years after his death, Tone seemed forgotten. No one knows for certain where he lies buried. Family tradition is that he was waked in Dublin and buried in his father's grave at Bodenstown, County Kildare.[69]

Epilogue

Plus Ça Change

The United Kingdom, France and America, January 1st, 1801 and after

> As to '98, we leave the weak and wicked men who considered force and sanguinary violence as part of their resources for ameliorating our institutions, and the equally wicked and villainously designing wretches who fomented the rebellion and made it explode [Camden's Government] ... We leave both these classes of miscreants to the contempt and indignation of mankind.
>
> *Daniel O'Connell, speaking in Dublin, May 1841*

THE DIRECT result of the rebellion was the Union with Britain, officially consummated on January 1st, 1801, six months after the Irish Parliament had agreed to vote itself out of existence.

The Union controversy split Ireland, with the exception of the Catholic hierarchy, who were solidly behind the Government, and the Orange party, who were effectively opposed, though officially neutral. Eventually, the Government's view, fortified by the promise of fifteen new baronies, fifteen promotions in the peerage and dozens of jobs, carried the day.[1] Castlereagh talked grandly of buying out "the fee simple of Irish corruption".[2] Cornwallis found it a hateful business.[3] In fact, these political arrangements were unusual but not without precedent. Pitt had created the same number of new peers in the British Parliament to smooth his path in the British elections of 1796.[4]

Among one section of the Irish people, however, there was not a flicker of interest in the great debates on the future of the nation. This was the submerged peasantry.

Those of them who had been caught up in the rebellion, continued to pay a heavy price. Most of them had now found their way back to their homes—or what was left of them. In some parts of the country, the cycle of violence continued sporadically in 1799. There were disturbances in Galway,[5] with widespread houghing of cattle, and a rising in Clare.[6] On the Wexford-Wicklow border there were shootings and chapel burnings.[7]

Dr. Troy, the Catholic Archbishop of Dublin, wrote confidentially to the Castle to complain that no "priest can appear in the N.E. parts of that distracted county nor in the neighbourhood of Arklow".[8] The root of the trouble seems to have been some unemployed Protestant yeomen who had taken to robbery, styled as the "Black Mob". No one dared prosecute them. They put up threatening notices—leases only for "true sons of Moll Doyle"—and for a time it looked as though a new round of persecution was beginning.[9] In the country as a whole the boom in rents and the slump in employment continued.[10] Snow fell in April, and the summer was as wet as the summer before had been fine. In many areas the harvest failed and people were on the verge of famine.[11]

Predictably, the result was a wave of emigration—to England and Scotland—rising soon to an average of 50,000 a year.[12] Compared with the tidal wave during and after the Great Famine, this was only a ripple. Still, the British industrial cities, where the Irish took refuge, had problems enough without them. Like all emigrants who lack capital and education, the Irish had to take the worst jobs and live in the worst ghettos. Many emigrants to Glasgow fell victims to the typhus epidemics of 1818, 1835–37, and 1847.[13] Their children went out to work as child labourers in the mills and the mines of the new Britain.

The political prisoners sent abroad generally fared worse than the voluntary emigrants. About five hundred were pressed into the navy, or sent overseas in the British army. To serve for any length of time in the West Indies was, for the rank and file, virtually a death sentence.[14] In fact, owing to overcrowding on the tenders, some of these new recruits died even before the *Hillsborough* arrived to take them to barracks in England.[15] A further group of 318 Irish convicts were sent to Emden in September 1799 on board the *Alexandria* and two other ships to serve in the army of the King of Prussia.[16] According to one account, they ended their days in the salt mines.[17]

Other political prisoners were transported, according to practice, to Botany Bay. In 1799 the *Minerva* and the *Friendship* sailed with two consignments of this sort, totalling about 230 prisoners.[18] Matthew Sutton, one of Roche's aides was among them. In a letter to his father he described the scene before the *Friendship* sailed; The prisoners were stripped, scrubbed, dressed in canvas shirts, and ironed together, 120 in one long room; already a malignant fever was sweeping the ship and several men had succumbed.[19]

A further consignment from Ireland followed in the *Atlas* and *Hercules*, mainly consisting of political prisoners. Conditions on board were bad even by contemporary standards. The Governor of the penal colony protested to Whitehall: "these ships have lost 127 convicts out of 320 put on board, and the survivors are in a dreadfully emaciated and dying state."[20] At the official enquiry it turned out that to carry more cargo for his own profit, the captain of the *Atlas*, had grossly overloaded the ship, and it was so low in the water that the ventilators could not be opened. In addition, according to the ship's surgeon, the captain had loaded the convicts "with heavy irons on their legs and one round the neck with a large padlock as an appendage".[21]

By 1802 Irishmen made up a quarter of the population of Botany Bay. Political prisoners included three Catholic priests: Father James Dixon, brother of the celebrated Captain Dixon of Wexford, Father James Harrold from Kildare and Father Peter O'Neill from Cork.[22] But the majority of them, like the hard core of the movement in the field, seem to have been artisans: weavers, carpenters, smiths, masons and so on.[23] The authorities were in constant fear of a rising, and in 1804 some sort of conspiracy was discovered, which led to the hanging of eight men.[24] The new prison governor sent out in 1805 was hardly the man to calm things down—he was Captain Bligh, late of the *Bounty*. (In fact Bligh was later deposed by the local military commander for ill-treating the prisoners, and himself imprisoned.)[25] In due course, some of the prisoners were released and found their way back to Ireland, Father O'Neill in 1802, Joseph Holt, the Wicklow partisan, in 1814.[26] Others were assimilated into Australian life, like James Meehan who became Deputy Surveyor-General of New South Wales. To-day there is a war memorial in Sydney to the men of '98.[27]

In Ireland in January, 1799, the third group of political prisoners—the seventy-six United Irish leaders who had signed the "Treaty of Newgate" with the Government—were still in custody, and still complaining bitterly about their treatment.[28] In fact the Castle's plan to ship them off to America had miscarried because President Adams regarded them as too dangerous to admit.[29] Instead, most of them were packed off to a Scottish fortress—Fort George in the Highlands—for the duration. At the Peace of Amiens in 1802 they were allowed to banish themselves to France.[30]

Next year renewed hostilities gave them renewed hopes of French help to liberate Ireland. Leader of this second revolutionary movement was Thomas Addis Emmet's twenty-four year old brother, Robert, who had been an undergraduate at Trinity in 1798, and escaped to France shortly after Lord Clare's purge of the college.[31] The older United Irish leaders were unenthusiastic; and so were the ordinary people of Ireland. Robert Emmet's rising ended in a scuffle in the streets of Dublin.[32] Years later, his speech before execution was to echo round the world. At the time he seemed to have thrown away his life in a fiasco.

By 1805 Britain's naval supremacy, finally confirmed at Trafalgar, had put an end to all hopes of French assistance. The survivors of the United Irish Directory now split. Thomas Addis Emmet, Neilson and Dr. McNevin went to America to find positions more congenial to their talents.[33] It appears that the personal antagonism between Thomas Addis Emmet and Arthur O'Connor, which had so much weakened the movement in the months before the rebellion, had never been far from the surface. In Fort George, Emmet had ineffectively challenged O'Connor to a duel.[34] Now he wrote to his friends from America to say that Arthur O'Connor was worse than Schimmelpennick—the current Dutch dictator. Indeed O'Connor planned to revive the ancient title of High King of Ireland.[35]

The United Irish colony in New York—Emmet, McNevin, Neilson, Sampson, Chambers and others—found the older republic much more to their taste. Two years after his arrival, McNevin edited a small book of their essays called *Pieces of Irish History* in which he denounced the French as one of the chief causes of their failure—"the corrupting, disuniting, debilitating interference of a foreign enemy, blindly deemed a friend." At the same time he advertised the prospectus for the history of the United Irish movement he proposed to write—"It possesses the interest of tragedy, and instructs by its catastrophe."[36] For some reason he never published it. Instead McNevin had a distinguished professional career; he became a professor of midwifery and chemistry in turn at the College of Physicians, and was appointed resident physician to the State of New York. His friend Thomas Addis Emmet became an outstanding member of the American bar, rising to the post of Attorney-General to the state of New York only seven years after his arrival. When he died, Governor Clinton pronounced a eulogy at his grave, and a marble monument, thirty foot high, was erected to his memory.[37]

Thomas Addis Emmet was undoubtedly the most talented and level-headed of all the United Irishmen, and a sincere nationalist. But, what perhaps endeared him as much to the American establishment, his own ideas on society were impeccably conservative. In a letter he wrote home in 1805, he confessed that he was "labouring under the most crying grievance of America, the badness of servants, of which, and the enormity of wages, you can scarcely form an idea. . ."[38]

Meanwhile, fortune had also smiled on the United Irish who stayed behind in France. Lewins, the ambassador, took a respectable job in the university. Other exiles found employment in the service of the Emperor. Surgeon Lawless, Lord Edward's friend, rose to the rank of major-general, despite losing a leg at the battle of Dresden. Hugh Ware, the Kildare leader, became second-in-command in the 1st Irish Regiment, which served with distinction against Sir John Moore's and Wellington's armies, in the Peninsula.[39] A new generation of Irish had become mercenaries in foreign armies, to fight against their own compatriots in the British armies. Indeed, by a final twist, some of the old royalists of the Irish brigade had returned to fight for Britain, just as the new republicans were going out to the Irish legion to fight for France.[40]

Strange to say, the United Irishman to achieve the highest honours in the French army never saw a shot fired. This was Arthur O'Connor, the last survivor of the Irish Directory. His force of character and social standing and above all his invincible belief in his own talents induced Napoleon to appoint him a general-of-division in 1804. His flair for conversation and aristocratic good looks won him a place among the *idéologues*—the intellectuals and anti-clericals for whom the Marquise de Condorcet formed and agreeable *salon*. She was a sister of Grouchy, an intimate of Lafayette, a translator of Adam Smith, and had a seventeen year old daughter called Eliza. O'Connor married Eliza in 1807, and made his home in a charming chateau in the Lorraine. And there he stayed, on the pay of a general-of-division, devoting himself to country pursuits, but happy to offer his services to each succeeding regime. He lived through the last days of the French Consulate, and all of the First Empire, the Restoration, the Hundred Days, the Second Restoration, the July Monarchy and the Second Republic to die tranquilly at the dawn of the Second Empire.[41]

In Ireland it soon emerged that the Union was not what its champions had hoped, nor its opponents had feared. Cornwallis was right. It was merely a union with the Protestant party in Ireland.

Perversely, this party had put up the most vigorous fight against it. But when they found they were not after all to be stripped of their power, they soon returned to the fold. Foster, pensioned off by Pitt with £2500 a year, was restored triumphantly as Irish Chancellor of the Exchequer in 1804.[42] John Claudius Beresford, the leader of the Dublin Orange lodge that had fought so hard for Ireland's freedom, was already reconciled; and the Beresford clan successfully resumed its pursuit of bishoprics.[43] All the High Protestants made it up with the Government: Enniskillen, despite his rebuke over the Woolloghan case; Downshire, despite being sacked from the command of his militia; even that improbable Judge, Jonah Barrington, who was to play such a heroic part in his own memoirs on the Union, now accepted a knighthood, although he was soon driven abroad by his debts and difficulties about a little matter of embezzlement.[44]

The other main group of anti-Unionists—the liberal opposition—soon dissolved their incongruous alliance with the Orange party. Yet they, too, were swiftly reconciled with the Government. Their fears about the Irish economy showed no immediate sign of being realised. In the first ten years of the nineteenth century Irish trade increased far more rapidly than in the last ten of the eighteenth. [45] Their professional prospects, that had seemed overshadowed by the Union, remained golden. The Irish bar (and indeed all Irish institutions except Parliament) remained at this time in Ireland. Irish barristers could also display their talents on the wider stage of the imperial Parliament. Bushe was soon Irish Attorney-General, Curran the Master of the Rolls, and Plunket Irish Lord Chancellor. When they spoke in Parliament on the need for a firm hand in the recurrent agrarian troubles, it was almost like the old days with Lord Chancellor Clare.[46]

Even the great Henry Grattan, though he never accepted office, and devoted the rest of his life to the struggle for Catholic rights, took his seat in London with the British Whigs and declared the Union irreversible.[47] He was buried in Westminister Abbey beside the greatest of British statesmen.

By contrast the main sponsors of the Union, both in England and Ireland, found their hopes blighted. As we saw, Pitt had planned to end the Catholic question once and for all by giving Catholics complete political equality with Protestants. He could also arrange, without fear of reprisal from the bigoted Irish Parliament, to abolish tithes and make some sort of establishment for the Catholic clergy. As soon as the Union had passed, Pitt had begun preparations.[48] But there was a grave flaw in his plans. It might be all right in future to let Irish Catholics into the United Parliament, safely diluted by British Protestants. But it certainly proved fatal at present to let Irish *Protestants* impose their view of Ireland on the United Parliament. The hundred Irish members in this assembly included, of course, the men who had consistently opposed Catholic claims in the Irish Parliament. The Union might be distasteful to them; Catholic emancipation would be political suicide. In alliance with their British counterparts they prepared to fight for their ascendancy.[49] The alliance was encouraged by George III, who claimed, with perfect truth, that the idea of Catholic emancipation drove him mad.[50] Pitt was forced to resign, and Foster's friend, Addington, took over. Pitt's partners in Ireland—Cornwallis, Castlereagh and Cooke—resigned in sympathy.[51]

After Pitt's death, Castlereagh was to serve for fifteen years as British Foreign Secretary, and Cooke served with him as under-secretary.[52] Cornwallis was appointed Viceroy for the third time in 1805, reluctantly agreeing to replace Wellesley in India; General Lake was the military commander and had learnt nothing from his Irish experiences; Cornwallis died of fever soon after his arrival, protesting about Lake's reckless treatment of the natives.[52]

Pitt was the first (but by no means the last) British Prime Minister to be broken by the Irish question. Not until 1829 did one of his successors summon the strength to carry Catholic emancipation—Wellington, who had got his first foothold on the political ladder in the Irish Parliament nearly forty years before.[54] By now Ireland, after years of political vacuum, was again on the brink of civil war. Tithes were commuted to a rent charge in 1838, and finally abolished when the Irish Church was disestablished in 1869. No arrangements were ever made to give state aid to the Catholic Church. Meanwhile, the failure to resolve these and the other Catholic grievances—the landlord system, and unemployment—had undermined the Union and proved a godsend to the new generation of anti-Unionists led by O'Connell. Ironically, the failure of the rebellion, which led to the Union, had put a weapon of enormous political potential in O'Connell's hands: non-violent agitation. If any immediate good came out of the rebellion it was this.

The Union failed for a whole number of reasons, including the way it was imposed and the tenacity of Irish nationalism.[55] If it had been followed by the Catholic concessions Pitt had planned, it might have had a chance. Instead, the Protestant Irish retained their political monopoly, and the British Government their inertia. The Union did, however, endure in the one part of Ireland where Protestants had a majority—the six counties of Ulster. The political descendants of Orr—the Protestant martyr of '98— now sit proudly on the Unionist benches. Yet in Ulster the price of assimilating Irish Protestants into the United Kingdom has been to leave Catholics out in the cold.

By a final twist, the second Irish war of independence of 1919-21 not only failed to win a united Ireland, but resulted in a return to a form of self-government in Ulster that had already proved disastrous in '98.

Forty years later the stench of history is overpowering. Catholics have remained poor, politically powerless, and alienated from government. Stormont has maintained Protestant ascendancy as stoutly as the Dublin Parliament. Successive British Governments have decided to let well alone, dodging the attacks of the Left with the same tactics Pitt used against Fox—Ireland is an Irish responsibility.

Perhaps the old wounds are healing. There are offers of help, at any rate, from Westminster—and high time, too. Yet when shall we lay the ghosts of '98?

Select Bibliography

ABBREVIATIONS

620	Irish State Paper Office, Rebellion Papers
BM Add MSS	British Museum, Additional Manuscripts
BNL	Belfast News-Letter
CRO	County Record Office
C/M	Court Martial
DEP	Dublin Evening Post
DNB	Dictionary of National Biography
FDJ	Faulkner's Dublin Journal
FJ	Freeman's Journal
HJ	Hibernian Journal
HO	Home Office Section of Public Record Office, London
IHS	Irish Historical Studies
ISPO	Irish State Paper Office
NAM	National Army Museum, Camberley, Surrey
NCEP	New Cork Evening Post
NLI	National Library of Ireland
PR	Parliamentary Register of Irish House of Commons
PRO	Public Record Office, London
PROI	Public Record Office of Ireland
RIA	Royal Irish Academy
RSCHC	Report of Secret Committee of [Irish] House of Commons 1798
RSCHL	Report of Secret Committee of [Irish] House of Lords 1798
SNL	Saunders News-Letter
TCD	Trinity College Dublin
UI	United Irishmen
WO	War Office Section of Public Record Office, London

A. MANUSCRIPT SOURCES
   DUBLIN
   Public Record Office of Ireland
   Bailey MSS
   Byrne MSS M 5 892a/81xx
   Frazer MSS (Kemmis) IA 40 112

   State Paper Office (at present kept in Public Record Office)
   Official Papers
   Prisoners' Petitions
   Rebellion Papers 620
   State of the Country Papers 1st and 2nd series 408, 30, 31
   State Prisoners' Petitions

National Library
　　Cullen MSS 9760
　　Dundas MSS 54A, 55
　　Grogan MSS 11077
　　Knox MSS ("Lake") 56
　　La Touche MSS and photostats 3151
　　Parsons MSS
　　Limerick MSS
　　Shannon MSS 13, 295–13, 306
　　Kilmainham Papers A

Kilmainham Hospital
　　Kilmainham Papers B

Royal Irish Academy
　　Charlemont MSS 12 P 20, 23–7
　　Haliday Collection 3 B 53–55
　　Bulletins and proclamations 24 D 37, 12 P 26
　　Little Diary 3 B 5 1
　　McSkimmin's notes 4 F 36

Trinity College
　　Connolly MSS
　　Commissary-General's letter book N 4 19–22
　　Court Martial Proceedings S 3 22, 6 2 19a
　　Cullen MSS S 5 19
　　Madden MSS 2 3 19–22
　　Musgrave Depositions G 2 19
　　and "bloody calendar" of Wexford
　　Sirr MSS N 41 2–10
　　Stock Diary etc S 3 17
　　Tone Diary, letters etc

BELFAST
　Public Record Office
　　Abercorn MSS
　　Clelland Depositions
　　Downshire MSS DOD 607
　　Drennan letters typescript
　　Gosford MSS
　　Massarene and Ferrard (incl. Foster) MSS
　　McCance collection DOD 272

PRIVATE COLLECTIONS IN IRELAND
　　Tullynally MSS, Castlepollard, Co. Westmeath
　　Leadbeater MSS 4 vols (Fuller than published version)
　　Longford MSS
　　Mountstewart MSS Co. Down
　　　Castlereagh MSS (A few unpublished items)

Leixlip MSS
Bunbury MSS (Ex-McPeake collection)

LONDON
Public Record Office
Home Office papers HO 100/47–89; HO 42/40; HO 1/769
War Office papers WO 1/922; WO 1/1101; WO 40/7, 9, 11
Pitt MSS 30/8

British Museum
Auckland MSS Add MSS 34, 454
Hardwick MSS Add MSS 35, 731–2; 35, 766; 35, 919–20; 35, 924–7
Handcock's narrative Add MSS 38, 102
Hodges MSS, Add MSS 40, 166
Ilchester MSS (Holland) Add MSS 51, 682; 51, 684
Pelham MSS Add MSS 33, 105–6
Percy MSS Add MSS 32, 335
Sunderlin MSS Add MSS 4, 192
Wellesley MSS Add MSS 37, 308
Windham MSS Add MSS 37, 844

EDINBURGH
Scottish Record Office
Melville Castle MSS
Dalguise MSS
Dundas of Arniston MSS (Colonel Durham's Diary)

SURREY
National Army Museum, Camberley
Nugent MSS (from Royal United Service Institution, London)
Cornwallis MSS

KENT
County Record Office, Maidstone
Camden MSS
Mann MSS (Cornwallis)

OXFORD
Bodleian
Edgeworth MSS (deposited by Mrs. H. Colvin)

WILTSHIRE
County Record Office
Cope MSS

STAFFORDSHIRE
Keele University
Sneyd MSS (Auckland)

PRIVATE COLLECTIONS IN BRITAIN
Kilmaine MSS at Mount House, Brasted, Kent
McPeake MSS at Frognal House, London NW
Wellington MSS at Apsley House, London SW1
Elmes MSS
Sutton MSS

PARIS
Archives de la Marine BB IV

* * *

B. PRINTED SOURCES
BOOKS

Abercromby *Sir Ralph Abercromby . . . a Memoir*, Lord Dunfermline Edinb 1861.

Adams, Mrs. narrative ed Thomas Crofton Croker *Researches in the South of Ireland . . . With an Appendix Containing a Private narrative . . . of the Rebellion of 1798* London 1824.

Alexander, James *Some Account of the first Apparent Symptoms of the Late Rebellion in the County of Kildare . . . with a succinct Narrative of Some of the Most Remarkable passages in the Rise and Progress of the Rebellion in the County of Wexford . . .* Dublin 1800

Aspinall, A. *The Later Correspondence of George III*, Vol III January 1798 to December 1801 Cambridge 1967, Vol IV January 1802 to December 1807 Cambridge 1968.

Aspinall, A. *The Correspondence of George, Prince of Wales 1770–1812* vol III 1795–8 London 1965.

Auckland, 1st Baron *Journal and Correspondence*, ed. William Eden 4 Vols London 1861–62.

Barrington, Sir Jonah *Personal Sketches of his Own Times* 3 Vols London 1827–32.

Barrington, Sir Jonah *Historic Memoirs and Secret Anecdotes of the Legislative Union* London 1833.

Barrington, Sir Jonah *Rise and Fall of the Irish Nation* Dublin 1833.

Beckett, J. C. *The Making of Modern Ireland 1603–1923* London 1966.

Beckett, J. C. & Moody, T. W. *Ulster Since 1800* 1st Series 1957.

Beresford, the Rt. Hon. John *Letters* ed W. Beresford 2 Vols London 1854.

Binns, John *Recollections of the Life of John Binns . . . written by himself* Philadelphia 1854.

Blacker's narrative ed. T. G. Paterson, "Lisburn & neighbourhood in 1798" in *Ulster Jn. of Arch.* i, pp. 193–8 1938.

Bolton G. C. *The Passing of the Irish Act of Union* Oxford 1966.

Bonaparte and the Invasion of England H. F. B. Wheeler & A. M. Broadley 2 Vols London 1908.

Bourke, F. S. "The French invasion of 1798: a forgotten eyewitness" in Ir. Sword ii 288–94.

Brownrigg, Mrs narrative *The War in Wexford* by H. F. B. Wheeler and A. M. Broadley London 1910.

Buckingham, Richard 2nd Duke *Courts and Cabinets of the Reign of George III* London 1848 Vol II

Bushe, Charles Kendal *An Incorruptible Irishman . . . Chief Justice Charles Kendal Bushe* E. A. O. Somerville & V. F. Martin London 1932.

Byrne, Miles *Memoirs* 1st ed. 2 Vols Paris 1863 New ed. Dublin 1906.

Carlisle MSS H. M. C. 1897.

Castlereagh, Viscount *Memoirs and Correspondence* ed Lord Londonderry 12 Vols 1848.

Caulfield, James *The Reply of the Right Rev. Dr. Caulfield . . . to . . . Sir Richard Musgrave* Dublin 1801.

Charlemont MSS H.M.C. Thirteenth Report: Appendix Part viii 1894.

Charlemont *Memoirs* Francis Hardy London 1820.

Cloncurry, V. B. Lawless 2nd Baron *Personal recollections of the Life and Times of Lord Cloncurry* 1849.

Cloney, Thomas *A Personal Narrative of These Transations in the County of Wexford, in which the Author was Engaged, during the Awful Period of 1798* Dublin 1832.

Coigly, James *The Life of the Rev. James Coigly . . . as written by himself* London 1798.

The Trial of James O'Coigly . . . Arthur O'Connor, J. Binns, J. Allen, and J. Leary for high treason . . . at Maidstone . . . May 1798 Taken in shorthand by J. Gurney London 1798.

Colchester, Lord *Diary and Correspondence edited by his son, Charles Lord Colchester* 3 Vols London 1861.

Cooper, George *Letters on the Irish Nation, written during a Visit to that Kingdom in the Autumn of 1799.* 1800.

Cornwallis *Correspondence of Charles 1st Marquis Cornwallis.* 3 Vols London 1859.

Craig, M. J. *Dublin, 1600–1860* London 1952.

Craig, M. J. *The Volunteer Earl* London 1948.

Crone, John Smyth *A Concise dictionary of Irish biography* Dublin 1937.

Crosbie, Sir Edward *An accurate and Impartial Narrative of the Apprehension, Trial, & Execution on the 5th of June, 1798, of Sir E. W. Crosbie . . . with Authentic Documents* 1st ed. Bath 1801 Dublin 1802.

Cullen, Rev. Br. Luke *Personal Recollections of Wexford and Wicklow Insurgents of 1798* Enniscorthy 1959.

Cullen, L. M. *Anglo-Irish Trade 1660–1800* Manchester 1968.

Curran, John Philpot 2 Vols *Life*, ed. W. H. Curran. Edinb. 1819.

(D'Arcy, Morgan) *A Vindication of the Roman Catholic Clergy of the Town of Wexford, during the Late Unhappy Rebellion, from the Groundless Charges . . . of . . 'Verax'* By Veritas 2nd ed Dublin 1798.

De Latocnaye *A Frenchman's Walk through Ireland (1796–97)* translated by J. Stevenson 1917.

Desbrière, E. Capt. *Projets et Tentatives de Debarquement aux Iles Britanniques* tomes I et II Paris 1902.

Dickson, Charles *The Life of Michael Dwyer . . .* Dublin 1944.

Dickson, Charles *Revolt in the North: Antrim and Down in 1798* Dublin 1960.

Dickson, Charles *The Wexford Rising in 1798: its causes and its course* Tralee 1955.

Dickson, Charles *The Battle of Vinegar Hill, 1798* In "Ir. Sword" i 293–5.

Dickson. W. S. *A Narrative of the Confinement and Exile of William Steele Dickson D.D . . .* 1812.

Drennan, W. *The Drennan Letters 1776–1819* ed D. A. Chart H.M.S.O. Belfast 1931.

Edgeworth, R. L. *Memoirs . . .* 2 Vols London 1820.

Emmet, T. A. & R., . . . *Memoirs . . .* 2 Vols New York 1915.

Emmet, T. A. *Life*, T. P. Robinson New York University thesis Ann Arbor microf AC–1 no 24, 452.

Falkiner, C. L. *Studies in Irish History* 1902.

Farrell, William *Carlow in '98: The Autobiography of William Farrell of Carlow* ed Roger J. McHugh Dublin 1949.

Fitzgerald, T. *The Trial of . . . on an action for damages, brought against him by Mr. Wright . . . With the proceedings in Parliament on his petition, praying indemnification* Dublin 1799.

Fitzgerald, T. *A Report of an Interesting Case, wherein Mr. Francis Doyle . . . was Plaintiff, and Sir Thomas Judkin Fitzgerald . . . was Defendant.* Dublin 1806.

Fitzpatrick, W. J. *The Sham squire, and the Informers of 1798* 3rd ed. Dublin 1866.

Fortescue, Sir John *History of the British Army* 13 Vols London 1899.

Fortescue MSS. H.M.C. 1892–1908 6 Vols preserved at Dropmore.

Fox, Charles James *Memorials and Correspondence of Charles James Fox* ed. Lord John Russell 4 Vols London 1853–7.

Frazer, George *Memoirs in the life and travels of . . .* 1808.

Glenbervie, Sylvester Douglas 1st Baron *The Glenbervie Journals* ed. W. Sickel 1910.

Gordon, Rev. James Bentley *A History of Ireland from the Earliest Accounts to the Accomplishment of the Union with Great Britain in 1801* Dublin 1805.

Gordon, Rev. James Bentley *History of the Rebellion in Ireland in the Year 1798 . . .* 1801.

Goff, Dinah Wilson *Divine Protection . . . during the Irish Rebellion of 1798* 1835.

Grattan, Henry jnr. *Life of Henry Grattan* 5 Vols London 1839–1846.

Grattan, Henry *The Speeches of the Rt. Hon. Henry Grattan* 4 Vols London 1844.

Guillon, E. *La France et L'Irelande pendant le Revolution* Paris 1888.

Hancock, Thomas *The Principles of Peace Exemplified in the Conduct of the Society of Friends in Ireland, during the Rebellion of 1798* London 1825.

Handley, J. E. *The Irish in Scotland (1798–1805)* Cork 1943.

Haughton, Joseph *Narration of Events during the Irish Rebellion in 1798* n.d.

Hayes, Dr. Richard *The Last Invasion of Ireland* Dublin 1937.

Hayes-McCoy, G. A. The Wexford Yeomanry and Miles Byrne. In "An Cosantoir". viii 3–10.

Hayes-McCoy, G. A. *Irish Battles* London 1969.

Hayes-McCoy, G. A. The Irish pike: additional notes on its history. In "Galway Arch. Soc. Jn." xxi 44–50.

Hayes-McCoy, G. A. The Red coat and the green. In "Studies" xxxvii 396–408

Hayes-McCoy, G. A. The topography of a battlefield: Arklow 1798. In "Ir. Sword" i, 51–6.

Holland, Lord *Memoirs of the Whig Party* ed. by his son London 1852–54.

Holland, Lady Elizabeth *Journal* ed the Earl of Ilchester 2 Vols London 1908.

Holt, Joseph *Memoirs . . .* ed from his original MS . . . by T. Crofton Croker 2 Vols London 1838.

Howell, Thomas Bayly Thomas Jones eds. A complete collection of state trials (vols 22–27) London 1811–26.

Hyde, H. M. *The Rise of Castlereagh* London 1933.

Jacob, Rosamund *The Rise of the United Irishmen 1791–1794* London 1937.

Jackson, Charles *A narrative of the sufferings and escapes of Charles Jackson late resident at Wexford in Ireland, including an account by way of journal of several barbarous atrocities committed in June 1798 by the Irish rebels . . .* 1798.

Jobit narrative. ed Nuala Costelloe 2 diaries of the French expedition Dublin Stationery Office. Ir MSS Comm. 'Anal. Hib.', no 11 1941. (1 by Capt. Jobit, Brest MS. 2 by Rev. Little RIA MS 31351).

Jones, John *An Impartial Narrative of the most important engagements which took place . . . during the Irish rebellion* 1799.

Jones, Commander E. Stuart, R.N. *An Invasion that Failed* London 1950.

Kavanagh, Rev. Patrick F. *A Popular History of the Insurrection in 1798* Dublin n.d.

Kiernan, T. J. *Irish Exiles in Australia* Dublin 1954.

Kiernan, T. J. *Transportation from Ireland to Sydney* (1791–1816) 1954.

Knox, Alexander *Essays on the political circumstances of Ireland, written during the administration of Earl Camden; with an appendix, containing Thoughts on the will of the people* 2nd ed. Dublin 1799.

Lake *Letters* (collection B. McPeake) "Ir. Sword", i, 284–7 1953.

Latimer, W. T. *Ulster biographies, relating chiefly to the Rebellion of 1798* Belfast 1897.

Leadbeater, Mary, and others *The Leadbeater Papers* 2 Vols London 1862.

Lenox-Conyngham, M. *An old Ulster House* Dundalk 1946.

Lett, Barbara Newton A '98 diary ed by Rev. J. Ranson. In "The Past", i no 5, pp. 117–49 1949.

Longford militia *A Short History of the Royal Longford militia*, H. A. Richey Dublin 1894.

Madden, R. R. *Down and Antrim in '98* Dublin n.d.

Madden, R. R. *The United Irishmen, their Lives and Times.* 4 Vols. (1st ed 1842–46) Dublin 1857–60. [This work referred to as "Madden" simply in notes].

Mason, William Shaw *A Statistical Account and Parochial Survey of Ireland* 1814–19.

Maxwell, Constantia *Dublin under the Georges, 1714–1830* London 1937.

Maxwell, Constantia *Country and Town in Ireland under the Georges* London 1940.

Maxwell, William Hamilton *History of the Irish Rebellion in 1798* London 1845.

Moody, T. W. The political ideas of the United Irishmen. In "Ireland To-day", vol iii no 1 pp. 15–25 1938.

Moore, Sir John *Diary* ed by Major-General Sir J. F. Maurice London 1904.

Moore, Thomas *The Life and death of Lord Edward Fitzgerald* (1st ed 1831) 3rd ed London 1832 2 Vols.

Musgrave, Sir Richard *Memoirs of the rebellions in Ireland* (1st ed 1801) 3rd edit 1802 octavo.

McAnally, Sir Henry The French invasion of Connaght 1798: Some problems in numbers In 'Ir. Host. Sc. Comm. Bull' no 37 1945.

MacCauley, James A. The Battle of Lough Swilly, 1798. In "Ir. Sword" iv 166–70.

MacDermot, F. *Theobald Wolfe Tone: a Biographical Study* London 1939.

McDowell, R. B. The personnel of the Dublin society of United Irishmen 1791–4. In IHS ii 12–53.

McDowell, R. B. *Irish Public Opinion 1750–1800* London Faber 1944.

McDowell, R. B. The United Irishmen of Dublin 1791–4 In "Bull. Ir. Comm. Hist. Sc." no 1 1939.

McDowell, R. B. ed United Irish plans of parliamentary reform—select documents. In IHS iii pp. 39–59 1942.

MacDonagh T. *The Viceroy's Post Bag* Correspondence of Earl of Hardwicke London 1904.

MacLaren, Archibald *A Minute Description of the Battles of Gorey, Arklow and Vinegar Hill; together with the Movements of the Army through the Wicklow mts* . . . 1798.

McNeill, Mary *The Life and Times of Mary Ann McCracken* (1770–1866) *A Belfast Panorama* Dublin 1960.

McNeven, W. J. *Pieces of Irish History* New York 1807.

McSkimmin, Samuel *A history of the Irish Rebellion* Belfast 1853.

Napoleon *Correspondence de Napoléon 1er* Vol III Paris 1859.

Newell, Ed. John *The Apostacy of Newell, . . . the Life and Confessions of that Celebrated Informer . . . Written by himself* London 1798.

Nicholson, Harold *The Desire to Please A Study of Hamilton Rowan & the United Irishmen* London 1943.

O'Brien, George *The Economic History of Ireland in the 18th Century* Dublin 1918.

O'Kelly, P. *General History of the Rebellion of 1798 &c* Dublin 1842.

Olson, Alison *The Radical Duke, The Career and Correspondence of Charles Lennox Third Duke of Richmond* Oxford 1961.

Paine, Thomas *The Rights of Man Being an Answer to Mr Burke's Attack on the French Revolution* Dublin ed 1791.

Palmer, R. R. *The Age of Democratic Revolutions* Vol 1 Oxford 1964.

Piondar, Sean President Moore of the first Irish Republic. In "Garda Review" pp. 535-8 1945.

Plowden, Francis *An Historical Review of the State of Ireland, from the Invasion of that Country under Henry II to its Union with Great Britain* 2 Vols in 3 London 1803.

Plunket, Hon. David *The Life, Letters and Speeches of Lord Plunket* London 1867.

Reynolds, Thomas *The Life of Thomas Reynolds by his Son* 2 Vols London 1839.

Roche, Jordan, *A Statement and observations, &c . . .* 1798.

Rosborough, S.: *Observations on the State of the Poor of the Metropolis* 1801.

Rowan, Archibald Hamilton *Autobiography 1840.*

Sampson, William *Memoirs* New York 1807.

Sarrazin, General John An Officer's account of the French campaign in Ireland in 1798. In "Ir. Sword" ii 110–18, 161–71 1955.

Senior, Hereward *Orangeism in Ireland and Britain 1795–1836* London 1966.

Sheares narrative *A Report of the Proceedings in Cases of High Treason, at a Special Commission of Oyez and Terminer* ... Dublin ... July 1798 (4 parts: 1 Henry and John Sheares; 2 John McCann; 3 Michael William Byrne; 4 Oliver Bond) Dublin 1798.

Simms, J. G. *Connacht in the eighteenth century* IHS vol XI no 42 p 116–33.

Snowe, William *Statement of Transactions at Enniscorthy on 28th May* (1798) 1801.

Stanhope, Earl *Life of the Right Honourable William Pitt* 3 Vols London 1862.

Stock, Joseph *Narrative of What Passed at Killala during the French Invasion of 1798* 1800.

Taylor, George *An History of the Rise, Progress and Suppression, of the Rebellion in the County of Wexford, in the Year 1798* ... *to which is Annexed, the Author's Account of his Captivity, and Merciful Deliverance* Dublin (1st ed 1800) Modern reprint n.d.

Tecling, C. H. *The History of the Irish rebellion of 1798, a Personal Narrative* 1828.

Thompson, E. *The Making of the English Working Class* 1963.

Tone, Theobald Wolfe *Life of . . . Written by Himself and Continued by his Son; with his Political Writings and Fragments of his Diary* ... ed by his son William T. W. Tone, 2 Vols Washington 1826.

Tone, Theobald Wolfe *Proceedings of a Military Court held in Dublin Barracks for the Trial of etc* Dublin 1798.

Wall, Maureen The rise of a catholic middle class in eighteenth century Ireland IHS vol XI no 42 1958 p. 91 f.

(Wall) MacGeehin, Maureen The catholics of the towns and the quarterage dispute in eighteenth century Ireland IHS viii 91–114.

Wallace, T. *An Essay on the Manufactures of Ireland* April 1798.

Wakefield, Edward *An Account of Ireland, Statistical and Political* 2 Vols 1812.

Wellesley, Richard Colley Marquis *The Wellesley Papers. Life and Correspondence* Vol I London 1914.

Whitelaw, Rev J.: *An Essay on the Population of Dublin* (1798) 1805.
Wilberforce, William *Life* ed by his sons 5 Vols London 1838.
Wilson, W. *The Post-Chaise Companion* 3rd ed Dublin 1805.
Windham, William *The Diary of the Right Hon. William Windham* ed Mrs Henry Baring London 1866
Wittke, C. F. *The Irish in America*
Woolaghan, Hugh *The Genuine Trial of Hugh Woolaghan ... by ... Court-martial ... Dublin ... Oct. 13 1798 for the Murder of Thomas Dogherty to which is added ... Lord Cornwallis's Order for the Court-martial to be dissolved* Dublin 1798.
Young, A. *A Tour in Ireland* Dublin 1780.
Zimmerman, George *Songs of Irish Rebellion* Dublin 1967.

PARLIAMENTARY PROCEEDINGS

The Parliamentary Register or the History of the proceedings and Debates of the House of Commons of Ireland Vols I–XVII, 1781–97 Dublin 1782–1801.
The Debate in the Irish house of Peers, on a Motion made by the Earl of Moira, Monday 19 February 1798 Dublin 1798.
Reports of the Secret Committees of lords and commons with the address of both houses to his excellency the lord lieutenant ... 1797 Dublin 1797
The Report from the Secret Committee of the House of Commons and of the House of Lords, with an appendix, 1798 Dublin 1798.
The Conduct of the Admiralty, in the Late Expedition of the Enemy to the Coast of Ireland, as stated by Ministers, in the House of Commons ... 3d of March, 1797: with ... the Official Papers ... printed by Parliament London 1797.
Report from the Committee of Secrecy ... relating to seditious societies, &c. Reported by Mr. Secretary Dundas, 15th March 1799 London 1799.

NEWSPAPERS & JOURNALS

Dublin Evening Post
Belfast News-Letter. Belfast
Northern Star Belfast 1792–7.
The Press Nos 1–67 Dublin, 1797–8.
New Cork Evening Post.
Saunders' News-Letter Dublin.
The Annual Register, or a view of the history, politicks and literature for the year London.
Irish Magazine: and monthly asylum for neglected biography Dublin 1807–15 (ed Watty Cox)
Faulkner's Dublin Journal ("the most correct in statement [of Irish newspapers] however sometimes faulty" Edward Cooke. HO 100/80/191).
Hibernian Journal Dublin.
Wilson's Dublin Directory.
Gentleman's and Citizen's Almanack (ed Samuel Watson).
Freeman's Journal Dublin.
Walker's Hibernian Magazine Dublin.

PAMPHLETS

Causes of the Rebellion in Ireland Disclosed, in an Address to the people of England ... By an Irish emigrant London 1798.

Considerations on the situation to which Ireland is reduced by the government of Lord Camden Dublin 1798.

A History of the Irish Rebellion in the year 1798 . . . The whole impartially collected from the best authorities . . .1799

Impartial Relation of the Military Operations which took place in Ireland, in consequence of the landing . . . of French Troops . . . 1798 Dublin 1799.

Narrative of a private soldier in His Majesty's 92nd Regiment of foot. Written by himself. Detailing many circumstances relative to the Irish Rebellion of 1798. . . Glasgow, 1820 (signed G.B.)

Notes

PART 1 PROLOGUE

1. The complete expedition totalled about 14,750 men in 45 ships. Desbrière *Projets I.* 135-81; E. Jones *Invasion* p. 106-8, 113-20.

2. Directors' instructions to Hoche June 19th 1798 printed Desbrière *Projets I.* 107-9.

3. Tone's journal for December 21st 1796 printed in *Life* II. 255-8 cf. Jones *Invasion* p. 165.

4. Tone's *Life* I. 38-58. See MacDermot *Tone* passim esp. 68-72, 83-7.

5. United Irish documents 1790-3 printed in RSCHC App. IV, V.

6. The first arrest of a United Irish leader—Hamilton Rowan—was in 1793. FDJ November 12th 1793.

7. Emmet, McNevin, O'Connor *Memoire* p. 3-4.

8. J. [Keogh] September 3rd 1795 printed in Tone *Life* I. 291-3. See also R. Simms—Tone September 18th 1795.

9. See A. Rousselin *Vie de Lazare Hoche* Paris 1798.

10. Tone's Journal for December 21st-2nd *Life* II. 255-8.

11. Ibid p. 259-60.

12. Ibid p. 257

13. Ibid p. 258.

14. Ibid p. 260-9.

15. DEP December 10th 1796. *Gentlemen's Magazine* December 1796.

16. For the abject situation of the Irish army see Irish House of Commons debate of January 18th 1797. cf HO 100/74 passim. Also Cooke-Auckland Sneyd MSS University.

17. Ld Castlereagh to his wife January 4th 1797. Londonderry MSS at Mountstewart.

18. Sir L. Parsons' speech in Irish Commons. DEP January 19th 1797.

19. FJ December 29th 1796.

20. Ld Shannon [January 1797] to his son. NLI 13, 303.

PART 1 CHAPTER I

At head of chapter: Bonaparte's remark, referring to the French Jacobins, is quoted in Tone *Diary* II. 462, 3.

1. William Pitt to the King January 22nd 1798. Aspinall *George III.* III 12-13.

2. The King to William Pitt January 23rd 1798. Stanhope *Pitt* III App XI.

3. e.g. The Duke of Bedford, an anti-Government Whig, who gave £100,000.

4. In Pitt's April budget it was estimated that tax would total £8·75m and Government expenditure £28·45m. Colchester *Diary* I. 151.

5. *Annual Register* 1798.

6. For a gloomy view of prospects see Cornwallis—Ross December 15th 1797. *Cornwallis Correspondence* II. 329-330.

7. *The Conduct of the Admiralty* printed by Parliament London March 1797; see E. S. Jones *Invasion* p. 181-94.

8. Camden—Pitt November 1797 PRO 30/8/326. See Bolton *Union* p. 46-7.

9. His health had begun to fail in 1797. See Stanhope III. 64.

10. Wilberforce *Private Papers of William Wilberforce*, London 1897 p. 45-81.

11. Aspinall *George III.* Vol III. xiii-xiv.

12. Ibid xi-xii.

13. Stanhope III. 23-48: Thompson *Making of the English Working-Class* p. 102-85.

14. Beckett *Ireland* p. 206-26.

15. Harlow *British Empire* I. 501–9.
16. Ibid I. 503.
17. Ibid I. 506 foll.
18. Barrington *Memoirs* I. 156, 164; *Rise and Fall* p. 288.
19. Harlow I. 519–26.
20. Wall, IHS 1958, p. 91 foll.
21. See Lecky IV. 120–123, etc.
22. Ibid III. 277, 493, IV. 407.
23. Ibid III. 61, 128, 151, 287.
24. For the latest study of the Fitzwilliam episode of 1794–5 see R. McDowell IHS vol 16 No. 55 p. 115–30.
25. FJ, FDJ passim 1795–6.
26. *The Times* May-June 1797; C. Gill *The Naval Mutinies of 1797* (1913) p. 301 ff.
27. Ibid.
28. Ibid.
29. Camden—Portland October 6th 1797. HO 100/72/283.
30. Desbrière I. 283–296. Wheeler and Broadley *Invasion* p. 74–103.
31. *New Cambridge Modern History* IX. 289–92.
32. Ibid IX. 291.
33. Bonaparte was appointed Commander of the "Army of England" October 26th 1797. Desbrière I. 283.
34. Bonaparte—Talleyrand October 18th 1797. *Correspondence de Napoleon I* III. 519–20.
35. Tone had interviews with Barras, Talleyrand and Scherer. His comment on Bonaparte's appointment was "Bravo! This looks as if they were in earnest." *Life* II. 451.
36. Ibid p. 406–441.
37. Ibid p. 443–6.
38. Ibid p. 454.
39. Ibid p. 454–6.
40. Tone's two memorials of 1795–6 are re-printed in the *Life* II. 181–204.
41. Ibid p. 457–8.
42. See Desbrière I. 383–391.
43. Ibid I. 387.
44. Forfait's report May 17th 1798 Archives de la Marine BBIV/121.
45. Report in Castlereagh *Correspondence* I. 165–8.
46. WO 11.

PART I CHAPTER 2

At head of chapter: 1798 Prophecy taken from McSkimmin *Rebellion* p. 100

1. Whitelaw *Population* p. 56–7. See also DEP June 7th 1798. There were 37,000 starving workers in Dublin acc. DEP August 31st 1797.
2. Malton *Dublin* introd. See C. Maxwell *Dublin* p. 59–79.
3. Abbot in 1801, Colchester *Correspondence* I. 289. See Hyde *Castlereagh* p. 209–214.
4. Sampson *Memoirs*.
5. Hyde *Castlereagh* p. 223–7 etc.
6. Camden—Portland January 22nd, March 6th 1798. H.O. 100/75/30–2; 100/75/163.
7. St. George—Kemmis January 24th 1798 PROI 1A/40/111a. cf ISPO 408/601/65.
8. FDJ February 3rd, 15th; FJ February 13th, 15th; SNL February 16th, 23rd 1798.
9. According Lord Glentworth. *The Debate in the Irish house of Peers . . . February 19th 1798*. Dublin 1798.
10. FDJ February 27th; DEP March 10th; NCEP March 8th 1798. William Cope March 2nd 1798. Cope MSS in Wiltshire CRO.
11. Lecky *Ireland* III–IV passim.

12. Sir J. Moore January 10th 1798 *Diary* I. 271.
13. Sir J. Carden February 15th 1798. 620/35/143. SNL May 9th 1798.
14. Lord Longueville—Charles Kippax March 30th 1798. ISPO 408/601/7.
15. Camden—Portland February 29th 1798. HO/75/116.
16. Camden—Portland March 6th 1798. HO/75/165-6.
17. Camden—Portland January 16th 1798. HO 100/75/32-3. Portland—Camden January 17th 1798. HO/100/75/23.
18. "J. W." (L. McNally) 620/10. Apparently enclosed with Camden—Portland February 26th 1798. HO 100/75/128.
19. "J.W. "March 4th 1798. 620/10.
20. "J.W." February 20th 1798. 620/10.
21. "J.W." December 7th 1797. 620/36/227.
22. "Richardson" (Turner) November 19th 1797 enclosed in Portland—Camden, January 6th 1798. HO 100/75/.
23. "J.W." January 7th 1798. 620/36/227. March 9th 1798. 620/10.
24. *The Press* No. 29 December 2nd 1797.
25. *The Press* No. 61 February 17th 1798.
26. *The Press* No. 58 February 10th 1798.
27. *The Union Star* extract reprinted in RSCHC App. XXVII p. ccxx
28. *The Union Star* Ibid p. ccxviii.
29. *The Union Star* Ibid p. ccxx.
30. *The Union Star* Ibid p. ccxix.
31. The Union Star Ibid p. ccxxiii.
32. Cooke—Pelham December 14th 1797. B.M. Add. MSS 33105/262-3. See also "F.H." (F. Higgins) November 29th 1797. 620/36/266.
33. *The Times* February 1798.
34. Camden—Portland March 7th 1798. HO 100/75/183.
35. "J.W." March 9th 1798. 620/10.
36. Printed Address of County Committee of Dublin City [U.I.] March 2nd 1798. Auckland MSS BM Add. MSS 34, 454/169. A very similar version is in RSCHC App. XXIV dated six months earlier
37. Ibid. See also printed Address of County Committee of Dublin City (U.I.) February 1st 1798. 620/43/9
38. Camden—Portland January 22nd 1798. HO 100/75/29-30. Portland—Camden January 29th 1798. HO 100/75/42.
39. Camden—Portland February 8th 1798. HO 100/75/71-72.
40. Ibid.
41. Portland—Camden February 15th 1798. HO 100/75/85.
42. Reynolds *Life* passim especially I. 186.
43. Ibid I. 187-8.
44. Ibid I. p. 203-5. William Cope—Charlotte. Cope MSS Wiltshire CRO. See also Cope's and Reynolds' statements on the affair (Ibid p. 229-33, quoted in W. J. Fitzpatrick *Sham Squire* p. 233-36).
45. William Cope July 29th 1798. Cope MSS Wiltshire CRO.
46. Info. [of Thomas Reynolds] enclosed with Camden—Portland February 26th 1798. HO 100/75/8 HO 100/75/128-34. Abbreviated in RSCHC App. XVII.
47. Info. [of Thomas Reynolds] enclosed with letter of March 11th 1798, below. Cooke's original note of March 6th 1798 is in 620/332/26.
48. Cope—Cooke March 10th 1798—including ground plan of Bond's house. 620/332/26.
49. Camden—Portland March 11th 1798. HO 100/75/195.
50. DEP, FDJ & FJ March 13th, March 15th 1798.

51. Statements of Mrs. Murray "derived from Traynor's own lips" to Dr. Madden. Madden MSS TCD S.3.19–33/166.

52. Reynolds *Life* I. 197.

PART I CHAPTER 3

Chapter heading: see notes 36 and 73.

1. Ly. Sarah Napier's journal entry March 1798. Extract printed in T. Moore *Fitzgerald* II. 26.

2. Clare—Auckland March 23rd 1798. Auckland *Correspondence* III 395.

3. FJ & FDJ March 13th 1798; NCEP March 15th & 19th 1798.

4. Camden—Portland March 12th 1798. HO 100/75/213–4. Camden claimed day "passed very quietly" despite crowds.

5. "J.W." (L. McNally) March 13th 1798. 620/10.

6. See also Jane O'Beirne—Anne Tottenham [March] 1798. La Touche MSS NLI 3151/17–22.

7. William Cope March 28th 1798. Cope MSS Wiltshire CRO. Also Ly. S. Napier's journal, op. cit, II. 21–22.

8. Ly S. Napier's journal op cit II. 39.

9. FJ., FDJ & DEP March 1798 passim. The Government believed he had gone North. Cooke—Auckland March 12 1798. Keele University, Sneyd papers.

10. Jane O'Beirne—Anne Tottenham. n.d. [March 1798] La Touche MSS NLI 3151/17–22.

11. Ly S. Napier's Journal op cit II. 26.

12. Ly S. Napier's Journal op cit II. 24. The phrase was Lord Castlereagh's.

13. Ibid.

14. Ibid.

15. Ibid II. 25

16. Ibid II. 58.

17. Camden—Portland March 11th 1798. HO 100/75/195.

18. Watty Cox interviewed by Cooke. See Cooke—Wickham March 10th 1798. HO 100/75/189.

19. Camden—Portland March 13th & 16th 1798. HO 100/75/217. Documents later published in RSCHC. App. XIX.

20. John Beresford—Auckland March 15th 1798. Keele University, Sneyd papers 3/1–3.

21. Camden—Portland March 26th 1798, enclosing Attorney-General's opinion. HO 100/75/293–6.

22. Documents no. 2 & 4 RSCHC, App. XIX p. cxlvii–cxlix.

23. William Cope's endorsement on Cooke's letter of March 29th 1798 quoted in W. J. Fitzpatrick *Sham Squire* p. 237.

24. "J.W." March 13th 1798. 620/10.

25. Cooke—Auckland March 19th 1798. Auckland *Correspondence* III. 392.

26. "F.H." (F. Higgins) March 15th 1798. 620/18.

27. "B". (Boyle) March 17th 1798. 620/36/228.

28. "B". April 3rd 1798 (Ibid). Similar anonymous report of March 23rd 1798 is in 620/36/52. (cf 620/18/18).

29. "M". (unidentified) March 26th 1798. 620/36/72.

30. Clare—Auckland March 23rd 1798. Auckland *Correspondence* III. 394.

31. Cooke—Auckland March 19th 1798. Ibid III. 393.

32. Portland—Camden March 11th 1798. HO 100/75/193.

33. Pitt—Camden March 13th 1798. PRO 30/8/325.

34. Auckland wrote to Beresford and presumably also to Cooke on March 10th 1798. Only their replies are preserved. See Beresford to Auckland March 13 1798. (Keele University, Sneyd Papers) and Cooke to Auckland of "12"th March (actually later) ibid.

35. Westmorland—Beresford March 15th 1798. Beresford *Correspondence,* p. 152–3. His first letter to Cooke on the subject was not apparently written till March 19th 1798.

36. Quoted in Dunfermline, *Abercromby* p. 93. For full text see RSCHC.

37. Abercromby to his son, March 23rd 1798. op cit p. 114.

38. Adjutant-General Hewitt—Gen. Sir Wm. Fawcett March 16th 1798. SRO Melville Castle Papers, 328. Another of Abercromby's friends, Colonel Craufurd, described the order as "unguarded, and very unfortunately worded." Craufurd—Wickham March 19th 1798. HO 100/66/76. Cornwallis shared the view.

39. DNB.

40. Dunfermline p. 22–3.

41. Ibid. (Other unpublished letters to and from Dundas are preserved in the Melville Castle Papers in SRO).

42. Ibid p. 74–5; *Diary of Sir John Moore* 1–127. Camden himself said the job had "little power but great responsibility". Camden—Pitt March 26th 1798. PRO 30/8/326/277. For a fuller account of this problem, see E. Johnston *Great Britain and Ireland, 1761–1811.* A similar, though less dangerous clash between C. in C. and Viceroy, had occurred in 1774.

43. Abercromby—Elliot December 25th 1797. BM Add MSS 33, 105.

44. Elliot—Abercromby December 26th 1797. HO 100/75/317.

45. Abercromby to un-named friend in England, December 11th 1797. McPeake MSS ("Lake Letters").

46. Quoted J. Moore *Diary* I. 271, entry January 10th 1798.

47. Abercromby—Pelham January 23rd 1798. Pelham MSS BM Add MSS 33, 105/334.

48. Abercromby—Lake December 13th 1797. HO 30/66/377.

49. Abercromby—Pelham January 23rd 1798. Pelham MSS BM Add MS 33,105/334.

50. Abercromby—Duke of York February 17th 1798. Quoted in Dunfermline op cit p. 92.

51. Ibid.

52. Dunfermline op cit p. 73–4.

53. Abercromby's "Remarks upon the South of Ireland" February 23rd 1798. HO 100/75/120.

54. Abercromby—Pelham February 21st 1798. Pelham MSS BM Add MSS 33, 105/345–6. He sent a copy of this letter to Colonel Brownrigg on March 16th 1798 with a note saying that it had originally "given offence" and a special meeting of the cabinet had considered it. SRO Melville Castle Papers, 327–3.

55. Camden—Portland February 24th 1798. HO 100/75/116.

56. Camden—Portland March 15th 1798. HO 100/75/225–7; Cooke to Auckland March "12th" (sic) 1798—"When I heard of it I disbelieved. When I read it I still disbelieved. It struck me in the moment as a fatal blow to the Government." Keele, Sneyd papers 1/1.

57. Wolfe Tone's old friend, Dr. Browne of Trinity College, raised the matter. Pelham answered that the C. in C.' orders "had merely for their object the discipline of the army, than which to perfect there was not an officer better qualified." FJ March 6th 1798.

58. Camden—Portland March 15th 1798. HO 100/75/225. Camden suppressed an earlier letter to Portland on the subject out of a feeling of "delicacy" towards Abercromby.

59. Ibid.

60. Abercromby—Camden March 15th, 1798. Enclosed with above. HO 100/75/229–30.

61. Camden—Portland March 15th 1798. HO 100/35/225–7. His reply to Pitt on the 17th was more hostile to Abercromby. He saw himself in a "cruel and unexpected and un-deserved situation" because of Abercromby's "almost criminal order." PRO 30/8/326/266–9.

62. Westmorland—Cooke March 19th 1798. 620/18A/12.

63. Dundas—Abercromby March 20th 1798. Melville Castle MSS SRO 327/5.

64. FJ March 15th 1798. Printed without comment under the heading "London 10th March". The first editorial reference to the famous order was not till April 5th 1798.

65. Clare—Auckland March 23rd 1798. Auckland *Correspondence* III 393–4.

66. Pelham—Portland [not sent] marked "April" [1798] BM Add MSS 33,105 Pelham fell gravely ill just *before* the crisis broke and was not much involved. Abercromby himself, and Moore in his turn, underestimated the force of the London-Irish lobby, and misunderstood Clare's role and that of Lords Auckland and Westmoreland. See Dunfermline p. 13, Sir J. Moore *Diary* p. 1, 284.

67. Beresford—Auckland March 24th 1798. Keele, Sneyd Papers 4/2.

68. Printed copy in NLI Melville MSS, 54A.

69. For text of Proclamation of March 18th 1797 see RSCHC App. x. p. lxxxvi. In fact Abercromby was not entirely accurate. General Johnson was not stopped from burning houses. See Johnson's letter in PRO I 1A/40. III.

70. J. Moore *Diary* I. 287.

71. Hewitt—Fawcett March 16th 1798. SRO., Melville Castle Papers 328/3. Lake—Knox March 2nd 1798. NLI 56/144. Portland [to Dundas]March 21st 1798. SRO Melville Castle Papers 327/6.

72. Lake—Knox January 7th 1798. NLI 56/121.

73. Lake—Knox February 25th 1798. NLI 56/143.

74. Beresford—Auckland March 24th 1798. Keele, Sneyd Papers 4/2.

75. Ross—Downshire March 27th 1798. PRONI., Downshire Papers, D.607/1456.

76. Craufurd to Wickham March 19th 1798. HO 100/66/76. J. Moore *Diary* I. 283-4.

77. Pelham's letter to Portland [not sent] marked "April" (1798). Pelham Papers, BM Add MSS 33,105

78. Craufurd—Wickham n.d. [April, 1798] HO 100/66/204); J. Moore *Diary* I. 288. Gen. Hope, just returned to England, wrote in still stronger terms on April 3rd 1798. NLI Melville MSS 54A/132.

79. Portland (to Dundas?) March 29th 1798. NLI, Melville MSS, 54A/129.

80. Camden—Portland March 26th 1798. HO 100/75/300. A fuller account of his personal feelings is in Camden—Pitt March 26th 1798. PRO 30/8/326/277. In the next fortnight Camden made half-hearted efforts to take back his decision of March 26th, but his Irish advisers gave him no encouragement, and anyway Abercromby was adamant.

81. Camden—Portland March 30th 1798. HO 100/75/343.

82. Camden—Portland March 28th 1798. HO 100/80/154-9 enclosing Fitzgerald's report p. 154.

83. Ibid p. 155 enclosing Lord Portarlington's report.

84. Ibid p. 156 enclosing Sir John Carden's report.

85. Camden—Portland March 30th 1798. HO 100/75/343.

86. Clare—Auckland n.d. (April 4th 1798). Auckland *Correspondence* III. 396.

87. Cooke—Auckland March 24th 1798. Keele, Sneyd papers 5/1.

88. Two letters of Camden—Portland on March 30th 1798. HO 100/75/346; HO 100/80/160. For text of the Proclamation of March 30th 1798 see RSCHC., App. XXXVI p. ccxcv. For its scope see Dunfermline p. 128.

89. J. Moore op cit p. 282; Camden—Portland March 31st 1798. HO 100/75/359.

90. Clare—Auckland n.d. April 4th, 1798. Auckland *Correspondence* III. 395-6.

91. Lees—Auckland April 2nd 1798. BM Add MSS 34, 454/197.

PART I CHAPTER 4
At head of chapter: *Songs and Recitations of Ireland* II. 27.

1. RSCHC App. XXV.

2. See Chapter 3 notes 24, 26, 28.

3. Madden *United Irishmen* IV. 227-247. The Sheares went to Wexford apparently to organise the movement there.

4. Ibid IV. 1-52.

5. RSCHC App. XXV; Farrell *Carlow* p. 64.

6. Fitzgeralds, Connollys, Keatings, Brownes, Lawless etc.

7. Reynolds *Life* I. 213. He lent Lord Edward 50 guineas in gold—and in return was given a letter of recommendation. 620/37/37.

8. Reynolds *Life* I. 214–60.

9. M. Leadbeater *Papers* I. "Brownie" was an alternative to "Moiley", presumably a bogeyman. There were frequent assassinations according to Farrell *Carlow* p. 51.

10. M. Byrne *Memoirs* I. 21.

11. Farrell *Carlow* p. 65.

12. Ibid p. 71–3.

13. Handbill of March 17th 1798 (St Patrick's Day) RSCHC App. XXV.

14. The date for invasion was mid-March according "F.H."—Cooke February 21st 1798. 620/18.

15. See Farrell's view *Carlow* p. 77.

16. Military commanders set their own dates.

17. Camden—Portland April 23rd 1798. HO 100/76/123.

18. W. Wellesley Pole—Mornington June 1st 1798. BM Add MSS 37, 308/114.

19. Ibid.

20. Camden—Portland April 23rd 1798. HO 100/75/129.

21. "J.W." April 8th 1798. 620/10.

22. Ibid.

23. Kemmis—Cooke March 28th 1798. 620/36/92.

24. Camden—Portland April 23rd, 1768. HO 100/76/127.

25. Ibid. See also Auckland—Mornington. BM Add MSS 37, 308.

26. Sir J. Moore *Diary* I. 289.

27. Abercromby's order dated April 3rd 1798. Four thousand copies printed. HO 100/80/177.

28. Camden—Portland April 23rd 1798. HO 100/76/122–6.

29. Camden—Pitt April 25th 1798. PRO/30/8/326.

30. Sir C. Coote April 15th 1798. 620/36/172.

31. Sir C. Asgill—Abercromby April 17th 1798. Castlereagh *Correspondence* I. 185.

32. See note 28.

33. Asgill's proclamation ibid p. 186–7.

34. W. W. Pole—[May-June]. BM Add MSS 37, 308/114/5.

35. Ibid.

36. Sir J. Moore, *Diary* I. 289.

37. Ibid p. 290.

38. Camden—Portland April 28th 1798. HO 100/80. Dundas—Abercromby April 23rd 1798. Castlereagh *Correspondence* I 187–8.

39. Leadbeater MSS. (Pakenham Collection) II. 208–9.

40. See informer's report in 620/51/122. In fact he was a loyalist. See Keating's own statements in 620/40/143 and 620/51/131.

41. See note 39.

42. Reynold's *Life* I. 223–4.

43. Ibid p. 224–6.

44. Ibid p. 225–229.

45. Ibid p. 228–230.

46. T. Fitzgerald December 20th 1802 quoted Madden I. 342. cf 620/37/118. His bill to Govt. is in 620/40/81, 620/57/108.

47. Col. Campbell April 22nd 1798. NAM Nugent MSS MM 174/425–7.

48. DEP April 24th 1798.

49. Dr. Drennan April 24th 1798. *Letters* p. 273.

50. Ld Wycombe—Ld Holland April 28th 1798. BM MSS 51, 683.

51. In Westmeath. *The Press* January 11th 1798. See also DEP September 23rd 1797.
52. See note 50.
53. Ibid.
54. Castlereagh—Lake April 25th 1798. Castlereagh *Correspondence* I. 189.
55. Lees—Auckland April 13th 1798. BM Add MSS 34, 494/218.
56. Ross—Downshire. Downshire MSS PRONI.
57. Lake—Pelham April 16th 1797. BM Add MSS 3310/3.
58. Flogging was still to be regarded as essential for military discipline for many years. See debate in House of Commons June 1815.
59. Flogging had not been used to discover arms before this—in Leinster at any rate—on an *official* basis. See DEP September 23rd 1797. cf DEP February 1st, March 20th 1798.
60. Asgill—Abercromby April 17th 1798. Castlereagh *Correspondence* I. 184–5.
61. Leadbeater MSS (Pakenham Collection) II. 208–10.
62. Reynolds *Life* I. 237.
63. See Anon's information to Govt. May 7th 1798. 620/37/35. Pike heads cost 2s 2d–4s 4d depending on quality, according to info. 620/36/218.
64. Leadbeater MSS (Pakenham Collection) II. 211–12. Printed version gives opposite sense.
65. T. Fitzgerald December 20th 1798 quoted Madden I. 342–3. See also Farrell p. 75.
66. Col. Campbell May 14th, 15th 1798. 620/37/67 & 78.
67. Anon. information May 14th 1798. 620/3/32/5.
68. Lecky IV. 265. Note the "scene of horrors" was not in fact opened till three weeks after the Proclamation of March 30th.

PART I CHAPTER 5
At head of chapter: D. O'Connell March 1st 1798 Fitz-Simons Papers (by kind permission of Lt. Col. M. O'Connell, Glencullen Co. Dublin).
1. Camden—Portland May 11th 1798. HO 100/76/170.
2. The United Irishmen claimed at the time that the Government's aim was to *provoke* a rising. See their handbill of March 13th. The legend has persisted to this day despite all evidence of the Government's confidential documents to the contrary, e.g. Camden—Portland May 21st 1798 "Large guards will be mounted . . . I doubt not by such precautions even the attempts to produce an insurrection will be prevented . . ." HO 100/76/236.
3. W. Cope [June-July] Cope MSS. Wiltshire CRO. Fitzpatrick *Sham Squire* is in error. See HO 100 75/175.
4. Confessions of Peter Germane and others. 620/37/48–50; 620/52/75.
5. Reynolds—Cope [May 5th] 1798 quoted Fitzpatrick *Sham Squire* p. 243.
6. See note 1. (it squares with Reynolds' own account in *Life* I. 249–51, 256 foll.)
7. See note 1.
8. Beresford—Auckland May 9th 1798. Auckland *Correspondence* II. 412.
9. Lees—Auckland April 2nd, May 1st, 3rd, 7th 1798. BM Add MSS 34, 454.
10. FJ April 24th, 26th 1798. Clare's own account is in Clare—Pitt PRO 30/8/326.
11. FJ May 12th 1798. A copy is in the NLI Proclamation file.
12. Cooke—Auckland May 1st 1798. BM Add MSS 34, 454/237.
13. The severe measures had alarmed the Dublin leaders. April 22nd 1798. 620/10.
14. See Higgins' letters to Cooke of January 5th, March 28th, May 1st, June 5th, 30th 1798. 620/18. cf HO 100/761.
15. Madden I. 393–4, IV. 577. Fitzpatrick *Sham Squire* p. 127 foll.
16. "F.H."—Cooke May 1st 1798. 620/18.
17. Confidential memo of May 21st 1798. 620/51/13 & 16. Published account in RSCHC App. XX.
18. Camden—Portland May 14th 1798. HO 100/76/170.

19. W. Farrell p. 82. cf "J.W." [May] 620/10 and many other reports of demoralisation e.g. 620/37/13.

20. The last handbill was dated late April.

21. J. Cormick's evidence RSCHC App. XXXII.

22. "F.H."—Cooke May 1st 1798. 620/18. Confirmed by Neilson RSCHC App. XXI.

23. T. Moore Fitzgerald I. 167.

24. Ibid p. 168.

25. Ibid p. 174-5.

26. Hughes' evidence RSCHL App. I.

27. Ibid.

28. Magan's story was broadly confirmed by the captured message from the Dublin executive to Ulster received on May 10th 1798. Printed in RSCHC App. XIV.

29. Ibid.

30. Handbill of March 31st 1798. RSCHC App. XXX. cf 620/43/4.

31. Ibid.

32. RSCHC App. XX p. clxix.

33. J. McManus—P. Gallagher May 2nd 1798. RSCHC App. XXXIV.

34. Attached to Sirr info.

35. Byrne *Memoirs* passim. Cullen MSS TCD. S.3.19 For Wexford liberals see Madden V. 461-69.

36. Camden—Portland May 11th 1798. HO 100/76/73.

37. E. Bayly—Sir J. Parnell September 21st 1797. 620/18A/6.

38. J. Hardy—Cooke January 16th 1798. 620/35/48.

39. Cullen MSS TCD S.3.29.

40. T. King March 25th 1798. 620/3/51/41. See also 620/36/105

41. J. Hardy January 19th, February 4th 1798. 620/35/48 and 620/35/115.

42. Lord Monck March 19th 1798. 620/36/27.

43. Magistrates' report of February 20th 1798. 620/35/146.

44. T. Parsons—L. Parsons April 17th, 24th 1798. Parsons MSS NLI cf Cullen MSS TCD S.3.19.

45. Info. of May 31st 1798. 620/3 32/6. cf captured Wicklow documents printed RSCHC App. XIX.

46. DEP May 15th 1798.

47. J. Hardy May 21st 22nd, 1798. 620/37/127 & 128.

48. Capt. J. Edwards May 17th 1798. 620/37/99.

49. Capt. Edwards May 30th, June 6th, July 25th 1798. 620/37/217, 620/38/63, 620/39/118.

PART I CHAPTER 6

At head of chapter: Zimmerman p. 133.

1. Ly Louisa Connolly—Wm. Ogilvie May 21st 1798 printed T. Moore *Fitzgerald* II. 95-101.

2. Piano had just been introduced into Theatre Royal. SNL January 29th 1798. For atmosphere of that week see Ric. Farrell MS Diary May 18th 1798 NLI 11, 941.

3. Barrington *Sketches* p. 104-7 [c.1900 edition].

4. FJ May 10th 1798.

5. "F.H."—Cooke May 18th 1798. 620/18.

6. "J.W."—Cooke [May] 1798. 620/10.

7. See note 9.

8. See accounts of Magan's services "F.H."—Cooke June 30th 1798; November 1st 1801. 620/18 and 620/49/137.

9. Emmet's statement in *Memoire* p. 33. See Neilson's ibid.

10. "F.H."—Cooke June 30th 1798. 620/18.

11. Neilson's statement in RSCHL App. V. T. Moore *Fitzgerald* p. 180. Sirr's statement quoted Madden II 408.

12. See note 10.

13. RSCHL App. XVIII. For Govt.'s glosses on them see HO 100/76 208.

14. T. Moore op cit p. 180–2. Madden II 406–8.

15. Murphy's own account published in Madden II. 412–6.

16. Ibid. See also Beresford—Auckland May 20th 1798. Auckland *Correspondence* II. 413–15.

17. Advt. in FDJ May 17th 1798.

18. See note 15.

19. See note 15.

20. Official version of capture published in *The Express* May 26th 1798.

21. See note 15.

22. FJ May 22, 1798.

23. Ibid & FDJ May 22nd 1798. cf Cooke's account in Auckland *Correspondence* II. 417–18.

24. Major Sirr—Ryan's son December 29th 1838. Castlereagh *Correspondence* I. 463–4.

25. FDJ May 22nd 1798.

26. *The Comet*, September 11th 1831, p. 152 quoted Fitzpatrick p. 116. See also Madden II. 407–8.

27. "F.H."—Cooke May 20th 1798. 620/18.

28. See note 1. and see Camden—Portland May 20th 1798. HO 100/76 203.

29. Col. Napier—Wm. Ogilvie May 21st 1798. Printed T. Moore *Fitzgerald* II. 102.

30. Clare—Auckland May 21st 1798. *Auckland Correspondence* I. 421–3.

31. No warning was sent to London, at any rate.

32. Cooke—Sirr [May 16th or 17th 1798] Sirr MSS TCD N.4.5/1. There is *no* evidence of a tip-off after Lord Edward returned to Thomas St.

33. Col. L'Estrange report May 20th 1798. HO 100/76/228. The Sheares' house was no. 128 (Madden IV. 340).

34. Armstrong's evidence at Sheares' trial. RSCHC App. XX.

35. In 1843 Capt. Armstrong came to see Madden and denied that he'd fondled the children. "Indeed I never was fond of children." Madden IV. 372 etc.

36. Camden—Portland May 21st 1798. HO 100/76/236.

37. See garbled version quoted by Bp Percy May 24th 1798. BM Add MSS 32,335/234.

38. Facsimile printed in RSCHC.

39. Camden—Portland May 20th 1798. HO. The other informers were N. Magin of Saintfield and S. Sproule of Dublin.

40. Camden—Portland May 11th, 14th, 18th 1798. HO 100/76/170, 190, 194.

41. Beresford—Auckland May 20th 1798. Auckland *Correspondence* II. 413–16.

42. Lees—Auckland May 22nd 1798. BM Add MSS 34, 454/266.

43. Two days later. DEP May 26th 1796.

44. Castlereagh—Lord Mayor May 21, 1798. Seward *Collectanea* iii. 238.

45. Col. Napier—Wm. Ogilvie May 21st 1798. Printed Moore *Fitzgerald* II. 101–2.

46. DEP, FJ May 22nd 1798.

47. Ric. Farrell *Diary* entries May 21st–23rd 1798. NLI 11, 941.

48. Beresford—Auckland May 23rd 1798. BM Add MSS 34, 454/272.

49. Lees—Auckland May 22nd, 23rd 1798. Ibid p. 266, 275.

50. Camden—Portland May 22nd 1798. HO 100/76/247–8.

51. Capt. T. Pakenham—Castlereagh April 1798. Castlereagh *Correspondence* I. 191–3.

52. General Vallancey's plan enclosed by Lake on June 14th 1798. 620/38/153.

53. DEP May 8th, FJ May 10th 1798.

54. Vallancey—Castlereagh April 14th 1798. Castlereagh *Correspondence* I. 190–1.

55. Cooke—Wickham May 22nd 1798. HO 100/76/244.

56. Cooke—Wickham May 26th 1798. HO 100/76/289.

57. Ibid.
58. Pitt, however, had not yet informed the Castle of the proposal. See Bolton *Union* p. 53.
59. Camden—Portland May 21st, 22nd 1798. HO 100/76/236, 248.
60. Sproule—Lees marked "rec'd ¼ past 4—23rd May [1798]. For Mr. Cooke immediate". 620/51/18.
61. Sproule—Cooke Monday [May 21st 1798]. 620/51/21.
62. Sproule—Lees May 23rd [1798]. 620/51/19.
63. Sproule—Cooke "9 at night" [May 23rd 1798]. 620/51/25.
64. "F.H."—Cooke May 20th 1798. 620/18.
65. Also an *earlier* report of Sproule enclosed in HO 100/76/122.
66. Anon. information of May 23rd 1798. 620/37/129, 130, 131. Information of May 24th 1798. 620/37/148.
67. Information to J. Ormsby May 23rd 1798. 620/37/131.
68. See Pt II Ch. 1 note 36.
69. Sir J. Barrington *Rise and Fall* p. 356-7.
70. Ibid p. 356.
71. Ibid p. 358 cf. FDJ May 24th 1798.
72. SNL, HJ May 25th 1798.
73. FJ May 29th, 31st 1798.
74. Ibid.
• 75. Bp Percy to his wife May 24th 1798. BM Add MSS 32, 335/23-4.
76. Musgrave himself saw the lights. *Rebellion* I. 267. For chalk marks see ibid p. 261.
77. Ld Wycombe—Ld Holland May 17th 1798. BM Add MSS 51, 684.
78. Musgrave *Rebellion* I. 264.
79. Ibid p. 262.
80. Ibid p. 259.
81. Ibid p. 262, 265.
82. Various informers' reports expecially "J.W." [May 24th 1798] 620/10.
83. Watty Cox's *Irish Magazine* 1807 p. 321-4.
84. Ibid.

PART II CHAPTER 1

At head of chapter : Zimmerman p. 259.
1. P. O'Kelly *Rebellion* p. 43-9. Fullest account of Kildare United plans.
2. Capt. Barker May 24th 1798. 620/37/159.   C/M evidence TCD G2 9a.
3. G. Lambert May 24th, 26th 1798. 620/37/138, 171.
4. Capt. Barker loc cit. Mrs. Mary Sutton's account, Sutton MSS.
5. HJ May 25th; FOJ May 26th 1798.
6. Byrne (Cullen) MSS PROI M 5892 a 1. FJ, FDJ May 26th 1798. For United plan see captured rebel's info., BM 33105/374. Also O'Kelly p. 43-62.
7. Neilson's evidence, RSCHL App. V. cf 620/38/67 plan for street fighting.
8. T. Moore *Fitzgerald* II. 213-14.
9. RSCHL App. VIII cf. 620/3/32/23. Reynolds claimed Cox was author.
10. "FH" May 18th 1798. 620/18.
11. T. Moore II. 210-13.
12. Madden I. 414-16; O'Kelly p. 21; Alexander *Rebellion* p. 22.
13. Reynolds I. 22.
14. See his letters to Govt. esp. 620/40/543. For Esmonde see O'Kelly p. 62.
15. O'Kelly p. 43, 58. Musgrave I. 289-300.
16. Gen. Dundas May 16th 1798. 620/37/90.
17. Barking May 9th 1798. 620/37/8. FDJ May 5th, 22nd, 24th 1798. Weldon MS diary entry May 21st 1798. See also 620/39/82.

18. See note 16.
19. Weldon MS diary entry May 24th 1798.
20. Musgrave I. 289–300.
21. So it appears from Weldon MS diary. See Mus. I 288 foll.
22. Farrell p. 224.
23. B. Duggan's accounts Madden MSS TCD S. 3. 19–22.
24. R. Griffith—Pelham June 4th 1798. BM Add MSS 33105/380–2.
25. Musgrave I. 277 cf Patrickson—Downshire May 24th 1798. PRONI D 607.
26. Byrne (Cullen) MSS. PROI M5692 a/1.
27. Ibid; SNL May 24th 1798; Musgrave I. 273–4; HO 100/76/258–265.
28. SNL May 24th 1798.
29. O'Kelly p. 58. Acc FDJ & FJ it was Cork coach, Leadbeater MSS Limerick coach, Gordon (p. 84) *both* coaches.
30. See note 24.
31. Ibid.
32. Ibid.
33. See note 23.
34. Musgrave I. 283–98. Cf. Jones p. 87–93. R. Griffith—Pelham July 13th 1798. BM Add MSS 33,106/10.
35. Camden—Portland May 26th 1798. HO 100/76/291–2. FJ May 26th 1798.
36. Musgrave I. 286. Lord Gosford—Camden May 24th 1798. HO 100/76/267.
37. Lord Gosford loc cit.
38. Lord Gosford July 15th 1798. 620/39/76. Musgrave I. 288.
39. Musgrave I. 319–20. See also 620/37/8.
40. Ibid.
41. Reynolds I. 225.
42. Dundas—Castlereagh May 25th 1798. HO 100/76/277. Musgrave I. 320 foll.
43. FJ May 26th 1798.
44. See note 42.
45. See note 42 and Leadbeater MSS II 214–15. Musgrave I. 310–12, 321–2.
46. Leadbeater MSS loc cit.
47. Robinson—Ld Aldborough June 5th 1798. 620.
48. Leadbeater MSS.
49. Musgrave I. 310–6.
50. Farrell p. 62–4.
51. Ibid p. 84–90.

PART II CHAPTER 2.
At head of chapter: FDJ July 12th 1798.
1. Camden—Portland May 24th 1798. HO 100/76/264.
2. Beresford—Auckland May 24th 1798. Auckland *Correspondence* I. 427–8.
3. Ibid.
4. Barrington *Memoirs* II. 260.
5. Cullen MSS PROI M 5842 a/1; FJ May 26th 1798.
6. Info. of Thomas Keogh [May 1798]. 620/52/156.
7. Musgrave I. 274.
8. Barrington *Memoirs* II. 259–62.
9. DEP June 14th 1798; Musgrave I. 274–5; Auckland I. 428.
10. FJ May 26th 1798.
11. HJ May 25th 1798.
12. Richard Farrell MSS NLI 11, 941.

13. RSCHC App. XXXVIII.
14. Text quoted Musgrave I. 271-3.
15. HJ May 30th 1798.
16. See note 8.
17. FJ May 29th 1798.
18. SNL June 12th 1798.
19. DEP May 31st 1798.
20. FJ May, June 1798.
21. Camden—Portland May 23rd, 24th 1798. HO/80/320; HO 100/76/258-9.
22. Camden—Portland May 26th 1798. HO 100/76/291-2.
23. Ibid.
24. *The Times* May 30th 1798.
25. Beresford—Auckland May 28th 1798. Auckland I 430-1
26 Musgrave I. 270.
27. FJ May 29th 1798.
28. FJ & FDJ May 26th 1798; Musgrave I. 277.
29. Musgrave I. 288-94; Jane Davis' deposition in TCD MSS G.2.19; other accounts in 620/40/174.
30. Musgrave I. 301-3; Mrs. Crawford's affidavit August 20th 1798, TCD MSS G.2.19.
31. Cooke—Wickham May 6th 1798. HO/100/76/289.
32. Camden—Portland May 24th, 25th 1798. HO 100/76 261-5, 269-70, 274-6.
33. Ibid.
34. DEP March 8th, 10th, 13th; Madden II. 297 foll; Howell *State Trials* XXVI-XXVII.
35. T. Moore *Fitzgerald* II. 20-21.
36. Howell op cit; King—Cooke January 6th, 12th, 21st 1798. HO 100/75/110; 620/18A/14.
37. Portland—Camden April 20th 1798. HO 100 76/95. The coat had also been worn by O'Connor, see Portland—Camden March 7th 1798. 620/18a/1.
38. Text printed in DEP May 29th 1798.
39. Howell op cit; Madden II 307.
40. Madden II. 303.
41. Grenville's intelligence May 4th 1798 in HMC Dropmore IV, 185.
42. DEP May 26th 1798.
43. Stanhope III. 129.
44. Stanhope III. 130-1.
45. *The Times* May-June 1798.
46. Wickham—Cooke May 28th 1798. "Town is not yet recovered from its panic." HO 100/76/304.
47. Musgrave I. 302; FJ June 7th 1798.
48. Lord Portarlington May 25th 1798. 620/37/161.
49. Maj. Leatham May 26th 1798. 620/37/179.
50. Col. Gordon May 26th 1798. 620/37/167.
51. George Cummins C/M TCD MSS G2-19-35.
52. Ly Louisa Connolly June 1st, 1798 quoted T. Moore *Fitzgerald* II. 112-18.
53. Edenderry magistrates May 27th 1798. 620/18/11 6.
54. Musgrave I. 310.
55. Ibid I. 309-14.
56. Ld Aldborough May 27th 1798. 620/37/182. Musgrave I. 299-301.
57. Leadbeater MSS Vol. II. Musgrave I. 339.
58. Rev. J. McGhee May 25th 1798. HO 100/76/277. Gordon *Rebellion* p. 91-7.
59. Hay p. 87; Musgrave I. 383.
60. Hay p. 76, 67; Gordon p. 222.
61. Camden—Portland May 28th, 29th 1798. HO 100/80/332; 244-7.

PART II CHAPTER 3

At head of chapter: Zimmerman p. 142–3.

1. Handcock's narrative BM Add MSS 38,102/13. Musgrave I. 471–2.

2. Watty Cox's *Irish Magazine* 1807 p. 417 foll.; Cloney p. 3.

3. Musgrave I. 393–4.

4. Handcock loc cit p. 9–10. DEP July 18th, 30th; FDJ August 1st 1793. Bishop of Wexford's *Relatio* in Wexford Diocesan Archives.

5. Handcock loc cit. John Colclough to Caesar Colclough, May 1st 1797 "I myself knew barley sold this year for five shillings per barrel which last year brought twenty-five shillings and everything else in like proportion"—McPeake MSS. And similar letter, S. Elmes, April 21st 1798 (Elmes MSS): "The farming business that flourished those years past is now declining fast . . . dairies are the only thing now that will stand."

6. J. Colclough letters in McPeake MSS 1797–8; Elmes MSS Letters 1797–8. The malt tax, according to the latter, had crippled the barley trade.

7. *The Times* 1797–8 foll. passim.

8. See note 6.

9. Capt. McManus—Cooke March 26th 1798. 620/36/78.

10. Kemmis—Cooke March 28th 1798. 620/36/92.

11. C. Colclough April 23rd 1798. BM Add MSS 33105.

12. Dr. Cleaver May 8th 1798. ISPO 30/191.

13. Handcock loc cit. Gordon p. 103–5. NB Ld Mountnorris specifically asked Govt. *not* to send troops.

14. Ibid.

15. Cullen MSS in TCD passim, summarised Madden IV. 550–1.

16. "JW"—Ld Downshire (sent on to Pitt) March 30th 1795. PRO 30/8/327/321–2. Madden IV. 464–8.

17. For political factions in Wexford see J. Colclough letters in McPeake MSS, Barrington *Personal Sketches* and FDJ August 10th 1797.

18. In November 1797 nineteen of the northern parishes were proclaimed. Musgrave I. 394–5. cf Miles Byrne.

19. Perry's confession May 26th 1798. 620/37/169. Byrne p. 6–21.

20. Musgrave II. 298, 331.

21. RSCHC App. XVI.

22. e.g. in nearby Carlow, where there was a Grand Lodge. FDJ Jan 13th 1798. And see Cooke—Pelham June 3rd 1798. BM Add MSS 33105.

23. Byrne p. 8–9.

24. Gowan claimed lodges had been set up at Carnew, Tinahely—in Wicklow—and Mt Nebo. There is no other record of their establishment. Gowan *Orangeism* p. 237–8.

25. See H. Senior *Orangeism* p. 8.

26. W. Morton—Lees May 22nd 1798. 620/37/125.

27. "A.B."'s Info. May 21st 1798. 620/3/32/6. M. Byrne p. 27–8. O'Neil, Graham etc. surrendered c. May 16th. See FDJ May 17th and DEP May 19th 1798.

28. Perry's confession Gorey May 26th 1798. 620/37/169. J. Kildal—Lees May 24th 1798. 620/37/141.

29. C. Morton May 24th 1798. 620/37/139; 620/37/141. cf Byrne p. 24.

30. J. Kildal—Lees May 24th 1798. 620/37/141.

31. Camolin cavalry order book quoted Wheeler and Bradley *Wexford* p. 81–2.

32. Hay p. 70–2. Alexander p. 28–9. "Severities" at New Ross may have started earlier.

33. Gordon p. 105–6. Hay p. 78.

34. Cloney p. 14–15. Hay p. 78.

35. Cullen MSS quoted Madden IV. 454. Cloney p. 14.

36. See Mus. I. 401, App. XVII. 10 priests had already signed address of loyalty. FDJ May 3rd 1798.

37. Mus. II. App. XVIII. 1. Acc. Gordon p. 107 "a fanatic".

38. Musgrave II. App. XVIII.

39. Madden IV. 475.

40. Cullen MSS TCD S.3.19. 12–14.

41. Ibid Cloney p. 10–11 Cf. Hay p. 76, 87 & Byrne p. 35, 6.

42. Byrne I. 29–31; Hay p. 87; Mrs Adams diary printed Croker *Researches* App. p. 347 Camolin cavalry order book p. 83.

43. Cullen MSS loc cit p. 14–16.

44. Camolin cavalry order book op cit p. 83–4. Gordon p. 107. Taylor p. 25.

45. Camolin cavalry order book op cit p. 85–6.

46. Camolin cavalry order book op cit p. 80. Byrne p. 34.

47. Musgrave I. 407–8.

48. Deposition of Wheatley in Musgrave App. XVIII. 2; affidavit of T. Burrowes App. XVIII. 4. Cullen MSS loc cit p. 19–31.

49. Deposition of E. Williams in Musgrave App. XVIII. 5.

50. Camolin cavalry order book op cit p. 85–6.

51. Ibid. T. Burrowes affidavit in Musgrave App. XVIII. 4.

52. Cullen MSS loc cit p. 23, 24. See also Ed. Roche's information August 25th 1798. 620/39/206.

53. Hay p. 78–9.

54. Ibid.

55. Hay 79–81.

56. Mrs. Adams' diary op cit p. 347.

57. Ibid.

58. Musgrave I. 419, 471.

59. Hay p. 82. Mrs Browning's diary printed Wheeler and Broadley Wexford p. 165–6. Jones *Impartial narrative* p. 80.

60. Hay p. 62. Cullen op cit p. 35.

61. The North Cork had arrived on April 26th see Musgrave.

62. Cullen MSS loc cit. p. 28–37.

63. Col. Foote's private a/c quoted Musgrave I. 421–2. Cf his official letter the day of the battle. Col. P. Foote—Ld Castlereagh May 27th 1798. 620/37/177.

64. Cullen MSS loc cit p. 35–7.

65. See note 63.

66. Mrs. Adams' diary op cit p. 348. Hay p. 65–6.

67. Mrs. Adams' diary ibid.

68. Ibid. For thatch stripping see claim for £64 compensation from shoemaker J. Edwards. 620/61/69.

69. Gordon p. 124.

70. Ibid p. 126–8. Camolin cavalry order book op cit p. 87.

71. J. Jones *Narrative* p. 320–1. Hay p. 90. Musgrave I. 428.

72. T. Hancock *Peace* p. 62–3.

73. Ibid.

74. Handcock. BM Add MSS 38, 102.

75. Snowe *Transactions* p. 5–8. Musgrave I. 429. Handcock (loc cit) estimated the insurgents' members at 5–10,000.

76. Musgrave I. 430.

77. Snowe op cit p. 7–8.

78. Ibid p. 8. Handcock op cit p. 31–3.

79. At Ferns, Clonegal, Enniscorthy and Wexford. See note 63.

PART II CHAPTER 4.
At head of chapter: BM Add MSS 51,684.

1. "A strong position" acc. Capt. Blanche's official report after battle. PRO/WO 40/11. See also Mus. I. 366.

2. Information from G. Lambert June 15th 1796. 620/31/139.

3. Cummins' C/M in TCD MSS G.2.190. Jones p. 162. Capt. Blanche loc cit. See also Alexander—Pelham June 3rd 1798. BM Add. MSS 33, 105/374.

4. Capt. Blanche loc cit. Jones p. 162. Evidence of highlander at Lawless' C/M July 2nd 1798. TCD G.2.19a.

5. Capt. Blanche loc cit.

6. Jones p. 163. Musgrave I. 366.

7. Capt. Blanche loc cit. Jones p. 166.

8. Clare—Auckland [May 30th] 1798. Auckland Correspondence III. 438.

9. 620/37/218.

10. Clare—Auckland op cit. Beresford—Auckland May 28th, 30th 1798. Auckland Correspondence III. 432–4. Cf. O'Kelly p. 69.

11. Camden—Portland May 29th, 31st 1798. HO 100/76/319, 80/340.

12. Camden—Portland ibid. O'Kelly p. 75–8.

13. Clare—Auckland op cit.

14. Sir J. Moore Diary I. 291–2.

15. M-Gen. Duff May 29th 1798. 620/37/211. Camden—Portland loc cit.

16. M-Gen. Duff loc cit. Musgrave I. 304–5.

17. M-Gen. Duff loc cit. Jones Narrative p. 137. Musgrave p. 323–4. Beresford loc cit.

18. Jones p. 138.

19. Madden MSS TCD S.3.19–22/275.

20. Camden—Pitt. PRO 30/8/32. Beresford—Auckland May 30th 1798. op cit. Camden—Portland May 31st 1798. HO 100/76/322.

21. M. Leadbeater's diary. Leadbeater MSS II. 214–21. A. Shackleton quoted Hancock Peace p. 107–8, 111.

22. Ibid.

23. A. Shackleton op cit p. 112–5. M. Leadbeater MSS II. 234.

24. M. Leadbeater Papers p. 99–101.

25. A. Shackleton op cit p. 112–5. M. Leadbeater MSS II. 251.

26. Musgrave I. 315. See also L-Col. Dunne—Lake May 29th 1798. 620/37/209.

27. Musgrave op cit. Cf. R. Marshall—Knox May 30th 1798. NLI 56.

28. Col. Longfield—Dundas May 29th 1798. 620/37/208.

29. Col. Longfield loc cit. Lake's orders were not to take prisoners. See R. Marshall loc cit.

30. R. Griffith—Pelham June 4th, 25th 1798. BM Add MSS 33, 105/446; 33, 106/4–7.

31. Gen. Lake—Pelham January 31st 1798. BM Add MSS 33, 105/336–8.

32. Clare—Auckland [May 30th 1798] op cit.

33. Cooke—Wickham. June 2nd 1798. HO 100/77/21.

34. Beresford—Auckland. June 1st 1798. Auckland Correspondence III. 442.

35. For account of Orangemen in 1798 see Senior Orangeism passim.

36. Cooke—Wickham May 28th 1798. HO 100/80/336.

37. Cooke—Wickham May 30th 1798. HO 100/76/313.

38. Camden—Portland June 1st 1798. HO 100/80/350. [Magin's] information enclosed with Camden—Portland June 5th 1798. HO 100/77/39 foll.

PART II CHAPTER 5
At head of chapter: Paddy's Resource, Belfast 1796 p. 7–8.

1. Ulster provincial and county reports from N. Magin. April 14th 1797–May 31st 1798.

Enclosed Camden—Portland HO 100/76–77. Edited, with names omitted, RSCHC. App.
XIV. For Magin's services see J. Pollock—Cooke July 13th 1798. 620/18A/4. N.M. was paid
off with £700 in August 1798. acc. secret service money list, RIA MSS.

2. Enclosed May 16th 1798. HO 100/76/222.

3. Camden—Portland June 5th 1798. Enc. N.M.'s report of provincial meeting of May
29th HO 100/77/44–5.

4. Ibid.

5. Until June 6th. Castlereagh—Nugent June 6th 1798. Nugent MSS NAM.

6. J. Hughes evidence August 3rd 1798. RSCHL App. I. J. Pollock—Cooke June 19th,
26th August 1798. 620/38/182; 620/39/213.

7. [Fox] letter c. 1799. 620/4/41. Jemmy Hope's account. Madden *Down and Antrim* p. 42–7.

8. See esp. letters of c. June 1797, May 12th and June 18th 1798 in Madden MSS TCD quoted
M. McNeil *Mary Ann McCracken* p. 151, 166–7 and 177–8. See also Jemmy Hope quoted
Madden *Down and Antrim*, p. 108 etc.

9. Fox loc cit.

10. Quoted Madden *Down and Antrim* p. 37.

11. Nugent—Knox June 6th and [June 7th] 1798 NLI 56/178, 184.

12. "Swineish" was a reference to Burke's celebrated pamphlet see E. Thompson *Working
Class* p. 90.

13. DEP June 16th 1798. For prosperity of North see H. Alexander—Pelham June 10th
1798. BM Add MSS 33,105/400 foll. J. Hamilton—Ld Abercorn May 9th 1798. Abercorn
MSS, PRONI 1.A.27.

14. C. Jackson *Narrative*, p. 2; Hay p. 94.

15. Rev. T. Handcock loc cit p. 32.

16. Snowe op cit p. 7–10; Capt. Philip Hay [1799] information. 620/56/98. Musgrave I.
420, 437; Jones *Narrative* p. 101 foll.

17. Ibid.

18. Ibid. Handcock loc cit. p. 38.

19. Handcock loc cit p. 37. NB After the rebellion Irish whiskey distilleries were closed by
the Govt.

20. Musgrave I. 490.

21. Handcock loc cit p. 43–6.

22. Hay p. 96.

23. Musgrave I. 442. Jackson p. 3. Hay p. 97.

24. Musgrave op cit (see map at end of book). Hay p. 97.

25. Ibid. Jackson p. 3.

26. Gen. Fawcett—Gen. Eustace May 31st 1798. 620/38/11. Lt. Birch July 23rd 1798,
quoted Musgrave I. 473–5. Hay p. 105–6.

27. Ibid.

28. Snowe p. 15. Hay p. 106–7. Musgrave I. 475–6.

29. Hay p. 107–8. Snowe p. 15–16.

30. Hay p. 107. H. called the people "a set of savages" acc. Mrs Brownrigg's diary quoted
in Wheeler and Broadley *Wexford* p. 173.

31. Snowe p. 16–18. See also Ld Bective—Gen. Eustace, May 31st 1798. 620/37/233.

32. Snowe op cit. See also Info. of May 31st 1798 in 620/37/234. Hay p. 109–110. Mrs
Brownrigg's diary op cit. p. 168.

33. Handcock, loc cit p. 49–52.

34. Mrs. Adams' diary op cit p. 356. Jackson p. 10.

35. Mrs. Brownrigg op cit p. 167–9.

36. Ibid p. 170.

37. Jackson p. 6–7.

38. Mrs. Brownrigg op cit p. 171–2; Musgrave I. 555, 557.

39. Jackson p. 10–11. Clearly designed as a set of passwords. A Dublin version gives "Ireland" instead of "Great Britain" in the last line.
40. Musgrave I. 490, 491.
41. Ibid p. 492–3.
42. Cooke—Wickham June 5th 1798. HO 100/81/23. Camden—Portland June 5th 1798. HO 100/81/21. Musgrave I. 494–500.
43. Gen. Loftus—Lake June 5th 1798. 620/38/49. Alexander—Pelham June 10th 1798. BM Add MSS 33,105/400/ foll. Musgrave I. 494–500. Jones Narrative p. 120–4.
44. Cooke—Wickham June 5th 1798. HO 100/77/50. Lake—Knox June 3rd 1798. Knox MSS NLI 56.
45. Cooke—Wickham ibid. Loftus retreated to Tullow in Co. Carlow.
46. Gen. Nugent—[Castlereagh] June 7th 1798. HO 100/77/78.
47. Castlereagh—Knox June 5th 1798. Knox MSS. NLI 56/176.

PART III CHAPTER 1
At head of chapter: Zimmerman, p. 144
1. Hay p. 112–13.
2. Jackson p. 6–7, 22.
3. Jackson p. 22.
4. Hay 112–13; 132–3. Jackson p. 19. Taylor Rebellion p. 13.
5. Hay p. 114, Musgrave I 556. Musgrave (1.549) claimed four others were killed that day.
6. Hay p. 121.
7. Hay p. 125, 1–89.
8. Hay p. 107–8.
9. Jackson p. 22 see Barrington Personal Sketches III. 296–300.
10. Hay p. 129–30.
11. Mrs Brownrigg's diary op cit p. 174. Hay p. 128–9.
12. Hay p. 130. Grogan had carried the Catholic petition to England in 1794–5.
13. Hay p. 128–9. Jackson p. 23. See Grogan MSS NLI and petition of John Grogan.
14. Hay p. 125–7; Jackson p. 10; Taylor p. 73–4; Mrs Adams' diary op cit p. 356–7; Mrs Brownrigg op cit p. 175.
15. Relatio of Dr Caulfield in Wexford Diocesan Archives.
16. Dr. Caulfield—Dr. Troy July 21st 1798 printed Plowden History 11. 749–51.
17. Mrs. Brownrigg op cit p. 175.
18. Dr. Caulfield—Dr. Troy September 2nd 1798 printed Plowden II. 717.
19. Hay p. 130–1.
20. Hay p. 131.
21. Hay p. 141–2.
22. see note 16.
23. Mrs Adams op cit p. 364.
24. Mrs Brownrigg's op cit p. 175.
25. Hay p. 142–5.
26. Jackson p. 12–14. Hay p. 145–6. For the title of the song see Zimmerman Rebel Songs p. 38, 40.
27. Cloney p. 29–300. Mrs Brownrigg op cit p. 176. Hay p. 140.
28. Hay p. 137–8.
29. Musgrave 1. 504–5.
30. Musgrave Ibid.
31. Ibid.
32. Cloney p. 33–4. Hay p. 149.
33. Cloney p. 34–5. Hay p. 149–50. Taylor gives "Citizen" in the text p. 49–51.
34. Musgrave 1 503 (see plan of town.)

35. Alexander p. 41–2, 45.
36. Cornwallis called him a "blockhead." He had a violent row with Col. Craufurd after the battle leading to the latter's court-martial.
37. DNB.
38. See his remarks quoted Alexander p. 50. New Ross garrison totalled 2,678 men exc. yeomanry. HO 100/77/52.
39. Col Robert Craufurd—Craddock June 7th 1798. HO 100/77/126.
40. Musgrave I. 503 foll.
41. Musgrave I 504 Alexander p. 31–2.
42. Alexander p. 53.
43. There may have been a longer interval between Furlong's death and the attack. Alexander p. 70, Taylor p. 51–2, Musgrave 1.504–5 Hay p. 150 Cloney p. 35.
44. Musgrave 1.525–6, inc. affidavits, App. XX. Nos. 5–12.
45. Ric. Grandy's affidavit of June 23rd 1798 printed RSCHC App. XXXV. Musgrave 1.525–8 Hay 156–8.
46. Taylor p. 60–1.
47. Wm. Fleming's, Elizabeth Dobbyn's affidavits September 20th 1798 and January 5th 1799 TCD MSS. The estimates of dead vary considerably. Hay (p. 156) says "nearly 80," Fleming (loc cit) gives a total of 199; Taylor and Musgrave (op cit) 221.

PART III CHAPTER 2
At head of chapter: P. J. McCall.
1. Alexander p. 54.
2. Ibid p. 55–7.
3. Cloney p. 35–6, 39. Taylor p. 52. Alexander p. 71.
4. Hay, p. 151.
5. Cloney p. 37.
6. Col. Craufurd—Lake June 5th, 6th 1798. HO 100/77/74–6.
7. Major Vesey June 5th 1798 HO 100/77/82–3. Alexander p. 73.
8. Cloney p. 35–6.
9. Ibid p. 38.
10. Hay p. 150. Major Vesey op cit.
11. Alexander p. 72–3. Taylor p. 53.
12. Cloney p. 38. Hay p. 651.
13. Cloney p. 37. FJ June 16th 1798.
14. Musgrave 1. 506.
15. Dr. Jordan Roche *Statement* quoted Dickson *Wexford* p. 253.
16. Alexander p. 62.
17. Ibid p. 75.
18. Ibid p. 76. Musgrave 1. 514.
19. Ibid p. 79–80. Taylor p. 54.
20. Alexander p. 63; Musgrave 1.507; Jones *Impartial Narrative* p. 39; Hay p. 151.
21. Ibid.
22. Hay p. 151–3; Cloney p. 39.
23. Cloney p. 39.
24. Musgrave 1. 507–8. Col. Craufurd op cit.
25. See list re captured artillery enclosed Gen. Johnson—Lake June 7th 1798 HO 100/77/108–10.
26. Alexander p. 84. Cloney p. 39, 41.
27. Alexander p. 84.
28. Musgrave 1.515. Alexander p. 84 (adapted).
29. Taylor p. 54 and Musgrave 1.507. But see Alexander p. 83 for the origin of the story.

30. Major Vesey—Gen. Lake loc cit. Cloney p. 40, 42.

31. Cloney p. 41.

32. Ibid p. 41-2.

33. Ibid p. 43.

34. "Quite ungovernable" was Craufurd's phrase after the battle. Col. Craufurd—Gen. Lake June 5th 1798 loc cit.

35. Alexander p. 67-8, 90, 95.

36. Ibid 91-2. For practice of shooting wounded cf Cullen, MSS TCD S.3 p. 36.

37. Major Vesey—Gen. Lake loc cit.

38. Alexander p. 91.

39. Ibid p. 93-4.

40. Ibid p. 64-5. Musgrave 1.514.

41. Taylor p. 57-8. The full text is given in Musgrave, and a scapular is preserved in his papers, TCD G.2.19.

42. DEP, FJ June 16, 1798.

43. Alexander p. 66.

44. Taylor p. 55.

45. Alexander p. 84-5, 125.

46. Official list printed DEP June 12th 1798.

47. In fact he returned another way to avoid the stench. Alexander p. 104-5, 125.

48. B. B. Harvey-Glascott June 9th 1798. Printed Taylor p. 69. See also Cloney p. 44, 48. Taylor p. 65.

49. Printed Taylor p. 65-6.

50. Cloney had little respect for him, and opposed the change. p. 54-5. For conflicting views on Fr. Roche cf. Gordon p. 143; Byrne 1.62.

51. A new camp was established at Sleevekitter above the Barrow. Cloney p. 45.

52. Ibid. p. 45-6.

53. Ibid p. 48.

54. Printed Musgrave 1. 537-8, said to be written by Fr. Michael Murphy.

55. For lack of liaison between units see, for example, Cloney p. 51. But note Harvey's proclamation did reach northern division; Taylor p. 79.

56. Byrne 1. 68-71, 85. Cloney p. 47, 51-2.

57. Byrne 1. 54, 71-2, 85, 94, 98-9, 125. Cloney p. 47.

58. Byrne 1. 94 Cloney p. 51.

59. See Harvey's and Roche's proclamation, printed Taylor p. 65-6, 96-7. But see also "Republic of Ireland" in "Father Murphy's journal" Musgrave App. XVIII. 1.

60. Proclamation of Edward Roche June 7th 1798 op cit.

61. Byrne 1. 118-19.

62. Ibid 1. 88, 93.

63. Ibid 1. 83, 87-8.

64. Cullen MSS printed as *Personal Recollections* (includes Cullen's Clondalkin MSS) p. 23, 25-7.

65. Henry Bayly to his father June 9th 1798, Ainsworth transcript NLI.

PART III CHAPTER 3.

At head of chapter: Zimmerman, p. 156-7.

1. Nugent—Castlereagh June 7th enc. with Camden—Portland June 9th 1798. HO 100/77/104-5.

2. Clare—Ld Auckland June 5th 1798. *Auckland Correspondence* IV. 3.

3. Castlereagh—Pelham June 8th 1798 BM Add MSS 33,105, 397.

4. Ibid p. 396.

AA

5. See note 2.
6. Including Francis Higgins' coach see "FH" (June 1st), 1798. 620 18.
7. Camden—Portland June 8th, 10th, 11th 1798. HO 100/77.
8. Duke of York—Portland June 9th 1798 enc. with Portland—Camden of same date HO 100/77/104, 114, 132.
9. Jemmy Hope account quoted Madden *Antrim and Down* p. 36 foll., 88 foll.
10. Ibid.
11. Fox's letter (c.1799) 620/4/61.
12. See the loyalist poem in FDJ July 16th 1798.
13. McSkimmin *Rebellion*; Dickson *Revolt in the North* p. 129–30; Musgrave II. 101.
14. Geo. Casement—Geo. McCleverty July 20th 1798. PRONI DOD/562/3038. Ed. Agnew memo November 26th 1798. McClelland Transcript PRONI.
15. Hudson—Charlemont June 19th 1798. HMC Charlemont II. 325.
16. See note 13.
17. Jones p. 117. Jemmy Hope op cit. McSkimmin op cit. Musgrave 11.
18. Jemmy Hope op cit.
19. There was a half-hearted attempt at ambush. See Jas. Dickey's C/M on July 5th 1798. 620/2/9/1.
20. Latimer *Ulster Biographies* p. 15. Jemmy Hope op cit. McSkimmin op cit.
21. Ibid. cf Col. Durham—Nugent June 7th 1798. 620/38/85.
22. Musgrave II. 100. McSkimmin op cit. J. Durham—Nugent June 8th 1798 op cit. He claimed 150 dead in the town. And see account in Durham MSS in SRO (Dundas MSS).
23. R. M. Young *Ulster* in '98.
24. FJ June 23rd 1798.
25. Jemmy Hope op cit. McCarten and Hope quoted Madden, cf Hudson—Haliday July 27th 1798 op cit.
26. Nugent—Knox June 6th, 8th NLI MS 56/178, 184. Nugent—Castlereagh June 8th, 10th 1798. HO 100/81/49.
27. Mrs. M. McTier—Dr. W. Drennan May 31st 1798. *Drennan Letters* 716.
28. Jones p. 172.
29. Jones p. 172–4. BNL May–June passim. For change of heart in the North see F. Archer June 3rd 1798. 620/38/36. Mass of the Presbyterians not Painites and now increasingly anti-Catholic. See also the series of letters in Downshire MSS esp. 1491, 1507, 1510, 1552.
30. BNL May–June passim.
31. Col. Clavering's proclamation June 8th 1798 NLI 56/186; Col. Clavering June 9th 1798 620/38/99.
32. Nugent—Lake, June 10th 1798. HO/10077/135-7.
33. Ibid.
34. W. Fox's letter loc cit.
35. Ibid.
36. J. Hope op cit. Madden MSS TCD 1317. At M.'s own C/M on June 16th, he claimed to have been forced to act as leader. 620/2/9/2.
37. Hudson—Charlemont July 27th 1798 op cit.
38. Text quoted Dickson, p. 147.
39. W. Fox's letter op cit.
40. [James Thompson] in *Belfast Magazine* 1825 vol. I. No. 1.
41. Ibid.
42. Lord Londonderry's steward at C/M of Miller on July 2nd 1798. 620/2/15/43. See also Hyde *Castlereagh*.
43. 620/2/15/26, 36, 43, 48.
44. W. Fox's letter loc cit.
45. Info of F. Conroy. 620/40/140.

46. J. Thompson op cit.
47. J. Jones, p. 177–8.
48. Nugent—Lake June (13th) 1798. 620/38/129. Ibid (later that day) HO 100/81/129–33.
49. M. Darby—Bp Percy June 13th 1798. BM Add MSS 32,335/48.
50. J. Thompson op cit. For the night attack see Teeling *Narrative* p. 255–6.
51. Musgrave II. 107.
52. Nugent loc cit. FDJ June 16th 1798. Musgrave II. 106. Teeling p. 256–7.
53. FJ June 16th 1798.
54. J. Thompson op cit.
55. Darby—Bp Percy June 13th 1798 loc cit. Rebel casualties estimated at 400. T. Whinney
—Lees June 13th 1798 620/38/138a.
56. J. McAllan claimed reward for collecting them. 620/7/76/6.
57. Ibid.
58. James Witherspoon's account Madden MSS TCD S.3.690 cf Teeling p. 258–60.
59. Evidence at Monroe's C/M loc cit. See also his proc. of June 12th 1798 for no rent for
landlords in the "National Liberty war." Nugent MSS NAM 463 1.
60. FJ June 16th 1798.

PART III CHAPTER 4
At head of Chapter: Zimmerman, p. 138.
1. Colchester *Diary* I. 155–7.
2. Ld Auckland—Ld Mornington July 19th 1798 BM Add MSS 37308/154 quoted
Wellesley *Papers* 1.60–1 See also note 7.
3. Pitt's first letters referring to it are Pitt—Camden May 28th 1798, Camden MSS Kent
CRO; Pitt—Mornington of same date in Roseberry's *Pitt*. Cf Bolton *Union* p. 53–4.
4. So one can infer from his later letters. See Pitt—Cornwallis November 17th 1798.
PRO 30/8/335/28.
5. Camden—Pitt June 6th 1798. PRO 30/8/326/308–12.
6. He was sent Camden's letter. See Pitt—George III. June 11th 1798. Aspinall *George III*
III p. 77.
7. George III Pitt 7 a.m. June 10th 1798. PRO 30/8/104/235.
8. DEP June 5th 1798.
9. According to Pitt's budget. Colchester *Diary* I. 151.
10. London report of June 6th, DEP June 12th 1798.
11. London report June 8th ibid.
12. Compare the bulletins in *The Times* etc. with the originals in HO 100.
13. See Letter of Jas. White London July 27th, reported SNL August 11th 1798.
14. Lees—Auckland June 5th, 6th, 8th, 10th 1798. BM Add MSS 34, 454.
15. Cooke—Wickham June 12th 1798. HO 100/81/76.
16. Bp Percy—his wife June 11th, 13th 1798. BM 32,335/39–40, 42. DEP June 14th
FDJ 16, 1798.
17. Camden—Portland, June 11th 1798. HO 100/81/61.
18. Ric. Farrell Diary p. XVIII NLI MS 11, 941.
19. Bp Percy—his wife June 20th 1798. loc cit p. 56. See Lady Antrim's diary entry of June
11th 1798 printed in *Two Centuries of Life in Down* p. 492–3.
20. DEP June 12th 1798, HJ June 23rd 1798. As late as June 2nd it was officially reported
that they could not return to Ireland because of the "danger of pestilence" through the
number of uburied bodies. HO/50/8.
21. SNL June 27th 1798.
22. See Bishop of Ferns, June 4th 1798. HO 100/66/101. Another "woman" was arrested in
mid-June at Carlisle. see J. Pollock—Cooke June 25th 1798. 620/38/236.
23. Grattan *Memoirs* IV. 380 see lampoon FDJ July 12th 1798.

24. FJ June 5th 1798.

25. Cloncurry *Recollections*, p. 68–9.

26. Ly Louisa Connolly June 1st 1798 printed Moore *Fitzgerald* II.

27. Duke of Richmond—Ly Louisa Connolly June 7th 1798 Bunbury MSS, McPeake Collection.

28. Prince of Wales—Wm Ogilvie June 6th 1798 printed Moore *Fitzgerald* II. 128–30.

29. D. of Richmond—Ly L. Connolly op cit.

30. C. J. Fox—Ld H. Fitzgerald June 7th 1798 printed Moore *Fitzgerald* II. 130–1. D. of Richmond June 7th 1798 op cit.

31. Ld H. Fitzgerald—Ld Camden June (6th) 1798 printed Moore *Fitzgerald* II. 135 foll. cf Ly Holland *Journal* I. 185–9.

32. C. Lock—W. Ogilvie June 4th 1798 printed Moore *Fitzgerald* II. 135 foll D. of Richmond—W. Ogilvie June 4th 1798 Ibid.

33. Ly L. Connolly—W. Ogilvie June 4th 1798. Ibid. See also memo quoted Moore 132. The 3 doctors' bills totalled £54 see secret service a/cs in RIA MSS.

34. Ly L. Connolly op cit. Cf letter of September 1801 Bunbury MSS: he said "Rebels would finally succeed."

35. Emily Bunbury's memo August 1832 (i.e. after Moore's *Fitzgerald* was published) Bunbury MSS McPeake Collection.

36. Ly L. Connolly—Ld H. Fitzgerald June (4th) 1798. Ibid. See description of funeral DEP June 7th 1798.

37. Olson *The Radical Duke*, p. 102.

38. See note 27.

39. D. of Richmond—Ly L. Connolly July 26th 1798. Bunbury MSS McPeake Collection.

40. Ly L. Connolly D. of Richmond July 18th 1798. Ibid.

41. See note 27.

42. One child, little Pamela, was brought up by her. Madden II. 539.

43. Ld Holland *Memoirs of the Whig Party*; Ly Holland *Journal* June 10th 1798 p. 187–9.

44. In private, that is. Ld Moira—Prince of Wales June 27th 1798 printed in Aspinall *Prince of Wales* III. 443.

45. Ly Holland op cit p. 190–1.

46. See the account of his debts in Aspinall *Prince of Wales* introduction.

47. See note 45 and Ld Moira—P. of Wales June 24th 1798 op cit. p. 440–2.

48. George III Pitt April 9th 1797 printed Stanhope III. App p. iii.

49. George III—Pitt April 10th 1797. op cit. App p. VI.

50. George III—Pitt May 30th (1798) op cit App. p. XIV.

51. Camden—Portland June HO/100/77.

52. George III—Pitt June 3rd 1798. PRO 30/8/104/231.

53. George III—Pitt June 10th 1798 ibid p. 235.

54. George III—Pitt June 13th 1798 ibid p. 239.

55. George III—Pitt June 11th 1798 ibid p. 237.

56. See for example Windham—Bp of Ossory [July] 1797. BM Add MSS 37878/118–9.

57. See Pt. IV Ch. 5.

58. See note 3, and esp. Pitt—Auckland June 4th 1798. "a good deal of discussion lately" Auckland *Correspondence* III 2.

59. Carlisle—Pitt June 9th 1798 HMC Carlisle.

60. See note 54.

61. Pitt—Grenville June 1st–10th 1798 HMC Dropmore IV. 230.

62. H. Dundas—D. of York June 2nd 1798; D. of York—D. of Portland June 25th 1798. HO 50/8.

63. M. of Buckingham—Ld Grenville May 27th, June 10th 1798. HMC Dropmore IV. 217–8, 231–2.

64. *After* despatch of latest reinforcements to Ireland. Only half of this body of 10,000 were Guards, and about half the rest were recruits.
Memo by Ld Grenville June 18th 1798. Ibid p. 237.
65. See note 61.
66. Extract of letter from M. de Dolmieu March 28th 1798 enc. with M. de Luc—Ld Grenville May 7th 1798. Ibid p. 192.
67. Ibid p. 189.
Prince Bouillon June 13th, 31st 1798. WO 1/922.
68. London (June 22nd) report, DEP June 26th 1798.
69. Ld Moira—P of Wales June 24th 1798 op cit.
70. Wilberforce *Life* diary entry July 16th 1798. It was suggested Pitt had gone mad. Stanhope *Pitt* III. 136.
71. Portland—Camden June [13th], 1798. HO 100/81/78-9.

PART III CHAPTER 4
At head of chapter: Zimmerman, p. 228.
1. Cooke—Pelham June 16th 1798. BM Add MSS 33105/437-8.
2. Camden—Pelham June 19th 1798. Ibid p. 441.
3. Camden—Elliot June 15th 1798. Ibid p. 431-2.
4. Gen. Needham—Gen. Lake June 10th 1798. HO 100/77/120-2. For full description of battle & bibliography see Hayes—McCoy *Irish Battles*.
5. Needham loc cit. See Capt. Philip Hay's account in 620/56/98 "The pikemen fled the instant the firing began."
6. Needham loc cit. See also Capt. Moore (Needham's ADC) account in HO 100/77/122. J. Jones *Narrative* p. 70-3 Musgrave 1.540-7.
7. Needham loc cit. Philip Hay loc cit.
8. Camden—Portland June 10th, June 11th 1798. HO 100/77/114-18, 132-4.
9. Castlereagh—Pelham June 13th 1798. BM Add MSS 33105/416-18.
10. Castlereagh—Elliot June 15th 1798. Ibid p. 427-8.
11. Johnson—Lake June 13th. 620/38/135.
12. Philip Hay op cit. Interview mentioned Castlereagh—Elliot June 15th 1798 op cit.
13. Info. of Rob Edwards enc. Camden—Portland June 10th 1798 HO/ 10077/128-31.
14. Lt. Hill's report re. expdt. 620/38/135. For Borris expdt. see Cloney p. 50-1.
15. Castlereagh—Elliot June 15th 1798 loc cit.
Cooke—Wickham June 13th 1798. HO 100/81/80.
16. Castlereagh—Pelham June 16th 1798. BM Add MSS 33105/439.
17. Cooke—Wickham June 14th 1798. HO 100/81/84.
18. Castlereagh—Elliot June 15th 1798 loc cit.
19. Lake—Castlereagh June 15th 1798. *Castlereagh Correspondence* I.224.
20. Wexford People's Proclamation of June 9th 1798. Printed Jackson p. 33-4. Edward Roche's Address to the People of Ireland June 7th 1798. 620/4/46.
21. Hay p. 163-4, 190-1.
22. Ibid p. 121-3.
23. Jackson p. 29.
24. Mrs. Adam's diary op cit p. 361.
25. Painite ideals appealed especially to artisan class. See Carlow movement 620/56/160.
26. The catechism is printed in full Musgrave App. XXI. 9.
27. Mrs. Adams op cit p. 336.
28. Ibid p. 365 For *British* rising in sympathy with Ireland see Jackson p. 24.
29. Hay p. 191-2.
30. Ibid p. 197-8; Jackson p. 30-2.
31. Ibid.

32. Hay p. 175-7.
33. Mrs. Adams op cit p. 367.
34. Ibid. For a characteristically absurd version of the incident see Barrington *Sketches*, III. 279-87.
35. Hay p. 195. For United Army's oath Wexford June 14th 1798 see Hay App. IX.
36 Hay p. 193.
37. Ibid p. 193-4.
38. Ibid p. 194-5 confirmed by Lieut Bourke—Hay June 3rd 1799 later endorsed Lord Kingsborough (Kingston) PROI/1A/40/112/55.
39. Dr. Caulfield—Dr. Troy July 21st 1798 printed Plowden II. 749-51.
40. Hay p. 204.
41. Ibid p. 205.
42. Sir Moore *Diary* I. 295-6.
43. Hay p. 213-15.
44. Charles Jackson *Narrative* p. 15-16.
45. Hay p. 215-17.
46. Ibid p. 218-19 Musgrave 11.20.
47. Mrs. Brownrigg op cit p. 186-7. Hay p. 220-1.
48. Dr. Caulfield op cit. Fr. Corrin's deposition printed Plowden II. 758.
49. Jackson p. 17-18. The total of victims is disputed cf Hay p. 219-21, Gordon p. 181-2, Taylor p. 107-8. Musgrave published the list in App. XX. 24 (original "Bloody Calendar" in TCD).
50. Hay p. 225-6, 2
51. Ibid p. 229-32. Ld Kingsborough June 21st 1798 encl. by Lake. HO 100/77/188. Jackson p. 18.
52. See note 49.
53. Lake—Castlereagh June 21st 1798. Ibid p. 184-5.
54. The Castle was well aware of the danger. See Cooke—Wickham June 25th 1798. HO 100/77/194.
55. Jones p. 75-7 see Dickson Wexford p. 155-65.
56. Musgrave II. 12-13.
57. Hay p. 235. Gordon (p. 174) says the fire was an accident caused by shooting the patients in their beds.
58. Ibid p. 242-3.
59. Sir J. Moore I. 294, 296.
60. Ibid I. 297.
61. Ibid I 298-9 cf Moore—Johnson June 23rd 1798. HO 100/81/163-4.
62. Mrs Brownrigg op cit p. 193-4. Musgrave II. 37.
63. Ibid p. 189-91.
64. Ibid p. 191-2.
65. Ibid p. 193.
66. Ibid.
67. FJ June 26th 1798.
68. Hay p. 231, 241-2.
69. J. Moore *Diary* I. 299.
70. Jackson p. 19.
71. J. Moore op cit. Musgrave II. 41.
72. Lake—Cornwallis June 23rd 1798. HO 100/81/173.

PART IV CHAPTER 1
Chapter head from Connolly MSS in TCD.

1. A review in the Park cancelled because of rain. DEP June 19th 1798. For July weather in Dublin see Kilmaine MS weather diary.
2. Hodges & Figgis MSS.
3. Lees—Auckland June 23rd 1798. BM Add MSS 34, 454/367.
4. DEP June 21st 1798 See also Ld Wycombe—Lady Holland June 21st 1798. BM Add MSS 51, 682. "He was asked whether he had a good passage. He replied he spewed a good deal . . . he's fond of quaint and memorable sayings."
5. DNB.
6. Cornwallis—Ross March 31st 1798. *Cornwallis' Correspondence* II.ʼ336.
7. Cornwallis—Ross July 1st, 9th 1798. Ibid II. 358, 363.
8. Cornwallis—Ross July 1st. Ibid II. 357.
9. Sir J. Moore *Diary* I. 327–8.
10. Cooke—Pelham June 16th 1798. BM Add MSS 3105/437–8.
11. Beresford—Auckland June 16th 1798. *Auckland Correspondence* IV. 20–1.
12. Cornwallis—Portland July 8th 1798. *Cornwallis Correspondence* II. 360–1.
13. DEP June 30th 1798, reporting Irish Commons debate June 29th.
14. Cornwallis—Portland June 28th 1798 loc cit II. 356–7.
15. Cornwallis—Ross July 1st 1798 loc cit II. 357.
16. Cornwallis—Portland June 28th 1798 loc cit II. 351.
17. Plowden Appendix CXII.
18. Gordon p. 105–6.
19. Hay p. 247–8; Cullen MSS TCD S.3.19/50–6.
20. Sir J. Moore *Diary* I. 303.
21. Near Scullogh Gap Cloney p. 86.
22. Hay p. 246–7, Byrne I. 121–2 broadly confirmed by Wellesley-Pole—Mornington August 24th 1798 *Wellesley Papers* I. 69–79. "In this horrible rebellion the king's troops never gave quarter to the rebels; hundreds and thousands of wretches were butchered while unarmed on their knees begging mercy . . ."
23. Byrne I. 125.
24. Hay & Cloney passim.
25. Hay p. 245.
26. Sir J. Moore *Diary* I. 301.
27. Hay p. 251.
28. Jackson p. 49.
29. Lt. Browne's petition for reward November 2nd 1799. 620/56/114.
30. Jackson p. 51–2. Musgrave II. 46.
31. R. Grandy's deposition RSCHC App.
32. John Knox Grogan—Ld Mountnorris October 24th 1801. His brother died "a victim to a violent Electioneering Party that exists in the County of Wexford." 620/59/73a. See also a petition to the Viceroy of November 21st 1798 in 620/56/117 and see Colclough MSS in McPeake collection esp. John Colclough July 1798.
33. Acc Rev. Vicarry, quoted Madden IV. 506.
34. Lake to men of Wexford June 22nd 1798. 620/38/218. Hay p. 166.
35. But see note on Edward Roche's Address to the People of Ireland Pt. III. ch V. note 20.
36. Byrne I. 118–9.
37. There was also a new hope of French assistance see Byrne loc cit. For false alarm of a French landing see FDJ June 26th 1798.
38. Byrne 1.158.
39. Gen. Asgill—Castlereagh June 26th 1798. HO 100/81/181–2. Byrne I. 154–76.
40. Byrne I. 167–9. The song recording the incident is in Zimmerman p. 147.
41. Ibid I. 193–204. Hay 258–63. Cornwallis—Portland June 28th 1798. HO 100/82/199.
42. Hay p. 263 cf Byrne I. 227.

43. Ld Castlereagh—Gen. Stewart June 25th 1798. *Cornwallis Correspondence* II. p. 355.
44. Cornwallis—Ross July 14th 1798. Ibid II. 370–1.
45. Cornwallis—Portland July 8th 1798. Ibid 359.
46. See note 44.
47. Marquis of Buckingham—Ld Grenville July 6th 1798. HMC Dropmore IV. 245.
48. See for example Clare—Beresford June 7th 1798 *Auckland Correspondence* and see Foster—Auckland October 21st 1798 Keele University III. 7. Sneyd MSS.
49. See Cornwallis to his brother March 12th 1801. Mann MSS Kent CRO.
50. Ross—Downshire June 27th 1798. Downshire MSS PRONI.
51. Sheffield—Auckland August 12th 1798. BM Add MSS 344454.
52. See note 47.
53. Cornwallis—Ross July 9th 1798. *Cornwallis Correspondence* II. 362–3.
54. See note 48.
55. See Clare—Castlereagh October 16th 1798. *Castlereagh Correspondence* I. 393–4.
56. Castlereagh—Wickham June 12th 1798. Ibid p. 219.
57. See note 12.
58. He was, however, in poor health and away from Dublin during many critical weeks of this year.
59. Cornwallis—Portland July 26th 1798. *Cornwallis Correspondence* II. 373.
60. Cornwallis—Ross July 24th 1798. Ibid p. 371.
61. Cornwallis—Portland June 21st 1798 HO 100/81/149 re Ld Castlereagh's brother, in action at Prosperous.
62. Ly S. Napier—D. of Richmond June 27th 1798 printed Moore *Fitzgerald* II.
63. For guerilla war in Kildare see also DEP June 21st R. Griffith—Pelham June 25th, 30th July 11th, 13th BM Add MSS 33105/453 foll; FDJ July 10th 1798.
64. Griffith—Pelham July 11th 1798 loc cit.
65. DEP, FDJ July 14th, 17th 1798.
66. DEP, FDJ July 12th, 14th 1798.
67. For their family connections see Madden *United Irishmen* Cullen MSS in TCD & 620/38/44.
68. See note 63, cf O. Kelly who claimed they were not to rise till after the attack on Dublin.
69. See note 71.
70. Four deserters from 4th Dragoon Guards acc C/M evidence 620/5/58/22.
71. For info. on Aylmer and the camp see 620/39/18–19, 629/38/145, 620/38/34, 620/38/44 esp. latter.
72. John Mitchell's info. June 8th 1798 620/38/93.
73. Rev. Chas Eustace June 7th 1798 620/51/59.
74. "They lay under the Ditches like pigs without a tent or any covering"—Barker's info. June 6th 1798. 620/38/73.
75. Buckingham—Grenville July 26th 1798. HMC Dropmore IV. 264–5.
76. See account of captured mail coach passengers in FDJ July 17th 1798.
77. Cullen *Recollections* p. 50–4, 57 cf Gough—Vereker July 12th 1798 printed p. 62–3.
78. Ibid p. 54–9.
79. Ibid. Loyalist account of this action—a kind of Rorke's Drift—is in FDJ August 2nd 1798.
80. Cullen op cit p. 76.
81. FDJ July 26th 1798 and see note 75.
82. Cooke—Wickham July 21st 1798. HO 100/77/268. See note 75.

PART IV CHAPTER 2
At head of chapter: Zimmerman, p. 133–7.
1. See also Sir Ed. Newenham, ex-member for Dublin, reporting on conditions from

inside—"perishing with cold . . . the large door leading to the Execution plank is just by my bed" October 21st 1800. ISPO P.P. 3/538.

2. J. Howard quoted C. Maxwell *Dublin* p. 155.

3. Ibid p. 154.

4. Rev. F. Archer's prison report. BM Add MSS 35,920/1–6.

5. Ibid p. 2.

6. Ibid.

7. Ibid p. 6–7.

8. Ibid.

9. For Kilmainham list see 620/7/79/31. For Newgate 620/13/174.

10. List of prisoners July 1798 620/54/30.

11. G. Renny—Capt. Taylor September 24th 1798. ISPO Official Papers 2nd series 515/82/9; report of S. Mason 620/14/204.

12. 620/51/72, 73, 76, 77 620/52/61–2; 620/35/109, 111, 114, 172.

13. Dublin C/M S in 620/3/16/1–19; 620/5/61–6; DEP June–July 1798.

14. Cornwallis—Ross See also Wellesley-Pole—Mornington August 24th 1798 *Wellesley Papers* I. 69–79.

15. See Lake's general orders in Limerick Militia book in Limerick MSS on loan to NLI.

16. I have added up the figures in the C/MS in 620. Cf chapter 6 note 39.

17. See numerous garrison reports in 620 e.g. Lord Longueville, Cork June 3rd, 6th 1798: hanged 10 people, flogging produced 1000 pikes. 620/4/38/1–2.

18. See W. Farrell *Carlow* p. 102–219.

19. DNB.

20. Asgill—Castlereagh June 21st 1798 620/38/215; W. Kemmis—T. Kemmis June 18th 1798 PROI 1A/40/111a/79.

21. W. Pole—Castlereagh June 16th 1798. 620/38/164.

22. Asgill—Dundas May 25th 1798. 620/51/53.

23. W. Farrell p. 139, 157.

24. Crosbie *Impartial Narration*. Farrell p. 123–7.

25. W. Farrell p. 138 foll.

26. For UI organisation in Tipperary see esp. 620/37/126.

27. Sir J. Carden—Ld Rossmore May 5th 1798 and see J. Fitzgerald—Castlereagh June 1st 1798 (ISPO 408/601/47) "I shall be merciful in a few days".

28. For Fitzgerald *Howell's State Trials* XXVII, 765–8, 787. For McCracken see M. McNeil p. 181–91.

29. Moore—Cooke August 17th 1798. 620/39/181. Moore—Castlereagh October 21st. ISPO 30/22/5.

30. Dundas—Castlereagh August 8th 1798. 620/39/158. See also Ld Ancram (July 4th 1798). He deplored severity. 620/3/51/7.

31. Capt. Taylor—Sir L. Parsons August 23rd 1798. (Parsons MSS) and see NLI 620/3/27.

32. Ld Altamont May–June 1798. 620/37/240.

33. Anon June 6th 1798. 620/51/165.

34. Holt *Memoirs* I. 298–301.

35. See Castlereagh—Mrs Emmet April 13th 1798. ISPO 30/179.

36. Cooke—Pelham August 9th 1798. BM Add MSS 33106/49–50. And see RSCHC App. XX.

37. See Pt. I ch. 3 note 31.

38. Curran *Life* II. 1–50. But see Madden IV–315.

39. Madden IV 364.

40. RSCHC App. XX.

41. Madden IV–281.

42. Barrington *Historic Memoirs* II. 266–7.

43. Printed in Madden IV. 296–7.
44. Curran *Life* II. 63.
45. Ibid II. 69–74.
46. FDJ July 19th, 21st, 24th 1798.
47. Cornwallis—Portland July 26th 1798 enc. prisoners' offer & list of names. HO 100/77/301–5.
48. McNevin *History* p. 176.
49. Alexander—Pelham July 26th, August 4th 1798. BM Add MSS 33106/24–26, 39–40.
50. See note 47.
51. Ibid.
52. McNevin p. 178.
53. Clare—Auckland August 1st 1798. *Auckland Correspondence* IV 37–41.
54. Cooke—Pelham August 9th 1798. BM 33106/48.
55. See note 47.
56. Elliot Pelham July 28th 1798. BM Add MSS 33106/27–30. Cooke—Wickham July 28th 1798. HO 100/77/311–12.
57. Alexander—Pelham July 26th. BM Add MSS 33106/26.
58. For terms see *Castlereagh Correspondence* I. 347–53 cf Madden III. 53–61.
59. See note 54 also Castlereagh—Wickham August 4th 1798. HO 100/78/13.
60. There are two versions of the memoir—the original MS one in HO 100/78/25–47 and one edited and published by McNevin etc. entitled *Memoire*. There are two versions of the replies to the Secret Case one included in the *Memoire*, the other published by the Govt. in RSCHC & RSCHL.
61. RSCHC App. XXXI.
62. Ibid.
63. Ibid.
64. Ibid.
65. Cornwallis—Portland July 8th 1798 loc cit II. 358.
66. Cornwallis—Ross July 29th 1798 loc cit II. 381.
67. Cornwallis—Duke of Leinster August 11th 1798. HO 100/81/307.
68. T. Moore *Fitzgerald* II. 281. The attainder was reversed in 1819.
69. See Grogan petitions in previous chapter.
70. DEP August 14th 1798.
71. Gen. J. Moore's report August 20th 1798. ISPO State of Country 1st series 408/601/64 cf J. Moore *Diary* I. 305–6.
72. J. Moore *Diary* I. 309, 11.
73. 23,000 rebels dead "at lowest estimate": W-Pole—Mornington August 24th 1798 *Wellesley Papers*, I. 69–79; 20,000 acc. another Castle estimate in 620/3/51/17a. See chapter 6 notes 40, 41.
74. List of arms captured pre August 19th 1798 RSCHC App. XXXIX.
75. Ibid.
76. Bouillon's report PRO WO/1/922. Wickham—Castlereagh August 14th, 15th 1798. HO 100/78/70–1, 87–8; Castlereagh—Wickham August 22nd 1798 referring to letter of 18th HO 100/78/95.
77. Capt. Taylor—W. Wickham August 21st 1798. *Cornwallis Correspondence* II. 389–390.
78. See for example series of letters of 1798 Major Mathews—Lord Downshire (Colonel of the Downshire militia) esp. July 8th 1798. The regt. "almost naked". PRONI D 607.
79. Cornwallis—Pitt July 20th 1798. PRO 30/8/327/183–4.
80. Ibid.
81. Cooke—Auckland [July] 1798. Sneyd MSS Keele University.
82. See Chapter 6 note 18.
83. See note 79.

84. Bp Percy—his wife August 16th 1798. BM Add MSS 32,335/76.
85. DEP August 18th, SNL August 15th 1798.
86. SNL August 22nd 1798.
87. DEP, BNL August 1798.
88. 620/36/71; 620/36/188; 620/9/100. Denis Browne August 22nd 1798. 620/37/195.
89. The fullest account of Mayo at this time is in Little's diary, published *Analecta Hibernica* (1941) no. 11.
90. See note 32 cf Anon report June 18th 1798 620/38/175. See also Ld Clanrickarde June 1st 1798 Clanrickarde MSS NLI 7333.
91. See note 93.
92. See his letters to Malone TCD MS.
93. For best account see Litton Falkiner *Studies* p. 267–70.
94. Stock *Narrative* p. 6.
95. Ibid p. 4 Jobit Diary printed in *Analecta Hibernica*. No. 11
96. Stock *Narrative* p. 4.
97. Text printed anon. author *Impartial Narrative* p. 45–7.
98. Stock MS diary, TCD MS.
99. Advt in HJ August 26th 1798. For first reactions in Dublin see Ross—Downshire August 24th 1798. PRONI D 607.
100. Ly Sarah Napier—D. of Richmond August 26th 1798. T. Moore *Fitzgerald* II. 230–2.
101. Cooke—Wickham August 25th 1798. HO 100/81/329.
102. DEP FDJ August 25th 1798.
103. J. Moore *Diary* I. 313.
104. The last land battle in Ireland was the Battle of the Aughrim in 1691.
105. Buckingham—Grenville August 26th 1798. HMC Dropmore IV. 286–8.
106. See for example Lees—Auckland August 28th 1798. BM Add MSS 34, 454/458.
107. D. Browne August 25th 1798. HO 100/78/205.
108. Cornwallis—Portland August 26th 1798. HO 100/78/189.
109. J. Moore *Diary* I. 313.

PART IV CHAPTER 3
At head of chapter: *Songs of the Irish Republic*, p. 66.
1. Desbrière II 69–83, 132–9.
2. Guillon *La France et L'Irlande* p. 366–7.
3. Savary's instructions July 30th 1798 printed Desbrière II. 78–9.
4. Humbert's instructions 1 Thermidor July 19th 1798 Archives de La Marine BBIV/122.
5. Ibid.
6. Capt. Jobit quoted Desbrière II. 85.
7. M. Tone to a friend in France 5, 6 Fructidor August 22nd, 23rd 1798. TCD M5 G2/19a/147–8.
8. Hardy's instructions 12 Thermidor July 30th 1798. Archives de La Marine BB IV/122.
9. Desbrière II. 76–7, 139–49.
10. Tone *Life* II. 473, 476.
11. Ibid II. 480–1.
12. Ibid II. 476, 478–9, 484.
13. Ibid II. 487.
14. Ibid II. 491.
15. Ibid II. 461–2.
16. Ibid II. 461.
17. For example, Tone knew nothing of the purpose of O'Connor's visit. Ibid II, 470–1.
18. Ibid II. 502.
19. Appeal of Orr, Teeling etc. June 16th 1798 printed Desbrière II. 40–1.

20. E. Lewins June 1798 printed Guillon p. 359–361.
21. Tone *Life* II. 466–7, 518–19.
22. It was planned to send a series of expeditions on the lines of Tandy's. Desbrière II. 136.
23. Gen. Humbert—Directory (trans.) August 27th 1798. TCD MS G2 19a/144. Stock *Narrative* p. 22.
24. Stock *Narrative* p. 15–16.
25. Ibid p. 16–17.
26. See note 4. Stock *Narrative* p. 1–2.
27. Stock *Narrative* p. 10.
28. Stock *Narrative* p. 35–6.
29. Ibid p. 37–8.
30. Ibid p. 23–4.
31. Ibid p. 24–5.
32. Ibid p. 25, 34.
33. See note 7.
34. Stock *Narrative* p. 30–1.
35. Ibid p. 27.
36. Ibid p. 31.
37. Ibid p. 31–2.
38. Stock MS Diary entry August 29th 1798. TCD MS 1960/7.
39. Ibid entry September 5th 1798 p. 12.
40. Ibid.
41. Stock *Narrative* p. 43–4.
42. Stock MS Diary entry August 26th p. 4.
43. Stock *Narrative* p. 41–2.
44. Stock MS Diary entry September 2–3, 1798 p. 11–12.
45. Capt. Jobit's Journal, *Analecta Hibernica* No. 11 p. 16–17 cf *Impartial Relation* p. 4–5.
46. Capt. Jobit's Journal loc cit p. 18.
47. Quoted Litton Falkiner *Studies in Irish History* p. 276 perhaps based on Musgrave II. 132.
48. M. Burke's info. 620/52/123. See also Hayes *Last Invasion* p. 44; Cooke-Wickham September 2nd 1798 HO 100/82/19.
49. Musgrave II. 151.
50. Fontaine's account quoted Lecky V. 50.
51. Jobit loc cit p. 20.
52. See note 56 below. The French were told the British had 16 guns. Jobit loc cit.
53. See Complete Peerage under Donoughmore.
54. DNB.
55. See Cornwallis—Hutchinson September 23rd 1798. *Cornwallis Correspondence* II. 413–4.
56. The Government forces numbers, often disputed, are clearly stated in Hutchinson's report September 21st 1798. *Cornwallis Correspondence* II. 411–12. See McAnnally IHS IV. No. 16.
57. Ibid see also Stock *Narrative* p. 44–5.
58. Hutchinson op cit. See also *Impartial Relation* p. 12.
59. J. Jones *Impartial Narrative* p. 215.
60. Musgrave II. 151–2.
61. Hutchinson op cit. Musgrave II. 152–3.
62. For fire power of the "Brown Bess" see Hayes-McCoy *Irish Battles* p. 281–2.
63. Lake's own accounts of the battle of August 27th, 28th 1798 are in HO 100/78/217, 221.
64. Jobit loc cit p. 21.
65. Ibid. McDonnell, however, fought bravely acc. Hayes op cit p. 44.
66. J. Jones p. 219.

67. Cooke—Wickham August 31st 1798. *Cornwallis Correspondence* II. 394-5.
68. Richey *Longford Militia* p. 29, 32 App. IX. (c). W. Maxwell *Rebellion* p. 235. *Impartial Relation* p. 15-18 cf Humbert's bombastic letter to the Directory after the Battle of Castlebar printed J. Jones p. 223-7.

PART IV CHAPTER 4
At head of chapter: Zimmerman, p. 160.
1. Cornwallis—Portland August 25th 1798. *Cornwallis Correspondence* II. 391.
2. J. Moore *Diary* I. 312-15.
3. Lake—Cornwallis August 28th 1798. *Cornwallis Correspondence* II. 363.
4. Hutchinson's report September 21st 1798. Ibid p. 412.
5. Taylor—Castlereagh August 31st 1798. Ibid p. 396.
6. Official figures printed in *Impartial Relation* p. 16-18. See also figures sent by Castlereagh August 30th 1798. HO 100/81/372. Cf Lake—Taylor August 27th 1798. HO 100/78/221. For number of troops cf Richie p. 29-30.
7. Castlereagh—Wickham August 27th 1798. HO/10078/207.
8. Buckingham—Grenville Aug st 28th 1798. HMC Dropmore IV 290-1.
9. Auckland—Beresford August 1798. *Beresford Correspondence* II. 180.
10. Auckland—Cooke quoted Lecky.
11. *Impartial Relation* p. 20-4. Cornwallis did not reach Tuam till September 2nd. See also J. Moore *Diary* I. 315-16, 318-20.
12. Cornwallis—Hutchinson September 23rd 1798. *Cornwallis Correspondence* II. 413.
13. Battle order of September 2nd 1798 printed *Impartial Relation* facing p. 24. For troops in other districts see p. 9-10. See also Buckingham—Grenville August 28th 1798 loc cit.
14. Buckingham—Grenville September 5th 1798 loc cit p. 300-1.
15. Buckingham—Grenville August 26th, September 1st 1798 loc cit p. 287-8, 299-300.
16. *Impartial Relation* p. 26-9. Cornwallis—Portland September 1st, 5th 1798. *Cornwallis Correspondence* II. 399-400.
17. General orders August 31st 1798. *Cornwallis Correspondence* II. 397.
18. J. Moore *Diary* I. 324.
19. Moore's own deposition in 620/51/240. For copy of assignat, signed by him, see Musgrave II. 164.
20. Gen. Humbert's proclamation August 31st 1798 printed J. Jones *Impartial Narrative* p. 221-3.
21. Gen. Humbert—Minister of Marine c. August 28th 1798 printed J. Jones p. 227-30.
22. Litton Falkiner *Studies in Irish History* p. 298-9. Hayes p. 369.
23. Hayes p. 32-3, 81.
24. Ibid p. 22, 260 cf Musgrave II 145-7 Stock *Narrative* p. 74-5.
25. J. Jones p. 220-1.
26. See note 20.
27. Acc. Moore 620/51/240 the contribution was originally to be 3,000 gns.
28. Humbert's instructions 1 Thermidor Archivesde la Marine BB IV/122.
29. Stock *Narrative* p. 74-5.
30. Musgrave II. 157-9. See list of "suffering loyalists" printed Hayes p. 358-61.
31. Musgrave II. 159 J. Jones p. 220-1.
32. Litton Falkiner p. 299-300.
33. See note 21.
34. Sergt Stanley's report August 31st 1798. ISPO 408/601/44.
35. Gen. Humbert—Executive Directory August 27th-8th 1798 printed J. Jones p. 226.
36. See note 21.
37. Ibid.
38. See especially DEP May 30th 1793; May 5th 1795; March 3rd 1796; FDJ March 3rd 1795.

39. Carrick, however, was a rendezvous for the Govt. troops see *Impartial Relation* p. 6–11.
40. Bp Elphin—Cooke June 16th 1798. 620/38/158.
41. FDJ, DEP, August 30th 1798 inc. Dublin Castle bulletin of August 29th.
42. See Dundas—Castlereagh August 27th 1798. HO 100/78/213. Col Longfield August 28th 1798. ISPO 408/601/29.
43. Ld Sunderlin September 4th 1798. ISPO 408/601/58.
44. G. Rochfort September 2nd 1798. Ibid No. 57.
45. Ld Belvedere August 6th 1798. 620/39/150.
46. Edgeworth *Memoirs* II. 181–4. H. Edgeworth October 6th 1798. Edgeworth MSS Bodleian.
47. Ibid II. 190–2.
48. R. L. Edgeworth August 24th 1798. Edgeworth MSS Bodleian.
49. Edgeworth *Memoirs* II. 193–4.
50. At Killashee on September 1st 1798. ISPO 408/601/37.
51. Edgeworth Memoirs II. 194.
52. Ibid p. 194–204. Maria Edgeworth September 5th 1798. H. Edgeworth October 6th 1798. Edgeworth MSS Bodleian.
53. Info. of "M" September 27th, December 1st 1803. 620/11/130. Capt. Cottingham November 30th 1798. ISPO 30/242.
54. Info. of A Montgomery May 31st 1798. 620/37/227. Exam of M. Smyth July 24th 1798. ISPO 30/335.
55. Desbrière II. 150 General Rey's proclamation. PRO WO/1192.
56. Desbrière II. 159–64.
57. Letter written by Tone August 14th 1798 is published in Hayes "Irish Swordsmen in France". I have not had access to the unpublished letters from Tone to his wife written at Brest July–September 1798. (Dickason MSS on loan to TCD).
58. Desbrière II. 164–5.
59. Tone *Life* II 522–3. See also note 57.
60. Litton Falkiner p. 306. FJ August 27th 1799. Note peerage also granted for political reasons.
61. *Impartial Relation* p. 33–4 J. Jones p. 265–9 Capt. Jobit loc cit p. 27–8.
62. Capt. Jobit loc cit p. 27–8.
63. Ibid. p 28.
64. Fontaine see ed's note on p. 28 of Capt. Jobit.
65. Capt. Jobit loc cit p. 28–9. Lake—Hewitt September 6th 1798. HO 100/78/304.
66. G. Rochfort September 5th 1798. ISPO 408/60159.
67. T. Shea September 5th, 6th 1798. 620/40/22. 24 Maj. Porter September 7th 1798. 620/4/34/1.
68. Maj. Porter loc cit. Col. Blake September 8th 1798. 620/4/34/2.
69. See note 67 see also J. Jones p. 253–64.
70. Capt. Cottingham September 6th 1798 printed J. Jones p. 245–9 cf Jones p. 249–53.
71. Anon. October 3rd 1799 printed J. Jones p. 263.
72. Capt. Jobit loc cit.
73. J. Moore *Diary* I 320, 234; Capt Taylor NLI MS 54a.
74. J. Moore *Diary* I 321 cf J. Jones p. 271.
75. *Impartial Relation* p. 34–9, printing Cornwallis—Portland September 9th 1798.
76. Ibid.
77. Lake September 6th 1798. HO 100/78/304. See also Capt. Jobit's second journal *Analecta Hibernica* no. 11.
78. Ibid.
79. Humbert's report quoted L. Falkiner p. 319.
80. DEP September 15th 1798.

81. FDJ September 15th 1798.
82. J. Moore *Diary* I. 323.
83. Portland—Cornwallis September 21st 1798. HO 100/66/363. DEP September 29th 1798.
84. Fullest account, giving names of the leaders of the Protestant fanatics, is in R. L. Edgeworth September 22nd, 29th 1798. Edgeworth MSS Bodleian.
85. Edgeworth *Memoirs*.
86. Capt. Jobit loc cit p. 29, 43.
87. FJ September 16th 1798.
88. Litton Falkiner p. 316
89. Cf Reay Fencibles order book in NAM (7 executed) with Maxwell p. 243 (17 executed) and Falkiner (70 executed).
90. Quoted Litton Falkiner p. 316.
91. DEP September 20th 1798.
92. Capt Keate September 17th 1798. HO 100/78/373. *Castlereagh Corr.* I. 374.
93. Richard Edgeworth September 22nd 1798. Edgeworth MSS Bodleian.
94. Edgeworth *Memoirs* II. 236.
95. Ibid.
96. Gen. Humbert—Milord L'Eveque October 26th 1798 printed Stock *Narrative* p. 181-2.

PART V CHAPTER 5
At head of chapter: Zimmerman, p. 168.
1. Stock *Narrative* p. 113-17.
2. Ibid p. 63-8.
3. Ibid p. 93-4.
4. Ibid p. 117-8, 127-8 Stock MS diary loc cit p. 24-5.
5. Stock *Narrative* p. 111. Little Diary printed *Analecta Hibernica* No. 11. 100-3.
6. Stock *Narrative* p. 118-19. See letter Col. Charost—Gen. Trench September 23rd 1798 HO/10082/176.
7. Stock *Narrative* p. 119-20.
8. Stock MS diary entry September 16th 1798 loc cit p. 25.
9. Gen. Rey's proclamation September 1798. PRO WOI/1101. Ameil's report printed Desbrière p. 150-7.
10. Ameil's report loc cit.
11. A. Waller September 17th 1798. 620/40/68a. See also F. Mansfield September 19th 1798. 620/40/73.
12. Ameil's report loc cit.
13. Letter from Ballyshannon September 24th 1798 enc. the proclamations PRO WOI/1101.
14. The most hostile account of this episode is Orr's printed *Castlereagh Correspondence* I. 406-8.
See also J. Murphy's account in ISPO State of the Country 31/3/68.
15. Stock *Narrative* p. 118-124. Stock MS Diary entry September 17th-18th loc cit p. 21-3.
16. Stock *Narrative* p. 132-4. For the tactful phrasing in text see Stock—Malone March 6th 1800 TCD MS photostat of Osburn transcript.
17. Stock MS Diary entry September 22nd loc cit p. 28. *Narrative* p. 136.
18. Stock *Narrative* p. 135.
19. Ibid p. 29 "during the whole time of this civil commotion, not a drop of blood was shed by the Connaught rebels, except in the field of war".
20. Stock MS diary loc cit p. 24.
21. Stock *Narrative* p. 137, 143-5.
22. See note 19.
23. Gen. Trench—Capt. Taylor September 24th 1798. HO 100/82/172. Stock *Narrative* p. 145-7.

24. Stock *Narrative* p. 147–50.
25. Ibid p. 148.
26. Ibid p. 147. Trench—Taylor September 26th 1798 loc cit.
27. Stock *Narrative* p. 144.
28. Ibid p. 151–2.
29. Ibid p. 157–8.
30. Ibid p. 153, 150–1. See also J. Kemmis September 25th 1798 "Such terrible slaughter as took place is impossible for me to describe" PROI/IA/40/111a.
31. Stock *Narrative* p. 163, 164–5.
32. Ibid p. 61–2, 158–62, 170–1. Stock MS diary entry September 26th, 27th 1798 loc cit p. 36–7.
33. Stock MS diary loc cit p. 34–5.
34. Stock *Narrative* p. 170–9. MS diary entry September 28th 1798 loc cit p. 37.
35. For Ld Portarlington's Letters see G. Clark *Gleanings From an Old Portfolio* (1896) p. 259–62.

PART IV CHAPTER 6
At head of chapter: Napoleon quoted Las Casas *Memoires* (ed. 1823) II. 335.
1. *The Times* October 2–13th 1798.
2. Ibid October 2nd 1798.
3. C. Oman *Nelson* (Sphere 1968 edit.) p. 267.
4. Lady Spencer October 2nd 1798 quoted O. Warner *The Battle of the Nile* (1960) p. 148.
5. *The Times* October 2nd, 4th 1798.
6. The King—Ld Spencer October 3rd 1798. Aspinall George III. Vol. III 134–5.
7. *The Times* October 6th 1798.
8. FJ, DEP October 6th 1798. For Derry and Waterford celebrations see FDJ October 13th 1798.
9. For Dublin reaction see Buckingham—Grenville October 15th 1798 HMC Dropmore IV. p. 344.
10. See J. Moore *Diary* I 326 entry October 14th 1798. FJ leader October 16th 1798 British Empire "at the summit".
11. The Brest fleet was sighted the day after sailing and then shadowed by Warren see Capt. Keate's message in HO 100/78/373 and Dela Boissière's info. in *Castlereagh Correspondence* I. 374. See also Castlereagh—Wickham October 14th 1798 HO 100/79/29.
12. Sir J. Warren—Castlereagh October 16th. HO 100/79/53. cf Ch Stewart's eye witness account loc cit p. 34. Not all ships were captured on the 12th see FDJ November 24th 1798.
13. Alexander—Pelham September 26th 1798. BM Add MSS 33106/85 foll. Downshire—Mornington March 20th 1798. BM Add MSS 37308/218 foll.
14. Cornwallis—Pitt October 8th 1798. *Cornwallis Correspondence* II. 417/8. The crucial paragraph is omitted in printed version of similar letter to Portland see HO 100/99/27.
15. Clare—Castlereagh October 16th 1798. *Castlereagh Correspondence* I. 393.
16. Clare—Auckland July 3rd 1798. BM Add MSS 34,454/386.
17. Note Clare's own words "Pitt is decided" (note 15) and Grenville's letter on subject printed Buckingham *Courts* Vol II.
18. Canning's memo October 23rd (1798). BM Add MSS 37844/273.
19. In late October he still hesitated. For the final decision see Elliot—Castlereagh October 24th 1798. *Castlereagh Correspondence*.
20. See note 17.
21. For a different view see Bolton *Union* p. 67, Pitt—Auckland October 11th, 15th and Auckland—Beresford October 17th 1798 *Auckland Correspondence* IV. 60–1.
22. Cornwallis—Dundas November 15th 1798 Melville Castle MSS SRO 331/4 "the

mischief which is done by the correspondence of half ministers, deputy ministers and all this is to be lamented . . ."

23. Ld Roden [autumn 1798] Roden MSS PRONI 147/9 Vol. 19.
24. Cornwallis—Pitt October 17th 1798. *Cornwallis Correspondence* II. 420–1.
25. Cornwallis—Ross November 15th 1798 op cit II. 435–6.
26. Cornwallis October 11th 1798 op cit II. 419.
27. Cornwallis—his brother James November 17th 1798. Mann MSS Kent CRO U 24/C2, 3.
28. Cornwallis—Dundas November 15th 1798. Melville Castle MSS SRO 331/4.
29. Even a "liberal" like Griffith was now violently opposed to the Government's policy of concessions see Griffith—Pelham September 6th 1798, BM 33106/68.
30. FJ October 16th 1798,
31. FJ October 1798.
32. FJ September 29th, DEP, FDJ October 13th 1798. Capt John Grogan Knox October 15th 1798. 620/40/173.
33. Capt. Taylor—Gen. Craig October 18th 1798. *Cornwallis Correspondence* II. 421.
34. Court martial evidence in 620/3/16. For similar cases see case of Lieut Hogg 620/17/30.
35. See note 33.
36. Sir G. Hill (Beresford's brother-in-law) November 15th 1798. 620/41/36.
37. McNevin, *History* p. 170, 195 cf 176.
38. Buckingham—Grenville October 2nd, 23rd 1798. HMC Dropmore IV. 330–1, 351–2.
39. *Cornwallis Corr.* III. 90.
40. That is up to August 1798. See ch 2 note 73. Total Govt. troops excluding yeomanry, killed in 1798 was 512 according to Army Medical Board report March 1st 1800 BM Add MSS 33119 For list of civilian loyalists dead see Musgrave App.
41. See ch. 2 note 73. cf FJ July 7th 1798 "30,000 rebels" killed; SNL August 8th 1798 "50,000"; Madden following Plowden II. 802.
42. Musgrave II. 206 cf earlier dated lists in NLI.
43. Ballynahinch was deliberately burnt by the Government troops as a reprisal.
44. For details see "Suffering loyalists" lists FJ, FDJ 1799 see also DEP October 23rd 1798.
45. G. Cooper *Letters;* Capt. T. L. Hodges' diary September 1798 BM Add MS 40, 166.
46. FDJ October 18th 1798.
47. DEP October 13th 1798 "never was there known in the memory of the oldest person living a more favourable harvest" At Wexford the wheat was *cheapest* despite devastation acc. DEP September 27th 1798.
48. *London New Monthly Magazine* quoted Tone *Life* II. 526.
49. Tone's Journal for December 25th 1796, *Life* II. 263.
50. Tone *Life* II. 524.
51. Ibid.
52. Castlereagh knew before Tone landed see W. Annesley—Ld Downshire November 2nd 1798 Downshire MSS PRONI DOD 607.
53. T. W. Tone—Ld Cavan November 3rd 1798 printed Madden II. 123.
54. DEP October 2nd 1798.
55. FJ November 13th 1798. Buckingham—Grenville November 10th 1798. HMC Dropmore IV. 369–70.
56. Curran *Life* II. 95–6. Tone *Life* II. 528–5.
57. *Dublin Magazine* November 1798 reprinted Madden II, 126–8. In the Govt. papers the speech was watered down see Buckingham November 13th loc cit p. 375.
58. Curran *Life* II 98–9.
59. Ibid p. 99–100 See Buckingham's sarcastic letter of November 12th 1798. HMC Dropmore IV. 373–4.
60. FJ November 24th–27th 1798 cf Tone *Life* II. 533.
61. Curran *Life* II. 100–1; Tone *Life* II. 534–5.

62. Tone *Life* II. 522.
63. Ibid p. 537–8, 536–7.
64. FJ November 15th 1798.
65. Dr. Lentaigne quoted Madden II. 140.
66. Sir G. Hill—Cooke November 15th 1798. 620/42/36. Cf Lord Cavan who on November 7th wrote that Tone's execution would be "amusing". 620/42/23.
67. See note on quotation at head of epilogue.
68. See page 125 para 2.
69. Madden II 142–3. DEP November 22nd 1798 merely states body given to his friends.

EPILOGUE
At head of chapter: O'Connell's speech in May 1841. FJ May 22nd 1841 quoted Madden III. 178–9.
1. See Bolton *Union* p. 205–6.
2. Castlereagh—Cooke June 21st 1800 *Castlereagh Correspondence* III. 333.
3. "I despise and hate myself every hour for engaging in such dirty work" Cornwallis—Ross May 20th 1799. *Cornwallis Correspondence* III. 101–2.
4. Bolton p. 205. Note there were *more* new Irish peerages in 1776.
5. C/MS in 620/9/96/7 & 21. Note the female revolutionary-Monemia Mahon. [sic]. See also DEP January 1799.
6. See C/M January 13th 1799 in 620/5/59/3. See also DEP January 1799; Lecky V. 251–4.
7. See also Bp of Ferns—Pitt May 9th 1800. PRO 30/8/327/335 foll.
8. Dr Troy August 3rd 1799. ISPO State Prisoners Petitions 2.
9. See Ed. Hay—Ld Moira March 20th 1800. PROI I. 40/112.
10. See interesting table in ISPO Office Papers 2nd series 525/162/14. Wages rose 30%, prices 50% in 1792–1802 acc. bakers' petition.
11. Lecky V. 338. M. McNeil *McCracken* p. 196.
12. Humboldt's estimate see J. Handley *Irish in Scotland* p. 153–4, p. 75–130.
13. Handley p. 231–5.
14. See Sir J. Fortescue *History of the British Army* IV. 638. Even at home recruits died in large numbers of disease see BM Add MSS 33,119.
15. J. Fitzpatrick November 18th 1798; January 8th 1798. BM Add MSS 33106/138, 162.
16. Capt. Schouler June 4th 1799 620/18a. For subsequent ship-wreck see ISPO Off Papers 515/84.
17. Byrne II. 279–80. Some were liberated by the French after being captured.
18. Lieut Sainthill (transportation agent) account April 1st 1798–March 2nd 1801. ISPO 526/166/7.
19. M. Sutton May 1799 enc Dr Troy June 1799. ISPO State Prisoners Petitions 2.
20. Kiernan *Transportation from Ireland to Sydney* p. 110–11 quoting HRA ii. 531.
21. Kiernan *Irish Exiles in Australia* p. 25–7 quoting HRA III. 556, 701–3.
22. Ibid. Appendix VIII p. 61–70 quoting convict list in Mitchell Library Sydney.
23. The list of occupations is published in HRA loc cit.
24. Kiernan *Exiles* loc cit p. 27–8.
25. DNB.
26. Kiernan *Exiles* loc cit p. 23.
27. Ibid p. 41 foll.
28. e.g. R. O'Connor—Ld Castlereagh September 25th 1798 "a narrative of my suffering would harrow up your soul" 620/4/29/7. See also Madden II 329 etc.
29. R. King—Portland September 13th 1798. HO 100/79/328. cf McNevin History p. 292–3.
30. Madden II. 329.
31. The warrant for his arrest is dated April 3rd 1799 see Madden I. 525.
32. MacDonagh *Post Bag* p. 289–94.

33. Neilson left for USA in 1802, Emmet in 1804, McNevin in 1805 see Madden Vols. III. IV.

34. The fullest account of this phase is in Robinson's thesis *Emmet* p. 185 foll.

35. T. Emmet—R. Simms 1805. PRONI D 1759/3B p. 26.

36. McNevin *History* p. 304–5.

37. Madden III. 141–77, 247–8.

38. See note 35.

39. Byrne II. 178, 274.

40. For Irish royalists see Lecky III. 523 foll.

41. I owe this passage to F. MacDermot *Arthur O'Connor* IHS vol 15 p. 48–69.

42. DNB. Note Foster's somersault he opposed emancipation as it would lead to the *repeal* of the Union see Bolton p. 214.

43. Lord John Beresford was created a bishop at 31, despite a reputation as a rake.

44. See the Parliamentary enquiry of 1829 (5 XIII).

45. See the dramatic increases in wheat, linen, barley and other exports in Smyth *Ireland Historical and Statistical* III. 302. See also Cullen *Anglo-Irish Trade*.

46. See Bolton p. 215–6; DNB; Becket p. 284–5.

47. He also made it up with Castlereagh. Grattan *Life* V. 553.

48. In September 1800. Lecky V. 438.

49. See Bolton p. 221. Elliot greatly exaggerated the support of the Irish members. See *Malmesbury Correspondence* IV 40.

50. The King—Pitt quoted Stanhope *Pitt* III App. XXVIII, XX.

51. Hyde *Castlereagh* 394–6, 409; Cooke resigned later; Cornwallis' comment was overset by a blast from St James'. Mann MSS Kent CRO.

52. DNB.

53. *Cornwallis Correspondence* III. 525–61. Lake threatened to resign unless given full powers of conducting the war see Lake—Cornwallis September 23rd 1805 *Correspondence* III. 555–7.

54. See (or, rather, buy!) E. Longford *Wellington: The Years of the Sword*. London 1969.

55. See Bolton p. 220–1, Becket p. 284–91 The most fundamental reason for the failure of the Union was its failure to solve the economic crisis created by the soaring population. Its success in Ulster owed much to the linen and ship-building industries.

Index

Thomas Pakenham is the author of *The Mountains of Rasselas*, *The Boer War* and, most recently, *The Scramble for Africa*, which won the W.H. Smith Literary Award (1992). He divides his time between a terraced house in North Kensington, London, and a crumbling castle in Ireland. He is married to the writer Valerie Pakenham and they have four children.